T5-BAL-360

Wissenschaftliche Untersuchungen
zum Neuen Testament · 2. Reihe
Begründet von Joachim Jeremias und Otto Michel
Herausgegeben von
Martin Hengel und Otfried Hofius
23

Enmity in Corinth: Social Conventions in Paul's Relations with the Corinthians

by

Peter Marshall

J. C. B. Mohr (Paul Siebeck) Tübingen

BS
2675.2
.M370
1987
cop.2

CIP-Kurztitelaufnahme der Deutschen Bibliothek

Marshall, Peter:

Enmity in Corinth: Social conventions in Paul's relations with the Corinthians / by Peter Marshall. – Tübingen : Mohr, 1987.
Wissenschaftliche Untersuchungen zum Neuen Testament : Reihe 2 ; 23)
ISBN 3-16-145070-1
ISSN 0340-9570
NE: Wissenschaftliche Untersuchungen zum Neuen Testament / 02

© 1987 by J. C. B. Mohr (Paul Siebeck), P. O. Box 2040, D-7400 Tübingen.

This book may not be reproduced, in whole or in part, in any form (beyond that permitted by copyright law) without the publisher's written permission. This applies particularly to reproductions, translations, microfilms and storage and processing in electronic systems.

Printed by Gulde-Druck GmbH in Tübingen; bound by Heinrich Koch KG in Tübingen.

Printed in Germany.

KRAUSS LIBRARY
LUTHERAN SCHOOL OF THEOLOGY AT CHICAGO
1100 EAST 55th STREET
CHICAGO, ILLINOIS 60615

CONTENTS

Preface

This study focuses upon Paul's relationship with the Corinthians and, in particular, upon the question of why his initial relationship so quickly turned to enmity. I examine the causes of the hostility, the form it takes, and Paul's efforts to win back the Corinthians, in the light of Graeco-Roman cultural traditions. Historically, Corinthian studies have been dominated by theological and literary concerns and the letters have not been subject to a thorough social analysis. Yet the social character of the Corinthian community and their interaction with Paul is more noticeable than in the case of any other of his churches and it is readily apparent that social attitudes and customs are integral to the interchange. Much success has been achieved in identifying the theological issues but I suggest that any such interpretation is incomplete without an adequate social understanding of the problems in Corinth.

The attempt to place Paul in his literary, cultural and social environment has been taken up again with new enthusiasm after many years of neglect. Projects such as the Reallexikon für Antike und Christentum and the Corpus Hellenisticum Novi Testamenti, among others, are systematically analysing and interpreting a wide range of aspects of Graeco-Roman society. The present state of this field of work is surveyed in four articles by the Australian ancient historian, E.A. Judge - St. Paul and Classical Society, JbAC 15 (1972), 19-36; Antike und Christentum: Towards a Definition of the Field. A Bibliographical Survey, Aufstieg und Niedergang der römischen Welt Vol. 2. 23.1, H. Temporini and W. Haase eds. (Berlin, 1979), 3-58; Gesellschaft und Christentum: Alte Kirche, Theologische Realenzyklopädie (Berlin and New York, 1984), 764-769; and, Gesellschaft: Neues Testament, Theologische Realenzyklopädie (Berlin and New York, 1984), 769-773. A more integrated treatment is offered by the American scholar,

A.J. Malherbe, in his Social Aspects of Early Christianity (Baton Rouge and London, 1977) 1-59 (2d ed., Philadelphia, 1983). This study follows this approach in that it attempts to explain the various aspects of Paul's relations with the Corinthians in terms of Greek social and cultural conventions.

The fruitfulness of a sociological analysis of the Corinthian letters has been shown by the German scholar, G. Theissen, in three important articles, now included in a collection of his essays, The Social Setting of Pauline Christianity: Essays on Corinth, ed. and tr. J.H. Schütz (Philadelphia, 1982). He explains the tension among the Corinthians in terms of an inner social stratification. He contends that the internal conflict was caused by the attempted social integration of people of different socio-economic levels into one association. His research indicates that a number of the leading Corinthians belonged to the socially well-established metropolitan ranks and that their behaviour is typical of what we might expect at this level in society. This study generally supports the conclusions reached by Theissen, though by a different route, that of an analysis of Paul's relations with these Corinthians.

V.P. Furnish's recently released commentary on 2 Corinthians (New York, 1984) is a superbly crafted and comprehensive entrée into the complex and mobile field of Corinthian studies. He most ably handles the variety of past and present historical, social, literary and theological views and adds his own considerable insights. Yet, rightly, he leaves us intrigued and open to the discoveries which we must make if we are to make this Corinthian story more complete.

This work is essentially a social enquiry and no attempt will be made to reconstruct a full historical context for the Corinthian letters. Such an enterprise requires the participation of a number of specialised disciplines, among which social analysis is only one contributor. The theological issues, therefore, will not be discussed. This emphasis does not diminish the importance of theology; rather it should complement and enhance our understanding of it and of other aspects by making it possible to view them from the perspective of social and intellectual history. This is not to say that our view of the theology in Corinthians will remain unaltered. Until now, scholars have directed their attention almost singularly to the theological position of Paul's detractors, arguing negatively from his responses to their supposed theology and identity. We must not take it for granted, though, that a reaction in theological terms indicates that the detractors held a different theological or philosophical viewpoint. It may point to a social situation, as I consider it does in many instances.

In fact we shall see that much of Paul's terminology in the conflict, however much it relates to and is informed by his theology, reflects normal social usage. This means, for example, that many of the ideas and practices traditionally associated with Paul's enemies will be redefined in social terms. We should, also, gain some insight into the interaction of culture and theology in Paul's practical and intellectual experience. It may be, if only in the future, that we shall be able as a result to define more exactly the socio-theological worlds of the parties involved in the dispute.

I have not pursued all the various philosophical, ethical, political and religious nuances which may be present in the terms and ideas under discussion. A Greek word or phrase may convey a wide range of meanings and its precise sense can only be determined from the context. Thus it is necessary to establish the literary and social levels of Paul and the various groups in his churches. As we shall see, the tendency has been to interpret the terms used by recourse either to the formal traditions of the philosophical schools, especially the Cynic-Stoic diatribe and, of late, to the Socratic tradition, or to ideas and concepts of a pneumatic/gnostic kind which are said to have been current in Paul's time.

The appeal to the Cynic-Stoic diatribe appears to demand for Paul and his detractors a degree of philosophical sophistication which was attainable by relatively few people. The philosophical nuances, however, may reflect only the general nexus of ideas and values (combining also social, economic, political, moral, legal and religious elements) which constitutes the mentality of educated people in society. While we cannot say precisely how such ideas were formed and exchanged or what conventions governed popular thought in the first-century Greek cities, I suggest that it is at this level that much of the interaction between Paul and the Corinthians took place. The language of what might be called embryonic gnosticism does not suffice to account for the range of nuances which are reflected in the interchange between Paul and his enemies. As we shall see, we can learn as much about this language and the associated behaviour from the social attitudes to hybris from the Greek literary tradition.

We come now directly to the task of this study. Our capacity to construct a contemporary social and intellectual framework for the New Testament, is, on the one hand, limited by the lack of first-century Greek literary sources. On the other, there is a substantial body of literature in the centuries next closest to the time of Paul which raises a difficulty as to how it should be related to first-century conditions. My approach, generally, has been to describe a select group of social institutions, conventions and traditions familiar to Greek and Roman authors, in an attempt to provide a background of typical behaviour against which we can view Paul's relations with the Corinthians.

I have referred frequently to the writings of Paul's contemporaries or near contemporaries such as Cicero and Seneca, Dio Chrysostom and Plutarch, though I have ranged widely through the literature from Homer.

While being concerned with the danger of importing too much from too far, we must take care not to distance Homer and other influential authors from the world of Paul. Homer's writings continued to influence writers throughout antiquity, and were read within the schools and became the basis of what appears to be one of the strongest literary traditions in Greek life and thought. We might term him an 'intellectual' contemporary of Paul.

This broad approach may appear to ignore the differences in perception of social ideas by these authors. But the common elements are substantial and I have endeavoured to show that the essential pattern of these conventions remained constant in antiquity whatever social, economic and political developments took place. In particular, we can see a general consistency in thought and practice in the authors of those centuries closest to Paul (1 B.C. - 2 A.D.). It is reasonable to assume that the Corinthian letters provide us with insights into the prevailing social conditions in a major first-century Greek city. Where, then, we can find evidence in them of similar patterns of thought and practice similar to the Graeco-Roman traditions, we may be justified in seeking an explanation in these terms.

In Section 1, comprising four chapters, I examine certain of the social institutions, terminology and ideas which I believe are central to the conflict between Paul and the Corinthians. Chapters 1 and 2 consist of a study of the nature and language of the reciprocal relationships of friendship and enmity. This includes an investigation into the conventions of giving, receiving, returning and refusing of gifts and services, and the traditional expressions of enmity such as invective and shame, as the background to Paul's refusal of the Corinthian offer of aid and the origin of the enmity relationship which followed. The familiar literary figure of the servile flatterer outlined in chapter 3 provides us with a context for the damaging charges of inconstancy made against Paul. In chapter 4, the practice of recommendation as a convention of friendship establishes the social setting for our understanding of recommendation in 2 Corinthians.

Section 1 is thematic in character in that each of the topics in chapters 2, 3 and 4 is associated with the notion of friendship in chapter 1 in one way or another: enmity as its traditional antithesis; the flatterer as the false friend; the custom of recommendation as a means of forming and maintaining friendship. Thus a certain amount of repetition is unavoidable. This network of associated ideas gives us a consistent context for recognizing the many relational nuances in the passages under discussion in 1 and 2 Corinthians. There are two other reasons for dealing with these topics in Section 1. First, as far as I can ascertain, there have been no comprehensive studies published on the subjects of enmity, the character of the flatterer, and the relational function of recommendation, in classical studies. These chapters are intended to contribute to our understanding of these topics in their own right. Second, to insert them at the relevant places throughout the study would seriously interrupt the flow of the argument.

Their prior treatment, however, creates a methodological problem. I only occasionally hint in these chapters as to how they might be applied to the New Testament and the amount of detail makes recalling to mind of the important features quite difficult. Therefore, I have prefaced the relevant discussions in the ensuing chapters with a recapitulation of the salient points of the particular convention that is in question. Discussions of other important conventions, which, with the exception of one, are brief, will appear in the context in which they arise.

Section 2 comprises two chapters which focus mainly upon the cause of the conflict in Corinth in terms of the conventions of friendship. Chapter 5 considers briefly the occurrence of friendship terminology in the non-Pauline writings, then, in greater detail, the various aspects of friendship and enmity in Paul's letters other than 1 and 2 Corinthians. This will show the conventional nature of Paul's relations with his churches and intimates, while pointing to some of the ways he diverges from common practice and his reasons for this. Of special importance is my discussion of the Philippian gifts as signifying a friendship relationship. It forms the background to my analysis in chapter 6 of the Corinthian offer of aid as an offer of friendship and the consequences for Paul in refusing it. This chapter comprises a lengthy investigation of the nature and consequences of Paul's refusal in the passages 1 Cor. 9:1-23, 2 Cor. 11:7-15 and 12:13-18 in the light of the conventions of gift exchange. I argue that the offer was in the form of a gift and was made by a group of wealthy Corinthians who wished to obligate Paul to themselves. His refusal dishonoured them and resulted in enmity. Also examined is the way the Corinthians viewed his variable conduct in relation to giving and receiving and the effect it had upon his relationship with them.

A substantial part of this chapter is devoted to the study

of the notion of ὕβρις and its application to the terminology and ideas expressed in 1 Cor. 4:6-13 and its wider context. I suggest that a. Paul relies on this traditional idea of excess to discredit the behaviour of his enemies; b. that this description indicates to us that they are people of rank and wealth and that the conflicts in Corinth are primarily social rather than theological or religious in character; c. that the excessive kinds of behaviour - sexual misconduct, disregard of others in relation to eating idol meat and the Lord's meal - associated as they are with notions of freedom, are typical of conduct of the hybris kind; d. that Paul adopts the same idea in 2 Cor. 10-12 to denigrate the rival apostles (an argument which we will explore fully in chapter 9); e. that the term 'hybrist' is a more appropriate appellation than 'gnostic' or 'pneumatic' for his Corinthian enemies. This idea will also explain in part what underlies Paul's adoption of the shameful figures of the socially humiliated person in 1 Cor. 4:9-13 and of the boastful fool in 2 Cor. 10-12.

Section 3 centres upon the forms in which Paul's enemies expressed their hostility towards him and his response to it. In chapter 7 I draw attention to the social significance of recommendation in 2 Corinthians for our understanding of Paul's relations with the Corinthians and of the alliance formed between them and the rival apostles. Chapter 8 investigates the nature of the invective against Paul alluded to in various passages in both letters. I suggest that it appears in the form of (1) charges of inconstancy in his conduct and relationships which are based on the familiar character of the flatterer, and (2) unfavourable comparisons according to the encomiastic topics of rhetorical convention. Chapter 9 looks at Paul's responses in the light of a number of the traditional techniques of rhetoric from which we will attempt to draw conclusions as to his familiarity with Greek rhetoric.

The argument in this section is as follows. I suggest that Paul's enemies commenced ridiculing him as a man who lacked culture (eloquence and its concomitants) and who behaved inconstantly in his relationships (the flatterer). They were able to persuade the majority of the Corinthians that Paul could not be trusted, and that he despised them and favoured other churches. In addition, they sought out by mutual recommendation rival apostles who quickly assumed control in Corinth and humiliated Paul when he visited there for the second time. I argue that the dispute is primarily a socio-cultural one and that Paul is discredited as a socially and intellectually inferior person, an invective which the Corinthians find persuasive. By contrast his opponents praised themselves as men of culture and thus superior to him.

I contend that Paul deliberately chooses the antithesis of rhetorical display and other socially accepted styles as the manner of expressing his apostleship in Corinth and that in so doing he runs directly counter to the standards of his opponents and of the majority of the Corinthians. This results in his being humiliated and shamed before them and in his own eyes also. 2 Corinthians represents his attempt to win back the Corinthians and I show that he ably uses a number of rhetorical devices to disparage his enemies. At the same time, he takes up the invective against him and develops it as a mark of personal shame and contrasts it with the honour of his opponents. I suggest that a. Paul's deliberate choice of a social style antithetical to that approved of by the rhetorical masters; b. his familiarity with Greek rhetoric; c. his dwelling upon shame; and d. the form and content of his enemies' invective, combine to reveal him as a man of high status who was probably trained in Greek rhetoric but who found both these conditions incongruent with the rejection and humiliation of Jesus, and his own practical and intellectual experience of humiliation in Greek society.

This work is a revision of my Ph.D thesis submitted to Macquarie University in 1980. The additions include the strengthening of my discussions of 1 Cor. 4:6-13 and 2 Cor. 10:12-18 and the inclusion of references to several pertinent articles published during the preparation of this revision.

Prior to commencing my thesis I was a marketing executive. The skills and understanding I acquired, together with the experiences of endeavouring to integrate my Christian faith with the daily world of business, contributed significantly to the ways in which I approached the study of early Christianity.

The application of these findings to modern public life remains my daily task.

My first words of thanks are for Archbishop Donald Robinson, Anglican Diocese of Sydney, who first encouraged me in 1974 to pursue my questions in the environment of the New Testament. The staff of Moore Theological College of that year, especially Dr Bill Dumbrell, introduced me to the unfamiliar skills and traditions of biblical scholarship.

Dr Robert Banks and Prof. Edwin Judge of the School of History at Macquarie University were my supervisors during the preparation of my thesis and I have continued to benefit from their enthusiasm and interest, friendship and scholarship.

The School of History at Macquarie University provided a unique environment for the study of Christianity and Graeco-Roman society. The varied special interests of the staff involved in the teaching of ancient history and the opportunities for the exchange of ideas contributed significantly to the development of my thinking. I am especially grateful to Dr Tom Hillard, Dr Alanna Emmett and Dr Raoul Mortley for their help and interest. I also thank Chris Forbes for the profitable interchange of ideas and insights, and Greg Horsley, editor of the New Documents Illustrating Christianity Series, for his advice and encouragement.

Prof. Abraham Malherbe of the Divinity School, Yale University, made a number of helpful suggestions and criticisms during the course of my work and I continue to be stimulated by his work.

I am most grateful to the staff of the Department of Studies in Religion, University of Queensland, for their valuable assistance and friendship at various stages in this work, particularly to Dr Michael Lattke, whose kindly reminders and care of my interests encouraged me to persist with preparation when other duties monopolised my time.

The Board and staff of the Zadok Centre: Institute for Christianity and Society, Canberra, of which I have been Director since 1983, have graciously given me time and support in the final stages of preparation of the manuscript. I would also like to thank Jill Mendham for compiling the indices and giving sound advice and Janine McCaffrey and

Krystyna Verhelst for their contributions.

I appreciate the willingness of Professor Martin Hengel and his fellow-editors to publish my work in the WUNT series and the help and patience of Rudolf Pflug of J.C.B. Mohr (Paul Siebeck) leading to its publication.

My wife, Pat, assisted me with numerous Latin passages and gave help and encouragement while fully involved in her own post-graduate studies and teaching career. My debt to her is profound and I dedicate the book to her.

Section 1

GRAECO-ROMAN CONVENTIONS OF FRIENDSHIP AND ENMITY

Chapter 1

THE RELATIONSHIP OF FRIENDSHIP

a. Friendship as giving for a return.

At the commencement of his de Beneficiis Seneca wrote : 'What we need is a discussion of benefits and the rules for a practice that constitutes the chief bond of human society"[1]. What follows in his essay is by no means original; it reflects the thoughts and practice of his predecessors over centuries on an institution which was a cornerstone of Greek and Roman society.

Innovative as the Greeks may have been throughout their history, gift exchange was not their invention. It is a universal institution. The anthropologist, Marcel Mauss, has shown that in primitive moneyless societies, many of which still exist today, gift exchange forms the whole basis of friendly relations and exchange of any kind. In this context he refers to it as a total social phenomenon embracing at the same time and giving expression to legal, economic, religious, moral, aesthetic and morphological institutions[2]. The exchange of goods and wealth are but two elements of this vast interchange of 'courtesies, entertainments, ritual, military assistance, women, children, dances, feasts'[3]. It is not the

---

[1] de Ben. 1.4.2.

[2] The Gift (ET:Glencoe, 1954), 1, 76-77.

[3] Ibid., 3, 11-12.

gift itself to which exchange refers but to the total nexus of relations involved in the giving and receiving, of which the gift is a part.

The offer of the gift, though in theory voluntary and disinterested, is in fact obligatory and interested[4]. The offer is intended to place the recipient under an obligation to repay - it can only be accepted with the offer of a counter-gift. As Mauss observes, this institution not only involves an obligation to repay, but two equally important obligations, to give presents and to accept them. The fulfilment of the obligations by all parties - to give, to accept, to return - fulfils the conditions of friendship. To refuse is the equivalent of 'a declaration of war; it is a refusal of friendship and intercourse'[5]. There is no middle ground : there must be 'either complete trust or mistrust'[6].

Two important considerations make acceptance imperative. The gift is intended to enhance the donor's status and win him public recognition and to establish security by a network of friendly relations or alliances. As a consequence, refusal of an offer is a serious affront and rarely occurs. This notion of increasing status and establishing superiority by a gift means that the acceptor, to avoid loss of face, has to outdo the donor in generosity to regain the advantage[7]. This internecine behaviour Mauss terms 'agonistic'[8] and it is 'always exaggerated and often purely destructive of the competitors' wealth'[9]. Failure to return on the part of either would lead to his becoming the dependant rather than the friend of the other [10] and in some societies the sanction applied is enslavement[11]. Servile notions always attend acceptance.

---

[4] Ibid., 1.

[5] Ibid., 10-11, 37-41.

[6] Ibid., 79.

[7] Ibid., 72-73.

[8] Ibid., 4-5.

[9] Ibid., 72; see also M.J. Herskovits, Economic Anthropology (New York, 1965), 155-179, and especially 162-164 where he describes the desire for prestige which motivates gift and ceremonial exchange in Polynesia.

[10] M. Mauss, The Gift, 51, 72.

[11] Ibid., 41.

Until the gift is reciprocated the recipient is considered to be the dependant of the other.

This institution of establishing friendship and affirming status by giving for a return is clearly reflected in the earliest Greek literature. M.I. Finley says that no single detail in the life of the heroes receives so much attention in the Iliad and Odyssey as gift-giving, and always with frank reference to adequacy, appropriateness and recompense[12]. I cite but three examples from the many.

As the goddess Athena, in the guise of Mentes, the Taphian chieftain, was preparing to depart, Telemachus offers her the customary gift from host to guest (οἷα φίλοι ξένοι ξείνοισι δίδουσι)[13]. She replies that she would accept, on her return journey, whatever gift (δῶρον) the φιλὸν ἦτορ prompted him to give, and that he should choose a beautiful one for he would not lose by it[14].

It is a mutual bond of guestfriendship between their grandfathers which prevents the outbreak of hostilities between Diomedes and Glaucus. Though they did not know each other previously, they honour and confirm this relationship founded on an exchange of gifts by a similar exchange. Thus they declare themselves to be friends from their fathers' days (ξεῖνοι πατρώιοι)[15].

Finley has shown that at a Homeric marriage, the bride was part of an exchange of gifts (ἔδνα) or services between a successful suitor and the bride's father[16]. When there was competition for a bride, a suitor's edna expressed his quality against other suitors. W.K. Lacey instances the occasion where Penelope's father and brothers were trying to persuade her to marry Eurymachus because he had gained the advantage in edna over the other suitors, besides outdoing them in δῶρα to her father[17]. For the unsuccessful suitors, to be outdone

---

[12] The World of Odysseus (Harmondsworth, 1954), 75.

[13] Homer, Od. 1.313.

[14] Ibid., 1.316-318.

[15] Il. 6.212-236

[16] 'Marriage, Sale and Gift in the Homeric World' RIDA 111. Vol. 2 (1955), 165 ff.

[17] 'Homeric ΕΔΝΑ and Penelope's ΚΥΡΙΟΣ', JHS 86 (1966), 57.

in edna and in dōra would 'incur a slur upon a man's rank and quality as an ἀγαθός'[18]. The successful suitor's gifts provoked counter-gifts, edna. These were intended to gain the advantage in prestige for the bride's family over the suitor's.

The origin and nature of this institution in Homeric society lies in what Finley describes as 'the basic ambivalence of the heroic world to the uninvited stranger, of rapid oscillation between deep well-warranted fear and lavish entertainment'[19]. The word ξένος implies this ambivalence : it means both 'guest-friend' and 'stranger' or 'foreigner'[20]. Like its Latin equivalent, hospes, it originally meant a 'stranger'; then it became used for a 'guest' and finally for a 'host'. ξενία (Latin, hospitium), which is difficult to translate into English, is the relationship between guest and host and implies 'ties of hospitality' or 'friendship of reciprocal entertainment'. Institutionally 'it was guest-friendship above all that weakened the tension between the poles'[21]. It helped to relieve the inherent rivalry between households.

The most common terms which denote this reciprocal relationship in Greek are φιλός and its derivatives φιλεῖν, φιλότης or φιλία). A.W.H. Adkins argues that they are closely related to the structure of Homeric society moulded by the Homeric use of αγαθός and ἀρετή and associated terms[22].

The individual Homeric oikos was a social, economic and religious entity presided over by the agathos, who is essentially a warrior-chieftain. It comprised his wife and children, servants and other dependants, his property and

---

[18] Ibid., 55.

[19] Odysseus, 117; see also J. Mathews, Hospitality and the New Testament Church : an Historical and Exegetical Study (Ann Arbor, 1977), 119.

[20] M.I. Finley, Odysseus, 116, see also J. Mathews, Hospitality, 70-72; H. Wagenvoort, Roman Dynamism (Oxford, 1947), 144-147.

[21] M.I. Finley, Odysseus, 118.

[22] '"Friendship" and "Self-Sufficiency" in Homer and Aristotle', CQ 13 (1963), 30.

possessions. These were his immediate _philoi_[23], those things which he possessed and could rely upon. About him was a hostile and competitive world and the qualities which he needed to survive were those commended by _aretē_[24]. In such an environment _aretē_ was seldom sufficient. Apart from his own _philoi_, he acquired external relationships by birth, marriage and services which were termed _philotēs_ or _xenia_. In Homer, a human being has no rights qua human being, but only in virtue of these relationships. This terminology of friendship then 'demarcated those persons and things which he can employ to ensure his continued existence. These things he possesses, they are his own : all else is hostile or indifferent'[25]. Outside these relationships he was an alien or stranger, regarded with suspicion and hostility and open to maltreatment by the _agathos_ into whose _oikos_ he had come[26]. To say that he had no rights qua human being is not to say that he had no rights at all. He had sacred rights to hospitality[27]. In the Odyssey the resident _agathos_ is morally obliged to welcome the visitor and to protect him from injury[28], to meet his needs[29] and to guard his life with

---

[23] φιλός can also be translated as 'dear' or 'own' or 'friend'. It is used in Homer to denote a man's own faculties and possessions and moves out to encompass a whole range of relationships. See A.W.H. Adkins, 'Friendship', 30-31.

[24] Ibid., 33; see also his discussion of _aretē_ in Merit and Responsibility: a Study in Greek Values (Oxford, 1960), 48.

[25] A.W.H. Adkins, 'Friendship', 32-33; cf. J. Mathews, Hospitality, 83-118, for 'Alien Existence as the lot of the Stranger'.

[26] Homer, Od. 6.119-121, 9.252-258, 13.200-202.

[27] Ibid., 14.56-58. In Homer, Zeus is the protector and avenger of strangers (Od. 13.213-214, 14.283-284; cf. Plato, Laws, 729E; Hesiod, W&D, 327-334; Aeschylus, Eum, 264-275) and is called Ζεὺς ξεῖνος , 'the stranger's god', and Ζεὺς ἱκετήσιος, 'the suppliant's god' (Od. 9.270-271). The stranger is said to be from Zeus who travels with him (Od. 6.207-208, 9.270-271, 14.57-59). The deities were assumed to disguise themselves as travelling strangers to test men's hospitality (Od. 17.485-487). Thus one should entertain a stranger and treat him with due reverence for he may be a god (Od. 9.269-271; cf. 7.162-165, 181). See also J.B. Mathews, Hospitality, 54-60.

[28] Ibid., 9.266-268, 14.56-59, 15.74.

[29] Ibid., 3.479-480, 13.72.

his own[30]. The stranger is thus granted the status of <u>philos</u> or <u>xenos</u>. This total act of hospitality is denoted by the verb φιλεῖν. Adkins notes two important aspects. First, <u>philein</u> is to 'do useful services for a man not in order to make him immediately useful to oneself but simply to secure his own existence in his own interest'[31]. In this respect, <u>philein</u> is disinterested. The stranger is the immediate beneficiary. Second, <u>philein</u> is intended to make the recipient 'a φιλόν-object on whose help one can rely when one needs it'[32] either immediately or in the future. Here the motivation is selfish. It is intended to enhance his <u>aretē</u>, bringing him 'honour', glory' and 'profit'[33] as the guest will always remember his host's kindness[34] and broadcast his reputation[35]. Conversely, failure to extend or to violate the obligations of hospitality was considered a disgrace[36], and an offence punishable by the gods[37].

For Adkins then <u>philein</u> is an act which creates or maintains a <u>philotēs</u> relationship based on reciprocal services between <u>philoi</u>. Friendly feeling is not necessary, since 'it is the action which is all important'[38]. As an institution it continued to function as a significant factor in the cash economies of Greece and Rome.

Within two centuries of the time that Homeric epics were written, the Greeks, now familiar with the use of coinage and a money market, did not understand the background of and were critical of a system in which a donor could openly

---

30 Ibid. 16.85-87, 18.61-65.

31 'Friendship', 36.

32 Ibid.

33 Homer, Od. 15.78.

34 Ibid., 15.55.

35 Ibid., 19.332-334.

36 Ibid., 14.402-405; cf. Cyclops, ibid., 9.106, 287 ff, 295, 10.80 ff; Heracles, ibid., 21.24-30.

37 Ibid., 17-483-484. See A.W.H. Adkins, '"Honour" and "Punishment" in the Homeric Poems', BICS 7 (1960), 25.

38 'Friendship', 36.

indicate in advance the return which he expected for his gift and would consider himself wronged if he did not receive it[39]. A superficial look at their critique suggests that they have made considerable advances in thinking and practice. The orator, Lysias, declares that it is a good man's part to benefit (ὠφέλειν) his friends, 'even if nobody was to know'[40]; and Demosthenes, that 'the benefactor ought to put it out of his mind at once', for, 'to remind a man of the good turns you have done to him, is very much like a reproach'[41]. Aristotle states that it is morally commendable (καλόν) to bestow a gift (εὐ ποιεῖν) without seeking a return[42], and the liberal man (ὁ ἐλευθέριος) gives for the nobility (καλόν) of giving[43]. This emphasis is also made by the Roman writers. Cicero maintains that true friendship (amicitia) emanates from natural love (amor) and giving of benefits (beneficia) - which may lead to reciprocal affection and services - rather than from the need to satisfy human weakness and want[44]. To put it more succinctly : advantage (utilitas) follows friendship rather than precedes it[45]. Terence finds it shameful for a benefactor to remind those who have forgotten a service (beneficium) done for them[46], while Cicero refers to such benefactors as 'a very disagreeable class of people'[47]. Generous and liberal people, like himself, do not give favours hoping for a profitable return[48].

---

[39] A.R. Hands, Charities and Social Aid in Greece and Rome (London and Southampton, 1968), 29-30.

[40] 19.59.

[41] de Cor. 269.

[42] EN 8.13.8 (cf. 9.7.5) where it is the act of benefitting which in itself is desirable or valuable to the benefactor.

[43] EN 4.1.12.

[44] de Amic. 8.26-32.

[45] Ibid., 14.51. However, see his de Inven. 2.45.166-167, where he concedes that as far as oratorical practice is concerned, friendship, like glory (gloria), rank (dignitas) and importance (amplitudo), is sought for both its intrinsic worth and advantage.

[46] Andria 43.

[47] de Amic. 20.71.

[48] Ibid., 9.31; cf. 8.27.

Likewise, Seneca advises that as a binding rule those who have bestowed benefits should immediately forget them, having no idea of a return[49]. He highly commends the anonymous donor who neither boasts nor mentions his benificence[50] and admits to difficulty in determining whether it is more shameful to deny that one has received a benefit or to ask for the repayment of one[51]. Much is made of the spirit in which the gift is given. It should be bestowed willingly, quickly and without hesitation[52], with kindness[53]. In accord with the Aristotelian dictum, the value of the gift should be assessed by the spirit of the giver and the resources at his disposal rather than the gift itself[54].

Though the different terminology and ideas, and the criticism of the Homeric practice reflect the different social and economic conditions in which these authors lived, the context of their thought reveals that in essentials giving continued unaltered. 'There remains basic to the discussion the assumption that the gifts, benefits or favours in question are to be conferred upon somebody who can make a return, so that a return, even though it may no longer decently be asked for, is confidently expected'[55]. This ambivalence is marked in Cicero's request for assistance : 'A man of any modesty finds it repugnant to address such a petition to one whom he thinks he has put under an obligation to himself, lest he should appear to exact rather than request what he wants, and to reckon the granting of it rather as a payment for value

---

[49] de Ben. 2.10.4; cf. 1.2.3-4, 4.5, 2.6.2, 31.2-5.

[50] Ibid., 2.11.1-3; cf. 2.10.1-4, 7.22.2.

[51] Ibid., 1.1.3.

[52] Ibid., 1.4.3, 2.1.1-4, 2.1-2, 3.1-3, 4.1-3, 5.1-4.

[53] Ibid., 2.11.4-6, 12.1-2, 13.1-3.

[54] Aristotle, EN 4.1.19; cf. Seneca, de Ben. 1.5.1-6, 6.1-3, 7.1-3, 8.1-2, 9.1.

[55] So A.R. Hands, Charities, 30-31. See also A.W.H. Adkins, 'Friendship', 40-41; G. Percival, Aristotle on Friendship, (Cambridge, 1940), XIV. Cf. Publius Syrus, 491, 515, for giving to those with good memories, or 93, for the observation that 'They are either rogues or fools who think benefits are merely gifts'.

received than as an act of kindness'[56]. Their discussions never reach the radical conclusion found in John Chrysostom : that if one gives it should not be to the rich who can give back; by implication giving should be to those who cannot return the favour[57].

b. The obligation to return.

While generosity is consistently encouraged, Greek and Roman writers place as much stress upon the moral duty of returning a favour as on the virtue of conferring one[58]. Aristotle says that as a general rule the recipient of a benefit ought to return services rendered (τὰς εὐεργεσίας ἀνταποδοτέον) before bestowing favours on friends[59]. While holding that it is more noble to benefit others without an eye to a return, he concedes that most give because it is profitable. So he counsels that a person should make every effort 'to return the equivalent of services rendered' (ἀνταποδοτέον τὴν ἄξιαν ὧν ἔπαυεν)[60]. Even though the recipient be unequal, he must repay what he can, namely honour (τίμην ἀνταποδοτέον)[61]. For Cicero, where an obligation has been incurred, 'no duty (officium) is more imperative than that of proving one's gratitude'[62]. Generosity (liberalitas)

---

[56] Fam. 2.6.1; however, cf. id., Att. 14.13a, Antony to Cicero: 'I feel a right to ask you this favour, for I have done all I could for your sake'.

[57] 2.126. Cf. Lk. 14:12-14.

[58] This is a major topos in a series of topoi on friendship in which Aristotle systematized and created the terminology found in later discussions (found in his EN 8, 9, EE 7.1-12, MM 2.11-17) : Does a good man need friends ? Is friendship only possible between good men ? Should one try to acquire many friends ? Is friendship of one kind or several ? Can friendship exist between unequals ? What are the claims of friendship ?

[59] EN 9.2.3.

[60] EN 8.13.8-9.

[61] EN 8.14.3, τίμη refers to the social and political support the recipient owes a benefactor. Cf. Cicero, de Off. 2.20.70.

[62] de Off. 1.15.47: nullum officium referenda gratia magis necessarium est.

consists both of giving and returning. However, while the giving of a benefit is optional, 'to fail to requite one is not available to the good man'[63]. Though Seneca enjoins his readers to forget immediately a benefit they have given, he decrees that the recipient should ever remember (meminisse mandavimus)[64]. In conjunction with his reiteration of the Stoic paradox, that a benefit has already been returned by the recipient who receives it gladly and graciously (i.e. shows gratitude - gratia),[65] he urges the recipient to 'return some gift similar to the one he received'[66]. Returning of gifts for him is essential to love and friendship (amor et amicitia). Failure in this regard means absence of loyalty (fides)[67] and is a greater sin than lack of generosity[68]. As with Homer, giving was the first act in a reciprocal relationship; the second was the counter-gift. The obligation to return gifts weighed heavily upon the recipient. Socially he is in an inferior position to the one who has taken the initiative even though he repays the debt. Thucydides observes that the one who takes the initiative is in the stronger position (βεβαιότερος), for the obliged recipient finds that he has lost the edge (ἀμβλύτερος) in friendship 'knowing that when he repays the kindness it will count not as a favour bestowed, but as a debt repaid'[69]. Aristotle refers to conferring benefits as a 'mark of superiority' as against the 'inferiority' of receiving them[70]. This is most hurtful to the latter for he wishes to be superior[71]. Pliny calls it the code of friendship; according

---

63 Ibid., 1.15.48.

64 de Ben. 7.22.1; cf. ibid., 2.10.4; Demosthenes, de Cor. 269.

65 de Ben. 2.30.2, and the ensuing discussion in 2.31-35; cf. 4.21.1-3, 5.4.1-2.

66 Ibid., 2.35.1.

67 Ep. 81.12.

68 de Ben. 1.1.13.

69 2.40.4.

70 EN 4.3.24.

71 EN 4.3.25.

to it 'the one who takes the initiative puts the other in his debt and owes him no more until he is repaid[72].

The disadvantage of the dependant is always present in discussions of the so-called 'disinterested giving' of the true benefactor. For Aristotle 'benefactors seem to love those whom they benefit more than those who have received benefits love those who have conferred them'. He likens the relationship to that of a craftsman who loves his work more than it would ever love him should it ever come to life. Yet he concedes that there is some truth in the popular, if cynical, analogy to the relations between a debtor and creditor who watches over his interests[73]. Seneca admits that it is more difficult at times to receive a gift than to bestow one, 'as greater effort is expended in guarding, than in giving, the objects that are received'[74]. The recipient must turn his thoughts immediately to repaying, needing 'to show great energy, great swiftness, if he is to overtake the other who has the start on him'[75].

To regain the advantage, the recipient is obliged not merely to reciprocate but to outdo his benefactor in generosity. This is one of the signs of Aristotle's great-souled man (μεγαλόψυχος). He repays with interest and reverses the roles; the original benefactor becomes the benefitted[76]. In a similar vein, Cicero asks, 'shall we not imitate the fruitful fields which return more than they receive?'[77]. From a bountiful harvest to the victor's wreath in Seneca's dictum : we should 'set before us the high aim of striving, not merely to equal, but to surpass in deed and in spirit those who have placed us under obligation, for he who has a debt of gratitude

---

[72] Letters, 7.31.7 : Neque enim obligandus sed remunderandus est in amoris officio qui prior coepit. See also Philo, de Virt. 118, in benefiting an enemy : ὃ τε γὰρ εὐ πεπονθὼς ἄκων ἄγεται πρὸς τὸ ἔνσονδον χάριτι δουλωθείς ; Publius Syrus 11, 61, 641.

[73] EN 9.7.1-2, 5-6.

[74] de Ben. 6.43.1.

[75] Ibid., 2.25.3.

[76] EN 4.3.24.

[77] de Off. 1.15.48.

to pay never catches up with the favour until he outstrips it'[78]. The person who fails to make every effort to do so is described as ingratus[79].

In Greek and Roman literature, this competition to outdo another in giving receives high praise. Quoting from the Greek philosopher, Chrysippus, Seneca lauds it as 'this most honourable rivalry in outdoing benefits by benefits'[80] and urges his readers to seek 'the secret of rivalry that is born in the hearts of the obligers and the obliged'[81]. Similarly, Pliny commends the one who wants 'friendship with you and vies with you in this best of rivalries, a reciprocated affection which will increase as time goes on'[82].

This continued agonistic attitude was only possible between those equals or near equals within the upper strata of society, where, as Hands remarks, 'the assertion of personal worth (ἀρετή/dignitas) through the maintenance of friendship remained of fundamental importance', an assertion which still depended not least on a claim to generosity (ἐλευθεριότης/liberalitas)'[83]. In this regard he cites Aristotle, who states that the liberal man (eleutherios) needs wealth in order to act generously and the just man (dikaios) also if he is to reciprocate gifts received[84]. It is evident that Aristotle is referring specifically to a particular class of people. Great public benefactions are suitable, he says, for those with ample means 'derived from their own exertions or from their ancestors or connections, and for the high born and famous and the like since birth, fame and so on all have an element of greatness and distinction'[85].

---

78 de Ben. 1.4.4.

79 Ep. 81.18 'A man is an ingrate if he repays a favour without interest. Therefore interest should always be allowed for, when you compare your receipts and your expenses. We should try by all means to be as grateful as possible.'

80 de Ben. 1.4.4 - hanc honestissimam contentionem beneficiis beneficia vincendi.

81 Ibid., 1.4.5.

82 Letters, 7.7.2.

83 Charities, 32.

84 EN 10.8.4; cf. 4.1.17.

85 EN 4.2.14.

This is not to say that all reciprocal relationships of this kind were the property of the upper classes. Mathews has shown that hospitality was incumbent upon the herdsman and prince alike in Homer[86]. It is difficult to assess to what extent other aspects of reciprocal *philia* existed among the lower classes. Given the viewpoint from which Aristotle and others write, I suspect that their denigration of friendship for utility is not simply restricted to the kind of relationship but includes the kind of people who form them. However, I shall deal with these relationships later. What is clear is that one of the prime requisites for this activity was adequate resources. Both giving and receiving for Aristotle were pleasant occupations. Receiving meant gaining what one desired. Giving, having larger means than the person benefited[87].

c. Refusal of friendship.

In principle within primitive societies gifts are always accepted. The obligation to receive is no less constraining than that of giving and repaying. One does not have the right to refuse a gift. Among the Kwakiutl, a North-West American Indian tribe, to refuse a gift or invitation was regarded as showing fear of having to repay or of being abased in default. It meant loss of status by admitting defeat in advance. In exceptional circumstances, a chieftain who considered himself superior could refuse a gift or invitation without hostilities ensuing. His refusal was an assertion of his superiority. Even then, it had to be accompanied by certain offers of gifts of his own[88].

The discussion of friendship in Greek and Roman literature centres on questions relating to the obligation to give, to receive and to return. Seldom is the refusal of an offer raised. From the evidence available, I doubt if refusal was generally practised and 'unusual' or 'exceptional' would best

---

[86] Hospitality, 50; cf. Homer, Od. 14.56-57, 15.74.

[87] Rhet. 1.11.22.

[88] M. Mauss, The Gift, 39-40.

describe such an occurrence. Certainly all gifts did not have to be accepted. But the circumstances in which one might properly refuse and the kinds of people to whom one could refuse an offer of friendship suggest that by and large the obligation to receive was observed. My contention is supported by what might be called themes in essays on friendship : those of 'the need for care in the choice of friends' and 'the problem of ingratitude'. Both of these topics refer to the difficulties resulting from acceptance, which indicates that the gift was received, despite the reservations or misgivings the recipient may have had. Subsequent behaviour points to the recipient's unwillingness, not to his refusal.

This is a crucial issue, for it points both to the binding nature of the obligation to accept an offer and to the consequences which attend refusal. Aristotle advises that the offer of friendship should not be accepted if the recipient is unwilling to return the favour. Because most offers are intended to return profit (ὠφέλεια) to the donor, one ought to consider at the outset from whom he will accept and to come to some agreement as to what is due in return, or else decline the offer. That is to say, to treat it as a commercial transaction[89]. He offers no comment as to the ensuing relations between the two parties but the context shows that his advice is proffered in view of the disputes which commonly occur after the gift is received. Cicero refers to this as acting praepostere : 'a negligence for which we are grievously punished for our carelessness in the choice and treatment of friends : for we deliberate after the event'. Thus after the relationships have been formed some cause of offence arises, and 'we suddenly break the bonds of friendship asunder when it has run but half its course'[90]. This notion of the careful choice of friends after testing or the

---

[89] EN 8.13.9.

[90] De Amic. 22.85

importance of judging a man before making him a friend features prominently in discussions on friendship. Cicero's praepostere warning is based on Theophrastus' On Friendship : τοὺς ἀλλοτρίους οὐ φιλοῦντα δεῖ κρίνειν ἀλλὰ κρίναντα φιλεῖν, but the sentiment appears in Theognis[91], Plutarch[92], Seneca[93], and elsewhere in Cicero[94], and in Publius Syrus[95].

Just as prominent are the warnings which revolve around the ingratitude of the person who has received the gift. Seneca pursues the general line when he says that the person 'who is too eager to pay his debt is unwilling to be indebted, and he who is unwilling to be indebted is ungrateful'[96]. In a similar vein, 'he who is unwilling to accept new benefits must resent those already received'[97]. If anyone denied or evaded the obligation to return a gift, the act of neglect was considered an injustice and a reasonable ground for dissolving the friendship. Ingratitude was the commonest kind of injustice which changed a friendly relationship into a hostile one. Seneca warns that one can go only so far in reminding an ungrateful person of his obligation 'for fear that I may turn an ingrate into an enemy'[98]. That he had shown insufficient gratitude was regarded by Mark Antony as the heaviest (gravissimus) of the charges he could lay against Cicero whom he accused of violating friendship (amicitia violata) with Caesar[99]. Amicitia violata is the equivalent of Seneca's description of ingratitude as beneficia violata, an act which renders a man cruel and wicked[100]. The protests show that ingratitude is failure in regard to an obligation incurred

---

91 125-128.

92 Mor. 94C-F.

93 Ep. 3.1-2.

94 de Amic. 17.62-63.

95 134.

96 de Ben. 4.40.5.

97 Ibid., 4.40.2.

98 Ibid., 5.22.3 - ne ex ingrato inimicum faciam.

99 Cicero, Phil. 2.1.2-3.5.

100 Ep. 81.32.

by acceptance. Yet with all the attendant problems and the serious social sanctions which followed such failure, acceptance prevailed over refusal. The question bears asking whether more dire consequences accompanied refusal.

Seneca says it is not necessary to receive from everybody, only from those to whom one would have chosen oneself to give. However, it is the nature of friendship and the nexus of binding personal obligations which concern him. One must be more careful in selecting one's creditor for a benefit than a creditor for a loan. For while repayment in full finalizes a loan, the acceptance of a benefit and its more than generous repayment commences a lasting reciprocal relationship[101]. For that reason Seneca did not want to be involved in a protracted relationship with someone he objected to, an unworthy person (indignus)[102]. For different reasons, though indicating again the nature and ties of friendship, he may refuse a worthy benefactor where the offer may result in some injury, inconvenience or risk to the benefactor himself. For instance, where the offer consists of services at the bar, the act of friendship would make him an enemy of a powerful opponent with terrible consequences[103].

While he admits that there are occasions where it is impossible to refuse - superior force or fear eliminates choice and coercing one to accept an offer ends in obedience not choice - in most situations one is free (liberum). It is for the individual to decide with some discernment whether he is willing or not[104]. He cites, as does Aristotle, Socrates' refusal of Archelaus' invitation and gives two reasons. First, Socrates did not wish to be placed in a position where he would be given gifts which he could not return. He exercises his right to choose and thereby remains free of an unwanted obligation. Second, and following on from the first, the man to whom freedom meant so much, declined to enter into 'voluntary servitude'[105]. Aristotle reasons similarly :

---

101 de Ben. 2.18.3-5.

102 Ibid., 2.18.5.

103 Ibid., 2.21.3.

104 Ibid., 2.18.6-7.

105 Ibid., 5.6.2-7.

Socrates refused as he could not reciprocate in kind, which would imply his being put to shame[106]. Though Socrates was free to refuse, Seneca candidly admits that his refusal would have made an enemy of the king 'who was arrogant and wished all his favours to be highly valued'. He was a loser in both ways. To refuse the invitation or to have been unable to return the gifts offered were alike rebuffs[107].

This exercise of choice, while highly commendable, had serious repercussions for Julius Graecinus, who, to finance the expense of public games, accepted gifts from his friends. However, he refused large sums of money from Fabius Persicus and a consular named Rebilus, men he considered to be of bad reputation. As a result, he earned the lasting hostility of the more powerful rebuffed donors[108]. A more realistic picture is painted by Cicero as he acknowledges the constancy of ever present obligations : 'For not only was I sick of it in the old days when I had youth and ambition to urge me on, and it was open to me absolutely to decline to defend a man I did not wish to defend' but now, 'there are times when I am obliged to defend men who have not deserved very well of me, at the instance of those who have deserved well of me'[109]. When we compare the weight of the discussion in Seneca on refusal as against the problems of unwilling friendship, Cicero's realism is sheeted home. In this regard, Seneca deals almost entirely with the ungrateful acceptor, who denies he has received a benefit, pretends he has not received one, fails to return one, receives one unwillingly or hastens to return it, or, worst of all, forgets a benefit[110].

Thus, although a person has the right to refuse an offer of friendship, and that right springs from his freedom as an individual (should he be free), acceptance rather than refusal was the social custom[111]. There were few like Socrates. Few

---

106 Rhet. 2.23.8.

107 de Ben. 5.6.7.

108 Ibid., 2.21.5-6.

109 Fam. 7.1.4; cf. Att. 1.12.1.

110 de Ben. 3.1.3.

111 See Diog. 6.36 refusal means breach of friendship.

were prepared to face the possible or likely hostilities inherent in a refusal. Rather, it was easier to accept an unwanted friendship and let the relationship take its unhappy course. The obligation to receive, then, was generally honoured, even though in many instances, carelessly, foolishly and begrudgingly.

d. Cessation of friendship.

It follows logically that the theme of 'cessation of friendship' should figure prominently in the discussions. Aristotle gives a number of legitimate reasons for breaking off friendship. a. In inferior kinds of friendship, for utility (τὸ χρήσιμον) or pleasure (τὸ ἡδύ) cessation may follow when 'our friends no longer possess the attribute of being useful or agreeable'[112]. Cicero, on the assumption that advantage (utilitas) is the cement of friendship, comments that where it is removed friendship falls apart[113]. b. Where blatant deception reveals that there never was an intention of friendship, the injured party can withdraw[114]. c. A person can disassociate himself from a friend who has been judged to be an immoral man and beyond restoration[115]. d. A friendship can be disbanded when one friend becomes superior in virtue and differences in tastes, likes and dislikes follow[116]. Friendship generally was considered a matter of equality. A friend who could not return a favour found himself in an inferior position and the relationship was in danger of being destroyed by the inequality. Aristotle laid great emphasis upon the importance of equality in friendship and found great difficulty in either maintaining friendship where equality had ceased or in making friends with unequals[117]. As we shall

---

112 EN 9.3.1.

113 de Amic. 9.32.

114 EN 9.3.2.

115 EN 9.3.3.

116 EN 9.3.4.

117 EN 8.7.1-6; cf. 8.6.6, 7.2-5, 13.1.

see, similarity of interests was a major element in true friendship and e. lack of it could bring it to an end[118]. As Cicero remarks : disparity in character and diversity of taste severs friendship (dissimilitudo dissociat amicitias). While such disparity does not make the relationship impossible, it cannot remain secure[119].

Cicero considered that no one was so bound that he could not withdraw from friends who were sinning in some important matter of public concern[120]. Serious disagreements ensue from such people demanding that their friends join them in their felonies. For refusal leads to the charge that the laws of friendship have been disregarded and so 'social intimacies are destroyed and everlasting enmities are produced' (familiaritates exstingui solere ... odia etiam gigni sempiterna)[121]. Still, there were considerable limits within which a friendship could be retained. Even should a friend wish something not altogether honourable but which involved his life or reputation, Cicero suggests that, provided one's own reputation or loyalty to the state is not questioned, 'we should turn aside from the straight path'[122]. This, however, as is the case with many of the anomalies in the principles of friendship, is at variance with a previous principle he had proposed : 'Therefore let this law be established in friendship : neither ask dishonourable things, nor do them if asked'[123].

Even in more difficult circumstances, unless it involves intolerable wickedness where withdrawal of affection and association should be immediate, 'ties of such friendship should be sundered by a gradual relaxation of intimacy'[124].

---

[118] EN 8.8.5-6; cf. 8.7.4-5.

[119] De Amic. 20.74.

[120] Ibid. 12.42.

[121] Ibid., 11.35.

[122] Ibid., 17.61.

[123] Ibid., 12.40.

[124] Cicero, de Amic. 21.76; cf. de Off. 1.33.120 'When friendship becomes no longer pleasing or desirable, it is more proper (so wise men think) to undo the bond little by little than to sever it at a stroke'.

Or, as Cicero had heard Cato reported as saying, 'They should be unravelled rather than rent apart' (dissuendae magis quam discindendae)[125]. Else, continues Cicero, it will not merely seem to be the case that friendships are put aside (non solum amicitiae depositae), but that 'open hostility has been aroused' (inimicitiae susceptae)[126]. Thus he counsels, 'you must be on your guard lest friendships be changed into serious enmities (gravis inimicitias) which are the source of disputes, abuse, and invective'[127]. Therefore the utmost caution was required and in fact, says Cicero, Scipio thought that even if one is unfortunate in one's choice of friends, it is better to endure the friendship than end it by planning hostile actions[128].

A graphic word from Plutarch on the problem reveals similar difficulties. He concedes that it is not easy to escape or to put aside an unsatisfactory friendship, for 'an unprincipled friend (φίλος πονηρός) either causes pain and intense discomfort by his continual association or else with accompanying enmity and hostility is forcibly ejected like bile'[129].

So far I have shown that a relationship of enmity can arise through a failure in the obligation to receive or return or through cessation of friendship however caused. Enmity can also arise out of the unfriendly acts of the benefactor, particularly in relation to the obligation to give to those who ask him for a benefit. Seneca warns the reluctant benefactor that a gift should not be given carelessly as it will be acknowledged in the same spirit as it is given[130].

---

125 de Amic. 21.76.

126 Ibid., 21.77.

127 Ibid., 21.78.

128 Ibid., 16.60.

129 Mor. 94D.

130 de Ben. 1.1.8.

Hesitant giving is next to refusal and wins no gratitude[131]. Unwillingness indicates 'the giver has not the courage to withstand the effort to extract it'[132]. So, cries the recipient in a burst of noble anger, 'if you are going to do anything, do it', and 'nothing is worth such a price; I would rather have you say no at once'[133]. 'Tardy goodwill smacks of illwill (tarde velle nolentis est)'[134]. The notion of enmity is an important one and I will examine it at length in the next chapter. Sufficient for the moment is it to notice that failure in the obligations of friendship, of giving, receiving and returning, can lead to enmity.

e. The reciprocal language of friendship.

By now much of the reciprocal vocabulary of friendship has emerged. Before analysing the nature and structure of the various kinds of friendship which appear in Greek and Roman literature, I will look at certain key relational terms with an eye to the nuance of reciprocity which always seems to be present when signifying a φιλία/amicitia relationship. In relation to friendship the Romans possess a more precise and almost technical group of correlative terms in contrast to the rich variety of the Greeks. But in each of the word groups which I will deal with - πίστις/fides,τὸ καθῆκον/officium, χάρις/gratia - the Latin and Greek words are equivalent.

πίστις and fides denote 'trust' or 'faith' and therefore 'trustworthiness' or 'faithfulness', and refer to a moral obligation and moral judgment. Epictetus held that man is born to πίστις (ὁ ἄνθρωπος πρὸς πίστιν γέγονεν) - to overthrow it is to overthrow the characteristic quality of man, and among other things, friendship[135]. Theognis sought to

---

[131] Ibid., 2.1.2.

[132] Ibid.

[133] Ibid., 2.5.2-3. Cf. Publius Syrus 591.

[134] de Ben. 2.5.4.

[135] 2.4.1, 3; cf. 2.22.27, 30, for philos/pistos, philia/pistis.

maintain it as the basis of his friendships[136] and it is what he looked for in a man who was to be his friend[137]. Without it (ἄνευ πίστεως) there can be no stable friendship and such πίστις comes only with time[138]. In Dio Chrysostom pistis is akin to εὐ πάσχειν, the act of being benefited, for which, he complains, one seldom receives gratitude (charis) from the recipient[139]. Failure in regard to it can lead to public censure, and the ἄπιστος and his ἀπιστία are included in Pollux' thesaurus of damaging invective which one can hurl against an opponent[140].

The reciprocal nature of fides can be seen where it is used in conjunction with such terms as patrocinium, praesidium and amicitia, amici, clientes, hospites and patroni[141]. It was a standard principle of Roman life which Cicero called 'the most sacred thing in life' (sanctissimam in vita)[142]. The Romans took great pride in their fulfilment of it, and Hieron describes them as men who continually talk about fidelity (pistis)[143]. By contrast, they considered the Greeks to be the moral antithesis of their own good selves. In Plautus, among many other examples, Graeca fides is used to describe the Roman's view of Greek unworthiness. All that is good in fides, becomes totally inverted in meaning[144].

---

136 529-30.

137 74; cf. his cynical comments as to the absence of pistis in others 811-813, 831-832.

138 Aristotle, EE 7.2.40; cf. Cicero, de Amic. 18.65.

139 Disc. 73.9. For numerous examples drawn from history, see his Disc. 73, περὶ πίστεως, and 74, περὶ ἀπιστίας, where he bitterly claims that it is dangerous to trust anyone, especially those who claim to be friends.

140 4.35, 38.

141 So M. Gelzer, The Roman Nobility (ET Oxford, 1969), 65-66 & nn. 72, 73 for numerous examples. See also Fustel de Coulanges, Histoire des institutions politiques de l'ancienne France Vol. 5 (Paris, 1922) 217-225; J. Hellegouarc'h, Le vocabulaire latin des relations et des partis politiques sous La Republique (Paris, 1963), 23-35; F. Schulz, Principles of Roman Law (ET Oxford, 1936), 223-238.

142 Verr. 2.3.3.

143 Diodor. 23.1.

144 Asinaria 199; see E. Segal, Roman Laughter (Cambridge, 1968), 37-39.

A man's reputation and honour were inseparably linked with it and defaulted to social disgrace (infamia)[145]. In connection with friendship, writers discussed the lengths a friend should go to maintain it[146].

Officium and τὸ καθῆκον are identical in meaning. περὶ καθήκοντος was a popular topic of the Stoics. Diogenes Laertius says that Zeno, the founder of the Stoics, was the first to use τὸ καθῆκον of conduct in his περὶ τοῦ καθήκοντος[147]. Panaetius and his student Posidonius produced similar works[148]. Diogenes describes one aspect of τὰ καθήκοντα as intercourse with friends (συμφέρεσθαι φίλοις), while it is παρὰ τὸ καθῆκον to 'disagree with friends')φίλοις μὴ συνδιατίθεσθαι)[149]. Cicero cites Panaetius' work as one of the sources for his de Officiis[150] and elsewhere in discussing the title of this work tells Atticus that τὸ καθῆκον is the nearest Greek equivalent to officium[151]. M. Gelzer renders social officium as 'reciprocal personal relationship' in the concrete sense of 'the performance of an action arising from such a relationship, and as a social and ultimately moral duty'[152].

Gratia and χάρις in the subjective sense can refer both to the response of gratitude or recognition by the recipient

---

145 Cicero, S. Rosc. 39.112 - 'The one who does not carry out a trust is guilty of a disgraceful fault, because he violates two things which are most sacred - friendship and good faith (duas res sanctissimas violat, amicitiam et fidem)'.

146 Cicero, de Amic. 11.36; Seneca Ep. 81.27.

147 7.124, 129.

148 Panaetius : Cicero, de Off. 1.3.8-9; Posidonius : Diog Laert, 7.124, 129.

149 7.108.

150 de Off. 1.3.8-9 - commune officium καθῆκον vocant.

151 Att. 16.11.4 - Quod de inscriptione quaeris non dubito quin καθῆκον officium sit. Cf. Ibid., 16.14.2; Pliny, NH Pref. 22; Aulus Gellius, 13.28.1; Servius, Aen. 548, who renders it as beneficium - beneficium est quod Graeci τὸ καθῆκον appellant.

152 Nobility, 66-67, esp. n. 75. See also, J. Hellegouarc'h, Le vocabulaire latin, 152-163.

of the favour shown[153] and to the kindness or goodwill of the donor[154]. In the concrete sense they mean the 'favour done' or 'favour returned'[155]. Both can refer to the favour in which one stands, one's popularity[156], and gratia at times could be translated as 'reciprocal good relations'[157]. Cicero terms it the foremost duty (officium)[158] and both gratia and beneficium are essential to the existence of amicitia[159]. Cicero defines it as 'that which has regard for remembering and returning services, honour and acts of friendship'[160].

f. Forms of friendship.

We have seen that _philos_ is used in Homer of those who are 'dear' or 'one's own', and by extension, refers to the things which a man possessed and relied upon, his _oikos_ and his external relationships[161]. _Philia_ is used by Aristotle not only of human relationships but also of those within animal

---

153 Gratia : Seneca, Ep. 81.19; Cicero, de Off. 2.13.63, Att. 1.1.4, 1.19.4, Brut. 209, Mur. 24, Agr. 2.1. χάρις : Dio Chrysostom, Disc. 73.9; Eur., Or. 244; Homer, Od. 4.695, 22.319; Xenophon, Cyr. 1.6.11.

154 Seneca, de Ben. 4.21.2.

155 χάρις : of the donor and the recipient, Thucydides, 3.63.4 - τὰς ὅμοιας χάριτας μὴ ἀντιδίδοναι αἰσχρόν ; cf. Arist. EN 9.2.1-3; of the donor, Aeschylus, Pr. 821; Sophocles, OC. 1489; Aristotle, Rhet.2.4.29; cf. χαρίζω, Homer, Od. 10.43; Aeschylus, Pr. 985; Euripides Or. 453; Lys. 12.60, 28.17, 31.24. Gratia : Seneca, de Ben. 2.25.3, 30.2, 33.2, 4.21.1-2; Cicero, Fam. 1.7.21. See also J. Hellegouarc'h, Le vocabulaire latin, 205-208; J.W. Franzmann, The Early Development of the Greek Concept of Charis (Ann Arbor, 1972).

156 Gratia : Cicero, A. Rosc. 15, Planc. 7.47, Verr. 2.1.136, 3.60, Att. 1.16.2, 17.6, 5.21.2, Fam. 2.6.3, 6.6.9, 11.16.3. χάρις : Plutarch, Lives 'Demos.' 849A.

157 Cicero, Verr. 2.1.21, Att. 1.14.7, 2.3.4, Fam. 1.9.4, 1.9.19; Aulus Gellius, 6.19.6.

158 de Off. 1.15.47.

159 Seneca, de Ben. 5.11.1; cf. Cicero, Planc. 33.80.

160 de Inv. 2.22.66 - gratiam quae in memoria et remuneratione officiorum et honoris et amicitiarum observantiam teneat. Cf. ibid. 2.53.161 - gratia, in qua amicitiarum et officiorum alterius memoria et remunerandi voluntas continetur.

161 See above n.23.

life in general[162] and of the parched earth's love for rain[163]. The term is comprehensive enough to encompass ' all relations in which things come together'[164]. His preoccupation, and that of many other Greek writers[165], is with those which are specifically human. Any human relationship based upon conscious reciprocity (ἀντιφίλησις) of goodwill(εὔνοια) constitutes <u>philia</u>[166].

However, not all friendships are of the same kind (εἶδος). Against popular opinion, Aristotle posits three distinct kinds of friendship (τρία φιλίας εἴδη)[167]- the good (τὸ ἀγαθόν), the pleasant (τὸ ἡδύ) and the useful (τὸ χρήσιμον)[168] - which three fold classification was followed by later Greek and Roman writers[169]. Moreover, each kind exhibits its own characteristic marks (φιλικά).

Perfect or ideal friendship is only possible between men who are <u>agathoi</u> and alike in <u>aretē</u>[170]. They alone are entitled to be called absolute or total friends (ἁπλῶς φίλοι)[177]. Aristotle lists its main characteristics. a. It is inclusive in that it incorporates the entire person for what he is in himself, namely good. In theory it is disinterested, for a good man has only an unselfish desire for his friend's well-being; he seeks only the good for him[172]. b. There is

[162] EN 8.1.3.

[163] EN 8.1.6.

[164] So, H.H. Joachim, Aristotle : The Nichomachean Ethics (Oxford, 1951), 244.

[165] Diogenes records a number of authors who wrote on περὶ φιλίας. Eg., 2.124, Simmias of Thebes, περὶ φίλου ; 4.4, Speusippus, περὶ φιλίας; 4.12, Xenocrates, a treatise in two books; 5.45, Theophrastus, in three books; 7.175, Cleanthes.

[166] EN 8.2.3-4.

[167] EN 8.3.1.

[168] EN 8.2.1.

[169] Eg., Plutarch, Mor. 8Eff; Seneca, de Ben. 1.11.1 - necessaria, utilia, iucunda; Cicero received a vast number of Greeks into his amicitia during his career (see R.J. Rowland Jnr. 'Cicero and the Greek World', TAPA 103, (1972), 451-461) and was undoubtedly thoroughly conversant with Greek concepts of friendship. P.A. Brunt, '"Amicitia" in the Late Roman Republic', PCPS 11 (1965), 1-20, shows that, while Cicero was not dependent on Aristotle or other Greek thinkers, he was familiar with Aristotle's triad. Cf. Cicero, de Amic. 6.22, 8.26, de Inv. 1.50.95, 2.55.176, Fam. 3.10.7-9.

[170] Aristotle, EN 8.3.6.

[171] Ibid., 8.4.6.

[172] Ibid., 8.13.2; cf. Cicero, de Fin. 2.26.78.

common or mutual attraction and interest based on being good and liking what is unqualifiedly good[173]. Common life was regarded as an essential element in all kinds of friendship, if somewhat more particularly marked in true friendship. Cicero regarded it as the essence of friendship, 'the most complete agreement in policy, in pursuits and in opinions'[174]; as 'accord in all things human and divine, conjoined with mutual goodwill and affection'[175]; and as 'equality and perfect reciprocity in all things'[176]. Plato comments simply, 'friendship is agreement' (ἡ φιλία ὁμονοία)[177] and Pliny likewise, 'a similitude of manners is the strongest cement of friendship'[178]. These sentiments were widely endorsed by other writers[179]. It is worth noting, however, even in this highest order of friendship, that one never loves another simply because he is lovable. Common life is reciprocal affection and action. c. True friendship tends to be lasting (φιλία διαμένει), for good men possess most of the virtues, and virtue is a stable quality[180]. Cicero speaks of the real and lasting friendship (verae amicitiae sempiternae) of the wise[181] in contrast with the impermanency of friendships of the ordinary kind (volgaris amicitiae).[182] He believed that true amicitia was achievable only between two morally perfect men - as he intends us to view the relationship between Scipio and Laelius[183] - or the good and

---

173 Aristotle, EN 8.3.6. Cf. Plutarch, Mor. 659F : φίλους δὲ ποιεῖσθαι τοὺς ἀγαθούς.

174 de Amic. 4.15.

175 Ibid., 6.20; cf. 17.61.

176 de Inv. 2.66.

177 Alcib. 127B.

178 Letters, 4.15.

179 Eg., Homer, Od. 17.218; Plato, Lys. 214A, Phdr. 240C; Aristotle, EE 7.1.7; Plutarch, Mor. 52A, 96D, E.

180 Aristotle, EN 8.3.6; cf. Plutarch, Mor. 659F : 'immutable & steadfast'.

181 de Amic. 9.32.

182 Ibid., 21.76.

183 Ibid., 15.82.

the wise[184]. For Seneca, 'the wise man alone is a real friend'[185]. Cicero qualifies this aspect of friendship. Unlike 'sophists' who take the maxim, 'no one is good unless he is wise', to extreme, thereby excluding all but philosophic sages from true friendship, he wants 'good' understood practically from 'the experience of everyday life' (i.e. good as the man in the street understands it)[186]. Friendships for the sake of τὸ ἡδύ or τὸ χφήσιμον merely approximate to perfect friendship. They exhibit degrees of the primary and principal (πρῶτος καὶ κυρίως) meaning and thus are called friendships by analogy (καθ' ὁμοιότητα)[187]. Aristotle regards friendship for τὸ ἡδὺ more highly than that for τὸ χρήσιμον[188] for it more closely resembles the perfect. While it exhibits many of the selfish characteristics of τὸ χρήσιμον -(a), (c), (d), (e) below - it reflects a more generous nature (τὸ ἐλευθέριον)[189] and is based on common pleasures.

τὸ χρήσιμον represents the commonest form of friendship, formed by bad men (φαύλοι)[190] who are denigrated as the commercially-minded (ἀγόραιοι)[191] whose motive for the association is some concrete advantage or profit (ὠφέλεια)[192]. Thus friendship for utility is presented as being entirely self-interested. H.H. Joachim summarises its characteristics

---

184 Ibid., 4.18; cf. 26.100 - amicitia perfectorum ... id est sapientium; de Off. 1.17.55-56.

185 Ep. 81.12.

186 de Amic. 5.18.

187 Aristotle, EN 8.4.4.

188 Ibid., 8.6.4.

189 Ibid.

190 Ibid., 8.4.6; cf. id. EE 7.2.14.

191 Ibid., 8.6.4.

192 Ibid., 8.13.4. Cf. Cicero, de Off. 2.20.69 : 'For as a rule, our will is more inclined to the one from whom we expect a prompter and speedier return'; de Amic. 14.51.

in Aristotle[193]. a. Its attraction arises out of a man's property or possessions rather than his whole personality. That is to say, κατὰ συμβεβηκός, 'incidental' friendship, which exists for some temporary rather than essential quality[194]. b. It occurs mostly between men with contrary needs (ἐξ ἐναντίων) 'for what is most useful to you is just what you do not possess yourself'[195]. c. It is generally of short duration, existing only in relation to the cause. When the cause no longer exists, the friendship dissolves[196]. In this regard Cicero comments, 'your friendship will last just so long as it is attended by expediency (utilitas). If expediency creates the feeling it will also destroy it'[197]. Seneca scathingly attacks such cases as 'fair weather friendships; one who is chosen for the sake of utility (utilitas) will be satisfactory only so long as he is useful'[198]. d. Even bad men can be friends for the sake of some advantage from each other[199]. e. The services required take little time. It is therefore possible to satisfy many people at the same time[200]. Intimacy and common life are not essential[201].

Aristotle's purpose, as A.W.H. Adkins observes[202], is to contrast <u>philia kat'aretēn</u> as sharply as possible with other types of <u>philia</u>. It is entirely unselfish; the others, completely selfish. While some of the distinctions are valid as to the degree of affection and quality of the relationships[203], nevertheless, as to the structure of the

---

193 Aristotle, 248.

194 Aristotle, EN 8.3.6, 4.6.

195 Ibid., 8.8.6.

196 Ibid., 8.3.3, 4.2.

197 de Fin. 2.26.78.

198 Ep. 9.9.

199 Aristotle, EN 8.4.2; cf. 8.4.6, 8.5, 9.6.4.

200 Ibid., 8.6.3.

201 Ibid., 8.3.4.

202 'Friendship', 40.

203 Cf. Aristotle, EN 8.3.1-3.

relationships, Aristotle is 'drawing a false distinction between them. The pattern of φιλία remains the same'[204].

Adkins reminds us that the agathos and his aretē to whom Aristotle is so drawn 'denote and commend a leisured social class'. They are not simply moral terms. These are the people of wealth and rank whose needs are met by each other in politics, the law courts and war. He continues,

> 'In Greek thought from the late fifth century onwards these are the fields in which ἀρετή is preeminently displayed : when help is needed by an Aristotelian ἀγαθός it is of the ἀρετή of the ἀγαθός that he has need, and it is on account of this ἀρετή that he φιλεῖ the other ἀγαθός. He will feel a strong and selfish emotion when he needs him under the φιλον-aspect : he need feel none when he φιλεῖ'[205].

While it may be possible to talk of lesser degrees of selfishness in Aristotle's friendship of the good, the structure of philia is the same for each kind of friendship and remains unaltered from what we saw in Homer.

Undoubtedly the distinction that Aristotle makes is a reaction to the theory and practice of his predecessors and contemporaries who saw utility as the source and continuing basis of friendship. Socrates, according to Xenophon, spoke of friendship solely in utilitarian terms[206], as a relationship of choice formed by services rendered and existing by the continuation of mutual service[207]. In Plato's only work on friendship, the Lysis, while he asserted the existing notion that friendship is only possible between the good[208], he held that the first position which should be maintained is :

---

204 'Friendship', 42.

205 'Friendship', 43. For his discussion of the notion of aretē see Merit and Responsibility, chs. 10-11.

206 Mem. 1.2.52-55; 2.6.4.

207 Mem. 2.6.5, 22-28; cf. id. Cyr. 8.7.13.

208 214D.

'whether a person will be loved depends upon whether he is useful'[209].

Diogenes tells us that the Cyrenaics, a minor Socratic school, held a similar position[210]. They were the pioneers of the thoroughgoing utilitarianism of Epicurus and his followers. Epicurus taught that 'friendship must always be sought for itself though it has its origins in the need for help'[211]. Similarly, 'the necessities of life give rise to friendship; it is indeed necessary to lay its foundation[212]. For him, interest was essential to friendship. However, a man concerned only with interest or, conversely, with no thought for utility, can not be a friend; 'for the one trades in favours so as to profit from them, the other cuts off at the root all good hope for the future'[213]. While utility is more pronounced in Epicurean friendship, bringing sharp censure from Cicero[214], nonetheless, though with various emphases, its presence in the popular thought and practice of Greek and Roman friendship cannot be denied.

By contrast, ideal friendship was extremely rare. Rarer than complete virtue in a man, admits Aristotle, for ἁπλῶς φιλία requires two of such character[215]. It existed 'between two only or at most a few'[216] and according to Seneca, was 'a rarity in all ages'[217]. The 'rarity' of which they speak may be due solely to the narrowness of the definition or the attempt to project the ideal. But not entirely so. It may also indicate the vast range of relationships into which one

---

[209] 210C; cf. 212D, C, where he declares that reciprocity is essential to friendship.

[210] 2.91 : τόν φίλον τῆς χρείας ἕνεκα

[211] Gn. 5.23.

[212] Life 120.

[213] Gn. 5.39.

[214] de Fin. 2.26.82-85.

[215] EN 8.3.8; cf. 9.10.6; Plutarch, Mor. 93E; Cicero, de Amic. 5.20; de Off. 21.79 - 'a rare class indeed'.

[216] Seneca, de Ben. 6.23.3.

[217] Ibid.

had to enter in political and social life in order to survive. For all their derogatory comments, it is clear that these writers had relationships in all categories and one can talk about a relational mix in which all kinds overlapped in the experience of each individual. The practicalities of life demanded it. Aristotle himself argues that we should limit the number of our friends in all three kinds of friendship[218]. Philia and amicitia are used to describe a vast range of relationships which varied almost imperceptibly in quality and degree[219]. In his supposed Handbook of Electioneering, Cicero pointed to one of the extended uses of amicitia. 'But the word "friends" has a wider application in a canvass than in the rest of life, for anybody who shows you some goodwill, or cultivates your society, or calls upon you regularly, is to be counted as a "friend"[220]. A vast complex of reciprocal services existed to meet the wide-ranging needs of individuals. Almost all of Cicero's letters to his friends either express thanks for a variety of services rendered or contain requests for services[221]. Whatever his needs, he turned to those philoi whose services he had secured in the past and who were morally obliged to respond. Whether it was for intimate friendship[222], social pleasure[223], a loan to finance a political campaign or to build a villa[224], advice[225],

---

218 EN 9.10.2.

219 Cf. Cicero, de Inv. 2.168. For the different forms of amicitia and the vocabulary commonly associated with it, see J. Hellegouarc'h Le Vocabulaire Latin, 63-90. For Cicero, see P.A. Brunt, 'Amicitia', 202-209.

220 5.16.

221 For an excellent recent study of the extent and variety of relations required to secure Cicero politically and socially, see B. Rawson, The Politics of Friendship : Pompey and Cicero (Sydney, 1978).

222 Eg., Cicero, Att. 1.18; Fam. 7.17.2; de Off. 1.17.58; Seneca, de Ben. 6.29.1.

223 Eg., Cicero, Fam. 3.13.2; 5.15.2; de Off. 1.17.58.

224 Eg., Cicero, Fam. 14.1.5; Seneca, de Ben. 1.2.4, 1.5.1-2, 11.5.

225 Eg., Cicero, Att. 3.15; de Off. 1.17.58; Seneca, de Ben. 1.2.4, 6.29.1.

the services of a lawyer[226], help in adversity[227], an appointment or promotion[228], an introduction[229], hospitality while travelling[230], or business commitments[231], one relied upon the friendships one had formed through past services.

g. Wealth and friendship.

Such services could never be paid for in cash. As A.R.Hands shows, among the aristocracy in Greece and Rome, the 'acceptance of payment in money remained shocking. It implied that the recipient was an employee of the other party, that he needed to accept such for his living and was not a man of quality at all'[232]. Only an equivalent service would suffice. Wealth was used to secure friends, never to respond directly to a benefit received. For the generous man (ὁ ἐλευθέριος), it was never an end in itself 'but as a means of giving'[233]. That is to say that wealth was to be 'used', which use consisted of 'spending and giving'[234]. By contrast, gaining and retaining riches were regarded as 'modes of acquisition'[235]. Being wealthy was not considered a wrong; it was desirable. But the retention of wealth was, and it is contrasted unfavourably with the correct use of wealth and, in particular, with that of its chief end, the acquisition of friends.

---

226 Eg., Cicero, de Off. 2.19.65-66; cf. ibid., 2.9.32.

227 Eg., Seneca, de Ben. 1.11.1, which he terms the highest benefit (necessaria); Cicero, Att. 8.14.1-2.

228 Eg., Ibid., 1.5.1-2, 11.5; these benefits (utilia) are : consulship, priesthood, public office, administration of a province, advancement for those striving for the higher positions.

229 See the many examples to which I refer in my discussion of recommendatio in Chapter 4.

230 Eg., Cicero, de Off. 2.18.64.

231 Eg., Plutarch, Mor. 95C; Publius Syrus, 53.

232 Charities, 33.

233 Aristotle, EN 4.1.20.

234 Ibid., 4.1.6-7.

235 Ibid.

This comparison of retention and use is a common one in discussions on friendship. Seneca writes, 'The wealth that you esteem, that, as you think, makes you rich and powerful, is buried under an inglorious name so long as you keep it. It is but house, or slave, or money; when you have given it away, it is a benefit'[236]. The truly wealthy person, suggests Aristotle, is the one who uses his money correctly rather than the one who simply possesses it[237]. Such is Menander's sentiment : 'while a person has control of his wealth, he should use it to secure the permanent good of friendship'; and again, unlike money, friendship lasts, for 'friends whom you have secured by generosity will make good a misfortune by repaying their debt of gratitude[238].

Speaking from bitter experience, Cicero asks if even the greatest wealth 'can stand without the services of friends'[239]. He regarded friendship as an 'absolutely indispensable relation' (maxime necessaria) on which all men thought alike - i.e. 'without friends, there is no life at all (sine amicitia vitam esse nullam), whether one is a statesman, a scholar, business man, or given up to sensual pleasures'[240]. It is this refrain with which Aristotle commences his discussion on friendship and in particular the question as to why one needs friends. He argues that not even the rich and powerful who possess all the other good things 'would choose to live without friends'. If he wishes to live a life of goodness (arete), he needs friends most of all (ἀναγκαιότατον), both to give benefits to, and an exercise of his arete, and to protect him against his enemies[241]. Finally we find the proverb in Greek

---

[236] de Ben. 6.3.4.

[237] Rhet. 1.5.7.

[238] Dysk. 5.797-812. Cf. these commercial connotations of friendship with Xenophon, Mem. 2.10.4, who advises the rich man to buy friends when they are cheap, and with Horace, Ep. 1.12.24 : vilis amicorum est annona bonis ubi quid deest.

[239] Planc. 33.81; cf. de Amic. 15.55.

[240] Ibid., 23.86.

[241] EN 8.1.1.

and Roman literature, 'friends are more necessary than fire and water'[242].

Wealth was not, however, given away indiscriminately. Each of the writers counsels that the benefactor should consider his own limited means and resources[243]. While the greatest privilege of having wealth is the opportunity it affords to do good, it should not be at the expense of one's fortune[244]. Indiscriminate giving is equivalent to ruining oneself, for 'wealth is the means of life'[245]. Thus in regard to 'giving and getting' (δόσιν καὶ λῆψιν) one ought to observe the mean[246]. The practice of Aristotle's truly liberal man provides us with the model all should try to emulate[247].

a. He gives to the right people. Cicero spells this out in more detail. The benefactor should 'take into account his moral character, his attitude towards us, the intimacy of his relations to us, and our common social ties, as well as the services he has hitherto rendered in our interest'[248].

b. He gives the right amount. This involves the donors becoming 'good calculators of duty able by adding and subtracting to strike a balance correctly and find out just how much is due to each individual'[249]. c. He gives at the right time and fulfils all the other conditions of right giving. All equally deplore the extravagant spender, no matter how honourable his intentions, 'for', says Cicero, 'many have squandered their patrimony by indiscriminate giving'[250].

---

242 Cf. Plutarch, Mor. 51B : πυρὸς καὶ ὕδατος ὁ φίλος ἀναγκαιότερος Cf. Cicero, de Amic. 6.22 : 'we do not use the proverbial "fire and water" on more occasions than friendship'.

243 Cicero, de Off. 1.14.44, 2.15.55; Seneca, de Ben. 2.15.3; Aristotle, EN 4.2.12; Publius Syrus, 54.

244 Cicero, de Off. 2.18.64; cf. ibid., 1.14.44.

245 Aristotle, EN 4.1.5.

246 Ibid., 2.7.4, 4.1.24; cf. Cicero, de Off. 2.17.59; Seneca, de Ben. 2.16.2.

247 EN 4.1.12.

248 Cicero, de Off. 1.14.45; cf. Seneca, de Ben. 2.15.3 : 'character and rank'.

249 Cicero, de Off. 1.18.59.

250 Ibid., 2.15.54. Cf. Aristotle's ἄσωτος, 'prodigal', who exceeds in giving but is deficient in getting : EN 2.7.4, 4.1.2, 29ff.

Chapter 2

THE RELATIONSHIP OF ENMITY

a. The idea of enmity.

I now return to the notion of enmity to investigate at length this hostile relationship, which is denoted by ἔχθρα/inimictia. As to whether it should be considered as an institution in its own right or subsumed under that of friendship, I am uncertain. In contrast to the many studies on friendship by scholars, I know of no study, major or otherwise, on enmity in Greek or Roman society[1]. This may be due to the almost total lack of discussion by Greek and Roman writers. Where it is dealt with, it is usually as a brief adjunct to friendship[2]. That is not to say that it is less important, or less a part of their social and political relationships. If anything, it indicates the general dread of such a relationship.

In early Greek literature, friendship and enmity are strongly contrasted in the traditional maxim, that one ought to do everything 'to help a friend and harm an enemy' (... κρατεῖν ἂν ἢ τὸν ἐχθρὸν ἢ φίλοισιν ὠφελεῖν ἔχειν)[3].

---

[1] That is not to say that it does not appear at all; but where it does, it is only treated briefly and mostly in conjunction with friendship; eg., 'Friends and Enemies', K.J. Dover, Greek Popular Morality in the Time of Plato and Aristotle (Oxford, 1974), 180-184.

[2] Plutarch's 'How to Profit from your Enemies', Mor. 863-92F, is the most detailed work in Greek literature on the subject. Cf. Aristotle's minor discussion, Rhet. 2.4.30ff. The associated idea of envy is more frequently discussed by ancient authors, see below 49-51.

[3] Aristophanes, Birds 420f.; cf. Plato Phdr. 240A in its various forms. See also : Hesiod, W&D. 351; Theognis 869-872; Solon, 1.3-6; Pindar, Pyth. 2.83; Xenophon, Cyr. 1.4.25, 6.28, 31, 8.7.28, Anab. 1.3.6, 9.11; Hiero. 2.2; Euripides, Med. 807-10; Aristotle, Rhet. 2.23.21. For its appearance in inscriptions, see Dittenberger, Syll 3 1268.I. 15-16, where it appears as part of a series of moral imperatives : φίλους εὔνει ἐχθροὺς ἀμύνου ; cf. P.Hib.170.

L. Pearson comments : 'the sharp distinction of friend and enemy as though the relation of enmity was natural and permanent, is a remarkable feature of Greek literature'[4]. There are numerous appeals to the maxim to justify and to determine behaviour. It was accepted by the Greeks as part of the fixed order of things. It was simply what a man must do. In Lysias, a soldier on trial tells the magistrate that he expected his enemies to be unjust in denouncing and abusing him as he considered it 'ordained (τετάχθαι) that one should harm one's enemies and serve one's friends'[5].

As a principle of conduct it could be applied to any situation or procedure and in its applications one was 'learning something good and excellent' (μαθεῖν τι καλὸν καὶ ἀγαθόν)[6]. Those who excelled in it were thought worthy of commendation (δοκεῖ ἀνὴρ ἐπαίνου ἄξιος εἶναι)[7]. Fulfilment of it would make a man 'appear to be a god among men'[8]. Tell-tale praise indeed, for it implies that this is indicative of the activity of the gods. Such a man has made up his mind 'that a man's arete consists in outdoing his friends in kindness and his enemies in harm' (ποιεῖν τοὺς ἐχθροὺς κακῶς)[9]. Euripides regarded its fulfilment as a matter of the first importance, over which nothing could take precedence. As the old servant contemplated the end of his mistress' enemy, he remarks, 'when you would wreak vengeance on your foes, there is no law that lies in the path' (ὁυδεὶς ἐμποδὼν κεῖται νόμος)[10].

As with friendship, enmity can be inherited from a previous generation. Demosthenes refers to such a relationship as

---

[4] Popular Ethics in Ancient Greece (Stanford, 1962), 87.

[5] 9.20.

[6] Xenophon, Mem. 4.5.10.

[7] Ibid., 2.3.14. Cf. Plutarch, Mor. 563D-E; id., 'Sulla' 38.4; Aristotle, EN 4.3.28.

[8] Theognis, 339-40.

[9] Xenophon, Mem. 2.6.35.

[10] Ion. 1045-1047.

ἔχθραν πατρικὴν[11], and Lysias describes an ancestral enemy as πατρικὸς ἐχθρός[12]. The handing down of quarrels from generation to generation is linked to the traditional maxim in Sophocles that it is 'the hope of parents that they may rear a brood of sons submissive, keen to avenge their father's enemies and to count his friends their own'[13]. K.J. Dover refers to this inherited enmity and the long-standing feuds of provocation and retaliation as 'a conspicuous phenomenon of the aristocracy'[14]. Enmity had almost become a technical term for a long and hostile relationship.

Though later Greek and Roman writers reacted against what they considered to be the injustice and inflexibility of the popular formula, there does not appear to be a lessening of its effect upon people's attitudes. Plato was the first to transcend it in his discussion of justice between Socrates and Polemarchus[15]. Polemarchus reduced Simonides' definition of justice, 'to render each man his due', to the accepted code of morality - τοὺς φίλους εὖ ποιεῖν ... τοὺς ἐχθροὺς κακῶς. In reply Socrates argues : 'It is not the function of the just man (δίκαιος) to harm either friend or anyone else, but of his opposite the unjust (ἄδικος)'[16]. But as Pearson observes, while the maxim was inadequate for Plato because it was not absolutely and universally valid, 'popular ethics does not abandon a traditional precept simply because it is found to be not universally applicable'[17].

Plato himself is not consistent in his treatment of the maxim. The Platonic Socrates affirms that it is not wrong to feel joy in the woes of enemies but it would be unjust to rejoice in the misfortunes of friends[18]. The sharp

---

11 19.222.

12 32.22

13 Ant. 643-646.

14 Greek Popular Morality, 182.

15 Rep. 331Eff.

16 Rep. 335D; cf. id. Crito 49B, C.

17 Popular Ethics, 17-18.

18 Plato, Phil. 49D.

distinction is retained in Aristotle. Revenge upon an enemy, rather than reconciliation, is a noble act : 'for to retaliate is just (δίκαιον) and that which is just is noble (καλόν)'[19]. Further, he utilizes the saying to define friends as 'those whose enemies are ours, those who hate (μισεῖν) those whom we ourselves hate, and those who are hated by those who are hated by us'[20].

In discussing the merits of benefits (beneficia) and injuries (iniuriae), Seneca takes exception to the popular opinion that Simonides' definition of justice meant 'thanks in return for a benefit and retribution, or at any rate, ill will in return for an injury' (beneficio gratiam, iniuriae talionem aut certe malam gratiam)[21]. Cicero has no such feelings when he describes Rufus as having been appointed by Fortune to enhance his prestige and to be the avenger of those who hate (inimicorum) and envy (invidorum) him, and to make them sorry[22]. Plutarch sums up popular sentiment when he says that slyness, deceit and intrigue are not bad (φαῦλον) or unjust (ἄδικον) when employed against an enemy, though for the training of one's own character, he advises, one would be better off without them[23]. Relationships then, in principle, were clearly defined. A person drew a distinction between his friends and enemies and knew how he should behave towards them, his behaviour being sanctioned by social practice and endorsed by writers of all ages.

Relationships, in practice, were not stable, a fact of life implicit in the various attempts to cope with the uncertainties of, and fluctuations in, friendship. In particular, there is a marked concern for the possibility of a friend becoming an enemy. It is reflected in the maxim attributed to Bias, one of

---

19 Aristotle, Rhet. 1.9.24.

20 Ibid., 2.4.7. Cf. Cicero, Planc. 1.1, where Cicero fears that Plancius' friendship with him will bring him into harm from Cicero's enemies.

21 Ep. 81.7. 'Talio, (from talis, 'just so much') is the old Roman law of 'eye for eye and tooth for tooth'. As the law was refined it gave way to fines' (R.M. Grunmere, Seneca Vol. 5 (Loeb), 222-223).

22 Fam. 2.9.3.

23 Mor. 91C.

the Seven Wise Men of Greece : "they love as if they could one day hate, and hate as if they would one day love' (φιλοῦσιν ὡς μισήσοντες καὶ μισοῦσιν ὡς φιλήσοντες)[24].
Aristotle applies the saying to old men, embittered and humiliated by their experiences of life, who no longer know how to love or to hate vigorously and thus cannot maintain proper relationships with friend or enemy. Bias was reported to have based his saying on the practical consideration that the majority of mankind were bad (τοὺς πλείστους εἶναι κακούς)[25]. One therefore must moderate one's behaviour accordingly. It became part of the general Greek doctrine of moderation and appears as a popular sentiment in guiding the course of relationships in the poets[26] and philosophers[27].

Unlike many of the sayings of the other Wise Men which were applauded, Bias' maxim offended some idealists. Cicero comments only on the first part of what he terms this 'commonly accepted belief'. With a concern for true friendship, he recalls Scipio's scathing condemnation : 'it was the speech of some abandoned wretch, or scheming politician or of someone else who regarded everything as an instrument to serve his own selfish ends. For how will it be possible for anyone to be a friend to a man who, he believes, may be his foe'[28].

Cicero's protest is well taken, but Bias was a realist to say the least. His saying reflects the nature of friendship and enmity, it does not determine it. It was not always possible to avoid offending a friend though this was done with the greatest reluctance. Behaviour provided a ready criterion for distinguishing a friend from an enemy.

---

[24] Aristotle, Rhet. 2.13.4. Cf. however, ibid., 2.21.13, where in rhetoric the maxim could create an impression of generality.

[25] Diog. Laert., 1.87.

[26] Sophocles, Ajax 679-683; Euripides, Hipp. 253-60. Cf. Aristotle, Rhet. 2.21.13-14; Cf. Publius Syrus, 284, 300; Philo, de Virt. 28.152-153, whose concern is with restraint in enmity, leading to reconciliation, and applies it to international affairs.

[27] Aulus Gellius, 1.3.30, where it is wrongly attributed to Chilon.

[28] de Amic. 16.59.

There was little room for individual choice or margin for error. An offence could be construed as an act of hostility and change a friendly relationship into a hostile one. Even cautious attempts to end an unsatisfactory friendship could be seen as planning ways to end it by hostile actions (inimicitiarum tempus cogitandum putabat)[29]. This note of caution appears also in Theognis. Though he bemoans the disloyalty of his friends[30] and is vexed by the dearth of true friends in the world[31], he warns not to let a friend's offence make an enemy of him : 'Don't destroy a friend on a trivial excuse'[32]. Dio Chrysostom oversimplifies the matter. The offender was never a friend as 'friends do not wrong friends'. All such wrong is suffered at the hands of enemies, 'friends in name, whom they did not know to be enemies'[33].

This reluctance to engage in action which could be considered as hostile by a friend underlies a note common in Greek and Roman literature; that of the anxiety caused by conflicting obligations in friendship. Diogenes provides another practical observation of Bias'. He would rather decide a dispute between two enemies than between two friends. The former would mean he would gain a friend; the latter, he would be certain to make a friend an enemy[34]. The indecision of Dionysus is quite understandable when he is faced with assessing the merits of two contestants who are his <u>philoi</u> : 'Both are my friends (ἄνδρες φίλοι); I can't decide between them : I don't desire to be at odds (δι' ἔχθρας) with either'[35].

Cicero faced a similar, if more dangerous, dilemma when he had to decide between Pompey and Caesar's friendship[36].

---

[29] de Amic. 16.60.

[30] 811-813.

[31] 415-418, 645-646.

[32] 323

[33] Disc. 3.113-114.

[34] Diog. Laert., 1.87.

[35] Aristophanes, Frogs 1411-1412.

[36] Att. 7.1, 10.8a. Cf. Varro's ties with Pompey and Caesar, Caesar BC 2.17.

His heart was with Pompey but the words of Caesar had an ominous ring when the emerging victor advised him either to remain neutral or to refrain from joining Pompey : 'For you will have done a serious injury (graviorem iniuriam) to our friendship and consulted your interests very little'[37]. It would not be long before to cease being an amicus Caesaris could have serious consequences - it came to mean the end of a man's public career; it could lead also to exile, confiscation of property or suicide[38]. Such was the nature of the Jewish leaders' threat to Pilate : 'If you let this man go you are no friend of Caesar' (οὐκ εἶ φίλος τοῦ καίσαρος)[39].

Dio Chrysostom defines friendship or enmity with the king in terms of imitation of his ways and conformity to his habits. Those who excel at it are his closest intimates and friends while those who are lacking 'would justly incur censure and disgrace' and be 'speedily moved from office as well'[40]. The threatening use of the friend or enemy alternative was patently an attempt to persuade the indecisive person to favour the party who made the threat. It was a persuasive argument especially when delivered by a more powerful opponent. It had its effect upon Flavius in his dispute over a debt with Cicero's brother, who made it blatantly obvious in a letter that Flavius' action would lead to his 'expressing his gratitude' to him as a friend or else 'making things unpleasant' for him as his enemy[41]. Cicero in his letter to Quintus does not dispute the justice of the alternative but only the facts about the debt itself. Seneca totally ignores this unpleasant prospect, that a friend may become an enemy, when referring to the saying. 'Ignores' may be doing him an injustice. Rather he acknowledges it by deliberately

---

37 Att. 10.8b.

38 See R. S. Rogers, 'The Emperor's Displeasure - amicitiam renuntiare', TAPA 90 (1959), 224-237.

39 John 19:12. Cf. Josephus, Ant. 15,167 : ἐν ἔχθρᾳ καίσαρος of Augustus and Herod's relationship.

40 Disc. 1.44.

41 Cicero, QF 1.2.10 : te aut quasi amicis tuis gratias acturum aut quasi inimicis incommoda laturam.

replacing it with the sentiment that one ought to do everything to stimulate love in a friend (in alio amorem incitet)[42]. It appears correct to say then that the Greeks and Romans alike had a distinct dislike for personal hostilities and where possible avoided actions which could be construed as hostile by their friends. One had enough enemies without adding to them[43]. At the same time, there would need to be good reason for a declaration of hostility.

'Love your enemies' is not a Greek or Roman sentiment. Enemies, though, did become friends and Seneca takes up the second part of Bias' saying, μισεῖν ὡς φιλήσων, when he encourages Lucilius to remember that an enemy could become a friend. By this he means that one should do everything to 'check hatred in the enemy' (in hoc odium moderetur)[44]. Seneca has more to say on this theme than others. As with true friendship, the attitude required for true reconciliation belongs to few. He believed that it was generally understood by all that it was the Stoics who taught that help should be proffered to all including enemies[45] and that one should act honourably when wronged[46]. But as J.N. Sevenster correctly concludes, Seneca is interested in individual not social ethics[47]. His is the wise man whose inner tranquility is invulnerable to either injury or insult[48]. His conduct towards his enemies demonstrates clearly his superiority.

Reconciliation, though, was not the exclusive province of noble conduct. It was motivated by any number of reasons -

---

[42] Ep 95.63.

[43] The evidence points to a reluctance to display overt hostility; cf. P.A Brunt, 'Amicitia', 11-13; Cicero, Fam. 11.28.2, 5.2.10; Ps Chion, ep 16.7.

[44] Ep 95.63; cf. id., de Ira 2.34.2,4.

[45] de Otio 1.4 See also Philo, de Virt. 23.117-118 for reconciling an enemy by benefitting him while he is in need.

[46] de Ira 2.31.6; eg. forgiveness, de Ira 2.32.1-3, de Vita Beata 20.5; judgment not anger, de Ira 1.6.1,3-4; moderation, de Clem. 1.14.3, 20.24, de Ira 2.17.2; clemency, de Clem. 2.7.2-5; counting a benefit more than an injury, Ep 81.4-17.

[47] Paul and Seneca (Leiden, 1961), 183; see his whole discussion on the motivation for Seneca's attitude towards his enemies, 180-185.

[48] de Cons. Sap. 2.1.3; de Ben. 2.25.2.

- patriotism, expediency, self-preservation - and is a notable feature of the political and social incidents in the Ciceronian collection of letters[49]. Cleobulus of Lindus' advice is more indicative of the nature of reconciliation : 'we should render a service to a friend to bind him closer to us, and to an enemy in order to make a friend of him. For we have to guard against the censure of friends and the intrigues of enemies'[50].

R. Syme states that amicitia (and presumably inimicitia can be similarly defined) 'was a weapon of politics, not a sentiment based on congeniality'[51]. Further, he writes that in politics it consisted of mutual services and mutual interests rather than unity of principle[52]. There are many examples to be found which support his point of view, but P.A. Brunt shows that his understanding is too narrow. It does not do justice to what he terms 'the bewildering kaleidoscopic combinations of relationships' denoted by amicitia[53]. Syme's definition, though, does underline the difficulty experienced in forming lasting and true friendships in public and political life in the Late Republic[54]. Today's amici might be the inimici of tomorrow[55].

It also highlights the pragmatic nature of the interchange of friends and enemies. One not only inherited personal enemies and made new ones but on occasions made peace with former enemies. Cicero paints a grim picture. The 'lust for money' (pecunia) and the 'struggle for office' (honoris contentio)

---

[49] See J.P.V.D. Balsdon, 'Cicero the Man', Cicero ed T.A. Dorey (London, 1964), 190.

[50] Diog. Laert., 1.91. Cf. Publius Syrus, 142 : 'When you forgive an enemy, you win several friends at no cost.'

[51] The Roman Revolution (London, 1939), 12.

[52] Ibid., 157.

[53] 'Amicitia', 199, 214. The use of amicitia may denote courtesy or be a polite form of address to someone who was not a close friend and even an opponent who was not an enemy (cf. Seneca, Ep. 3). It may indicate readiness to give help and support. Cf. Plutarch, Mor. 659E-660F.

[54] Cicero, de Amic. 17.63-64.

[55] Caesar, BC 1.4.

frequently led to 'the deadliest enmities (inimicitias maximas) between dearest friends (amicissimos)'[56]. Conversely, hostilities ceased and enemies became friends. This deliberate setting aside of the traditional principles of conduct for advantage earned Sallust's rebuke that men came 'to value friendship and enmity not by desert but by profit'[57]. It is possible that a censure of this kind is implied by Luke when he records the reconciliation of Herod and Pilate as a result of the trial of Jesus. He writes, 'Herod and Pilate became friends (φίλοι); till then there had been a standing feud (ἔχθρα) between them'[58]. However interested the motives for reconciliation may appear, a clear picture emerges from this discussion. Every effort was made to retain and to extend friendships and to keep enmities to a minimum.

Desirable as this may have been, there were few, if any, of whom it could be said that they had no enemies. In Greek and Roman social and political life, <u>philia</u>/amicitia presupposes <u>echthra</u>/inimicitia. Dio Chrysostom yearned to be free of the 'fatiguing burden of enmity'[59]. Perfect happiness for him was having a large number of friends and few enemies, or none at all[60]. 'Not so', retorts Plutarch. 'Our very friendships, if nothing else, involve us in enmities'[61]. He explains : 'For enmities follow close upon friendships and are interwoven with them, inasmuch as it is impossible for a friend not to share his friend's wrongs or disrepute or

---

[56] de Amic. 10.34. In Cicero's case it was often imposed on him in the principle of having the same friends (or enemies) as one's (new) friends. Cf. T.A. Dorey, 'Honesty in Roman Politics', in id. (ed.), Cicero 27-45.

[57] Cat. 10.5. For censure of inconstancy in enmity and friendship, see also Philo, de spec. leg. lib. 4, 15.88 : 'They form friendships and enmities recklessly so that they easily change each for the other'.

[58] 23:12.

[59] Disc. 41.12.

[60] Disc. 3.103.

[61] Mor. 86C, 96A-B, especially in public life. His essay, 'How to Profit from One's Enemies', belongs thematically to his group of works on friendship, though it is closer than the others to the world or politics. So D.A. Russell, Plutarch (London, 1973), 96.

disfavour; for a man's enemies look at once with suspicion and hatred upon his friend'[62]. Not even men of such outstanding reputation and character as Themistocles and Aristides could avoid them[63]. With good humour, Plutarch cites Chilon's remark to the man who boasted that he had no enemies : 'The chances are that you have no friend either'[64].

Drawing upon a statement which he attributes to Antisthenes[65] and to Diogenes[66] that 'as a matter of self-preservation, men have need of true friends or else of ardent enemies' so that they might learn the truth about themselves either by admonition or by reviling, he concludes that it is helpful to have some enemies[67]. Citing an old adage, the sentiment of which is expressed in various forms by others, he advises that what one must do is learn how to profit from them[68]. This involves, for instance, commending an enemy when he deserves it. Such an act wins the greater commendation. His reasoning here, like Seneca's befriending of an enemy, belongs to the Stoics. The act is self-regarding. As a process of training (ἄσκησις) it produces great benefits for the soul[69]. Best of all (κάλλιστον), it enables one to act with greater generosity towards one's friends[70] and, at the same time, will bring distress to one's enemies[71].

Plutarch's morale booster apart, there is revealed in my discussion of enmity so far what might be called a genuine fear of hostilities, and in particular, of what Cleobulus described as 'the intrigues of enemies'[72]. These activities

---

62 Mor. 96A-B.

63 Mor. 809B.

64 Mor. 96A; cf. Aulus Gellius 1.3.30; Publius Syrus 355, 'It's a very poor fortune that has no enemy.'

65 Mor. 89B.

66 Mor. 74C, 82A.

67 Mor. 91F-92A.

68 Mor. 86C, 87B; cf. Xenophon, Oec. 1.15; Philostratus, Lives of the Sophists 628 : 'even from the enemy one can learn something worthwhile' (cited from Aristophanes, Birds 375) where an antagonist's eloquence is improved by reciprocal censure.

69 Mor. 91B. Cf. Philo, de Virt. 23.117.

70 Mor. 91A-B, E.

71 Mor. 88C.

72 Diog. Laert. 1.91.

are referred to explicitly in the second part of the maxim, 'help your friends, harm your enemies'. Plutarch gives a graphic account of 'the most harmful element in enmity' : 'Your enemy, wide awake, is constantly lying in wait to take advantage of your actions, and seeking to gain some hold on you, keeping up a constant patrol about your life!'[73]. Further, our enemies ferret out information even from our friends and are often the first to know about our sickness, debts, conjugal difficulties, especially our failings, and 'pounce upon them and seize them and tear them to pieces'[74]. It is this untiring vigilance and constant attention of the enemy which Dio Chrysostom calls 'a grievous thing in all circumstances of life'[75].

A corollary of the popular convention ('help your friends and harm your enemies') appears frequently in Greek and Roman writings : 'friends share one's joy while enemies gloat over one's misfortunes'[76]. The positive aspect of this appears in Homer where the happiness of a married couple is said to bring 'great sorrow to their enemies and joy to those who love them'[77]. It is the negative application with which I am most concerned and its concomitants, of shame, dishonour and ridicule. Theognis deplores his sufferings for they have become a source of mockery (κατάχαρμα) for his enemies but woe to his friends[78]. Death is a terrible thing for Megara, but to die in a manner which would give their enemies the chance to mock (ἐχθροῖσιν γέλων διδόντας) would be a greater evil than death (τοῦ θανεῖν μεῖζον κακόν)[79]. Likewise, Demosthenes claims that men do not dread death but a dishonoured end; he asks, 'Is he not indeed to be pitied

---

[73] Mor. 87B. Cf. Plutarch's use of Hesiod's advice, W&D. 342, in Mor. 530D, 707C.

[74] Mor. 87C, D. See Cicero's claim, Inv. ag. Sallust, 2.3 : 'For as a rule the state is advanced by the quarrels of individuals, which allow the character of no citizen to be hidden.'

[75] Disc. 41.13.

[76] Disc. 3.103.

[77] Od. 6.184-185.

[78] 1107-1108.

[79] Euripides, HF 285ff. Cf Philo, Flacc. 18.147.

who must look upon the sneering face of an enemy and to hear with his ears his insults?'[80].

This use of the second element of the convention appears regularly and always with reference to the shame one feels before a triumphing enemy. For Theognis, it is the disgrace of surrender which delights his opponents[81]. It underlies Hesiod's advice that one should not marry a wife who would make one a laughing stock of the neighbours[82]. It explains the shame of Electra who, in her address to the departed Orestes, says that he is dead and gone and their enemies are laughing[83]. An examination of its uses in other passages reveals a similar pattern[84]. Both conventions are used by Sophocles when he refers derogatorily to sons as 'unprofitable' who do not know how to take revenge upon their father's enemies for they bring 'his foes much laughter' (πολὺν γέλων)[85].

As a counterpart to this shame and ridicule theme, there appears the advice given by Euripides that one should do everything to conceal one's misfortunes[86]. Menander also suggests that they should be kept to as few witnesses as possible[87]. Plutarch speaks of this fear of an enemy's ridicule as a 'peculiar mark of vice that we feel more ashamed (αἰσχύνεσθαι) before our enemies than before our friends'[88]. He counters that the presence of an enemy is helpful for a person becomes more heedful of himself and exercises more caution in the way he acts. While this may be regarded as a positive educational factor, the building of a better character, the notion of shame and ridicule are

---

80 Aeschines, Emb. 181-182.

81 1033

82 W&D. 701.

83 Sophocles, El. 1152ff.

84 Id., OC. 1399, Phil. 1023, Aj. 367; Euripides, Ba. 842, 1080. Cf. Xenophon, Anab. 1.9.12, Cyrus never allowed his enemies to laugh at him.

85 Ant. 646-648.

86 Fr. 460.

87 Farmer 79-89.

88 Mor. 88A.

still present. Greeks and Romans shunned any course which could make them an object of contempt, especially in the eyes of an enemy[89]. Cicero, who had already experienced Dionysius' ridiculing of his bad fortunes[90], asks that Dionysius be prevented from gaining further advantage, for 'I should prefer that discomforts as great as mine should not be seen by a man who is not my friend'[91]. A Socrates may have had the courage to cry in defiance, 'let them mock'[92], but few emulated him.

It must not be forgotten that both the ridiculer and ridiculed are enemies of each other. Shame indicates, among other things, the disadvantaged position of one in relation to the other. The situation could easily be reversed and the 'shamed' would become the 'ridiculer'. Like friendship, enmity was a reciprocal relationship and one sought always to have the upper hand over an enemy. To attempt revenge upon him was accepted as a 'most lawful act' (νομιμώτατον)93 or just (δίκαιος)[94]. None could begrudge (ἐπιφθονεῖν) a person doing in fact what was his duty (δεῖ)[95]. There was no fairer task than successful retaliation[96]. It gave not only the 'greatest of pleasures' (ἥδιστόν ἐστιν)[97] but a person could almost forget his illness to see his enemy dead[98].

Success won great honour. This is implicit in Thucydides'

---

[89] Sophocles, OC. 902. Cf. R.L. Kane, 'Oedipus Tyrannus, 1084-85 : "I'll not deny my nature"', AJP 103 (1982) 137-143. Oedipus does not fear facing the truth of his lowly origins.

[90] Att. 9.12.

[91] Att. 10.2; Cf. 9.15.

[92] Plato, Euthyphro 3C.

[93] Thucydides, 7.68.1.

[94] Aristotle, Rhet. 1.9.24.

[95] Demosthenes, 59.15.

[96] Euripides, Ba. 878-880.

[97] Thucydides, 7.68.1; similarly, Xenophon, Mem. 4.5.10; Aristotle, Rhet. 1.12.24; Publius Syrus, 270, 310, 326. Contrast Philo, de Virt. 23.116, who suggests that the injunction to help even an enemy's beast when it is distressed implies τὸ μὴ τοῖς ἀβουλήτοις τῶν ἐχρανάντων ἐφήδεσθαι.

[98] Sophocles, Phil. 1040-1043.

claim that an agathos fights when he is wronged[99]. Though his reference is to national enemies, the pattern is the same for personal foes. Aristotle reasons : 'to retaliate is dikaion and that which is just is kalon; and further, a courageous man ought not to allow himself to be beaten. Victory and honour are also noble'[100]. Conversely, failure brought distress[101] and dishonour[102]. A fragment of Epictetus' writing which criticizes these attitudes, at the same time illustrates the normative nature of this behaviour. 'To fancy that we shall be contemptible in the sight of other men if we do not employ every means to hurt the first enemies we meet is characteristic of extremely ignoble and thoughtless men'[103].

A contrasting opinion to that of Epictetus is given by Tacitus. He describes the interminable rivalry among the Roman aristocracy as ipsa inimicitiarum gloria[104]. A nobleman could take great pride in successfully establishing and defending his rank, prestige and honour, and that of his friends, at the expense of his enemies. This behaviour is understandable in a society which K.J. Dover describes as 'addicted to comparison and competition'[105]. In chapters 8 and 9 I will look at the traditional values concerned with this competition for status. Let it suffice for the moment to mention some of the techniques and ways by which one 'hurts' an enemy.

'Enmity' (ἔχθρα/inimicitia) is often linked with 'envy' (φθόνος/invidia) and 'hatred' (μῖσος/odium). At times invidia and odium are equivalent in meaning - hate, hatred, illwill - but though Greeks and Romans regarded them as similar

---

99 1.120.3.

100 Rhet. 1.9.25.

101 Aeschines, Emb. 182.

102 Euripides, Phoen. 509-510; eg., ἀνανδρία, 'unmanliness', and αἰσχύνομαι 'feel shame'.

103 Fr. 7 (Stobaeus 3.20.61, Musonius fr. 41(ff)).

104 Dial. 40.1.

105 Greek Popular Morality, 237.

passions, they were not considered to be the same[106]. Cicero frequently refers to his opponents, jointly and separately, as inimici and invidi[107]. The terms were not synonymous for not all invidi were inimici[108]. The association of 'envy' with 'enmity' is interesting. Envy has its roots in the old superstition of the 'evil eye' and the fear its power provoked at all levels of society. By it a person sought to bring his opponents to ruin and archaeological evidence of crude drawings and mosaics of disfigured eyes, and the wearing of amulets, point to the attempts to ward off or break its power[109]. We can only speculate as to its connection with the consistent notion of the 'watchful enemy' from whom one must conceal his misfortunes. I suspect it lies beyond Plutarch's description of the enemy's constant patrols, though as a superstition it may have lost its force for the more educated man, or at best was retained at the level of the subconscious[110]. Envy was regarded as the worst of evils and most destructive of human relations. It is consistently opposed to friendship and is said to have brought many to ruin[111]. Plutarch, in his essay on 'Hate and Envy', argues that each is 'contrary to

---

[106] See the discussions in : Aristotle, Rhet. 2.4.30ff; Plutarch, Mor. 536E-538E, who seems to follow Aristotle; Dio Chrysostom, Disc. 77 & 78 : περὶ φθόνου.

[107] Inimici and invidi : Mur. 7.17, Att. 3.9, Fam. 1.9.16, 2.9.3, Planc. 1.1; invidi : Att. 4.5, Fam. 7.2.3, Planc. 24.59.

[108] So P.A. Brunt, 'Amicitia', 13-14.

[109] See J. Engemann, 'Zur Verbreitung magischer Übelabwehr in der nichtchristlichen und christlichen Spätantike' JbAC 18 (1975), 22-49, and Talfen 8-16. His illustrations show that even people rich enough to have mosaics feared the evil eye. Cf. also the use of amulets : Virgil, Ecl. 3.103, Persius, 2.34. For the custom of the triumphator carrying or attaching to his chariot a rat's foot or a dried up cockerel's comb or a red-painted phallus as an amulet against the evil eye, see R. Payne, Hubris, a Study in Pride (New York, 1960), 42-43; Pliny, NH 28.7.139; Maerobius, Sat. 1-6.9.

[110] For the degree to which Plutarch himself reflects popular superstition see F. E. Brenk, In Mist Apparelled : Religious Themes in Plutarch's Moralia and Lives (Leiden, 1977), 184-213.

[111] Eg. Xenophon, Mem. 3.9.8.; Plutarch, Mor. 538E; Plato, Phil. 49D, 50A.

friendship' (ἐναντίαν τῷ φιλεῖν)[112].

Enmity is also discussed in relation to its causes and effects. It is produced by anger (ὀργή), spitefulness (ἐπηρεασμός) and slander (διαβολή)[113], envy (φθόνος), rivalry (ζῆλος) and contention (φιλονεικία)[114], and 'leaves as its residue jealousy (ζηλοτυπίαν), joy over others' misfortunes (ἐπιχαιρεκακίαν), and vindictiveness (μνησικακίαν)'[115]. Plutarch regards these causes as concomitant with public or political career[116]. This brief look at enmity and its associated terms already indicates to us what is involved in κακῶς/ποιεῖν, the duty of a man towards his enemy[117]. Plutarch defines 'hate' in a similar way as 'a certain disposition and intention awaiting the opportunity to injure (τοῦ κακῶς ποιῆσαι)'[118]. The Latin noun iniuria serves an identical purpose to describe the injury or wrong suffered at the hands of an enemy[119]. Seneca opposes it to beneficium in a maxim that I have previously quoted which sets out one's reciprocal duty : 'thanks in return for a benefit and retribution for an injury (beneficio gratiam, iniuriae talionem)'[120].

b. Enmity and invective.

(1) The purpose of invective.

The popular cliche, 'nothing is sacred', is hardly adequate when applied to the nature and content of κακῶς/ποιεῖν.

---

112 Mor. 536F.

113 Aristotle, Rhet. 2.4.30ff. Cf. Xenophon, Mem. 2.6.21 : 'Strife and anger lead to hostility, covetousness to enmity, jealousy to hatred'.

114 Plutarch, Mor. 86C.

115 Ibid., 91B.

116 Ibid., 86C.

117 Similarly, Lysias, 9.20; Xenophon, Cyr. 1.6.28, 31, Mem. 2.6.35; Plato, Rep. 331E.

118 Mor. 538E; cf. Aristotle, Rhet. 2.5.3-8.

119 Seneca, Ep. 81.4 and frequently in this letter; cf. Cicero, Att. 9.15.

120 Ep. 81.7.

Plutarch describes one aspect of the attitudes and practices of an enemy as behaviour that is 'scurrilous, angry, scoffing, and abusive'[121]. He summarily observes that 'biting jests' are part of the orator's business against enemies and legal opponents[122] and are used to inflict pain and to excite or provoke laughter (γέλως) among the onlookers[123]. It is this aspect of the enmity relationship, that of ridicule or invective, to which I now particularly direct my attention.

Generally speaking, the use of ridicule against an opponent is twofold; a. to show by contrast how much more favoured in every way the ridiculer is than is his enemy (such self-commendation may be direct or, as is more often the case, implied by the unfavourable comparison made with the enemy); b. to ensure the public humiliation and disgrace of the enemy. Aristotle, the architect of formal rhetoric and the formulator of the philosophical and ethical precepts on the use of the laughable[124], states the aim of the orator's epilogue : 'To dispose the hearer favourably towards oneself and unfavourably towards the adversary; to amplify and depreciate. For after you have proved that you are truthful and the adversary is false the natural order of things is to praise ourselves, blame him, and to put the finishing touches. One of two things should be aimed at, to show that you are either relatively or absolutely good and the adversary either relatively or absolutely bad'[125]. Elsewhere he lists the τόποι of ἀρετή which are the source of encomium 'by which one proves goodness - justice (δικαιοσύνη), courage (ἀνδρεία),

---

[121] Mor. 90E.

[122] 'Cicero', 27.1; cf. Cicero, Brut. 47: Gorgias deemed an orator's task to be 'rem augere posse laudando vituperandoque rursus affligere.'

[123] 'Cicero;, 27.1.

[124] So M.A. Grant, The Ancient Rhetorical Theories of the Laughable (Madison, 1924), 24.

[125] Rhet. 3.19.1. Cf. Cicero, de Or. 2.43.182.

self-control (σωφροσύνη), magnificence (μεγαλοπρεπεία), magnanimity (μεγαλοψυχία), liberality (ἐλευθεριότης), gentleness (πραότης), practical and speculative wisdom (φρόνησις, σοφία). Badness is proven from their contraries (τὰ ἐναντία)[126].

Direct self-commendation was used effectively by Cicero against Piso. He compares and contrasts his own and Piso's careers, and argues that he has merited his consulship by his own efforts whereas Piso attained his by ancestry, an appearance of austerity and the confused political situation[127]. Further, he proclaims his own achievements[128] and attacks Piso's[129]. Implied self-commendation is evident in Aeschines' attack on Nicoboulos : 'Nicoboulos is objectionable and walks hurriedly and has a loud voice and uses a stick'[130]. These detractions are in clear contrast to Aeschines' impressive physical stature and beauty, which we know would have been obvious to the listeners.

(2) σύγκρισις as a form of invective.

Formal comparison (σύγκρισις) as a device of invective has an important bearing on my discussion of Paul and his opponents. The verb συγκρίνω appears in 2 Cor. 10:12. Comparison was a rhetorical exercise practised in schools along with the associated exercises of encomium and commonplace[131]. Quintilian summarises comparison as 'which of two characters is the better or the worse, which, though it is managed in a similar way, yet doubles the topics, and treats

---

126 Rhet. 1.9.4.41. Cf. Cicero, de Or. 2.11.45-46. The superior things by which a man should be praised are 'race, wealth, connections, friendships, power, good health, beauty, vigour, talent, and the rest of the attributes that are either physically or externally imposed'; after these 'instances of conduct ... wisdom, generosity, valour ...'.

127 In Pisonem 1-3.

128 Ibid., 4-7.

129 Ibid., 8-11.

130 Demosthenes, 37.52-55.

131 See D.L. Clark, Rhetoric in Greco-Roman Education (New York, 1957), 198-199.

not only the nature, but the degrees of virtues and vices'[132]. I have already noted the virtues which Aristotle considered were the sources fo encomium[133]. Hermogenes, in his discussion of comparison, extends the topoi. Comparison is not only the 'means of amplifying misdeeds' and 'good deeds' but also involves the encomiastic topics of a man's city, race, upbringing, pursuits, affairs, external relations and the manner of death[134]. In addition, physical qualities such as beauty, stature, agility and might were appropriate topics[135]. He defines comparison as follows : 'Now sometimes we draw our comparisons by equality, showing the things which we compare as equal either in all respects or in several; sometimes we put the one ahead, praising also the other to which we prefer it; sometimes we blame the one utterly and praise the other, as in a comparison of justice and wealth'[136].

The definition of his contemporary, Theon of Alexandria, is more comprehensive both as to the form and content of sygkrisis. Comparisons present the better or the worse and are effective when made between similar persons and things. Marked disparity would be ridiculous. Topics comprise birth, education, fertility, positions held, reputation, state of body, and general physical appearance. Actions chosen are the finest and most enduring, done freely and without any kind of compulsion. They should be rare deeds achieved by strivings, especially done beyond the normal age for active life[137]. A later writer, Nicolaus the Sophist, says that

---

132 2.4.21.

133 See above

134 Hermogenes, προγυμνάσματα, Rhetores Graeci Vol. 2, L. Spengel ed. (Frankfurt, 1966), 14-15. Translation by C.S. Baldwin, Medieval Rhetoric and Poetic (New York, 1928), 23-38.

135 Hermogenes, Rhetores Graeci, 11-14.

136 Ibid., 14-15.

137 Theon of Alexandria, προγυμνάσματα, Rhetores Graeci Vol. 2, 112. I am indebted to C. Forbes, "Strength" and "Weakness" as Terminology of Status in St. Paul : the Historical and Literary Roots of a Metaphor, with Specific Reference to 1 and 2 Corinthians, unpublished BA Hons. thesis, Macquarie University, 1978, 86-90, whose discussions with me led to our recognition of the importance of formal comparison in 2 Cor. 10-12, for details of the definitions of sygkrisis by Theon and Nicolaus. (See his 'Comparison, Self-Praise and Irony : Hellenistic Rhetoric and the "Boasting" of Paul, NTS forthcoming.)

when a comparison is made, particularly in relation to the encomiastic topics, it is done either with respect to equality or to inferiority and superiority. The form consists of point for point comparison of individual pairs of virtues and vices from the topics. Superiority will then emerge, not through exaggerating the 'superior'side nor denigrating the 'inferior', but through praising the inferior so that the superior appears even greater still[138]. In these discussions, comparison is usually a third person rhetorical technique, but Nicolaus has Themistocles making first person comparisons. This is true of many of the instances of comparisons which are cited throughout this study of enmity and invective. The most notable example of comparison in Graeco-Roman literature is Plutarch's Lives, where sygkrisis supplies the pattern of the work and finds particular expression in the comparisons appended to each pair of parallel 'lives'; nineteen such sygkriseis are extant[139].

(3)The use of laughter.

The use of laughter against an opponent was a topic debated by the Greeks[140] and there appears to have been a number of books onthe subject which Cicero claimed to have studied[141]. The person who excelled in wit was highly respected[142] and Cicero prided himself on his skilled use of it. He expands

---

[138] Nicolaus the Sophist, προγυμνάσματα, Rhetores Graeci Vol. 3, 485. Cf. the similar definition of Aphthonius, προγυμνάσματα, Rhetores Graeci Vol. 2, 42, both either of the fourth or fifth centuries. Forbes' "Strength" and "Weakness", 102 n. 50, argues that it is most probable that the definition and practice of sygkrisis remained constant over the centures between Paul and Nicolaus due to '(1) the rigorous standardisation of the προγυμνάσματα, even to the order of the topics studied, and the extraordinary similarity of treatment between the various authors ..., (2) the strong "classicising" flavour of literature in the period generally, and (3), the survival of the educational tradition generally, both in and after this period'.

[139] See D. A. Russell, Plutarch, 109ff.; 'On Reading Plutarch's Lives', Greece and Rome 13 (1966) 150-151; P. A. Stadter, 'Plutarch's Comparison of Pericles and Fabius Maximus', GRBS 16 (1975) 77-85.

[140] Eg. Aristotle, Rhet. 3.18.7, EN 4.8.3-11; Theophrastus, περὶ γελοίου; Diog. Laert. 5.46.

[141] de Or. 2.53.216.

[142] Eg., Cicero, Planc. 14.33; of Granius, proverbial for his caustic wit.

on it at length in his exposition of rhetoric which includes numerous examples of the laughable (de ridiculis)[143]. Laughter served a number of purposes. It relaxed the audience; it neutralized the emotions aroused by his opposition; most importantly, it was intended to reflect the humane character of the speaker so that the audience would be favourably disposed towards him[144]. Persuasion of the onlookers in his favour he saw as the true end of wit rather than the pain inflicted on an opponent or the cleverness per se. There were conventions which one must follow and by which one could determine the difference between legitimate or malicious invective, good-natured or ill-natured laughter[145]. Generally speaking, the invective against personal enemies disregards the proprieties, and Cicero in court and in social matters does not always live up to the standards of the de Oratore. However, he does concede that certain principles can be put aside where the person is particularly bad or the person is an enemy and more so if he is also stupid[146].

(4) The truthfulness of invective.

An important aspect of comparison is raised by Aristotle's words that the speaker's aim is to 'amplify and depreciate', namely the question of the truthfulness of the invective. The schools of rhetoric did not give any significant training in the investigation of facts. Aristotle, and those who followed him, considered that the establishing of facts, either by witnesses or documented evidence, did not belong to the art of rhetoric[147]. Rather it was the speaker's personal character (ἦθος) and his powers to stir the emotions (πάθος) of his hearers[148]. By creating a favourable

143 de Or. 2.53.216-71.291.

144 Cicero, de Or. 2.58.236; Quintilian, 6.3.1.

145 See M.A. Grant, The Laughable, 39-148.

146 de Or. 2.56.229 : stultitia; cf. id., Or. 89; Quintilian, 6.3.28; Plato, Rep. 452D - for Plato, deserved ridicule is legitimate. Plutarch, Mor. 545A-B, the use of self-praise against an enemy is justified.

147 So D.L. Clark, Rhetoric, 72. Cf. Aristotle, Rhet. 1.2.2. See also E.E. Ryan, 'Aristotle's Rhetoric and Ethics', GRBS 13 (1972), 296-302, for deliberative epideictic rhetoric in this regard.

148 Aristotle, Rhet. 1.2.3-6.

impression he inspires trust in his audience; by arousing the emotions which he requires in his hearers he can persuade them towards himself[149]. Cicero regarded πάθος as the highest function of oratory and its powers to persuade the audience as of the utmost importance. By means of it, together with ἦθος, the minds of the hearers could be 'won over, instructed and moved' (conciliare, docere, movere)[150]. In Plato, the public speaker is urged to know the truth. However, it is the case that the speaker's task is to persuade his hearers as to what is true and false and to be able to distinguish between the truth and error in his opponent's arguments. It is not required that he speak the truth himself[151].

While invective might contain elements of truth, much of it was exaggerated or invented. It was not necessary for it to be truthful at all. Though Cicero came from a well-known family of Arpinum, he was denigrated as the son of a fuller[152]. Such charges provoked counter charges. Antony snidely remarked that Octavianus' great-grandfather had been a freedman and a ropemaker and his grandfather a moneychanger[153]. He called the father of the equestrian-born consul of 45 B.C.,

---

149 Ibid., 2.1.1ff. Aristotle recognizes ten πάθη which he individually defines and describes the conditions in which they are likely to occur, the kind of people in whom they are likely to be aroused, and against whom they can be directed. The ten are : εὔνοια, ἔλεος, φιλία, χάρις, ὀργή, μῖσος, φθόνος, φόβος, αἰσχυνή, τὸ νεμεσᾶν, ζῆλος. Cf. the list in Cicero, de Or. 2.42.178.

150 de Or. 2.28.121; cf. ibid., 2.27.115; movere, audientium, animos; πάθος, its importance, Or. 128; cf. concitatio, de Or. 2.49.201; ἦθος as conciliating the audience towards the speaker, as reflecting his humanity, dignity, culture and intellect, Or. 128; de Or. 2.43.182; 2.45.189; cf. commendatio, de Or. 2.49.201. See F. Solmsen, 'Aristotle and Cicero on the Orator's Playing upon the Feelings', CP 33 (1938), 390-404.

151 So D.L. Clark, Rhetoric, 35-37. Cf. Cicero, de Or. 2.42.178 : 'For men decide far more problems by hate, or love, or lust, or rage, or sorrow, or joy, or hope, or fear, or illusion, or some other inward emotion, than by reality, or authority, or any legal standard, or judicial precedent, or statute'. Cf. ibid., 2.43.182, 44.185

152 Plutarch, Lives, 'Cicero', 1.2; Cicero, Leg. 3.36; Dio Cassius, 46.4.2.

153 Suetonius, Aug. 2.3; Ps. Cicero, ep. Oct. 9.

C. Trebonius, a buffoon[154]. Cicero reciprocated by defoliating the family tree of Antony's wives, Fadia and Fulvia[155].

The use of generalizations[156] or defamatory conjecture was as good as historical fact if it would sharpen the point of invective[157]. If the family or facts were so well known as to render invective ineffective, then other detrimental charges had to be fabricated. Where an enemy has lived a blameless life or his reputation has nothing to do with the case, Cicero advises that one should concoct a charge that he has been 'concealing his true character'[158]. Conversely, one could show that one's enemy was a habitual dealer in deliberate fabrication. Cicero claimed that Verres told the enemies of Sthenius to rig up some charge to bring before him. When they could not think of anything to say, Cicero asserts that Verres openly and positively told them that any charge (forging a document) they chose to bring before him would succeed[159].

The successful dealer in misrepresentations was admired and it was a commendation to this effect which was attached to Thrasymachos who was praised as 'most powerful in devising and abolishing calumnies'[160]. The Gospel trials of Jesus and the charges laid against him by his opponents appear to

---

154 Cicero, Phil. 13.23.

155 Ibid., 2.3, 3.16, 13.24.

156 For the use of general arguments in particular cases, see Cicero, de Or. 2.31.133-135. For the use of popular anti-Epicurean polemic against Piso, see P. DeLacy, 'Cicero's Invective Against Piso', TAPA 72 (1941), 49-58.

157 So D.L. Clark, Rhetoric, 198.

158 de Inv. 2.10.34 : nam eum ante celasse nunc manifesto teneri. See also P. Red in Sen. 15, where Cicero says that Piso concealed his vices behind a vultum inportunium; cf. in Pisonem 70. However, cf. id., Reg. Deiot. 11.30, where Cicero says it is humane to fabricate charges against a personal enemy who is innocent.

159 Verr. 2.2.37.

160 Plato, Phdr. 267D.

contain an element of this, as Pilate was fully aware[161]. 'These embroideries', writes Nisbet, 'were the fashion of the day' and, as conventions, 'were meant to cause pain and hilarity, not to be believed' [162]. Similarly, Gelzer comments that such insults 'belong to the arsenal of rhetoric' and 'where we are able to control such testimony, it is usually possible to discard everything out of the way'[163].

R. Syme observes correctly that the victims of invective did not always suffer discredit or damage. He points to the feeling for humour and the strong sense of the dramatic possessed by the Romans and of the point of honour to take invective gracefully. He suggests that they developed an immunity. 'They were protected by long familiarity, by a sense of humour, or by skill at retaliation. Certain charges, believed or not, became standard jests treasured by friends and enemies'[164].

In spite of this long familiarity, the conventional nature of invective, the reluctance to enter into hostile relations, and the respectability and acceptance of invective as a rhetorical device, there remained much that could not be passed off lightly. Personal abuse, injury to a man's status or dignity, an injust legal decision, prosecuting or testifying against a man on charges involving his caput and existimatio would almost certainly create a relationship of enmity[165].

Cicero clearly distinguishes between contendo inimicus and contendo competitor. The latter case is simply that of a struggle for the sake of honos and dignitas; the former, for the sake of caput and fama[166]. Here caput doesn't simply mean his life itself. It denotes his civil and political right which could be lost by infamia, if

---

[161] Eg., Luke 23:1-25.

[162] R.G.M. Nisbet, Cicero in Pisonem (Oxford, 1961), 196-197.

[163] Nobility, 15. Cf. J.R. Dunkle, 'The Greek Tyrant and Roman Political Invective of the Late Republic', TAPA 98 (1967), 167-168.

[164] Roman Revolution, 151-152.

[165] So P.A. Brunt, 'Amicitia', 13. Cf. Publius Syrus, 114, 330.

[166] de Off. 1.12.38.

judgement were given against him and his goods sold[167]. The hostilities which arose in the normal course of public affairs could be relinquished more readily and with more honour than those issuing from personal insult (Honestius enim et libentius deponimus inimicitias rei publicae nomine susceptas quam contumaciae)[168].

The reader will be able to anticipate that my discussion of friendship, enmity, and especially of invective to this point raises serious questions as to the nature of the attacks which are made against Paul by unnamed opponents, and which will be the subject of further study in Section 3. I mention here only some of the key questions.

a. Do the attacks upon Paul fall within the scope of conventional invective ?

b. How susceptible are the observers of the hostilities to the persuasion inherent in the invective ?

c. How conventional or otherwise are Paul's responses ?

d. Can we assess from the responses, or lack of response, the validity of the accusations ?

e. What do the persistent stress on social values and, in particular, the strong emphasis upon 'shame' tell us about the nature of the criticisms and Paul's opponents ?

I will argue that Paul's opponents' attacks are conventional and that, while his responses are also conventional, they take an original direction.

If my argument holds, then it poses serious problems for Pauline studies. I raise but a few. I suggest :

a. that we can no longer assume that the criticisms of Paul are in fact true.

b. We may have to disregard various aspects of our picture of Paul and adopt new ones, if they are available.

c. The common method of arguing negatively from Paul's responses to the identity of his detractors and their theological position is open to serious question until we

---

167 Caput as synonymous with status, cf. Quintilian, 3.6.2, 21, 89; 3.11.3, 27.

168 Cicero, Att. 14.13a.

can determine the conventions with which his responses are formed. Once sufficient control has been achieved over this framework of conventions, we may be able to proceed cautiously in this direction again.

(5) Conventional themes of ridicule.

Thus far I have briefly considered the use of ridicule in relation to comparison and laughter. I now turn my attention to the content of the ridicule, and in particular to the 'contraries' of the encomiastic topics by which invidious comparisons are made. The many court cases recorded in Graeco-Roman literature provide ample evidence of what appears to us to be an extraordinary use of invective against personal enemies[169]. Cicero's scurrilous attacks upon Piso are grossly abusive even by standards of ancient usage[170] but they are merely the head of the boil. The fifth century Athenian exponents of the art, Demosthenes and Aeschines, lacked nothing by comparison. Ridicule marked the hostile relations in politics of both Greece[171] and Rome and political invective was at its peak in the Late Republic[172].

The writers of iambics were noted for their personal abuse which was motivated predominantly by a desire for personal revenge[173] and as such earned the censure of Aristotle[174]. Playwrights made use of it to good effect and gave it expression in the mouths of people from all ranks of society. The personal abuse and invective in Old Comedy matched that

---

169 Cf. Cicero, QF 2.3.2ff.

170 Cf. in Pisonem 1.

171 On personal abuse in Demosthenes see C.D. Adams, Demosthenes and His Influence (London, 1927), 63-66.

172 So R.G.M. Nisbet, Cicero in Pisonem, 193. For numerous examples of personal abuse in this period, see R. Syme, Roman Revolution, 149-152; M. Gelzer, Nobility, 15-18; J.R. Dunkle, 'The Greek Tyrant and Roman Invective, 151-171 for the exaggerated employment of the well recognized type of the tyrant - its synonyms and associated vocabulary - against personal enemies.

173 So M.A. Grant, The Laughable, 40-43. Cf. Archilochus, fr. 24 who assailed Lycambes; Alcaeus reviled Pittacus for a number of physical defects, Diog. Laert. 1.81; loose behaviour, fr. 70; craftiness, fr. 72; unequal marriage, fr. 69.

174 Poet. 4.10-13.

of Old Ionian Iambic in comparison with the milder approach of Middle and New Comedy[175]. Warring sophists and their partisan students in the second century AD denounced each other with erudition in public speeches and polemical tracts[176].

Barristers, politicians, poets, dramatists, sophists - invective is part of the language of the professionals. But did it belong also to the man who was not rhetorically trained ? Invective appears to have been a common language. For example, the harsher ridicule and sarcasm of the iambic and comic writers, as against the style of the heroes and heroic deeds of epic and tragedy, belongs to 'the events of everyday life written in plain everyday language'[177]. The thirty character sketches by Theophrastus are of ordinary people. The flatterer, the obsequious man, the garrulous person, are types which, though derived from earlier tragedy and comedy, 'are brought down to the level of everyday life and were familiar and common in the urban society of the Greek world'[178].

The conventional themes of ridicule are easily discernible : social background, immorality, physical appearance, religious and philosophical belief, speech, avarice, personal activities[179]. K.J. Dover gives a selective list of the ridicule of individuals which he calls the 'common property' of fifth and fourth-century Greek comedy and oratory[180]. He lists three ingredients of ridicule : where the opponent

---

175 M.A. Grant, The Laughable, 43-46.

176 Invective as a characteristic of sophistic animosity, see Philostratus, Lives, Aelius Aristides 584-585, Herodes 561. Cf. G.W. Bowersock, Greek Sophists in the Roman Empire (Oxford, 1969), 89-100, on professional quarrels.

177 See M.A. Grant, The Laughable, 40.

178 See E.C. Evans, 'Physiognomics in the Ancient World', TAPS 59 part 5 (1969), 38-39.

179 See W. Süss, Ethos (Leipzig and Berlin, 1910), 245-267; R.G.M. Nisbet, Cicero in Pisonem, Appendix vi, 'The in Pisonem as an Invective', 192-197.

180 Popular Morality, 32-33.

or his family are of foreign or servile birth[181]; have followed menial callings[182]; or are sexually deviant or loose[183]. Further, one ridiculed an enemy's real or alleged lack of education[184], of eloquence[185], of courage[186], of manners[187], and of family background[188].

Background is an important feature of ridicule. Cicero's accusers would speak of the newness of his family (de generis novitate accusatores esse dicturos)[189]. His 'ignoble' origin - he came from municipal nobility - was often thrown at him. As the first of his family to gain the consulship he was a novus homo[190]. Catiline labelled

---

181 Eg., Aeschines, 2.78, 3.172 : Demosthenes' mother is called a Scythian nomad; Demosthenes, 18.129 : his father is called a slave. Cf. Plutarch, Cic. 27.5 : Marcus Gellus is said to be of servile birth, οὐκ ἐξ ἐλευθέρων. For numerous examples, refer W. Süss, Ethos, 247.

182 Eg., Aeschines, 2.93 : Demosthenes, 'son of a knife-maker'; ibid., 3.173 : ridiculed as a λογόγραφος, 'speech writer'; Aristophanes, Frogs, 1083ff : 'clerks' used derogatively; cf. Hypereides, Ath. 3.4; Plato, Phdr. 257C, D. Refer W. Süss, Ethos, 248.

183 Eg., Aeschines, 3.174; Aristophanes, Clouds 1093f., Eccl. 111ff.; Demosthenes, 19.287; Plutarch, Lives 'Cicero' 26.9-10; Metellus Nepos' parents unchaste; ibid., 29.5 : Clodius, 'incest'; ibid., 7.7 : Cicero, 'effeminate' (cf. Dio Cassius, 46.18.4-6); id., Mor., 88C : reviling an enemy as 'lewd, effeminate, licentious, vulgar or illiberal'. Refer W. Süss, Ethos, 249-250.

184 Eg., Sallust, BJ. 85.39 : Marius claims he was derided as 'sordid and uneducated' because he showed lack of taste in the arrangement of dinner parties, knew nothing of the theatre, and paid no more for his cook than for the manager of his estates, ironically turning their prejudices into an invective against them. Cf. Aeschines, 3.117,; Demosthenes, 20.119; Plutarch, Mor. 88D : ἀπαίδευτος; id., Cic. 26.9.

185 Eg., Philostratus, Lives 594 : Pausanius' coarse and heavy accent led to his being ridiculed as 'a cook who spoiled expensive delicacies in the preparation'; ibid., 577 : on Hermogenes' loss of eloquence, his detractors described his words as once having been 'winged' but now 'moulted'.

186 Eg., Plutarch, Mor. 88D : δειλός, 'a coward'; Aeschines, 3.175, 214; Philostratus, Lives 626.

187 Eg., Cicero, in Pisonem 13, 92 : on Piso's wearing soleae (sandals partly open on top) when on formal occasions calcei should have been worn (cf. id., Verr. 2.5.86; Phil. 2.76); id., Phil. 2.77; Mark Antony's open expression of affection towards his own wife made a mock of Roman decorum and decency.

188 See above n.181 & 182, p63.

189 Cicero, Mur. 7.17.

190 See H.H. Scullard, 'The Political Career of a Novus Homo', Cicero, ed. T.A. Dorey, 1-25.

him an inquilinus, an 'immigrant foreigner'[191] and in court a patrician opponent called him a peregrinus rex, a 'foreign dictator'[192]. This abuse is implied by Metellus Nepos' repeated (πολλάκις) taunt : τίς σου πατήρ έστιν[193].

Physical deformity or peculiarities figured prominently in invective. Greek and Roman writers consistently maintained that laughter had its origin in the study of the ugly or defective. Cicero reiterates the theory in his de Oratore as can be seen from the following example : 'caricatures also provoke loud laughter. As a rule they are levelled against ugliness or some physical defect and involve comparison with something unseemly'[194]. It is also important to notice that it is only the defects of the weak which are presented as being truly ridiculous[195]. At the same time, as a general rule, it could not be directed against the unfortunate[196], though the rule could be set aside if the unfortunate behaved with undue arrogance[197].

Great significance is attached to right proportions in the human body and especially in association with aretē[198]. The Auctor ad Herennium defines physical attributes as the merits or defects given by nature and names them as agility, strength, beauty, health, and their opposites (velocitas, vires, dignitas, valetudo, et quae contraria sunt)[199].

---

[191] Sallust, Catil. 31.7.

[192] Cicero, Sulla 22-25.

[193] Plutarch, Cic. 26.9.

[194] de Or. 2.66.266.

[195] M.A. Grant, The Laughable, 19 :'That laughter had its origin in the contemplation of the ugly or defective is a fundamental and frequently recurring definition in Greek and Roman theories of the laughable, and it is equally significant that usually only the defects of the weak are presented as truly ridiculous.' See Aristotle, Poet. 5.1-2; Cicero, de Or. 2.58.235, 59.238, 59.239, 61.248; Plato, Phil. 48-50.

[196] Chilon, Diels, 521.24. Cf. Democritus, Diels, 405.15; Cicero, de Or. 2.59.238, Or. 88; Quintilian, 6.3.28, 31.33.

[197] Cicero, de Or. 2.58.237.

[198] See A.C. Pearson, The Fragments of Zeno and Cleanthes (London, 1891), 148.

[199] 3.10.

As to opposites, Timarchus was ridiculed for the deterioration of his physique[200]; Nicobulus for his ungainly gait and loud voice[201]; Cicero for his varicose veins[202]; Leo of Byzantium for the weakness of his eyes[203]; L. Piso for his unkempt hair and inappropriate dress, to say nothing about his eyebrows[204]; Hiero for his offensive breath[205]. With a sense of humour, Plutarch relates that when Hiero berated his young wife for not telling him, she 'being virtuous and innocent said, "I supposed all men smelt so"'.

The comparison could only be made if one is free from such deformities or physical defects oneself. One might revile an enemy who is bald or humpbacked provided it did not give an opportunity for a reciprocal remark and laughter at one's own expense[206].

Cicero was particularly adept at drawing inferences from physical ailments to other shameful characteristics to slight a person's character. Vatinius, who was suffering from swollen glands in his neck was dubbed a 'tumid orator'[207]. The servile connotations are clear in his ridicule of Octavius, said to be of African descent. When he mentioned harmlessly that he could not hear Cicero, Cicero contemptuously responded, 'And yet your ear is not without a perforation' (... οὐκ ... τὸ οὖς ἀτρύπητον)[208].

Certain mannerisms were standard fare for opponents who used them for derogatory characterizations or to make slanderous assertions. The physiognomical details of the upturned hand, a certain posture, a thin neck, a particular style of walk and dress, are alluded to in charges of

---

200 Aeschines, 1.26, 118, 120.

201 Demosthenes, 37.52-55.

202 Dio Cassius, 46.18.2.

203 Plutarch, Mor. 88F.

204 See E. C. Evans, 'Physiognomics', 42-43 for references.

205 Plutarch, Mor. 90B.

206 Ibid., 88F.

207 Id., Cic. 26.3 : οἶδος, 'swelling'; tumidus 'puffed up'.

208 Ibid., 26.5 : ἀτρύπητος,'unperforation', alluding to the perforation of the ear which often marked a slave.

effiminancy. The hair style and mincing gait of Lacydes, King of the Argives[209] and Pompey's habit of scratching his head with one finger caused both to be ridiculed as unmanly[210] The notion of servility implicit in the charge of behaving womanishly is evident in Prometheus' defiant retort that he would never be coerced by fear to ape women's ways with upturned hands simply to gain release from the bonds of his hated enemy[211].

A detailed examination of the origins and extent of ridicule is beyond the scope of my work. The aspects which I have chosen from this vast field and commented on briefly relate directly to what I consider to be the nature of the attacks on Paul by his opponents. In this regard much profit could be derived for a better understanding of the hostile relationships evident in Paul's letters by :

a. a deeper understanding of the physiognomic consciousness of the early Christians (that is, to see what evidence there is for their interpreting character from physique)[212];

b. a greater awareness of the influence of traditional theatrical masks of stock characters upon invective at all levels of society[213];

c. an examination of the vocabulary of abuse, the derivation and application of its elements, such as contained in the thesaurus of rude names (ψόγος) compiled by the second-

---

209 Id., Mor. 89E. Cf. Lucian, RL Pr. 11-12; Dio Chrysostom, Disc. 33.52; Anonymous Latin Handbook, Physiog. 2.98.123; Plutarch, Mor. 46E.

210 Ibid., 89E; cf. Mor. 800D; Pompey, 645A; Caesar, 709B.

211 Aeschylus, Pr. 1001-1005; cf. Ps. Aristotle, 808a; E.C. Evans, 'Physiognomics', 34, 71.

212 For a detailed study of five Greek authors' views on the physical attribute of strength, see C. Forbes, 'Strength' and 'Weakness', 10-73; and more generally, E.C. Evans, 'Physiognomics'.

213 Masks provided a ready source of invective and reference to them could evoke an immediate response from the hearers who would have been familiar with them in the theatre and their use in literature. For familiar mask types, see E.C. Evans, 'Physiognomics', 34, 37, 38, 42. For the use of the mask of the tragedy-tyrant in invective, see J.R. Dunkle, 'The Greek Tyrant and Roman Invective', 170-171.

century rhetorician, Julius Pollux[214].

(6)Withdrawal of friendship.

κακῶς ποιεῖν went beyond ridicule. One tried to deprive an enemy of his friends[215], to secure his public humiliation and disgrace[216], the loss of rank, job or privilege[217], confiscation of property[218], exile[219] or death[220]. Cicero for all his considerable connections, wealth and eloquence could not withstand his inveterate personal enemy, Clodius, in 59 BC. Plutarch records that Clodius 'having escaped his peril and having been chosen tribune at once began to attack Cicero, arraying and stirring up against him, all things and all men alike'[221].

Before Clodius' intrigue and slander, Cicero had already tasted the bitterness of fickle friendship and of his isolation from true friends. In 63, his powerful friends dissociated themselves from him in the face of a threat from the powerful and established Metelli family and its connections. He complains to Atticus : 'So utterly am I deserted (destitutus) that the only moments of repose I have are those spent with my wife ... For my grand and showy friendships bring some public eclat but of private satisfaction they are none. And so when my house has been crowded by the morning levee[222]

---

214 4.35 : ψόγος

215 Eg., Cicero, Att. 11.9 : 'Balbus' letters to me are becoming daily cooler and it may be he receives dozens against me'; Caesar, BC 1.7.

216 Eg., Cicero, Att. 11.9 : 'ruin and humiliation secured by law'; Sallust, Catil. 49.2.

217 Philostratus, Lives 601 : loss of the privileges of exemption from taxes and expensive public services; ibid., 613 : loss of a professorial chair of rhetoric at Athens.

218 Eg., Seneca, de Ben. 5.172.

219 Eg., Cicero, Sall. 1.1, 31.88ff; Philo, Flac. 18.50-53. Cf. Plutarch, Mor. 607A, exile is a term of reproach like terms of abuse : pauper, bald, foreigner.

220 Eg., Seneca, de Ben. 2.21.5.

221 Lives, 'Cicero', 30.4.

222 See M. Gelzer, Nobility, 104-105, for the major occupation of rising politicians of the daily morning call at the homes of their protectors; cf. Polybius, 31.29.8.

and I have gone down to the forum among a throng of friends, I cannot find in the whole company a single man with whom I can jest freely or whisper familiarly'[223]. He was mistakenly confident that his old and new friends would support him against the Clodius faction. 'I hope that we shall meet force with force thanks to the enthusiastic support not only of my friends but of others as well'[224]. Clodius' intrigue contributed to both Caesar and Pompey turning against Cicero[225] and when he was threatened with exile, many of his supporters deserted to Clodius. 'I found those my cruelest enemies who I thought had my salvation at heart'[226]. In exile he wrote to Atticus, 'I mourn the loss not only of my wealth and my friends but of my old self, for what am I now?'[227].

Withdrawal of friendship or the transfer of allegiance was one of the realities of politics in the Late Roman Republic. As we have seen, many political friendships were based on common interests and reciprocal services. It is understandable then, as R. Syme suggests, that the continuance and complications of mutually destructive hostilities played havoc with the most binding ties of personal allegiance[228]. For advantage and security, friendships were renounced and enmities resolved or postponed[229]. Suitable terminology was available to justify and ennoble such behaviour[230]. Efforts were made to persuade an enemy or his supporters to join the 'better side'[231] by helping him to 'see reason'[232].

---

223 Att. 1.18; cf. Fam. 5.2.1ff.

224 QF 1.2.16.

225 Plutarch, Cic. 30.1-7.

226 Cicero, Att. 3.13 and similarly, 3.15 : simulationem, 'false friendship'; cf. Vibius and Caius Vergilius' refusal of hospitality after the edict, Plutarch, Cic. 32.1-2.

227 Att. 3.15; cf. 3.5, 10.

228 Roman Revolution, 157.

229 Cicero, Phil. 5.50; cf. Tacitus, Ann. 1.10.

230 So, R. Syme, Roman Revolution, 157-158.

231 Cicero, Att. 15.5.

232 Ibid., 14.20.

Isolated from effective support, without a strong amicitia, as Cicero discovered, one was helpless against a powerful enemy.

The shame of defeat, the fear of humiliation, the loss of reputation at his hands and the consequent withdrawal of friends, weighed heavily upon Greeks and Romans alike[233]. Success or failure was the criterion of honour or shame. Speaking about the political scene in Rome, 43 BC, Dio commented : 'Those who were successful were considered shrewd and patriotic, while the defeated were called enemies of their country and accursed'[234]. In a society generally unsympathetic to losers, there was no middle ground, no benefit of the doubt. Failure almost always meant the destruction of a man's status and reputation in public estimation, sometimes temporarily, often permanently[235].

There is no direct line which can be drawn between the hostilities of this turbulent political situation and the hostile relations in Paul. I have used it as an illustration, though it may be somewhat magnified, of the various elements in a hostile relationship in a not unrelated period. Such elements, as we have seen, are typical of the enmity relationship of Graeco-Roman society. Should some of these occur in Paul, we may be justified in seeking an answer within this convention.

---

[233] See above 45-49.

[234] 46.34.5. The reference here is to civil war, not political enmity of the normal type.

[235] Cf. Deinarchus, 2.2.

Chapter 3

THE CHARACTER OF THE FLATTERER

a. The figure of the friend of many.

The acquisition of many friends (polyphilia) was a practice widely endorsed by the Stoics but opposed by both Aristotle and Plutarch. Aristotle's grounds for objection I have already considered : true friendship consists of common life[1]. This underlies Plutarch's criticism that friendship consists of companionship, not herding[2]. Therefore a person should seek to limit his friends to 'a circle of associates with whom one can meet constantly'[3]. Apart from the obvious difficulties arising out of having many friends[4], what is important for my discussion is the manner in which they describe the 'friend of many'. Aristotle's assessment of the <u>polyphiloi</u> is that of the 'hail-fellow-well-met with everybody are thought to be the friend of nobody'. This is the category of people generally denigrated as 'obsequious' or 'weakly complaisant' (ἄρεσκοι - 'servile' or 'fawning'[5]. Plutarch's description is more detailed and colourful. He concludes his treatment of the subject by asking :

---

[1] EN 9.10.3-4; see my previous discussion, 25-26. Contrast, however, Aristotle's view in Rhet. 1.5.16 that <u>polyphilia</u> is one of the elements which makes for happiness; ibid., 2.9.9 : an advantage. For the Stoic viewpoint see Diog. Laert. 7.124 : τὴν πολυφιλίαν ἀγαθόν, said of Posidonius Necato.

[2] Mor. 93E.

[3] EN 9.10.5

[4] See Plutarch, Mor. 95B-E.

[5] EN 9.10.6. The phrase, 'hail-fellow-well-met', appears to be a characteristic reference to the flatterer. See Cicero, Fam. 1.9.19.

'What man is there, then so indefatigable, so changeable, so universally adaptable, that he can assimilate and accommodate himself to many persons without deriding the advice of Theognis when he says : Copy this trait of the cuttlefish, which changes its colour so as to seem to the eye like the rock where it clings. However, the changes (αἱ μεταβολαί) in the cuttlefish have no depth, but are wholly on the surface, which owing to its closeness or looseness of texture, takes up the emanations from objects which come near to it; whereas friendships seek to effect a thorough-going likeness in characters, feelings, language, pursuits, and dispositions. Such varied adaptation were the task of a Proteus, not fortunate and not at all scrupulous, who by magic can change himself often on the very instant from one character to another, reading books with the scholarly, rolling in the dust with wrestlers, following the hunt with sportsmen, getting drunk with topers, and taking part in the canvass of politicians, possessing no firmly founded character of his own (ἴδιαν ἤθους ἑστίαν οὐκ ἔχοντος) ... so the possession of a multitude of friends will necessarily have, as its underlying basis, a soul that is very impressionable, versatile, pliant, and readily changeable. But friendship seeks for a fixed and steadfast character (στάσιμον καὶ βέβαιον ἦθος) which does not shift about, but continues in one place and in one intimacy. For this reason a steadfast friend is something rare and hard to find'[6]. In brief, the friend of many's chief characteristics are inconstancy and insincerity displayed in his deliberate change of character to that of his friend's.

b. The figure of the flatterer.

While discussions of the *polyphilos* are few, he is almost indistinguishable from a commonplace character in Greek and Roman literature, the flatterer. The flatterer is the

[6] Mor. 96F-97B.

subject of a number of essays[7] and plays[8] and features regularly in the discussions of many writers on a broad range of subjects. Athenaeus records snippets from a vast array of writers and presents us with a sort of 'Who's Who of Flatterers' in antiquity[9]. The flatterer is almost always discussed within the context of friendship and is presented as a false friend who is impossible at times to detect from a true friend. He skilfully gives the appearance of being one[10]. He was strongly and vehemently censured and always with an array of denigrating terms[11]. Writers expressed alarm for the great harm he did to his associates. Anaxilas called them 'worms in rich men's property' who, after devouring the wealth, 'bite another'[12]. Despite the harm recognized by

---

[7] Eg., Theophrastus, Characters 2, περὶ κολακείας - the flatterer, as with the other character sketches of Theophrastus, presents us with a person well known on the streets of Athens; Philodemus, περὶ κολακείας; Plutarch, Mor. 48E-74E.

[8] Terence, in his prologue to Eunuchus (1.30ff), acknowledges his obligation to Menander's κόλαξ for the characters of the flatterer-parasite. In the same prologue (1.25ff), he mentions an old play by Naevius and Plautus called 'Colacem', 'The Flatterer'. The names, Gnatho and Struthias, became stock names for flatterers and parasites; cf. Lucian, Fugitivi 19 (P. Oxy. 10, p. 93) : 'being on the score of flattery to outbid Gnathonides and Struthias'; Athenaeus, Deipn. 12.524A, where the property owners referred derogatively to the populace as Gergithes. Gergithius was the name of a parasite in Athens (ibid., 6.255C-257C) and his name became a contemptuous term for manual labourers.

[9] Deipn. 6.248C-262A.

[10] Aristotle, MM. 2.11.4-5 : φαίνονται φίλοι εἶναι; id., Rhet. 1.11.18 : θαυμάστμς καὶ φαινόμενος φίλος ὁ κόλαξ ἐστίν; Seneca, Ep. 45.7 : adulatio quam similis est amicitiae; Plutarch, Mor. 13C: ὑποκριταὶ φιλίας.

[11] Eg., Aristotle, Rhet. 2.6.2, 8 : among things considered as 'shameful', id. EN 10.3.11 : a 'reproach'; Plato, Rep. 590B, 'censured'; Gorg. 464C-465A, 'shameful'; Phdr. 240B, 'a horrid creature'; Dio Chrysostom, Disc. 3.17, 'most mean of all vices'; Cicero, de Amic. 24.89, 'handmaiden of vice' (cf. ibid., 25.91); Seneca, Ep. 59.11, 'shameless flattery'; Terence, Eun. 490-491, 'the meanest of the mean'; Plutarch, Mor. 13A : 'There is no class of persons more pernicious.'

[12] Athenaeus, Deipn. 6.254C.

the critic and the sufferer[13], human nature being what it is, he was popular and acceptable to the majority of people whose company he sought[14], even above that of true friends[15].

While the flatterer is the friend of many he is not necessarily the friend of all. He associates with those only where it is to his profit or advantage (ὠφέλεια). This motive is one of the major characteristics of the kolax and it is precisely this which differentiates him from a similar figure, the ἄρεσκος ('obsequious'). Both indulge in excessive (ὑπερβάλλων) praise but the areskos merely sets out to be pleasant and has no ulterior motive; the kolax seeks his own advantage (ὠφελείας τῆς αὐτοῦ)[16]. This distinction is observed by Athenaeus[17] who objected strongly to those who perverted the meaning of ἀρεσκεία, 'willingness to oblige', and made it the equivalent of κολακεία, 'flattery'[18]. The character who corresponds to the flatterer is the parasite (παράσιτος), who, as the analogy suggests, drew nutriment from others and engaged in all kinds of servility, including flattery, to hang on to his source of life. Athenaeus says that κόλαξ and παράσιτος are close in meaning[19]. In fact, the two characters merge into the one and a person may be termed a flatterer-parasite or the terms may be used interchangeably of the one person[20].

c. The flatterer as a servile person.

The notion of servility and its accompaniments of shame and

---

13 Eg., Plato, Phdr. 240B, Rep. 538B; Dio Chrysostom, Disc. 3.18; Athenaeus, Deipn. 6.256B, 259F; Cicero, de Amic. 26.97; Seneca, Ep. 59.13, de Ira 2.21.7-8. de Ben. 6.30.3-6, de Tranq. An. 1.16, NQ 4, Prol. 3; Menander, κόλαξ 79.

14 For the consideration of self-love and the flatterer, see Plutarch, Mor. 49F; Aristotle, Rhet. 1.11.26.

15 Aristotle, EE 7.4.7.

16 Id., EN 2.7.13; cf. 4.6.9.

17 Deipn. 6.255A-B.

18 Ibid. For similar kinds of substitutions, see Thucydides, 3.82.4; Plato, Rep. 560E; Aristotle, EN 2.7.13; Athenaeus, Deipn. 6.258C.

19 Deipn. 6.248D, 255B; cf. 6.236E.

20 Terence, Eun. 30 : Colax Menandrist : in east parasitus Colax. Cf. Plutarch, Mor. 547D : κόλαξ καὶ παράσιτος : Athenaeus, Deipn. 6.258A.

and dishonour are always present in the various terms used to describe the flatterer and his activities - by analogy with the behaviour of dogs, by reference to slavery and self-debasement, and cowardice. The common Latin word for flattery, adulatio, literally means the fawning or cringing of a dog[21]. Aristotle draws an analogy between the smooth forehead of a fawning dog and the characteristic smooth brow of the flatterer[22]. θωπεύειν and its cognates are used both of the fawning of dogs and of the person who flatters[23]. The parallel is evident in Aristophanes' description of Paphlagon, who, on finding out his master's weaknesses, cringes down before him and 'flatters and fawns and wheedles and cajoles' (αἰκάλλω, θωπεύω, κολλακεύω, ἐξαπατάω)[24]. Similarly, Athenaeus records that three men - Ortyges, Irus, Echarus - were entitled 'Fawning Dogs', i.e. 'Flatterers' because of the attentions they bestowed on eminent persons[25].

The abhorrence felt by Greek and Roman writers to the flatterer is most distinct where they describe flattery as a form of slavery or of self-debasement. Aristotle describes the task of flattery (ἔργον κολακείας) as associating humbly (ταπεινῶς) with those who enjoy being flattered[26]. It was believed that flattery debased the character of flatterers because the very ones they praised regarded them with contempt (τὴν κολακείαν ταπεινὰ ποιεῖν τὰ ἤθη τῶν κολάκων καταφρονητικῶν)[27]. Proof of this debasement, suggests Athenaeus, can be found in the way they submit to anything though cognizant of the kind of treatment which people

---

21 Eg. Cicero, ND 2.63.158 : canum tam fida custodia tamque amans dominorum adulatio.

22 Phys. 6 (811b.37).

23 Of dogs : θωπευτικός, 'fawning', Aristotle, HA 1.1.21-22. Of persons : θωπεία, 'flattery', Aristophanes, Eq. 890; Euripides, Or. 670; θωπεύω, 'to flatter', Sophocles, OC 1003, 1036; Aristophanes, Eq. 48, Ach. 657.

24 Eq. 48; Dio Chrysostom, Disc. 77 & 78.34.

25 Deipn. 6.259A.

26 Pol. 5.9.6; cf. ibid., 4.4.5.

27 Athenaeus, Deipn. 6.255D.

committed against them[28]. By contrast, Aristotle's great-souled person could never debase himself for 'he is incapable of living at the will of another, unless a friend, since to do so is slavish (δουλικὸν)' So Aristotle concludes, 'flatterers are always servile and humble people flatterers' (πάντες οἱ κόλακες θητικοὶ καὶ οἱ ταπεινοὶ κόλακες)[29].

Both notions of servility, the dog-analogy and slavery, are present in Dio Chrysostom's denigratory remarks about the philosopher who will change his character (μεταβαλεῖ τον ἀυτοῦ τρόπον) and become a flatterer and a cheat (κόλαξ καὶ γόης), fawning and grovelling (σαίνοντα καί ταπεινὸν) about the courtyards of the wealthy like Circe's lions, timid and cowering[30]. To be guilty of flattery was for him to be guilty of uttering a word which was both ignoble and servile[31]. Socrates similarly equates the work of a flatterer with the way of a politician who seeks to serve the whims of the public[32]. Indeed, the flatterer appears to be used consistently in a derogatory manner to describe both the popular politician and the populace in Athens. Athenaeus reports Hegesander as saying that the popular leaders at Athens during the Chremonidean War (268-263 BC) resorted to politics by flattery[33]. Conversely, the Athenian public became notorious for flattery, especially towards Demetrius, and he describes them as 'flatterers of flatterers' and 'Dionysus-flatterers'[34]. The servile connotations were

---

28 Ibid., 6.255E. Cf. Plutarch, Mor. 64E : 13C.

29 EN 4.3.28ff. Cf. Seneca, de Ben. 6.30.4 : obsequium servile submissa. Plutarch, Mor. 13C : τῇ τυχῇ μὲν ἐλεύθεροι τῇ προαίρεσει δὲ δοῦλοι.

30 Disc. 77 & 78.33-35. σαίνω literally refers to a dog 'wagging the tail' or 'fawning' : see Homer, Od. 10.217, 16.16; Epictetus, 2.22.9; Athenaeus, Deipn. 3.99E. Circe's lions : Homer, Od. 10.212-219.

31 Disc. 50.8.

32 Plato, Gorg. 521A-B.

33 Deipn. 6.250F.

34 Ibid., 6.253A-254B. Cf. Aristotle, Rhet. 3.2.10.

retained even when the words were used in a more respectable form. In post-Augustan historians, adulatio was used frequently for servile respect to a superior exhibited by bowing the body[35]. Flattery lay at the heart of the charges of servility in the anti-epicurean polemic. Epicureans were accused of forming friendships for utility, as I have previously shown[36], with the rich and powerful whom they flattered and served in other ways. Epicurus himself was said to have flattered Mithras and Idomeneus simply for his own pleasure[37]. He responded in turn by denigrating Plato's followers as 'the toadies of Dionysius'[38]. The symposiums of Epicurus were represented by their enemies as an assembly of flatterers who excessively praised each other[39]. Cicero used to advantage this popular criticism to account for Piso's supposed servility. Piso had close friendships with Epicureans, especially with Philodemus, the flatterer, who sought his patronage and never departed from his presence[40].

As can be seen from the preceding examples, either explicitly or implicitly, freedom and flattery are implacably opposed. This is clearly evident in two accounts in Athenaeus. Thrasydaeus, the greatest flatterer (κόλαξ μέγιστος), whom Philip favoured and placed in a position of authority, is contrasted with Arcadion, 'who was no flatterer', who went into voluntary exile rather than submit to Philip[41]. The same Philip was said to be stern towards the dignified and flatterers but good-tempered towards those who joked at his expense. The reason - he thought 'that only these men are free, even if they be slaves'[42]. This important contrast

---

35 Eg., Tacitus, Ann. 3.2, 4.6.

36 See above n.23.

37 Athenaeus, Deipn. 7.279F; cf. Diog Laert. 10.4-5.

38 Diog. Laert. 10.8. 'Dionysus-flatterers' is a common servile term of derision in Athenaeus, Deipn. 6.249F, 254C, 485E, 588F.

39 Athenaeus, Deipn. 5.182A.

40 Cicero, In Pisonem 28.70-29.71.

41 Deipn. 6.249C-D.

42 Ibid., 6.260C-D.

of freedom and flattery as servility underlies most of the ensuing discussion and, as we shall see in chapter 8, the charge of inconstancy against Paul in 1 Cor. 9.

Finally, servility and cowardice were characteristics of the flatterer in physiognomics and theatre masks. In the former, I have already referred to Aristotle's 'smooth brow' analogy. Quintilian provides us with this further insight into the inner nature. He suggests that, as a rule, it is unbecoming to raise or contract the shoulders. This shortening of the neck is indicative of a mean and servile person and when accompanied by flattery, admiration (bad sense) and fear it denotes a fraudulent person[43].

As to masks, Pollux describes forty-four masks used for stock characters in New Comedy in the second century AD[44]. The parasite and the flatterer are of dark complexion which according to Pseudo-Aristotle is a mark of cowardice[45]; both have hooked noses, which for them is a sign of shamelessness as against its indication of greatness of soul in a noble person[46]; to complete a not entirely favourable frontispiece, he had raised, malicious-looking eyebrows, a sign of conceit[47].

Diodorus Siculus relates two stories about Prusias, 'a man unworthy of royal dignity', which incorporates all the elements of flattery so far discussed. Diodorus claims that Prusias' entire life consisted of acts of abject flattery to his superiors. Prior to the visit by a Roman embassy, he put aside all the insignia of royalty and went to meet the envoys in the guise of a newly emancipated freedman at Rome and declared himself to be a freedman of Rome. Diodorus could not conceive of a more ignoble act. On another occasion, Prusias, on entering the senate, lowered both his hands and kissed the threshold in obeisance and greeted the

43 11.3.83.

44 Onom. 4.13.

45 812a. These references from Pseudo-Aristotle appear in 'Physiognomics', 38.

46 811a.

47 811b.

members with 'Hail, ye saviour gods'. Diodorus' terse and vitriolic comment : he thereby achieved 'unsurpassable depths of unmanly fawning and effeminate behaviour'. His speech in the senate, of a similar nature, offended the Romans. 'For', says Diodorus, 'the Romans desire even the enemies whom they conquer to be men of high spirit and bravery'[48].

d. The flatterer as the inconstant friend.

I have already mentioned the close relationship between friendship and flattery and the deliberate character changes of the flatterer. I now intend to deal with them in more detail. In relationships where pistis/fides is paramount, the flatterer is not to be trusted. Cicero calls such people fickle and falsehearted men (leves homines atque fallaces)[49], whose hypocrisy (simulatio) is 'especially inimical to friendship' (amicitiae repugnat maxime) for it destroys sincerity[50]. He aims at giving immediate pleasure through excessive praise and ignores the truth[51]. Aristotle, in describing the areskos, claims that he 'complaisantly approves of everything and never raises an objection and thinks it is his duty to avoid giving pain to those with whom he comes in contact'[52]. In fact, says Cicero, if people wish to know the truth about themselves, they would be better served by the acid comments of enemies than by their sweet smiling

---

[48] 31.15.2-3. See also Polybius, 30.18.1-7, for a similar account. I have already drawn attention to the allusion to servility in charges of effeminancy (see above, 66). The flatterer is also denigrated as being servile and effeminate. See Diodorus Siculus 31.15.3; and Athenaeus, Deipn. 12.535A, where Eupolis in the play, 'The Flatterers', ridiculed Alcibiades in these words : 'Let Alcibiades cease to be a woman'; cf. ibid., 535B.

[49] de Amic. 25.91; cf. ibid., 25.92 : varius, commutabilis, multiplex.

[50] Ibid., 25.92. Cf. Plutarch, Mor. 142C : 'you cannot use me as a friend and flatterer both'.

[51] Eg., Aristotle, EN 4.1.35, 10.3.11, EE 2.3.8, MM 1.31.1, Rhet. 2.6.8; Plato, Gorg. 464C-465A; Dio Chrysostom, Disc. 3.2-3; Cicero, de Amic. 25.92.

[52] EN 4.6.1.

friends (ei amici, qui dulces videantur)[53].

This contrast was an important element in the teaching methods of the Cynics. Solon's conventional morality, expressed in his prayer as, ἔιναι δὲ γλυκὺν ὧδε φίλοις, ἐχθροῖσι δὲ πικρόν, τοῖσι μὲν αἰδοῖον, τοῖσι δὲ δεινὸν ἰδεῖν[54] was amended in part by Crates to ὠφέλιμον δὲ φίλοις, μὴ γλυκερὸν τίθετε[55]. Sweetness led to flattery which was anathema to the Cynics who claimed to speak the truth in all circumstances. κολακεία, with its notions of servility and falsehood, stood in contradistinction to their highly-valued παρρησία, the freedom of speech[56]. In contrast to the harm caused by flattery, they sought to teach and educate, their truthfulness taking on the nature of a doctor's instrument; as he would heal the ill so they by censure and reproach would educate man as to his faults[57]. However, the line between blame and insult is a thin one indeed in such a society, and their good intentions were not always welcomed by their hearers.

There runs throughout the discussions of friendship the question as to how frank one should be with a friend, particularly in pointing out his faults. The entire second part of Plutarch's essay on 'How to tell a Flatterer from a Friend' is devoted to this topic[58], and he strongly favours παρρησία within friendship. While opinion differed on this point, for some doubted friendships capacity to withstand reproach by a friend[59], no one doubted that an enemy would use

---

[53] de Amic. 24.90; cf. Plutarch, Mor. 89B-C.

[54] Fr. 13 Bergk.

[55] Diels, 220.5.

[56] Diog. Laert. 6.69.

[57] Ibid., 6.4.

[58] Mor. 59Cff. Cf. Seneca, de Ben. 6.30.3-5.

[59] The line between ridicule and reproach was a thin one indeed and one should never ridicule a friend; Cicero, de Or. 2.58.237, 59.238, Or. 89; Quintilian 6.3.28; Democritus, Diels, 405.19; Publius Syrus, 634. However, cf. Socrates, Xenophon, Mem. 1.2.52, who suggests that helping a friend did not necessarily mean being gentle with him; Plutarch, Mor. 51C; Cicero, de Amic. 13.44; Publius Syrus, 625.

it to full advantage. Some thought it was evidence of an enemy rather than a friend[60]. The bluntness of Diogenes' speech led to his being called the 'dog'[61] and he is reputed to have said of himself that while other dogs bite their enemies he bites his friends to save them[62].

The silken tongue of the flatterer had a long history[63] as had the acid tongue of the enemy. The Cynic, especially of the earlier school, assumed the role of an enemy whom he regarded as less harmful than a false friend[64]. Plutarch was in full agreement with this assessment. 'What your best friend would never tell you' could often be found among the barbs of the enemy if one was prepared to listen and learn[65]. However, he would not agree with the simplistic distinction of the sweet talking false friend and the parrēsia of the enemy. While parrēsia is not one of his more obvious characteristics, the more subtle flatterer may become skilled at this also. He speaks with the openness and candidness permitted to only the closest of intimates[66]. But even in this guise, his aim is still to provide pleasure and to achieve his own ends[67].

Plutarch's awareness of various kinds of flatterers is important to note. The obvious characteristics of a Gnatho

---

60 Plutarch, Mor. 56A-B; Cicero, de Amic. 24.89; Quintilian, 8.5.4 : 'Complaisance wins us friends, truth enmity' (from Terence, Andr. 1.1.41).

61 Dio Chrysostom, Disc. 9.

62 Stobaeus, Flor. 3.13.44.

63 Cf. Theognis, 851.

64 Anton. Mel. 1.25 (sp. 853B) : Later Cynics reacted in favour of a milder approach and sought to convey truth with a gravity braced with laughter; like a physician who smears the rim of the cup with honey to lessen the bitterness of the medicine; cf. ibid., 2.32 (sp. 1084D). For the connection between the serious and the laughable and its formal union into σπουδαιογέλοιοι see Plato, Laws 810E, 838C.

65 Plutarch, Mor. 89B-C.

66 Ibid., 59A-F. Cf. Cicero, de Amic. 26.99, who describes the 'deep crafty' flatterer, who is hard to recognize 'since he often fawns even by opposing, and flatters and cajoles pretending to quarrel'.

67 Plutarch, Mor. 60B-C.

so skilfully created by a playwright are misleading. The compliant laugh, the 'right', 'excellent', 'splendid' of the actor[68] provide us with the more popular, if exaggerated, conception of the flatterer. His praise, agreement, exaggeration, imitation and capacity to please are well documented in literature. But it does not do justice to the 'subtle' flatterer, as will emerge from the ensuing discussion, nor to the real dilemma which Greeks and Romans faced in dealing with anomalies in a person's character. It is to the complex question of deliberate character change, αἱ μεταβολαί, in relation to the flatterer to which we now turn.

By both action and words (πράξεις καὶ λόγοι)[69], the flatterer adapted himself to the character and circumstances of his associates and is reputed to have had an almost inexhaustable repertoire[70] and to be thoroughly professional in his adaptations[71]. For this character change, as with the polyphilos, the charge of inconstancy was consistently made against him[72]. Cicero asks, 'What can be as pliant and erratic as the soul of a man who changes not only to suit another's humour and desire but even his expression and nod ? 'He says "nay", and "nay" say I; He says "Yea", and "Yea" say I; in fine, I bid myself agree with him in everything'.'[73]. Cicero is quoting from and commenting on the self-disclosure of Gnatho in Terence's Eunuchus. There Gnatho prefaces this statement of his practice

---

68 Terence, Eun. 494, 773ff.

69 Aristotle, MM 1.31.1. Cf. Athenaeus, Deipn. 6.238F : ἔργοι and λόγοι.

70 Cf. Theophrastus, Char. 2; and the many accounts in Athenaeus, Deipn. 6.248Cff.

71 Plutarch, Mor. 50E : 'with adroitness and skill'; flattery was actually called a profession, Athenaeus, Deipn. 6.258D; Lucian, Parasite 2; See however, Plato, Gorg. 465A.

72 Eg., the absence of τὸ βέβαιον Plutarch, Mor. 97A-B, 53A.

73 de Amic. 25.93. Cf. Cicero's references to Gnatho, Fam. 1.9.19.

of accommodation with : 'I smile on them and stand agape at their intellects. Whatever they say I praise; if again they say the opposite, I praise that too. If one says no, I say no; if one says yes, I say yes. In fact, I have given orders to myself to agree with them in everything'[74].

Various attempts were made to account for how the flatterer was given the name of kolax. The physician, Androcydes, believed it came from the way in which he glued himself (κολλᾶσθαι) to his associates[75], while Clearchus thought it came from his easy good nature (εὐκολία), the dexterity with which he submitted to all kinds of treatment and took upon himself another's character, 'never restive under anything, no matter how degrading'[76].

Change of character is the mark by which Plutarch distinguishes the flatterer from a friend. I quote at some length :

> 'What, then, is the method of exposing him, and by what differences is it possible to detect that he is not really like-minded, or even in a fair way to become like-minded, but is merely imitating such a character ? In the first place, it is necessary to observe the uniformity and permanence of his tastes, whether he always takes delight in the same things, and commends the same things, and whether he directs and ordains his own life according to one pattern, as becomes a free-born man (ἐλεύθερος) and lover of congenial friendship and intimacy; for such is the conduct of a friend. But the flatterer, since he has no abiding-place of character (ἦθος) to dwell in, and since he leads a life not of his own choosing but another's, moulding and adapting himself to suit another, is not simple, is not one, but variable and many in one,

---

[74] Eun. 250-253.

[75] Athenaeus, Deipn. 6.258B.

[76] Ibid., cf. Plato, Laws 942D, from which Clearchus borrows. In Athenaeus' opinion, Deipn. 6.261F-262A, κόλαξ is derived from κόλον, 'food', and with reference to ψωμοκόλαξ 'crumbflatterer', i.e., a person who flatters to obtain a piece of bread. The notion of servility is present in all these attempts to account for the origin of the word.

and like water that is poured into one receptacle after another, he is constantly on the move from place to place, and changes his shape to fit his receiver. The capture of the ape, as it seems, is effected while he is trying to imitate man by moving and dancing as man does : but the flatterer himself leads on and entices others, not imitating all persons alike, but with one he joins in dancing and singing, and with another in wrestling and getting covered with dust; if he gets hold of a huntsman fond of the chase, he follows on, all but shouting out the words of Phaedra : "Ye gods, but I yearn to encourage the hounds, as I haste on the track of the dapple deer." He does not trouble himself in regard to the quarry, but he goes about to net and ensnare the huntsman himself. But if he is on the track of a scholarly and studious man, now and again he is absorbed in his books, his beard grows down to his feet, the scholar's gown is the thing now and a Stoic indifference, and endless talk about Plato's numbers and right-angled triangles. At another time, if some easy-tempered man fall in his way, who is a hard drinker and rich, "Then stands forth the wily Odysseus stripped of his tatters"; off goes the scholar's gown, the beard is mowed down like an unprofitable crop; it's wine-coolers and glasses now, bursts of laughter while walking in the streets, and frivolous jokes against the devotees of philosophy ... A further testimony is to be found in the action of the great flatterers and the demagogues, of whom the greatest was Alcibiades. At Athens he indulged in frivolous jesting, kept a racing-stable, and led a life of urbanity and agreeable enjoyment; in Lacedaemon he kept his hair cropped close, he wore the coarsest clothing, he bathed in cold water; in Thrace he was a fighter and a hard drinker : but when he came to Tissaphernes, he took to soft living, and luxury, and pretentiousness. So by making himself like to all these people and conforming his way to theirs he tried to conciliate them and win their favour. Not of this type, however, was Epameinondas or Agesilaus, who, although they had to do with a very large number of men and cities and modes of life, yet maintained everywhere their own proper character in dress, conduct, language, and life. So, too, Plato in Syracuse was the same sort of man as in the Academy, and to Dionysius he was the same as to Dion. The changes of the flatterer, which are like those of a cuttle-fish, may be most easily detected if a man pretends that he is very changeable himself and disapproves the mode of life which he previously approved, and then suddenly shows a liking for actions, conduct, or language which used to offend him. For he will see that the flatterer is nowhere constant, has no character of his own (αὐτὸν οὐδαμοῦ βέβαιον οὐδ᾽ ἴδιον) that it is not because of his own feelings that he loves and hates, and rejoices and grieves, but that, like a mirror, he only catches the images of alien feelings, lives and movements'[77].

Alcibiades is Plutarch's exemplary κόλαξ (ὁ μέγιστος)[78] though a deterrent example, and he develops the theme of the cuttlefish[79] or chameleon[80] in his biography of Alcibiades. In this, he points to many of the anomalies between Alcibiades' public and private life and concludes that public opinion was undecided about him by reason of the 'unevenness' (ἀνωμαλία) of his nature[81]. Plutarch was not the first by any means to comment on Alcibiades' renowned versatility. The Alcibiades legend was well known and discussed and opinions as to his true character were quite diverse[82]. Nepos was well aware of the anomalies : 'All men marvelled that one could have so varied and contradictory a character' (dissimilitudinem tamque diversam naturam)[83]. Though

---

77 Mor. 52A-53A. Plutarch, in this essay, is describing flatterers of some status who associate with influential men.

78 Mor. 52E.

79 Mor. 97A, 52F.

80 Mor. 53D.

81 Alcib. 16.1-6.

82 See D.A. Russell, 'Plutarch : "Alcibiades" 1-16', PCPS 12 (1966), 37-47, esp. 37-38.

83 Alcib. 1.

Alcibiades' reputation had been assailed by many writers, Nepos considered him to be a truly great man with unusual though remarkable qualities and he enlists the support of three noted historians who praised his versatility - Thucydides, who was Alcibiades' contemporary, Theopompus, and Timaeus[84]. However, Plutarch leaves us in no doubt as to his opinion of the enigma. The indecision of the Athenians as to 'his erratic and unpredictable style', is now seen to be a capacity for infinite changes of style to suit changed circumstances[85]. Again, I quote at length from Plutarch's description of Alcibiades' chameleon-like skills.

> 'At Sparta, he was held in high repute publicly, and privately was no less admired. The multitude was brought under his influence, and was actually bewitched, by his assumption of the Spartan mode of life. When they saw him with his hair untrimmed, taking cold baths, on terms of intimacy with the coarse bread, and supping black porridge, they could scarcely trust their eyes, and doubted whether such a man as he now was had ever had a cook in his own house, had ever so much as looked upon a perfumer, or endured the touch of Milesian wool. He had, as they say, one power which transcended all others, and proved an implement of his chase for men : <u>That of assimilating and adapting himself to the pursuits and lives of others, thereby assuming more violent changes than the chameleon</u>. That animal, however, as it is said, is utterly unable to assume one colour, namely, white; but Alcibiades could associate with good and bad alike, and found nought that he could not imitate and practice. In Sparta, he was all for bodily training, simplicity of life, and severity of countenance; in Ionia, for luxurious ease and pleasure; in Thrace, for drinking deep; in Thessaly, for riding hard; and when he was thrown with Tissaphernes the satrap, he outdid even Persian magnificence in his pomp and lavishness. It was not that he could so easily pass

---

84 Ibid., 11; cf. Athenaeus, Deipn. 12.534B, for a further account of Alcibiades' versatility.

85 D.A. Russell, Plutarch, 123.

> entirely from one manner of man to another, nor that he actually underwent in every case a change in his real character (ἤθει μεταβολήν); but when he saw that his natural manners (φύσις) were likely to be annoying to his associates, he was quick to assume any counterfeit exterior which might in each case be suitable for them'[86].

The calculated and unprincipled changes of the kolax are directly opposed to the commendable behaviour of those who remain true to their character in all circumstances of life and are the antithesis of the steadfastness and reliability of a true friend. I have previously commented on this aspect of friendship[87] but the deliberate contrast is worth noting. For Pliny, what commends a true friend is 'unfailing loyalty in his affections' (habet maximam in amore constantiam)[88] and Cicero says he will be 'firm, steadfast and constant' (firmi et stabiles et constantes)[89]. Like Plutarch, Cicero believes that a fawning friend (simulatus) can be distinguished from a true friend (sincerus) and he contrasts the 'smooth-tongued, shallow citizen' (assentatorem et levem civem) with the friend who is stable, sincere and serious (constantem et verum et gravem)[90]. Such is his distaste for the former that he reckons it to be a sign of inconstancy to have a flatterer for a friend on any terms[91].

To use constancy as the criterion for true friendship does

---

[86] Alcib. 23.3-5. Cf. Athenaeus, Deipn. 6.238B-F for numerous other examples of the flatterer's accommodation to varying circumstances; 6.258A, '... he assumes every kind of shape and of speech as well, so varied are his tones.'

[87] See above 25-27.

[88] Letters 7.8.3. Cf. Aristotle, EE 7.2.39 : βέβαιον γάρ τι δοκεῖ ἡ φιλία; Plutarch, Mor. 563E : ἤ βεβαιότερον φίλοις 659F : ἀμετάπτωτος καὶ βέβαιος ; 169F-170A - Plutarch would rather have man say that he should not have been born or did not exist rather than that he was 'an inconstant, fickle person' (ἄνθρωπος ἀβέβαιος εὐμετάβολος).

[89] de Amic. 17.62; cf. ibid., 17.64, de Off. 1.80. For a discussion and numerous examples of constantia /amicitia /fides, see J. Hellegouarc'h, Le vocabulaire latin, 283-285.

[90] de Amic. 25.94-96.

[91] Ibid.

not exclude versatility in the friend who has, like everyone else, to cope with the various contingencies of life. However, like Epameinondas and Agesilaus, he will maintain the principles of his nature (ἦθος) as he does so. Each person is an individual and his set of characteristics unique; what might be right for one may be wrong for another, reasons Cicero. But as to propriety (decorum), for the individual it must mean 'uniform consistency in the course of our life as a whole and all its individual actions' (aequabilitas cum universae vitae tum singularum actionum). Such is impossible if one apes the personal traits of others and eliminates one's own. What commended Cato, however much one might like or dislike the various aspects of his personality, was his 'unswerving consistency' (perpetua constantia). By this, Cicero means, he was true to his character, his purpose and fixed resolve[92]. Therein lies the real contrast[93].

The question as to whether a man could change his character has a long history in Greek literature and is inseparably linked with their understanding of inherited characteristics, those which nature (φύσις) imposed. They had a somewhat deterministic and inflexible view of character[94] which Aristotle systematized, setting the pattern for the understanding of <u>physis</u> which appears in later Graeco-Roman literature[95]. He taught that a man is born with certain traits or capacities (φύσεις) to which, as he matures, are added further characteristics (ἤθη). Though his <u>physis</u> can and should be developed by education and thus enhanced, it cannot be altered or eradicated by it. It fundamentally remains the same throughout life. <u>Physis</u> and <u>ethos</u> represent his total pattern of conduct, known to himself and to others. Thus predictions could be made with some degree of certainty about

---

92 de Off. 1.31.111-112; cf. ibid., 1.33.120; 1.26.90.

93 See A. Wardman, Plutarch's Lives (London, 1974) 49-57, for Plutarch's comparison of the ideal leader, Politicus, and the flatterer-demagogue.

94 Eg., Demosthenes, 20.141, 37.56, 61.8, 14.

95 EN 2.1.1ff. Cf. A.W.H. Adkins, From the Many to the One (London, 1970), 178-181, for <u>physis</u> in Aristotle.

how he might behave in most circumstances. What was required of him was consistent adherence to his known character, to what people expected of him[96].

The immutable physis, however, presented great problems. How could apparent changes in character be accounted for ? Anomalies in character or the enigma were perplexing and where they occurred they had to be explained. The extent to which either 'nature' or 'nurture' determined the components in a person's character was much discussed by pre-Aristotelian writers[97], evidencing the dilemma in which their deterministic views had placed them. Plutarch recalls Theophrastus' attempt in his 'Ethics' to answer the problems of character-change in relation to Pericles[98].

Polybius faced the same problem with the character of Hannibal and most of the elements of the discussion appear there[99]. He concedes that most men at some time in life act contrary to nature and exhibit a disposition which is the opposite to their real nature[100], either by 'compulsion' or 'force of circumstance' or by the influence of friends[101]. Two diametrically opposed solutions are proffered. First, that the circumstances bring out the real character. That is to say, that he has disguised his real character till now. Second, and the one Polybius favours, that μεταβολή obscures rather than reveals physis[102].

These traditional solutions are used by Plutarch in his secondary comparison of Marius and Sulla. Marius the elder had always been cruel and power did not change him; rather it intensified his cruelty. By contrast, Sulla's childhood and early days of power had been consistent with a merciful

---

[96] Cf. Plutarch, Sert. 10.1-3.

[97] See K.J. Dover, Greek Popular Morality, 88-95, for heredity and environment as determinants of moral capacity.

[98] Pericles 38.2.

[99] 9.22.1-26.11.

[100] 9.23.4.

[101] 9.22.10, 26.1.10.

[102] 9.23.4

disposition. As to his later capriciousness and cruelty, Plutarch leaves it open as to whether it was due to 'change and a reversal of nature, brought about by fortune, or rather a revelation, when a man is in authority, of underlying baseness'[103]. Both solutions, though, attempt to maintain the immutability of the physis.

By contrast, the acquired characteristics can change, and are more easily explained. Sertorius' change of ēthos was due to unfavourable circumstances[104]. Not so was the change in Alcibiades who deliberately and consciously changed this aspect of his character to gain his own ends[105]. Plutarch's criticism of Alcibiades in this regard is not new. However, it does spell out more clearly what is implicit in many of the discussions of the flatterer to which I have referred. The kolax deliberately and calculatedly violates the demands made by his character and with chameleon-like skills adapts himself to the different characters of those whom he wishes to gain for his own advantage. Such behaviour is servile and the opposite of freedom. Unlike the slave who has no choice in the matter, the flatterer willingly surrenders his freedom for gain.

For this, he earned the almost universal censure of Roman and Greek writers of all ages. It was regarded as an act of great shame and Aristotle emphatically denies that the just man (δίκαιος) in his social relations could ever 'assimilate himself to the character of those with whom he converses for such conduct is that of a flatterer'[106]. In a similar vein, is Hesiod's indictment : 'He is a worthless man (δειλός) who makes one and now another his friend. But as for you do not let your face put your heart to shame'[107]. To be

---

[103] Sulla 30.4-5. Cf. Dio Cassius, RH. 33.109.2, for his view of Sulla's character change.

[104] Plutarch, Sert. 10.4

[105] Ibid., Alcib. 23.5. See D.A. Russell, 'On Reading Plutarch's Lives', 146-147.

[106] MM 2.3.3.

[107] W&D 713-714.

charged, then, as a flatterer went to the heart of all that the Greeks and Romans most despised in society, carrying with it all those nuances of social disapproval[108]. Both the terms which signify this change of character - μεταβολή/μεταβάλλων and αὐτομολία/αυτόμολος - are included in Pollux' thesaurus of invective[109].

It seems not all surprising to me that Russell in his discussion of Alcibiades appeals to Paul's self-description, 'I am all things to all men' as a succinct summary of Alcibiades' versatility[110]. Whether this is a conscious reference to Paul, or whether he is using it as the popular maxim it has become with its derogatory connotations, I do not know. As I understand the saying in Paul, the popular maxim more accurately represents its meaning than the interpretation given by biblical scholars and it forms part of the serious accusations that have been made against him by his opponents.

---

108 διαβάλλειν κόλλακεις : Dio Chrysostom, Disc. 3.25; cf. Aeschines, 3.162.

109 4.35, 38.

110 Plutarch, 107.

Chapter 4

THE CUSTOM OF RECOMMENDATION

a. Recommendation as a form of friendship.

The form and structure of Greek letters of recommendation have been the subject of two studies : the seminal investigation of C.W. Keyes in which he examined the form of thirty private and fourteen literary letters and two samples from manuals of letter writing[1]; the dissertation by Chan-Hie Kim in which he analysed the form and structure of eighty-three published private letters[2]. Both Keyes and Chan-Hie refer to the numerous parallels between Greek and Latin letters of this kind, notably those of Cicero[3]. The cumulative weight of these parallels led Keyes to suggest that Cicero was not only acquainted with the Greek style but that he used some of the conventional Greek forms in his own letters. Further, he claims that Cicero's letters became models for later writers of letters of recommendation in Latin[4]. It is also possible that Latin formulae underlie some of the Greek letters from

---

[1] 'The Greek Letter of Introduction' AJP 56 (1935), 28-44.

[2] Form and Structure of the Familiar Greek Letter of Recommendation, SBL Series 4 (Missoula, 1972). The eighty-three letters (six are Latin) are reproduced in an appendix, III, and consist of either complete papyrus letters or letters which contain passages of recommendation. Two articles on Christian papyrus letters of recommendation are also worth noting : K. Treu, 'Christliche Empfehlungs-Schemabriefe auf Papyrus' in Zetesis : Festschrift de Strijcker (Antwerp/Utrecht, 1973), 629-636; H. Leclercq, 'Litterae Commendatitiae et formatae' in DACL 9.1 (Paris, 1930) Coll. 1571-1576. I have been unable to sight the study of Latin letters of recommendation by H.M. Cotton, Letters of Recommendation from Cicero to Fronto, (Listed in BICS 24 (1977), 167) which has now been successfully submitted as a doctoral dissertation at Oxford University.

[3] C.W. Keyes, 'The Greek Letter', 43; Chan-Hie Kim, Familiar Greek Letter, 38 n.9, 49-50, 67-72, 81, 90-92.

[4] 'The Greek Letter' 44; he suggests Cicero's influence can be seen in Fronto's letters of recommendation, the Latin papyrus letters and P. Oxy. 32.

the first century AD onwards[5].

It is not my intention, however, to look further into the form and structure of these letters. Rather, I wish to examine the convention which I believe underlies many of them, that of friendship. Fustel de Doulanges was the first to notice that relationships based on fides were initiated by commendation[6]. He was followed by M. Gelzer who briefly commented on this observation[7]. To my knowledge, no other work has been done on it since. Gelzer warns that 'it would be quite perverse to look for ties of fides behind every commendation'[8]. Letters of recommendation were written for a number of reasons :

a. as a form of introduction[9];

b. to support a candidate for office[10];

c. to publicly acclaim a citizen[11];

d. as a testimony to the character of a person on trial[12];

e. to recommend favoured athletes by the emperor or Romans of high status[13].

It is not easy to draw a line where fides is concerned because of its vast range of meaning and whether a relationship is denoted or intended depends upon the individual assessment of each context.

In the vast majority, if not all, of Cicero's letters of recommendation, commendare, 'recommend', is linked in one

---

[5] See Chan-Hie, Familiar Greek Letter, 69-70, for ἔχειν συνιστάμενον as a Latinism; for the appearance of two phrases in Greek papyrus letters first introduced in the Roman period : ibid., 68-70, request formula with ἐρωτέω ; ibid., 85, appreciation formula with μαρτυρέω .

[6] Histoire des institutions politiques de l'ancienne France Vol. 5. (Paris, 1890), 205-225.

[7] Nobility, 67-69.

[8] Ibid., 69.

[9] Xenophon, Anab. 3.1.8; 6.1.23; P. Petrie 2.11.1.

[10] Commendatio/suffragatio : see J. Hellegouarc'h, Le vocabulaire latin, 158-159; M. Gelzer, Nobility, 107-110; L. R. Taylor, Party Politics in the Age of Caesar (Berkeley and Los Angeles, 1961), 39ff., 64-66; E.S. Staveley, Greek and Roman Voting and Elections (London, 1972), 106, 195, 221ff., 261 n. 423.

[11] Cicero, Parad. 29.

[12] Fronto, Amic. 1.1.1; Pliny, Letters 10.58.3, 6; 10.60.

[13] Dio Chrysostom, Disc. 31.111.

degree or another to amicitia[14]. Its Greek equivalent, συνίστημι is related to philia in a number of the Greek letters[15]. Several of Pliny's letters, while not adhering to accepted formulae, are intended as recommendations in much the same way as Cicero's[16]. Fronto's collection, likewise, contains a number of more orthodox letters of recommendation[17]. The connection in both Pliny and Fronto with amicitia is most apparent.

The extant letters of recommendation are merely the tip of an iceberg in what was a familiar daily practice. Direct references and allusions are numerous in both Greek and Latin literature[18]. Cicero admits to three of his friends that, because of his known relationship with them, he was besieged with numerous requests from people who wished to be recommended to them. He concedes that he had been somewhat indiscriminate, even though obliged to do so, in granting their requests[19]. Only a few items of the implied mass of correspondence with these three friends are in Cicero's collection[20]. Epictetus claims that Socrates' recommendation was much sought after and that he used to take people with him to recommend them

---

[14] Cicero's Fam. 13 (excluding 13.68) consists only of letters of recommendation. 6 refer to communities (4, 7, 9, 11, 18b, 40) and 72 to individuals. Others are scattered throughout his correspondence : Fam. 1.3; 3.1.3; 5.5; 6.9; 7.5.3; 8.9.4; 12.21, 26, 27, 29; Att. 15.14; Brut. 1.6, 8; QF 2.14.3.

[15] Papyrus : P. Cairo Zen. 59052, 59192; P. Oxy. 743, 787, 1424; P. Mich. 33; P. Col. Zen. 48; PSI.359, 415, 520, 969; P. Sorb.49; P. Herm. 1; SB.8005. Literary (from R. Hercher, Epistolographi Graeci (Amsterdam, 1965)): Aeschines 6; Chion 2, 8; Dion 2; Plato 14, 15; Socrates 21; Socratici 25.

[16] With commendare : Letters 7.31; 10.58.6; without commendare but recommendations just the same : 2.13; 3.2; 4.4, 15; 6.8; 10.86b, 87.

[17] M. Caes. 5.37; Amic. 1.1, 4, 6, 8, 9, 10.

[18] Latin : Cicero, Fam. 1.10; 2.14, 2.19.2; 3.1.2; 5.11.2; 6.8.3; 7.5.2, 7.6, 7.17.1, 2; 8.2; 11.6.1; 12.25b.6; Att. 4.16.1; 6.1.3; QF 1.2.11; Pliny, Letters 3.8; 6.9, 6.12; 10.58.3, 6, 10.60.1. Greek : Diog. Laert., 5.18; 8.1, 8.3, 8.87; Epictetus, 2.3.1

[19] Fam. 13.5.1 (Valerius Orca); 13.70.1, 71.1 (Servilius Isauricus); Brut. 1.8.1 (Brutus); cf. Fam. 12.30.1; 13.32.1, 40; Pliny, Letters 6.12.

[20] Valerius Orca : Fam. 13.4, 5, 6a, 6b; Servilius Isauricus : Fam. 13.66, 67, 68, 69, 70, 71; Brutus : Brut. 1.6, 8.

in person[21]

Frequency and familiarity pose a problem with regard to the study of the relationships connected with the letters. The almost rigid adherence to the standard formula raises the question as to whether these letters were intended to be or were taken seriously by the writer and the recipient. Even much of the very intimate vocabulary of some of Cicero's letters appears rather common and formal as one reads through the collection. This is not a problem unknown to us : we write with studied propriety and read with cynical benevolence.

The writers and recipients, though, were aware of the problem. Cicero does make some distinction between intimate friends and others whom he recommends[22] and he attempted on occasions to create a deeper impression on the recipient by extending praise of the recommended's character, motives and reputation or recitation of his circumstances and needs[23]. More particularly, he commented directly that his letter was no stereotyped recommendation (non vulgarem esse commendationem) or that he had made conscious stylistic changes to make the recipient aware of its importance[24]. Sometimes he appended to the letter a previously agreed upon private mark which indicated to the recipient that the recommendation was to receive special attention, and one of these letters is simple, short and formal[25].

The stereotyped nature of other letters can be misleading and alone cannot be the test for the importance of the recommendation or the degree of intimacy between the writer and the recommended. Cicero's recommendation of M. Fadius

---

[21] 3.23.22; 4.8.2, Ench. 46.1.

[22] Eg., Fam. 13.70, 71.

[23] Praise : Fam. 13.10.2-3; 16.1-4, 55.1; circumstances : Fam. 13. 1.2-4, 19, 29, 56.

[24] Non vulgarem esse commendationem : Fam. 13.15.3; cf. 13.35.1, 69.1; nec ea vulgaris : Fam. 7.6.1; ut mihi verba deisent : Fam. 13.63.1; Caesar ridiculed him on one occasion for, in Cicero's words, using that vetere verbo, 'hackneyed expression' and he determined to avoid it in future - Fam. 7.5.3. Stylistic changes : Fam. 13.6a.3, 27.1, 63.1-2.

[25] Friends of Cuspius : Fam. 13.6a, 6b.

is quite ordinary even by his standards[26] but he is an old and highly valued friend to whom Cicero is indebted if Fam. 7:23-26 are any indication. Similarly, the recommendations of Manius Curius and Mescinius Rufus, while more elaborate, are not a good indication of Cicero's relationships with either simply on the basis of the style of recommendation he wrote[27].

An analysis of other personalities who appear in Cicero's or Pliny's recommendations, I am sure, will reveal a like situation. Unfortunately, there are no similar collections in Greek but there is no reason to suppose that the situation would have varied greatly. This supports my contention which I will argue later, that it is the relationship between all the parties concerned which is of prior importance for recommendation, not simply the style or formality of the letter.

Further evidence in this regard can be found in the interchange of information in Cicero's collection. Cicero tells one friend that, though he has recommended so many to the latter, they and he are totally satisfied with what the latter has done. That is, he always treats the letters as genuine and responds accordingly[28]. Further, he warmly thanks his friend Servio Sulpicius for acting on behalf of those he had moderately commended (mediocriter commendati)[29]. Much of the interchange arises from his explicit or implicit requests for assurance from all parties as to the success of the recommendation. Either he sought a letter bearing proof that his recommendation had been followed from the recipient[30] or the recipient wrote himself[31] or the recommended informed him[32]. He wrote letters of thanks to friends who had acted

---

[26] Fam. 13.59.

[27] Manius Curius : Fam. 13.17.1; 16.4.2-3; Mescinius Rufus : Fam. 13.26; 28a; 5.19, 20, 21.

[28] Fam. 13.32.1.

[29] Fam. 13.28a.1.

[30] Fam. 12.24.3, 13.10.4, 73.2.

[31] Fam. 13.44, 75.1.

[32] Fam. 13.24.1, 27.2, 28a.1, 41.1, 42.1, 43.1, 44.1, 54.1, 64.1; Att. 15.14.

as he had asked[33] and informs others he had followed their recommendations[34].

A familiar request phrase, 'has requested me to write', appears in both Greek and Latin letters[35]. Keyes and Chan-Hie have suggested that the phrase somewhat diminishes the force of the recommendation[36]. It is doubtful, however, if any letter of recommendation was written without a request by the recommended or someone on his behalf. If the request is not stated it certainly is implied; the writer and the recipient are aware of the practice which was proper and acceptable within the convention of friendship. In a Greek literary letter, the writer comments, 'he asks of us what is just and what a friend may properly ask, assistance'[37]. In fact, the request may well be indicative of friendship. The numerous references in Cicero's letters to which I have previously referred[38] ought to make one wary of using this common practice as evidence of a depreciative force. To concentrate on the familiar form in this regard is to miss the crux : the nature of the relationship which the letter or other evidence reveals.

It is my contention that letters of recommendation were an essential and fundamental element in the establishing,

---

[33] Fam. 1.3; 12.26.1; 13.25.2, 28a.1; 15.14.1-2, Att. 15.14.3.

[34] Fam. 3.1.2; 5.11.2; 12.25b; 15.14; 16.12.6; Att. 2.22; 4.16.1; Pliny, Letters 3.8; 6.9, 12.

[35] Greek : P. Cairo Zen. 59045, 59192; BGU 1297; P. Oxy. 746; PSI 520; Chion 8; Latin : Cicero, Fam. 13.1.3, 75.1; see above n.18, 19, 21, for other request passages.

[36] C.W. Keyes, 'The Greek Letter', 42; Chan-Hie Kim, Familiar Greek Letter, 57.

[37] Plato, 15.

[38] See above n.19 21.

extending, and maintaining of friendship[39]. I have already shown the wide range of relationships, of both kind and degree, and the associated obligations denoted by <u>philia</u> and amicitia. Many of the letters of recommendation accurately reflect this situation and contain many of the elements outlined earlier. I have been able to trace only two statements as to the origin of the practice. In the second century AD Fronto recalls : 'The custom of recommendation (commendantis mos) is said in the first instance to have sprung from good will, when every man wished to have his own friend made known to another and rendered intimate with him'[40]. He then goes on to relate the extension of the practice to the sphere of public or private trials. In the courts of law these letters were preceded and influenced by the old custom of bringing forward, after all the evidence had been heard, witnesses to character who gave their own private opinion of the defendant. Thus these 'commendatory letters (commendantium litterae) seemed to discharge the function of a testimony of character'[41].

A similar explanation as to the origin of Greek letters of recommendation prefaces the sample letter in Demetrius Phalereus : 'The introductory type (ὁ συστατικὸς) which we write to one person for the sake of another, inserting (words of) praise, and speaking of those previously unacquainted as if they were acquainted'. Or, as a variant translation expresses it : 'making acquainted those previously

---

39 During the absence of a friend, friendship was largely maintained by private letters. Prolonged absence was considered detrimental to even the most intimate friendships, for without the reciprocal affection and services of which it consisted, it was difficult to sustain (eg., Aristotle, EN 8.5.1). Frequent letters stimulated the relationship of parted friends and in Cicero one can detect criteria for friendship in letter-writing. Eg., frequency of letters were a sign of or a test of friendship (Fam. 11.10.1; cf. Fam. 6.6.1; 12.17.1, 30.1; 15.14.3) and were evidence of good manners (Att. 7.1; Fam. 7.14.1, 2; 16.4.2). Non-replying to a letter could be taken as the aligning of oneself with the writer's opponent (QF 3.1.11). See H. Koskenniemi, Studien zur Idee und Phraseologie des Griechischen Briefes (Helsinki, 1956) 37, who traces the idea to Aristotle and his concepts on the nature of community in Nichomachean Ethics.

40 Amic. 1.1.1.

41 Ibid.

unacquainted'[42]. I have been unable to evaluate the accuracy of these claims as to the origin in friendship[43] but it will become clear from what follows that friendship remains the primary basis of recommendation whatever other developments have taken place. It is certainly the ground on which person to person recommendations are built (I will refer to these later in the chapter).

Two or more of the following friendship ingredients are present in many letters of recommendation :

a. the recommendation arises out of the request of a friend;
b. the request is based on the friend's awareness of a friendship between the recommender and the recipient;
c. the recommender's appeal is directed to his friendship with the recipient;
d. the intention of the recommendation is to create friendship between the recommended and the recipient;
e. the intention of the recommendation is to enhance the relationship between the recommender and the recommended.

b. The friendship of recommender and recommended.

The recommendation arises out of a request of a friend, either for himself or for someone else, and it is to this friendship that the recommender is obliged to respond[44]. The recommender uses a wide variety of terms to describe the nature and degree of intimacy of his relationship with the recommended and embellishes it with further explanations

---

[42] V. Weichert ed., Demetrii et Libanii (Leipzig, 1910), 3, 2.17-18.

[43] See H. Koskenniemi, Studien, who argues that, while the form and structure of Greek letters has become stereotyped, they were linguistically rooted in the _philia_ relationship.

[44] The obligation to respond is expressed in a variety of ways in Cicero : Fam. 13.71.1; Brut. 1.8.1: commendem necesse; Fam. 13.8.1 : quod mihi petendum esset; Fam. 13.10.2 : debere; Fam. 13.11.3 : praecipae ad meam curam officiumque pertinet; Fam. 13.39: officio.

where he deems it necessary[45]. In addition, the writer often makes it clear that the recommendation is part of the reciprocal services of the friendship and a wide range of common relational terms are used[46]. Many of the Greek letters, more so than the Latin letters, identify the person as a family relation[47]. I have found only one letter where it is explicitly stated that there is no existing friendship between the recommender and the recommended. But the writer welcomes the opportunity afforded by the recommendation to make this person his friend[48].

Only three letters refer to the recommended simply in terms of his occupation or private business without indicating the relationship[49]. Chan-Hie overstates his conclusion that from this we can observe that 'the social status or personal qualification of the recommended does not count for

---

[45] Familiaris or familiarissimus meus : Cicero, Fam. 1.3; 5.2; 6.9.1; 12.21, 24; 13.12, 13, 15, 24, 35, 38, 42, 44, 58, 60, 69, 74, 77, 78; cf. Fam. 13.27, 50, 75; Pliny, Letters 2.13; Fronto, Amic. 1.1.2, 1.9. Amicius or amicitia : Cicero, Fam. 13.1.2, 13, 16.2 (fidem atque amicitia), 17.1 (amicitia pervertus), 77.2 (veterem amicum); P. Oxy. 32.5 (amicum meum); Pliny, Letters 2.13; Fronto, Amic. 1.9. Necessarius or necessitudo : Cicero, Fam. 13.11, 12, 15, 27, 30.2, 37, 71, 79; Fam. 13.29.1 (paterna necessitudine); Fronto, Amic. 1.1.2, 4. Intimis : Cicero, Fam. 13.3, 30.2. Coniunctio : ibid., 13.7.5. Hospitium or hospes : ibid., 13.9.1, 24.1, 25.1, 32.1, 34.1, 35.1, 37.1, 52.1, 67.1, 78.1. Frater : ibid., 13.1.3, 62. Philos/philia : papyrus - P. Cairo Zen. 59042, 59248; P. Col. Zen. 7 (with anagkaios) P. Mich. 33; P. Herm. 1 (with ana[gkai]os); literary, Plato 14, 15; Socratici 25; Socrates 2 : Dion 2. See also the various pronouns which denote intimacy : papyrus, P. Cairo Zen. 59042; PSI 359; PSI 520; P. Sorb. 49; SB 8005; P. Oxy. 1424; P. Oxy. 787; P. Mich. 82b; PSI 969; P. Cairo Goodspeed 4; literary - Dion 2; Plato 14.

[46] Eg., Cicero, Fam. 12.29.1; (multa .. officia); 13.27 (magnis meis beneficiis devinctus); 13.32 (officiis benevolentia); 13.43.1 (cum consuetudine ... officiis plurimis masimisque mihi); 13.45 (etiam officia magna et mutua nostra inter nos esse); 13.50.1 (summus inter nos amor et mutuus); 13.63.1 (plurimus eius officiis); 66.7 (studiis officiisque); 6.9.1 (non solum officiis amicitiae sed etiam studiis communibis); Brut. 1.6.2 (hoc ego ad meum officium privatarum rerum aeque atque ullam rem pertinere arbitror); cf. Pliny, Letters 2.13; Aeschines 6; Chion 2.

[47] Chan-Hie Kim, Familiar Greek Letter, 48-49.

[48] Chion 8.

[49] P. Osl. 51; Dion 1; Appollonius Tyaneus 107.

much'[50]. He is of course referring mainly to Greek private letters. In the Latin letters, status and reputation are often highlighted and clearly form an important part in character presentation[51], and as such are of value to the recipient in his evaluation of the person's worth to himself[52]. However, he is correct when he says that it is the relationship with the recommender that is regarded as more valuable than one's own credentials[53]. This is particularly so where the person recommended is of low social status[54].

The credentials of friendship are pointed in Cicero's response to Q. Cornificius who complained that Cicero only sent letters of recommendation and no private letters of friendship. He replies, 'There are heaps of letters, since you have managed to make everybody believe that unless he has a letter from me, he has brought no recommendation to you'[55]. By stressing his relationship with the recommended, the writer intends the recommendation to be taken as if he himself were the recommended. The sender hopes the recipient will treat the person whom he has recommended just as he would himself[56].

c. The friendship of recommender and recipient.

The request for recommendation is based on the friend's awareness of the friendship between the recommender and the one to whom he wishes to be recommended. This does not appear as a stylistic element in the letters. However, Cicero states openly that numerous friends have sought him out

---

50 Familiar Greek Letter, 51.

51 Eg., Cicero : his frequent mention of the equestrian order, Fam. 13.14.1, 31.1, 33, 38, 45, 51; reputation or honour, Fam. 1.9.9; 12.17.3, 21; 13.51; S. Rosc. 113; Quinc. 20.62.

52 Cicero, Fam. 12.26.2; 13.28a.2.

53 Familiar Greek Letter, 51.

54 Freedman : Cicero, Fam. 13.21.2, 23.1, 52, 60.1, 69.1; Fronto, M. Caes. 5.37; Plato 13. Slave : Cicero, Fam. 13.45. Trader : Chion 2, Chion 8.

55 Fam. 12.30.1.

56 Cf. P. Osl. 55 (ὑποδεξάμενος ὡς ἂν ἐμέ); P. Oxy. 32 (peto domine ut eum ant[e] oculos habeas tamquam me); Cicero, Fam. 13.62 (cura ut habeas quo me); 13.74 (si mea res esset).

because of his connections with the recipient[57] or because of the evidence of reciprocal good will between them[58].

This is implicit in many of his letters and the Greek letters also, and may be inferred from the consistent request that the recipient give ample proof to the recommended that the friendship is of the highest order. That is, that the friendship is all that the recommended expected it to be, or in accord with what he had heard of it from the writer[59]. This notion, in my opinion, underlies the 'witness' purpose clause, μαρτυρέω - μοι, of the Greek papyrus letters of the Roman period[60] although both Keyes and Chan-Hie see it as a promise indicating that the recommended will repay services done for him by the recipient[61].

d. Recommendation as an exchange of mutual services.

The recommender's appeal is based on his friendship with the recipient. One of Cicero's more whole-hearted appeals encompasses the whole course of friendship, and provides us with many of the elements of which these appeals consist. He writes, 'I ask you ... in the name of our hereditary connexion, our mutual affection, our common pursuits, and the close resemblance of our whole lives throughout their course' (pro paterna necessitudine, pro nostra amore, pro studiis, et omnia cursu nostro totius vitae simillimo)[62].

---

[57] Fam. 13.5.1 (necessitudinem), 71.1 (nostra necessitudo); cf. 13.8.1, 10.1, 19.3, 26.1.

[58] Fam. 1.3; 13.5.1, 45; 13.70.1; 13.71.1; Brut. 1.8.1.

[59] Eg., Cicero, Att. 15.14 : in response to Cicero's recommendation of Atticus to Dolabella : Cicero claims that all of the many favours and services which Dolabella had done for him, the highest and most gratifying is that 'you have shown Atticus how great my affection is for you, and yours for me'. Cf. Fam. 13.4.4; 13.67.2; 12.27.1; amor etc. : ibid., 13.44, 47, 74, 75.2; cf. Aeschines 6 'not entirely lacking in friends'.

[60] P. Osl. 55; P. Flor. 173; P. Oxy. 1064, 1424; P. Giss. 71 (ἀνθομολογέομαι, 'to bear proof'); cf. Cicero, Fam. 13.10.4 (ut quam primum intellegam) and ibid., 12.24.3, 13.6a.4.

[61] C.W. Keyes, 'The Greek Letter', 41; Chan-Hie Kim, Familiar Greek Letter, 85-86.

[62] Fam. 13.29.5. Contrast Cicero's scathing condemnation of those who become friends without business connections or recommendation, Verr. 3.3.22.

In the Latin letters the nature of the relationship and/or the evidence and obligations of it are made the basis of the appeal. Cicero asks the recipient to act towards the recommended 'in view of our close association' (pro nostra necessitudine/coniunctione)[63] or friendship (amicitia)[64]. On occasions it is the recipient's affection (amor) for him[65] or the mutual good will or services they have shared[66]. It may be that the recipient owes gratitude for previous services[67] or, as appears once in a Greek literary letter and five times in Cicero, that the recommender wishes it to be regarded as another of the many services which the recipient has already done for him[68]. In this regard Cicero writes : 'Although there are numberless circumstances in which I hope I may have clear proof - and indeed I have long since had proof enough - of your affection for me (me a te amari), yet here you have a case offered you in which you can easily make manifest your kindly feeling for me (tuam erga me benevolentiam)'[69].

Requests based on friendship appear also in Pliny and Fronto. Pliny writes, 'I ask therefore nay demand in friendship's name'[70], while Fronto, less assertive by equally assured, suggests, 'our friendship is a guarantee of your loyal love for me and (will bring it about that) whatever I ask should seem to you but one word'[71]. Finally, in both

---

[63] Necessitudo : Fam. 13.4.4, 11.2, 31.2 (familiaris et ..), 49,55, 57, 73.2, 74; coniunctio : ibid., 13.7.4.

[64] Fam. 13.77.3; cf. Pliny, Letters 6.8.

[65] Ibid., 13.7.4 (tuus amor in me); 13.7.5 (in me perpetua et maxima benevolentia); 13.43.1 (me a te amari and tuam erga me benevolentiam); 12.21, QF 1.2.11 (si me amas); Att. 15.14.3 (amares).

[66] Fam. 13.4.4 (mutua benevolentia); 13.55 (plurimisque officiis paribus ac mutuis).

[67] Ibid., 5.5.1 (gratia).

[68] Dion 2 : πολλῶν χαριζόμενος.

[69] Fam. 13.43.1; cf. ibid., 13.47 (omnium tuorum officiorum quae et multa et magna sunt); 13.52 (ita magnum beneficium tuum magno cumulo auxeris); 13.54.1 (ego quoque tibi imponam pro tuis in me summis officiis); Att. 15.14 (Ex omnibus enim ... studiis in me et officiis, quae summa sunt, hoc ...).

[70] Letters 6.8.

[71] Amic. 1.2.4.

Greek and Latin letters, the appeal may be simply that the recipient should do it 'for my sake' or 'on my account'[72].

Cicero leaves us in no doubt as to the nature of the obligation and what it involves for the recipient. It will at least oblige the recipient to show as much respect for the writer's friends as his own[73]. A response by Cicero to a recommendation utilizes much of this appeal's language and sentiment : he promises a friend who recommends his wife to him, that he would do all she wanted 'with the utmost energy and attention' (summo studio curaque facturum); if necessary he would call upon her himself; nothing would be so unimportant or insignificant as to seem too difficult or beneath his dignity; whatever he does for her he would regard it as 'a labour of love and an honour' (laboriosa mihi et honesta)[74].

By acting on his recommendation, the writer assures his friend that he will 'do him the greatest favour'. This is a common feature in both Greek and Roman letters. In the Greek letters it is often expressed by χαρίζω and its cognates as a preface to the request or as the closing appreciation[75]. It is present in the Latin letters as a statement of appreciation for the service done or about to be done or the pleasure the deed had brought and is denoted by various

---

[72] Papyrus : P. Merton 62, P. Oxy. 787 (εἰς τὴν ἐ[μ]ὴν); P. Petrie 2.2.4 (δι᾽ ἡμᾶς); Covenaile Corpus Papyrorum Latinarum 257 (meum honorem). Literary : Plato 14 (πρός ἡμᾶς); Plato 15 (ἕνεκα ἡμῶν). Cicero : honoris mei causa - Fam. 13.26.2, 31.7, 37, 65.1, 69.2, 76.1; mea causa - ibid., 13.1.2, 5.3, 28a.3, 73.2.

[73] Fam. 13.49; Cf. id., de Amic. 22.82; Attic. 12.37.3.

[74] Fam. 5.11.2.

[75] Papyrus : χαριεῖ μοι P. Cairo Zen. 59038, 59042, 59603, 59805; P. Col. Zen. 48; PSI 376; P. Cairo Goodspeed 4; P. Tebt. 20; εὐχαριστήσεις μοι or ἡμῖν - P. Petrie 2.2.4; P. Cairo Zen. 59192. SB 7178; P. Mich. 6; cf. also P. Oxy. 292; P. Herm. 1; P. Merton 62. Literary : Socrates 2; Dion 2.

constructions of gratia or pergratum[76]. Admittedly, the clause may simply be a polite or formal way of asking for a favour[77] or may indicate appreciation for placing the recommended under a further obligation to the recommender. However the nuance of reciprocity is usually present and the clause can be understood as an acknowledgement of indebtedness.

Cicero stresses this reciprocal element when he says that he will regard any service (officium) or benefit (beneficium) done for those he recommends as done for him[78]. This will place him under an obligation (obligatum)[79] to his friend and he will show due gratitude (gratia)[80]. Reciprocity is directly intimated in nine of the papyrus letters where the recommender asks the recipient to let him know how he might demonstrate his thanks by a reciprocal favour[81]. As Chan-Hie correctly observes, the object of the offer of reciprocal services is the promotion of good friendship between the two correspondents[82].

In Cicero, the note of reciprocity is in the nature of a promise in three of his letters. He promises in return for the recipient's services, 'For my part I shall attend with zeal and assiduity to whatever I think you desire or that affects your interests'[83]. That the note of appreciation or promise of reciprocal services is included before the action is carried out may indicate confidence on the part of the writer in his

---

[76] As part of the request formula : gratissimum mihi feceris si ... Cicero, Fam. 13.2, 4.3, 22.2, 38, 44, 64.1, 2, 67.2, 74, 75.2; vehementer mihi gratum feceris si ... - ibid., 13.15.3, 20, 67.2, 70; pergratum mihi feceris si ... - ibid., 12.27, 13.23.2, 25, 26.3, 60.2, 61, 71, 77.2, cf. 75.2. As a final note of appreciation : erit mihi gratissimum - ibid., 12.21, 13.3, 8.3, 14.2, 42, 47, cf. P. Ryl. 608; erit id mihi maiorem in modum gratum - Cicero, Fam. 13.16.4, 35.2, 78.2; erit mihi vehementer gratum - ibid., 13.20, 23.2, 32.2, 37, 39, 67.2, cf. 13.13, 27.3, 28b.2, 31.1, 46, 64.1, 77.

[77] Chan-Hie Kim, Familiar Greek Letter, 65.

[78] Fam. 13.11.3, 53.2; cf. Pliny, Letters 3.2.

[79] Fam. 13.18.2; Pliny, Letters 3.2; obligatum - Pliny, Letters 2.13; 4.4, 15.

[80] Fam. 7.8.1; 13.11.3, 50.2; cf. Pliny, Letters 3.2.

[81] See Chan-Hie Kim, Familiar Greek Letter, 96, Table 18.

[82] Ibid., 95.

[83] Fam. 13.6a.5; cf. ibid., 13.69.2, 50.2.

friend. It could also imply obligation to respond to the request.

Where the relationship between the two correspondents is strained, the recommendation has little value. Such was the case between Cicero and Gaius Antonius. Cicero maintained that those who sought G. Antonius' friendship came to him because they knew of Cicero's great energy and numerous services (studiorum et officiorum) on his behalf. Most had properly assumed that he owed Cicero summa officia, but Cicero complained that he had returned no practical gratitude (gratiam). Thus, despite all efforts on Cicero's part, the friendship had lapsed and he resolved to send him no more letters, except for letters of recommendation. Even with these Cicero had his doubts, for his past recommendations had had little influence (valere) upon him. However, he had continued to recommend people to him simply to prevent them having any reason to suspect that there had been any lessening of the ties between them(nostra coniunctione imminutum)[84]. This pretence at friendship with letters of recommendation on the part of Cicero confirms the point I have been making : recommendations are an observable indication of the friendship between the two correspondents - here retained as a last resort - and are regarded by them as part of the wider reciprocal services and affection which constitute their relationship[85].

I have found only one letter of recommendation where a friendship did not exist between the two correspondents. The purpose of this letter is especially noteworthy, for the writer wished it to be regarded as an offer of friendship. Fronto acknowledged to Passienus Rufus that they had never been on the terms of correspondence (implying friendship) although he knew of his good reputation through friends. He prefaced his first letter to Rufus, a letter of recommendation : 'I could find no fairer prospect of establishing a close friendship with you than the occasion of

---

[84] Fam. 5.5.

[85] Cf. ibid., 13.50.1-2, where Cicero deems it necessary to rehearse all the various facets of reciprocity in his approach to the recipient.

recommending to your favour an excellent young man'[86].

e. The friendship of recommended and recipient.

The intention of the recommendation is to create friendship between the recommended and the recipient. Cicero advises M. Brutus that in forming new connections (novis çoniunctionibus) it is crucial to consider 'the details of the first approach, and the value of the recommendation that throws open, so to speak, the door of friendship. That is, what I wished to effect by this letter'[87]. This concept of the recommendation or of the recommender as a friendship-maker is also found in Xenophon. In Antisthenes' recommendation of a stranger to Socrates, he so whetted Socrates' appetite by his praise of the man that he commended Antisthenes as an excellent go-between : 'for the man who can recognize those who are fitted to be mutually helpful and can make them desire one another's acquaintance, that man in my opinion, could also create friendship between cities'[88].

As I have said before, the request for friendship with the recipient arises with the recommended. This is generally implied in the request for a recommendation itself although Pliny states explicitly to Cornutus Tortullus that Claudius Pollio wanted his friendship[89]. The desire, flattering as it may be to the recipient, in itself is not sufficient. Friendship with the recipient in most instances depends upon friendship with the writer. Cicero told Caelius Caldus that the careful elaboration in the recommendation had greatly influenced him 'as the studied recommendations of men who are emphatically my friends is bound to have' (sicuti debet hominum amicissimorum diligens commendatio[90]. Similarly, he wrote to Atticus, 'I have shown Paccius both by word and deed the weight a recommendation (quid tua commendatio ponderis haberet) from you carries. Accordingly he is among my intimate friends (intimis) now though I did not know him before'[91]. The weight

[86] Amic. 1.8.

[87] Fam. 13.10.4; cf. 13.78.2.

[88] Syn. 4.63-64.

[89] Letters 7.31; cf. Cicero, Fam. 5.5.1; 13.1.3.

[90] Fam. 2.19.2; cf. 13.55.1. cf. Quintilian, 12.7.5.

[91] Att. 4.16.1.

that friendship-credentials have upon the recipient appears in Fronto also. He mentions that one new friend was brought to his notice by his learned and close friends whose personal wishes rightly had the greatest weight with him[92]. Again, he told M. Aurelius that when the freedman, Aridelus, presented himself and he didn't recognize him, to remember that he had been 'commended to you by me' (a me tibi commendatum)[93].

In the Latin letters, the desire for friendship is made by the writer either as a direct request or in the form of a commital. Pliny urged Priscus that, though he was in a position to give the highest benefits, he could give the recommended 'nothing more valuable than your friendship'[94]. Cicero simply asks, 'receive him into your friendship[95] or 'receive him into your trust/confidence'[96] or commends the person as being 'worthy of your friendship'[97]. Fronto somewhat more intimately says, 'Love him, I beseech you'[98],

---

[92] Amic. 2.6.

[93] M. Caes. 5.37.

[94] Letters 2.13.

[95] in amicitiam tuam receperis : Fam. 13.23.2; habeasque in numero tuorum : 13.21.2, 35.2, 69.2; cf. ibid., 8.9.4 (in tuorum numero habeas); 13.78.2 (in tuis habeas); 15.14.1 (mihi amicum tua commendatione); 13.19.3 (recipias in necessitudinem tuam); 3.1.2 (Biduo factus est mihi familiaris) 1.3 (se apud te gratiosum fore); Att. 2.22 (Numerium Numestium libenter accepi in amicitiam ... et dignum tua commendatione cognovi); Caesar, BC 3.57.1 (quem ab illo traditum initio et commendatum in suorum necessariorum numero habera instituerat); Pliny, Letters 6.18 (Proinde Firmanis tuis ac iam potius nostris obliga fidem meam).

[96] in tuam fidem recipias : Fam. 13.49, 51, 67.2, 69.2, 78.2; fidem et necessitudinemque recipias : Fam. 13.19.2; cf. Fam. 13.4.3 (fidei, iustitiae, bonatatique commendo); Sallust, Catil. 35.6 (commendo tuaeque fidei trado).

[97] tua dignum amicitia : Fam. 13.7.5, 17.3, 51; dignum tua amicitia atque hospitio and dignum tua amicitia hospitioque : Fam. 13.78.2; tua amicitia dignissimum: Fam. 13.3, 14.2, 40; perdignum esse tua amicitia : Fam. 13.6a.4; tua necessitudine dignissimos : Fam. 13.7.5, 25; cf. ibid., 13.11.3 (Bonos viros ad tuam necessitudinem adiunxeris municipiumque gratissimum beneficio tuo devinxeris); Pliny, Letters 2.13 (cuius esse eum usque ad intimam familiaritatem capacem quo magis scires).

[98] Amic. 1.8 : ama eum, oro te.

and 'he deserves your love'[99], or 'count and love him as your own'[100]. A second century AD papyrus letter suggests, 'he is such a man that he may be loved by you'[101].

The common life between the recommender and recommended is often included in the appeal and underlies the reciprocal element which is present in all the aforegoing requests. For instance, Pliny commends Rufus in this vein : 'If therefore you esteem Tacitus and myself, you cannot but have the same favourable sentiments of Rufus; for a similitude of manners is, you know, the strongest cement of friendship' (cum sit ad connectendas amicitias vel tenacissimum vinculum morum similitudo)[102]. Or more to the point is Cicero's assurance that, if the recipient follows his recommendation, he 'will bind Capito, that most excellent and obliging of men, in the bonds of fellowship to yourself by your own excellent good services'[103]. Cicero, Pliny and Fronto alike regard the service of the recipient as giving patronage to the recommended[104].

The direct request for friendship, as far as I have been able to determine, occurs on three occasions in Greek letters and conforms with what precedes. The writer, possibly Dio Chrysostom, asks on behalf of his long-time friend : 'You who have done me many favours, would do me a great favour if you would consider Herrenius as your own (σαυτοῦ i.e., 'friend')[105]. Hierokles asks Zeno to (become better) acquainted (with him)[106], and, in an early first century AD

---

99 Amic. 1.6 : dignus est quem diligas.

100 Amic. 1.10 : nostrae numeras ac diligas.

101 P. Oxy. 32 : est enim tales omo ut ametur a te.

102 Letters 4.15.

103 Fam. 13.29.8 : Hanc rem ... si effeceris ... ipsum Capitonem, gratissimum, officiossimum, optimum virum, ad tuam necessitudinem tuo summo beneficio adiunexeris.

104 Cicero, Fam. 13.64.2 (si te fautore usus erit); Pliny, Letters 2.13 (quem rogo pro ingenio, pro fortuna tua exornes), 6.12 (quos tuendos putas); Fronto, Amic. 1.6 (suffragis).

105 Dion 2. See also Dio Chrysostom, Vol. 5, Letters 2. The Loeb Classical Library and see 353 for the likelihood of Dio being the author.

106 P. Cairo Zen. 59284.

Letter, Theon asks Tyrannos for Heraclides : 'I most urgently beg you to take him under your patronage'[107]. In another letter, a previous letter is referred to as the one which brought about friendship : 'Krinis ... has long been your philos as well as mine. But since your acquaintance (with him) was originally due to us, I think it proper now, as if I were introducing him to you a second time ...' (ὥσπερ ἑτέραν ἀρχὴν ποιούμενος συστάσεως)[108]. The only committal to friendship of the kind I have noted above in the Latin letters, and it reflects the Latin formula, is the fourth century AD letter of Synesius : 'συνίστημι τῇ φιλίᾳ καὶ τῇ προστασίᾳ τῇ σῇ τὸν θαυμάσιον Σωσηνᾶν'[109]. The use of παρατίθημι σοι or συνίστημι σοι in the Greek letters, by which the writer entrusts the recommended to the care of the recipient, corresponds to the very common Latin committal, commendo tibi[110]. That in itself is no indication of the creation of friendship and the requests which accompany committal need also to be examined. In the majority of cases, the request in the Greek letters is for general assistance : the recipient is asked to help the recommended in his endeavours with all sincerity and earnestness[111].

The most frequent specific request, and one which lends itself to testing, is for the recipient to extend hospitality

---

[107] P. Oxy. 292 : διὸ παρακαλῶ σε μετὰ πάσης δυνάμεως ἔχειν αὐτὸν συνεσταμένον.

[108] Socratici 25.

[109] 102.

[110] First noticed by C.W. Keyes, 'The Greek Letter', 43. Papyrus : παρατίθημι σοι - P. Giss. 88; PSI 96; P. Oxy. 1663 ; συνίστημι σοι - P. Strassb. 174. Literary : συνίστημι σοι - Chion 8; Dion 1; Plato 14 (cf Rom. 16:1). Commendo tibi : Cicero, Fam. 8.9.4; 12.21, 24, 27; 13.6a.3, 9.1, 12.1, 13, 15.1, 16.4, 17.3, 20, 21.2, 23.2, 25, 30.1, 33, 34, 37, 38, 39, 40, 43.1, 44, 45, 46, 47, 51, 52, 53.1, 58, 60.2, 63.2, 70, 71, 74, 77.2, 79; Att. 15.14; QF 1.2.11; 2.14.3; Brut. 1.8.1,2; Latin papyrus, CPL.257; Fronto, M. Caes. 5.37; Amic. 1.8, 9; Pliny, Letters (commendas mihi) 6.9, 12; cf. Cicero, Fam. 12.25b.1.

[111] Chan-Hie Kim, Familiar Greek Letter, 72-77.

to the recommended[112]. One of these is no more than a request for an overnight stay for an official[113] and other requests for hospitality may be of this kind. However, as I have previously shown[114], hospitality is one of the cornerstones of friendship and to extend hospitality was the first step in initiating a reciprocal relationship. It is conceivable then, that some of these requests for hospitality are akin to the direct request for friendship.

There are two cases where this is clearly so in Cicero. First, is the request : 'deem him worthy of your hospitality' (dignum hospitio tuo iudicares)[115], which is undoubtedly equivalent to the friendship request. By it, Cicero goes on to expand, 'take him under your protection (receperis eum in fidem tuam) and assist him'. Second, is the request which appears twice in the one letter : 'pronounce him worthy of your friendship and hospitality' (dignum tua amicitia atque hospitio iudicabis)[116]. In this letter, the request immediately follows the statement that the recommendation is 'opening the door and paving the way to your acquaintance'. In both letters Cicero describes the person as 'a hospitable friend' (hospes)[117].

In one Greek literary letter, the pattern is the same. Ariston had extended hospitality (ὑποδεξάμενος) to the writer; he wishes the recipient to receive him kindly (ὑποδέξῃ φιλοφρόνως) and to help him in other matters 'so that he may learn that he has entertained a man who is not entirely lacking in friends'[118]. Undoubtedly the

---

112 Papyrus : ξενίαν ἔχειν/ποιεῖν - P. Flor. 173; P. Oxy. 1064; P. Ryl. 691; προσδέξομαι - P. Mil. Vogl. 76; P. Osl. 51; ὑποδέξομαι - P. Osl. 55; P. Princ. 105. Literary : ὑποδέξομαι - Aeschines 6; Chion 2; εἰσδέξομαι - Chion 8; cf. ξενίων - Socrates 2.

113 P. Princ. 105.

114 See above, 2-5.

115 Fam. 13.67.2.

116 Fam. 13.78.2

117 Fam. 13.67.1 (hospites), 78.1 (hospes); cf. Att. 4.16.

118 Aeschines 6.

hospitality signified by ὑποδεξάηενος between the writer and the recommended is the basis of their friendship. I can only speculate that ὑποδέξη φιλοφρόνως is a request for friendship. In another letter the request that the recipient receive the recommended hospitality is based on a debt of charis which the writer owes the recommended[119]. Both requests express the writers' self-interest, but that also underlies the Latin letters as I will shortly show. The request 'to grant hospitality', I suggest, is clearly that of philia in the sample letter of Demetrius Phalerus : 'kindly grant him hospitality both for my sake and for his, and indeed also for your own'[120].

Where there is no direct request for friendship or other explicit evidence in the letter, whether a friendship has resulted or was intended can only be tested by external evidence. There is no such evidence with the Greek letters for we have none of the collections such as Cicero's or Pliny's to turn to. Where it is possible to examine a relationship which appears to have been initiated by a letter of recommendation, then I presume that it is correct to say that the relationship is within the purpose of the letter and that we should look for the various associated components of recommendation. In particular, it is my contention that we shall find the relationship between Paul's opponents - certain Corinthians and the rival apostles - was initiated by the letters of recommendation referred to in 2 Cor. 3:1-2 and is of the nature of the relationships we have been considering.

One such study of a friendship which was initiated and nurtured by letters of recommendation and which is available to us is that of Cicero, Trebatius and Caesar (Fam. 7.5-22). As a rising young lawyer, Trebatius committed himself to Cicero's friendship and protection (sed com te ex adulescenta tua in amicitiam et fidem meam contulisses) (7.17.2) and thus

---

[119] Chion 8.

[120] V. Weichert, Demetrii et Libanii, 3.2.21-22 - 4.2.1 : καλῶς ποιήσεις ἀποδογῆς ἀξιώσας καὶ δί ἐμὲ και δι᾽ αὐτόν, ἐτὶ δὲ καὶ διὰ σαῦτον; cf. ibid., Libanius, 22.4.12-14 : δεξάμενος ξενίσαι.

commenced a friendship which was to last throughout Cicero's lifetime (7.19.2). Cicero took it upon himself to 'guard his interests and promote his advancement and distinction' (7.17.2) but his own plans for his protegé were frustrated; then he received an invitation from Caesar in Gaul to recommend someone to him (7.5.2). He took the chance to commend Trebatius to Caesar's 'general goodwill and generosity' (benevolentiam tuam et liberalitatem peto) : 'In short, I hand him over to you absolutely, from my hand (as they say) to yours - a hand as distinguished for its triumphs in the field, as for its loyalty in friendship' (7.5.3). But soldiering was not Trebatius' strong point. Life in Gaul was too severe (7.10.2, 16.1) and he longed for the comforts of Rome (7.6.1, 17.1).

Cicero's letters show a consistent anxiety for his young friend, for his personal welfare, and for what he considered to be his jeopardizing a rare opportunity (7.8.1-2). His short time in Gaul had been financially rewarding, but Cicero admonishes him : 'you were in a hurry to snatch the money and return home, just as if what you brought the commander-in-chief was not a letter of recommendation but a bill of exchange' (Tamquam enum syngrapham ad imperatorem non epistolam attulisses sic, pecunia ablata, domum redire properabas (7.17.1). The object of the recommendation had been to make Trebatius one of Caesar's friends (in familiaribus Caesaris) (7.7.2, 17.3) and Cicero insists that, while other close friends could assist, Trebatius must make every effort to ensure by his own modesty and hard work the success of the friendship (7.7.2). Trebatius' main complaint in this regard was that Caesar had been somewhat dilatory in responding to Cicero's recommendation (7.17.2). Not that Cicero was lacking in his support, for he told Trebatius that he attached to all his letters to Caesar 'a sort of statutory appendix, to wit, my recommendation of you' (7.6.1), which in time he had to cease else he cause Caesar to think he mistrusted him[121]. Caesar was somewhat conscious of

---

[121] Fam. 7.10.3; cf. 7.18.1.

Cicero's riders and he intimated to him that the pressure of his work had prevented his becoming as intimate with Trebatius as he could wish (7.8.1). The enterprise bore fruit and Trebatius told Cicero that Caesar had summoned him because of his juristic excellence[122] and later, that he was now 'on familiar terms with Caesar' (te esse Caesari familiarem) (7.14.2) and that the cold, grey skies of Gaul had taken on the blue of Rome[123].

A prominent feature in the creation of friendship is the use of relational terms to describe its reciprocal nature. In the Latin letters the action taken by the recipient on the recommended's behalf is called a 'benefit'[124]. As is usual with many of the discussions on the reciprocal nature of friendship, this action is described in commercial language. The recipient will be investing his generosity in grateful people[125] and he should regard it as a 'sound' or 'brilliant investment'[126], a source of 'immense profit and infinite pleasure'[127], or simply, the kind of profit which one expects in return for services rendered[128].

The emphasis upon the moral obligation of the recommended to respond is marked. Pliny assures the recipient that his kindness (beneficium) will place all parties under an obligation (obligatio), especially the recommended, 'who is as solvent a debtor as you reckon me to be' (non minus

---

[122] Fam. 7.10.1; cf. 7.11.2.

[123] Fam. 7.13.2, 15.1, 18.1.

[124] summo beneficio : Cicero, Fam. 13.7.5, 29.8; cf. ibid., 8.9.4; 13.26.4, 28a, 53.2, 54; Att. 15.14.3; Pliny, Letters 4.4 (officii).

[125] Cicero, Fam. 13.22.2.

[126] Ibid., 13.26.4 (beneficium bene apud Mescinium positurus esses); 13.28a.3 (ita bene collacturum); 13.41.2 (teque apud eos praeclare positurum); 13.55.2 (quam bene positurus sis studium tuum atque officium); 13.64.2 (apud ipsum praeclarissime posueris).

[127] Ibid., 13.50.2 (maximum fructum summamque voluptatem esse capturum); 13.10.3 (voluptati et usui tibi).

[128] Ibid., 13.65.2 (maximum fructum capies); 13.22.2 (quem soles fructum a bonorum virorum officiis exspectare esse capturum).

idoneum debitorem quam nos putas)[129]. Cicero similarly advises his brother : 'Pray make a point of laying him under an obligation to you by treating him handsomely' (quem fac ut tua liberalitate tibi obliges)[130]. The response of the recommended is intimated in the promise that he would be most grateful or would show due gratitude[131] and he would consider himself bound by the strongest ties of obligation and respect[132]. While these assurances are both formal and courteous, reciprocity is clearly intended.

The reciprocal element in the Greek letters is mainly restricted to the writer's own promise of his appreciation for favours done. However, reciprocity is implicit in the writer's statement that the recommended 'is the sort of person who will consider your interests'[133] and is alluded to in the qualification, 'if he proves useful (χρήσιμος) to you[134]. Reciprocal usefulness also appears in the Demetrius Phalereus sample letter as 'you will praise him to others when you have learned how useful he can be in everything[135]. In one other letter, ἀντιχαρίζομαι is used to express the appreciation the recommended himself would show for the recipient's help - ἀντιχαρίεται παρὰ πάντα δὲ χαρίῃ τὸν σώματος ἐπιμελόμενος ἰν' ὑγι[α]ίνης[136]. Chan-Hie is correct in seeing this as an offer to reciprocate for services received[137].

A number of letters of recommendation, rather than creating

---

[129] Letters 4.4.

[130] QF 2.14.3.

[131] Gratia/gratissimos : Cicero, Fam. 7.8.2; 8.9.4; 13.7.5, 11.3, 28a.3, 29.8, 40, 41.1, 54, 60.2, 65.2, 77.2; QF 1.2.11; 2.14.3; Att. 15.14.3; Pliny, Letters 7.31.

[132] Cicero, Fam. 13.3 (summo officio et summa observantia tibi in perpetuum devinxeris); 13.30.2 (officio et observantia); cf. observantia : ibid., 12.26.2; 13.23.2, 65.2; obligatio : ibid., 8.9.4; Pliny, Letters 4.4.

[133] P. Cairo Zen. 59046.

[134] P. Cairo Zen. 59192.

[135] V. Weichert, Demetrii et Libanii, 4.2.2-4.

[136] BGU 1871.

[137] Familiar Greek Letter, 94.

friendship, strengthen an existing relationship between all the parties concerned. The recommended is the friend of both. I quote two examples. Cicero writes : 'I beg of you ... so to manage matters by your kind feeling, influence and devotion as to convince M. Anneius not only of your existing friendship for him (te et sibi amicum esse) - of that he has often told me, he has no doubt - but also of the enhancement of that friendship by this letter of mine (et multo amiciorem his meis litteris esse factum)[138].

And at some length we meet M. Fadius again, long time friend of Cicero[139] and himself recommended by Cicero[140]. Cicero responds to Cassius : 'By your recommendation you present M. Fadius to me as a friend; well, I gain nothing by that. As a matter of fact he has been for years entirely at my disposal, and I have liked him for his extreme kindness and the respect he shows me. But for all that the discovery that you are extraordinarily fond of him has made me much more a friend to him. And so, although your letter has had its effect, yet what recommends him a great deal more is that I have come fully to see and understand his kindly feelings for yourself'[141]. Here there can be no sense of 'being introduced'. Instead, the recommendation of a mutual friend serves to promote and extend the existing relationships, both as to intimacy and mutual services[142].

Subsequent letters of recommendation on behalf of the one person also serve to foster and encourage the development of friendship initiated in the first letter. I have previously referred to the appended recommendations from Cicero to Caesar on Trebatius' behalf. While not always required, subsequent recommendations were sought by the recommended. Avianus considered that frequent letters from Cicero were important for his affairs with T. Titius. Probably with some

---

[138] Fam. 13.55.2.

[139] Fam. 7.23-26.

[140] Fam. 13.59.

[141] Fam. 15.14.1.

[142] For other examples of this kind of recommendation, cf. ibid., 12.24.3; 13.16.3; 13.47.1; 16.12.6; cf. 13.1.2, 66.1, 64.2; 3.1.2, 3; Att. 16.3; Pliny, Letters 6.8, 9; Dion 2; Socratici 25.

justification. While Cicero apologises for acceding to Avianus' request lest Titius should think his own constancy is doubted, Cicero suggests that, though Avianus does not doubt his affection for him, Titius should make it his object to convince Avianus of his love for Cicero[143]. Like Trebatius who attached himself to Cicero, Q. Pompeius had made a practice of soliciting recommendations from him which had been instrumental in bringing about 'his fortunes, his reputation and influence'[144]. Pliny records that Archippus sought and won from Domitian a series of letters of recommendation testifying to his character when seeking reinstatement to his former position. These of course had nothing to do with the initiation of friendship[145].

Subsequent letters did not only arise from the request of the recommended. The writer himself could take the initiative, through becoming aware of additional needs which required attention by the recipient. In his second recommendation of Lyso to Sulpicius, Cicero refers to his first letter[146] and thanks him for fulfilling the request. At the time however Lyso's fortunes were in the balance and Sulpicius may have been reluctant to put his full weight behind the recommendation. Now Lyso's civil status was assured and Cicero urges : 'I make no abatement in the strength of my recommendation to you, as if I had got all I wanted, but I press you all the more to admit Lyso into your confidence and intimacy'[147]. A note of caution appears in this letter as it did in Cicero's letter to Titius. Cicero is concerned that if Sulpicius did not give Lyso his full support 'he may suspect me of not having written warmly enough and not of you having forgotten me'[148]. Cicero later wrote a note of appreciation to Sulpicius in which he acknowledges his kindness,

---

143 Fam. 13.75.1-2.

144 Fam. 13.49.

145 Letters 10.58.3; cf. 58.6, 60.

146 Fam. 13.19.1

147 Fam. 13.19.2.

148 Fam. 13.19.3; cf. Pliny, Letters 6.8.

and while Lyso says that he now needs no more recommendations, Cicero encourages Sulpicius to continue his efforts[149]. Recommendations of a common friend or subsequent recommendations are generally conceded to be unnecessary by Cicero in whose letters most instances occur. Yet, he continues to write them on request. It says something of the fundamental importance of these letters for friendship.

f. The enhancing of friendship.

The intention of the recommendation is to enhance the friendship between the recommender and the recommended. I have already shown that the recommendation arose out of friendsip and was considered as part of the mutual services between the two friends. A successful recommendation enhances this relationship. Cicero tells P. Silius : 'You will have bound the company more closely to me' (societatem mihi coniunctionem feceris)[150]. The notion of reciprocity appears in the formal and familiar request in Cicero that the recipient take every step to make the recommended aware of how instrumental the recommendation had been in the action he has taken. This appears most commonly as a request that the recipient 'be careful to make him feel that this recommendation has been of the greatest service to him'[151].

There are numerous variations on this theme : that the recommended be made aware how much weight was attached to the letter[152]; that he may realise that the recommendation of him was no conventional formality[153]; that the recommendation had

---

[149] Ibid., 13.24; cf. similar patterns : L. Lucceius - ibid., 13.41.1,2,42; Lucius Oppius - 13.43, 44; Arpinates & Q. Fufidius - 13.12.1; Nero - 13.64.1, 2; Strabo Servilius - 13.64.1; Cacrellia - 13.72.1; community at Buthrotum - Att. 15.14.3; Socratici 25.

[150] Fam. 13.65.1.

[151] Fam. 12.29.3 : mea putes esse curesque, ut intellegat nanc commendationem maximo sibi usui fuisse; cf. ibid., 13.30, 34, 35, 38, 39, 46, 52, 71.

[152] Fam. 12.27; cf. ibid., 13.25.

[153] Fam. 1.3.

not been the most negligible factor in his success[154]; that the recipient should convince the recommended 'that I had taken special care in writing about him and that my recommendation has been of substantial service to him'[155]; that the recommendation has 'conferred great distinction on him'[156]; that the recipient may see to it that the thanks Cicero receives 'may be as cordial and as prompt and as frequent as possible'[157]; that the recommended be made to 'feel that my friendship even when I am far away is of benefit to him[158].

The only similar request in the Greek letters carries the same meaning : 'make it clear to him that we have written to you about him'[159]. I have previously noted the numerous responses of gratitude which Cicero received from those he recommended[160]. As with the creation of friendship, the recommendation can be called a 'benefit'[161] for which the recommended is obliged to return gratitude[162].

A further important feature of letters of recommendation is what I shall term 'multiple' commendations. This may refer to the practice of recommending the one person to more than one friend[163], thus surrounding him with as many supporters as warranted. More particularly, it refers to the individual recommendation of a person by a number of his friends to a common friend, and to the pool of correspondence that seems to be generated. In its most simple form, it consists of a dual recommendation : while Varro Murena

---

[154] Fam. 13.26.4.

[155] Fam. 13.20.

[156] Fam. 13.37.

[157] Fam. 13.6b.

[158] Fam. 13.58 - cf. ibid., 13.59.

[159] P. Cairo Zen. 59101.

[160] See above n.32.

[161] Beneficium : Cicero, Fam. 13.28a; Pliny, Letters 2.10; 3.2.

[162] Gratia : Cicero, Fam. 13.6b, 27.2; Brut. 1.8.2.

[163] Eg., Cicero's letters to Caesar, Balbus and Quintus on behalf of Trebatius : Fam. 7.5.3, 6.1, 7.1; QF 2.14.3; cf. P. Cairo Zen. 59045, 59046; P. Oxy. 292.

is confident that his recommendation of T. Manlius will be well received by Sulpicius, he considered that a recommendation from Cicero would enhance his prospects. Cicero not only accedes to the request but adds that his own anxiety for Manlius stimulated his letter[164].

A more complex situation is presented by the recommendation of L. Flavius, a friend of Cicero. Flavius considered himself to have been unjustly treated by Cicero's brother, Quintus, in a matter of debt over an estate he had inherited. He complained bitterly to Cicero that he had had no influence with Quintus, either as to friendship or justice. In fact, he had received a letter from him which had left him in no doubt where he stood. Quintus would express his gratitude to him as a friend if he complied with his wishes or else make things unpleasant for him as his enemy. Flavius sought recommendations from Pompey, Caesar and Cicero while at the same time engaging in correspondence with Quintus. The outcome is unknown[165].

As could be expected, apart from the interchange of correspondence between the parties to which I have already referred, there was a significant interchange of letters and discussions. Negotiations between the recommender and the recipient preceded the recommendation itself and essentials were worked out and agreed upon. The recommendation reminded the recipient of the negotiations as well as recommending the person in the normal way[166]. Two friends could come to some mutual arrangement as to the recommendations of their friends to each other, especially where they considered their positions would enable them to be mutually helpful[167]. People in high positions could invite their friends to recommend people to them, not simply to reflect upon their own status, but as a sign of friendship[168]. Conversely, people appealed

---

[164] Fam. 13.22.1

[165] QF 1.2.10-11.

[166] Cicero, Fam. 6.8.3 (cf. 6.9); 13.3, 6a.1, 7.1, 55.1, 57.2.

[167] Ibid., 13.6a, 6b.

[168] Cf. Caesar's invitation to Cicero : Fam. 7.5.2 - si vis, tu ad me alium mitte, quem orne.

to friends to use their position of advantage to advance the cause of their own friends, as they did their own[169]. In one letter of recommendation, Cicero asks the recipient who apparently was in Rome at the time, to send the recommended a letter to be handed back to the recipient in the province. The contents should be so constructed, advised Cicero, as to jog his memory as to the care Cicero had taken in writing the recommendation[170]. Last, the recipient himself may be asked to recommend the person by letter or in person to others[171].

g. Forms of character praise.

Praise is not essential to letters of recommendation and, as I have said before, credentials of friendship are of first importance. Still, the various elements of character, status, background, ability and pursuits which appear in the letters are important. They serve not only to enhance the reputation and prospects of the recommended, but to outline the potential reciprocal services the recipient could expect. Pliny writes, 'I have sent you a short sketch of his tastes, his manners, in fine his whole character'[172]. It is this character sketch which Cicero terms the 'careful elaboration' (accuratissime scripsit) and the 'studied recommendation' (diligens commendatio) of his closest friends which had such an important part in the influence of a recommendation upon him[173].

Complimentary phraseology is more elaborate in the Latin letters and reference is sometimes made about excessive use of praise. Cicero admits to Caesar that in his recommendation of Trebatius he was inclined 'to lay it on with a trowel'[174].

---

[169] Eg., Cicero, Fam. 13.49; Pliny, Letters 2.13; 3.2.

[170] Fam. 13.43.

[171] Fam. 13.19.3; P. Ryl. 691; cf. P. Cairo Zen. 59045, P. Tebt. 20 : εἰσάγω ; Synesius 102.

[172] Letters 2.13 : breviter tibi studia, mores, omnen denique vitam cius expressi.

[173] Fam. 2.19.2.

[174] Fam 7.5.3.

Yet it is anything but uncommon in his other letters. In only one letter of Cicero's is there a negative qualification to the praise. He candidly concedes to Lentulus : 'L. Valerius the lawyer, I strongly recommend and that too even if he is - well, no lawyer'. Here Cicero's appeal is based solely upon his intimacy with Valerius and his unfailing gratitude to the recipient[175]. The problem was not a new one to Cicero or Lentulus. Two years earlier Cicero had recommended this aspiring lawyer to Lentulus. As Cicero's letter to Valerius himself shows, his efforts to become learned in the law in the province were unsuccessful. Though he tactfully praises Valerius as 'learned in the law' and as one who seems 'to be the only man who knows anything at all', he asks him not to make further use of the letter of recommendation and to come home[176]. It is worth noting that letters of recommendation can be withdrawn by the writer.

Excessive praise of a person appears almost to be synonomous with recommendation. Diogenes says of Aristotle : 'Beauty he declared to be a greater recommendation than any letter of introduction' (τό κάλλος πάντος ἔλεγεν έπιστολίου συστατικώτερον)[177]. This introduces another important aspect of character praise in recommendations, i.e. that a person's character commends itself. This lies at the heart of Diogenes' response to a request for γράμματα συστατικά, that it was a person's qualities which recommend themselves without a written commendation[178].

This appears to have become a formal element in letters of recommendation, and it is difficult to decide whether it represents a true account of the outstanding character of the person or an apologetic note for excessive praise, or whether it serves to heighten the praise. I favour the last of these alternatives for the normal praise element is never replaced by it, but rather, it becomes part of the normal praise element. This can be seen in the following examples from Cicero :

---

175 Fam. 3.1.3.

176 Fam. 1.10.

177 Diog. Laert. 5.18.

178 Epictetus, 2.3.1-2. Cf. Ep. Diogenes, 18.

'If you have met him prior to the arrival of this letter ... for such is his courtesy and civility that I expect that he has already been his own recommendation to you'[179]; 'For I feel sure that he would succeed by his own character and culture, unaided by anybody's recommendation in winning your esteem no less than mine and that of all his other friends'[180]. It takes other forms also : in the assurance that the recipient will be able to verify the character-praise for himself when he becomes well acquainted with the recommended[181]; or in the variety of pledges that the recipient will find the recommended as described[182] to his own advantage.

Other facets of a person's background or career may obviate the need for written recommendation. First is Cicero's concession that the route ad gloriam is much easier with commendatio maiorum : 'self-started and self-supported, I have worked my way to my present position, but his shining virtues will be reinforced by the recommendation of illustrious ancestors'[183]. With not disinterested praise, he says Quintus Pompeius gained recognition on his own merits and won the highest honours without commendatio maiorum[184]. Conversely, it was noble birth alone, accuses Cicero, which commended another to public opinion and misled people as to his real character[185].

Second, is the office of quaestor, to which were elected young men of distinction. Cicero considered M. Varro did not require a written recommendation as he was sufficiently recommended by the practice of our ancestors' (satis enim commendatum tibi cum arbitrabar ab ipso more maiorum) which

179 Fam. 13.17.2 : Ea est enim humanitate et observantia, ut eum tibi iam ipsum per se commendatum putem.

180 Fam. 13.21.1 : Perficeret enim ipse profecto suis moribus suaque humanitate, ut sine cuis quam commendatione diligeratur, abs te non minus, quam et a me ceteris suis familiaribus.

181 Cicero, Fam. 13.10.4 : cum bene cognoris iudicanda sunt; cf. ibid., 7.5.3; 13.6.4, 19.3, 28a.3, 78.2.

182 Ibid., 13.10.3, 17.3, 28a.3, 31.2.

183 Planc. 27.67 : hoc facilior fortasse, quod ego hoc, a me ortus et par me nixus, adscendi; istius agregia virtus adiuvabitur commendatione maiorum.

184 Brut. 25.96.

185 Sest. 9.21-22 : erat enim hominum opinioni nobilitate ipsa blanda conciliatricula commendatus ... et falsa opinione hominum ab adulescentia commendatum sciebam.

assumed that a quaestor's connection with the consul closely approximated that of a father to his son[186]. Though Cicero concludes that the bond of quaestorship should open the door of friendship unaided, Varro still sought a written recommendation. Cicero agreed on the basis that it would strengthen the traditional ties[187]. Third, and akin to Quintus Pompeius, is the recommendation that issues from a person's achievements. Somewhat tongue in cheek, Cicero told M. Antony : 'in these days public affairs have so recommended you to me that there is no one for whom I have more regard'[188]. Fourth, are the rights and merits of nationalities (iura et merita populorum). The Lacedaemonians did not doubt that they were sufficiently recommended 'by their own high claims and those of their ancestors' (ipsi sua maiorumque suorum auctoritate)[189].

To return to the point I made at the beginning of this discussion of praise of character. While praise is not essential to letters of recommendation, it is an important element in the relationship between the recommended and the recommender and between the recommended and the recipient. Where praise of character is clearly unnecessary, it is still given unabashedly. In a similar vein, where it appears that no written recommendation is necessary - existing friendships, subsequent recommendations, ancient traditions, a character which commends itself - letters are still sought and given. These considerations illustrate the importance with which written recommendations were regarded by all parties in forming a relationship and the fundamental importance of

---

186 Fam. 13.10.1; cf. ibid., 2.19.2 for the recommendation of a quaestor to Cicero; 13.26.1 for Cicero's relationship with his quaestor, L. Mescinius; Pliny, Letters 4.15 in relation to the choice of a quaestor. This office was normally elected to young men of distinction but in a tradition as ancient as the office itself, a magistrate could choose a quaestor outside the election for personal reasons. If attached to a magistrate, the quaestor served out his appointment for the duration of his consul's term and remained morally tied to him as a client for life.

187 Fam. 13.10.4.

188 Att. 14.13b : tum his temporibus res republica te mihi ita commendavit, ut cariorem habeam neminem; cf. id., Inv. ag. Sall. 2.4 : quam eos res suae gestae et vita innocentissime acta commendavit.

189 Fam. 13.28b.

friendship in its wide range of intimacy and services to this practice.

h. Self-commendation.

Two important and interrelated aspects of recommendation remain to be considered : self-recommendation and commendati in fidem. I have dealt so far with written recommendations by a third party. Now I turn to the act in which a person recommends himself to another. In the first instance is the use of συνίστημι or commendo in forming a reciprocal relationship with or without mutual connections. Polybius relates (1.78.2-8) how Naravas, a young Numidian nobleman, took advantage of Hamilcar's precarious battle position to meet and commend himself to him (πρὸς ἔντευξιν αὐτῷ καὶ σύστασιν). Though he wished all the Carthaginians well (εὐνοεῖν) - he had long-standing family ties with them (πατρικὴ ἔχων σύστασιν) - he particularly wanted Hamilcar's friendship and for this reason he had come to introduce himself and offer his services. An impressed Hamilcar reciprocated by not only offering an association (κοινωνός) but ties of marriage if he remained loyal to Carthage.

A second incident of this kind took place prior to a major battle during Caesar's Spanish campaign. Soldiers under Petreius and Afranius sought after acquaintances and fellow-townsmen in Caesar's camp and inquired after the 'good faith of the general' (imperatoris fide) to see whether they would be justified in committing themselves to him (quaerunt, rectine se illi sint commissuri). Similarly, many military tribunes and centurions came to Caesar and commended themselves to him (compluresque tribuni militum et centuriones ad Caesarem veniunt seque ei commendant) and Spanish chieftains sought out acquaintances and guestfriends through whom they might have an opportunity of being commended to the attention of Caesar (Hi suos, notos hospitesque quaerebant, per quem quisque eorum aditum commendationis haberet ad Caesarem)[190].

---

[190] Caesar, BC 1.74.

From perilous military situations to parlous affairs of the heart. Terence's Chaerea, who loved Pamphila and got himself into a fine predicament as a result, entreated Thais 'to stand by me in this matter. I entrust myself wholly to your honour, I take you as my champion' (in hac re mi ... ut adiutrix sies, ego me tuae commendo et committo fidei te mihi patronam capio)[191]. Likewise Thais, who loved Chaerea's brother, placed herself under the protection and patronage of his family' (patri se Thais commendavit, in clientelam et fidem nobis debit se)[192].

Self-recommendation also occurs where a relationship already exists. In seeking restoration, Cicero wrote to Curio : 'As it is I simply entrust and hand over to you the whole business, the cause of Milo and my own interests without reserve' (Nunc tibi omnem rem atque causam meque totum commendo atque trado)[193]. The difficult political situation of the late republic accounts for many of the self-recommendations which appear in Cicero[194]. But political fortunes do not exhaust the possibilities. Cohorts in crime may commit themselves to the protection of the most powerful member[195]; one's public and private affairs, while travelling abroad, can be commended to a friend[196]; entering into a business partnership is described as committo me in fidem[197]. Of a similar nature, though they are third party recommendations, are the commendations of a wife or family (or estate and property) to a friend during political exile

---

191 Eun. 885-887.

192 Eun. 1039-40.

193 Fam. 2.6.5. Cf. Fam. 3.9.4; QF 1.3.10.

194 Eg., Att. 3.20.2; Fam. 11.6.1; 12.17.3.

195 Cicero, S. Rosc. 37.106: the Roscii : ac se in Chrysogoni fidem et clientelam contulerunt.

196 Id., Quinc. 20.62 : cui tu et rem et famen tuam commendare proficisiens et concredere solebas.

197 Id., S. Rosc. 40.116 : ad cuius igitur fidem confugiet cum per eius fidem iaeditur, cui se commiserit.

or long absence from home[198] and the committal of a son to a friend for his education[199]. Thus we are presented with a wide variety of recommendations of this kind and I have no doubt that the range would be extended considerably by a more detailed study than my limited one. It appears that a person could commend anything to do with his own security or interests to the care of a friend, or those with whom he hoped to form a relationship, and that they had a moral duty to respond to the act of committal[200].

As the use of συνίστημι σοι and commendo tibi in written recommendations shows, and as I have just observed from self-recommendations, the notion of trust is implicit in the use of συνίστημι and commendo. This nuance in commendo is often strengthened by other Latin 'trust' words - committo, trado, concredo, confero, confugio - which are virtually synonymous with and can do service for commendo[201]. There appears to be no Greek equivalent to the peculiarly Latin stock phrase commendo in fidem, though Plutarch appears to translate it into Greek as ἐκείνῳ πιστεύοντες αὑτοὺς μόνῳ to describe the Lusitanians' act of entrustment to Sertorius[202].

A brief examination of its use will show that it has the same meaning as the committals and requests for friendship in written recommendations. Commendo in fidem is variously translated as 'I commend' or 'entrust' or 'commit' myself into your 'trust', 'confidence', 'loyalty', 'honour' or 'protection'.

---

198 Sallust, Catil. 35.6 : from Lucius Catilina to Q. Catulus - Nunc Orestillam commendo tuaeque fidei trado; Cicero, QF 1.3.10 : Cicero's family - quid ego, mi frater, tibi commendo ... sed, te incolumi orbi non erunt . ... Etiam Terentiam velim tueare; cf. id. Fam. 14.2.2; Catil 4.23; Plautus, Trin. 1.2.113.

199 Cicero, Cael. 17.39; cf. 4.9. Cf. Diog. Laert. 7.183 : τίνι συστήσω τὸν υἱόν; εἰπεῖν, ἐμοί.

200 Id., Fam. 12.17.3; Cicero calls commendo me in fidem a 'universal custom' (omnium mores).

201 Commendo et committo : Terence, Eun. 886; committo : Caesar, BC 1.74; Horace, Sat. 2.7.67; commendo et trado : Sallust, Catil. 35.6; Cicero, Cael. 17.39; Fam. 2.6.5; commendo et concredo : id., Quinc. 20.62; S. Rosc. 39.113; Plautus, Trin. 1.2.141-143. Confero : Cicero, S. Rosc. 37.106; Fam. 7.17.2; confugio : id., S. Rosc. 40.116; cf. Quinc. 2.10 - to a judge; Scaur. 8.17 - to a jury.

202 Plutarch, Lives 'Sert.' 10.1. See also fn 199 above, Diog. Laert.7.183

Though fidem is the common term, it is at times accompanied by other relational terms such as amicitia[203], amor[204], necessitudo[205] and clientela[206]. While denoting various aspects of the relationship in a specific way, they are not necessary and are implicit in the stock phrase. The same may be said for other associated words such as tueri[207], salutem[208] and defendas[209] which serve to qualify more precisely the form of protection required[210]. Commendo me sufficiently connotes the total entrustment of oneself but it is more usual for the phrase to be accompanied by terms which emphasise the reputation, status, or stance of the person. It involves then the committing of one's dignitas and existimatio[211], fama and res[212], or causa[213], to a relationship based on fides.

All these associated terms are components of the act of entrustment in written commendations and it takes the same form as commendo me. In Cicero's letters of recommendation, in tuam fidem may refer to the advancement of a young man's career[214], the protection of a man's interests and reputation[215], the protection of the total rights of a community[216],

---

203 Cicero, Fam. 7.17.2; Plautus, Trin. 1.2.153.

204 Id., Att. 30.20.2.

205 Id., Fam. 13.19.2.

206 Terence, Eun. 1039.

207 Cicero, Fam. 11.6.1; QF 1.3.10.

208 Id., Brut. 1.16.1.

209 Sallust, Catil. 35.6.

210 Eg., ibid., Eam ab iniuria defendas.

211 Dignitas : Cicero, Fam. 11.6.1; cf. 11.4.1; dignitas et existimatio: ibid., 12.17.3.

212 res et fama : id., Quinc. 20.62; res : id, Fam. 2.6.5.

213 Id., Fam. 2.6.5; cf. 1.9.20.

214 Ibid., 13.49.

215 Ibid., 13.51; in tuam fidem recipias ciusque rem famamque tuaere.

216 Ibid., 13.4.3 : Eorum ego domicilia, sedes, rem, fortunas, ... tuae fidei, iustitiae bonitatique commendo.

protection in a court case[217], and giving a hospitable man hospitality[218]. In relation to status terms, the writer can simply commend the recommended's reputation to the recipient[219]. There seems then to be no essential difference in meaning and intention between commendo me and commendo aliquem tibi/ συνίστημι σοι. Particularly when one remembers that commendo me is implicit in many of the written recommendations. The writer asks the recipient to act towards the recommended as if he were recommending himself[220].

In relation to the references to recommendation in 2 Corinthians, I shall argue that Paul's self-commendation to which he refers in 3:1a - Ἀρχόμεθα πάλιν ἑαυτοὺς συνιστάνειν - is the same as commendo me in tuam fidem. Essentially, it is no different from the letters of recommendation which his opponents wrote to each other to initiate their association - ὥς τινες συστατικῶν ἐπιστολῶν πρὸς ὑμᾶς ἢ ἐξ ὑμῶν. It is not the practice which Paul condemns but the nature of the relationship which they formed and their intention to oppose him and exclude him. By examining these relationships and the emphasis placed by both Paul and the hostile alliance upon recommendation, I may be able to throw some light upon the influence of social conventions in the life of the early church and in particular in its relations with its leaders. Further, and importantly, I may be able to provide some clue as to Paul's practice as he travelled into old and new communities, in relation to hospitality and support, and to the relationships he formed with these communities.

Three aspects of self-commendation remain for brief comment -

---

217 Ibid., 13.69.2 : eum recipias in fidem, habeasque in numero tuorum. Cf. ibid., 13.19.2 : ut eius ipsius hereditatis ius causamque tueare; 13.30 : hanc hereditatem fraternam, et omnia eius tibi commendo. Cf. Quintilian, 12.7.5.

218 Cicero, Fam. 13.67.2, 78.2.

219 Ibid., 12.21 : dignitatem eius tibi commendo; cf. ibid., 11.6.1.

220 Cicero regarded Brutus' self-commendation (mihi meam commendas dignatatem) as being no less important than mihi meam dignatatem commendare : Fam. 11.6.1; this is the language of friendship. Similarly, Cicero refers to the mutual love between himself and P. Cornificius as the prior reason for conceding to Cornificius' self-commendation; Fam. 12.17.3 : ... me cum amori, quem inter nos mutuum esse intellegam.

obligation, servility, and praise. In many instances self-commendation forms part of the mutual services and obligations of the relationship. Therefore, though uncommon and unnecessary, the self-recommender can tactfully remind the friend of past mutual services or of his indebtedness[221]. Commendo me between friends assumes an obligation on the part of the second party to which he has a duty to respond[222]. At stake was not just the self-recommender's concerns. In fidem involved the honour and reputation of the second party and a failure in this regard would bring him into disrepute[223].

Where the self-recommender is of lower rank, or is unknown, or is in difficult straits, the notion of servility is present in commendo me. It was strongly felt by Brutus when he learned that Cicero had commended himself and Brutus to Octavius. He angrily wrote to Cicero " 'For this is how you offer him thanks in matters of state, in such a suppliant and humble tone (suppliciter ac demisse) : What am I to write ? I am ashamed at being in such a position - I'm ashamed at my lot - and yet write I must. You entrust him with our protection'.[224].

Finally, the praise element is entirely missing in many self-recommendations. While this may have much to do with the appropriateness or inappropriateness of self-praise in Greek and Roman society, it is also indicative of the note of humility or servility that appears to be present in many instances of commendo me. In these situations, the disadvantaged person can only entrust himself; the important consideration being the fides of the second party.

---

[221] Ibid., 2.6.1-2.

[222] Ibid., 11.5.3 : ... faciam illud, quod meum est, ut tibi omnia mea officia, studia, curas cogitationes pollicear, quae tuam laudem et gloriam pertinebunt; cf. ibid., 11.6.1; and over a considerable period of time, Cicero's response to P. Cornificius, ibid., 12.17, 18, 19, 20, 22; esp. 12.17.3, 22.2-3. See also Diog. Laert. 4.10 : 'a suppliant must not be betrayed'.

[223] Id., Cael. 17.39, implied in : ob hanc causam tibi puerem parens commendavit et traditit.

[224] Id., Brut. 1.16.1.

Section 2

THE CAUSE OF ENMITY IN PAUL'S RELATIONS WITH THE CORINTHIANS

Chapter 5

FRIENDSHIP IN THE NEW TESTAMENT

a. In the non-Pauline writings.

W.M. Rankin commences his article on friendship with the comment : 'It is an old and almost a stock objection that friendship occupies a subordinate place in the New Testament, compared with the prominence assigned to it in ancient authors'. Further, that in the New Testament it 'is nowhere made the subject of formal discussion and of express precept'[1]. A. Grant is more emphatic : 'Christianity ignores friendship'[2]. In relation to Paul's writings, the point has been made that the notion of friendship is absent and that the apostle does not resort to the regular social terminology of friendship to describe his relationships with others[3].

In other New Testament authors, the _philia_ relationship appears infrequently in comparison with other kinds of social relationships such as master and slave, teacher and pupil, parents and children, etc. But wherever terms denoting it are used they appear to be used in quite ordinary ways and reflect the wide range of meanings found in Greek authors. _Philos_, for instance, is used as a polite form of address[4], to indicate

---

[1] 'Friendship', Encyclopaedia of Religion and Ethics 6 (Edinburgh, 1913), 133.

[2] The Ethics of Aristotle 2 (London, 1885), 250. Though it is not clear whether his reference is to the New Testament or to Christianity in general.

[3] Eg., J.N. Sevenster, Paul and Seneca, 177-178; E.A. Judge, 'Paul as a Radical Critic of Society', Interchange 16 (1974), 196; J. Moffatt, The First Epistle of Paul to the Corinthians, (London, 1938), XIII.

[4] Lk. 12:4; 14:10.

various levels of friendship[5], patronage[6], and intimate relationships[7]. In Matthew, the term ἕταιρος, which refers to friendship has a similar range of meanings[8]. On two occasions philos is used where we might have expected the term adelphos[9]. It occurs in the normal sense in association with terms which describe other kinds of social relationships - parents, brothers, kinsmen, neighbours - and the standard nuances of reciprocity and obligation are present[10]. James follows normal usage when he opposes philia/-os to their traditional antitheses, echthra/-os. Friendship with or being a friend of the world must result in enmity with or being an enemy of God[11]. It is not the friendship relationship itself which is attacked here but the kind of person or thing with whom one forms the relationship. Indeed, Abraham is commended as a friend of God[12] while in the gospels Jesus is ridiculed as a friend of publicans and sinners[13].

In John's Gospel, Jesus names his disciples as friends[14]. This is most important, for the kind of relationship which Jesus proposes is akin to that of being an amicus Caesaris, as in the case of the New Testament example of that between

---

[5] Lk. 23:12, of Herod and Pilate : ἐγένοντο φίλοι; cf. Lk. 7:6; 15:6, 9; 16:9; Acts 19:31.

[6] Jo. 19:12 - οὐκ εἶ φίλος τῷ καίσαρος.

[7] Jo. 11:11, Jesus called Lazarus : ὁ φίλος ἡμῶν; Acts 10:24, Cornelius called together his kinsmen and close friends (τοὺς ἀναγκαίους φίλους) (cf. P. Col. Zen. 7; P. Herm. 1); Ja. 2:23; 3.29.

[8] Polite form of address : Mt. 20:13; 22:12; term of endearment : Mt. 26:50, Jesus to Judas : ἑταῖρε, ἐφ' ὃ πάρει.

[9] Acts 27:3; 3 Jo. 14; A. von Harnack, Expansion of Christianity 2 ET (London, 1905), 31-34, suggests that the early Christians preferred the warm and close term adelphos to that of philos.

[10] Lk. 14:12; 21:16; Acts 10:24; reciprocity, see Lk. 11:5-8; 14:12-14.

[11] Ja. 4:4; for details of this antithesis see above 35-36.

[12] Ja. 2:23.

[13] Mt. 11:19; Lk. 7:34.

[14] Jo. 15:13-16.

Caesar and Pilate[15]. Many of the elements of the relationship which Jesus mentions - status and power, inequality, intimacy, the making of conditions by the more powerful, the obligation of the lesser to fulfil the conditions in order to maintain the friendship - are common to patronal friendship[16]. The distinction between a slave and a free person as a friend in whom one can confide and with whom one can share common interests appears as a topic in Aristotle's essay on friendship[17]. Thus, while the use of philia/-os is limited in the New Testament, the fact that the normal sense of these terms is found suggests that there is no attempt either to subordinate or ignore the institution. I agree with Rankin on this point. But I cannot find any evidence, as he goes on to say, of the process of assimilation, absorption and transformation of the institution by New Testament Christianity[18].

Like other biblical scholars who have commented briefly on friendship, he limits his remarks to the 'rare' or 'ideal' kind of friendship so admired by Greek and Roman philosophers. He has failed to recognize the fundamental importance of this institution in Greek and Roman (and indeed Jewish) social, political and economic life, the many grades, kinds and combinations of friendship, and the wide range of services and gifts which it comprises. What we require now are detailed sociological studies of the social institutions and conventions which appear in the New Testament. I suggest that a study of friendship in the Gospels would reveal the presence of this institution in numerous passages and its importance for Jesus' followers in their relationships with each other and

---

15 Jo. 19:12. Suggested by E.A. Judge, 'Paul as a Radical Critic', 196. Pilate is not listed by J.A. Crook in Consilium Principis (New York, 1975), 148-190 among the important amici or comites of the Caesars, the definitive treatment of this phenomenon.

16 Cf. E.A. Judge, 'Paul as a Radical Critic', 196. For friendships of disparity, of the patronal kind, and patronage, see below, 142-144.

17 EN 8.11.6 : 'For a master and slave have nothing in common'.

18 'Friendship', 133.

their normal social relations[19].

b. In the Pauline letters.

The terms <u>philia</u>/-os do not appear in the writings of Paul. Not even where we might have expected to find them, where he refers to people with whom he has had a long and intimate relationship[20]. To describe these relations, Paul resorts to terms which are drawn from the language of servitude or the household. He calls his associates σύζυφοι (Phil. 4:3) or more frequently, σύνεργοι[21], δοῦλοι[22], σύνδουλοι (Col. 1:7, 4:7) [23], διάκονοι[24], ὑπηρέτας (1 Cor. 4:1), or οἱ κοπιῶτες[25]. He also describes himself and his apostolic activity in similarly servile terms[26]. Further, he uses familial concepts drawn from the ancient household, of the father and his children[27], of conception (1 Cor. 4:15), and of 'brother' (1 Cor. 16:12, 2 Cor. 2:13; 8:18, 22), 'sister' (Ro. 16:1) and 'mother' (Ro. 16:13).

J.N. Sevenster argues that the reason for the absence of the terms <u>philia</u>/-os was that Paul considered them to be inadequate to describe what he felt to be of fundamental importance in his relationships with others. He states :

19 Eg., Lk. 11:9 : 'Ask, and it will be given you; seek, and you will find; knock, and it will be opened to you'. Notice how this follows the parable of the importunate friend (vv. 5-8) in Luke. Cf. however, G. Theissen, 'Wanderradikalismus', ZThK 70 (1973), 260, who calls this 'eine ausgesprochene Bettlerweisheit'. See also Lk. 6:34-35; 10:5-7; 17:11-19.

20 Eg., Prisca and Aquila : Ro. 16:3; 1 Cor. 16:19; and see other intimate relationships in Ro. 16:1-16.

21 Ro. 16:3, 9, 21; 1 Cor. 3:9; 2 Cor. 8:23; Phil. 2:25; 4:3; Col. 4:11; Phlm. 1, 24. Cf. συωέργω, 1 Cor. 16:16.

22 2 Cor. 4:5; Col. 4:12. Cf. δουλοῦν, Phil. 2:22.

23 For its literal use in inscriptions see G. Horsley, New Documents Illustrating Early Christianity 2 (Sydney, 1982), 54.

24 1 Cor. 3:5; 2 Cor. 6:4; Eph. 6:21; Col. 1:7; 4:7. Cf. διακονία : 1 Cor. 16:15; 2 Cor. 6:3.

25 Ro. 16:12a; 1 Cor. 16:16; 1 Thess. 5:12. Cf. Ro. 16:6, 12b.

26 δοῦλος: Ro. 16:1; 2 Cor. 4:5; Gal. 1:10; Phil. 1:1; δουλεύω : 1 Cor. 9:19; διάκονος: 1 Cor. 3:5; 2 Cor. 6:4; Eph. 3:7; Col. 1:23,25; οἰκονόμος : 1 Cor. 4:1, 2; 9:17; οἰκονομία : Eph. 3:1; ἀνάγκη : 1 Cor. 9:16; and I suggest also ἄκων : 1 Cor. 9:17; κόπος καὶ μόχθος: 1 Thess. 2:9; 2 Thess. 3:8; κόπος : 2 Cor. 6:5, 11:23; ἔπγον : 1 Cor. 9:1.

27 Eg., 1 Cor. 4:14, 15, 17; 2 Cor. 12:14b-15; Phil. 2:22; 1 Thess. 2:11; Phlm. 10.

'For Paul this relationship was not anthropocentric, still less egocentric, but Christocentric. Friendship and friends are words whose meaning is too greatly restricted to the human plane alone'[28]. Undoubtedly differences can be detected between Greek views of friendship and Paul's concept of relationships, and value judgments can be made in favour of one or the other. But such an approach is too general and most certainly does not represent the way in which Paul understood institutions and conventions of his day. We need to take full account of Paul's selectivity in such areas. In doing so, I suggest that we will find that Paul does not dismiss the practice of friendship and that many of its conventions continue to govern his relationships with others.

But Paul does seem to deliberately avoid friendship terms to describe his relationships with others and resorts to terms which denote servile status. Why does he do this, and what does their use have to say about Paul's view of certain aspects of friendship ? E.A. Judge suggests, persuasively, that it may have been due to the status implications of <u>philia</u>/-os. He considers that we 'must watch with great care the way in which Paul talks about his relations with people and their relations with each other, and watch as he draws the line between what would have been the natural outworking of the status system and the outworking of the quite different principle of relationships which he is promoting'[29]. While Paul in the course of his mission participated in the patronal order of society, both as sponsor and sponsored, 'he clearly has no value to place upon patronal relationships as such'[30].

We could have expected Paul to use the language of friendship to describe these patronal relationships but instead he refers to his patrons as 'fellow-workers'. I do not doubt his patrons conceived of their duties and obligations towards Paul in terms of friendship and it must have been startling for them to be addressed in servile terms. In a

---

[28] Paul and Seneca, 178-180.

[29] 'Paul as a Radical Critic', 196.

[30] Ibid.

similar manner, Paul refers to those in positions of leadership or authority as 'slaves' and 'ministers' instead of using the regular vocabulary of leadership[31]. These people are among the cultivated elite of their society and Paul reserves this language for them almost exclusively.

It may well be, then, that Paul is very conscious of the connotations of _philia_ and _philos_, as terms of status and discrimination, and that he is deliberately countering them by rejecting status as a distinguishing element. There is no superior and inferior status in Christ; it is of no consequence to God's call through the gospel. However, the time and effort that he gives to countering status notions, especially in Corinthians, suggests that it is still of great importance for many in the new community. Broadly speaking, I suggest we find in Paul's writings the idea of unity based on the notions of servitude and subordination to Christ and to each other. Where Paul is in conflict with those of rank and influence, the idea is expressed more sharply, polemically and personally.

This offsetting of status distinctions is not directed towards the formation of a classless society. The conventional social distinctions were retained within the household, even though there is a softening process[32]. It is probable that the heads of these converted households exercised the same authority over their dependants as before (though ideally in a different way, i.e. through service). Where a number of households were involved, authority seemed to fall naturally upon the head/heads of the wealthier families[33]. However, all members of the household were to be regarded as one based on their being in Christ[34]. This idea of unity also underlies the body metaphor which Paul uses to describe the relations between Christians. They form a community bound together by gifts of the Spirit and all are individually involved in the

---

31 Ibid., 196-197.

32 Eg., 1 Cor. 7:20-24; Eph. 5:21 - 6:9; Col. 3:18 - 4:1.

33 Eg., Ro. 16:23; 1 Cor. 16:15-16.

34 Eg., 1 Cor. 12:12-13; Gal. 3:27-28; Col. 3:11.

service or benefit of each other and the community as a whole whatever the distinctions of status and honour and function may be[35]. It does appear that Paul is endeavouring to challenge certain conventions which supported the prevailing notions of social status. This is true of the friendship institution as I will show presently. Clearly, though, major studies of the social institutions which appear in Paul's letters are required before we can say with confidence how Paul views fundamental issues in his society, what is the extent and nature of his attempts at amendment, and what the social implications were for the early Christians with whom he associated. In regard to questions of status in Greek and Roman society, we shall find that, in certain respects, Paul's approach is both startling and novel and that he is a radical and discerning critic of the society of his day.

While it is true to say that Paul never uses the word philia or philos in his letters, it is wrong to suggest on these grounds that the notion of friendship is absent. This fixation with words to the exclusion of ideas has long hampered biblical scholarship. I have also pointed to the too limited understanding of friendship with which scholars have approached Paul's writings and the subsequent failure to recognize many aspects of this institution in them. Again, I have suggested that friendship underlies many of the social relationships formed by Paul and that it continues to govern the expectations and conduct of the Christians in his churches. I shall argue in the next chapter that it lies at the heart of his conflict with the Corinthians. In the ensuing discussion I shall look at aspects of friendship as they appear in some other of his letters as a background to this conflict.

Five distinct, though interrelated, aspects of friendship appear in Paul's letters : hospitality, patronal relations, recommendation, the antithetical relationship of enmity, and giving and receiving. A valuable and extensive study has been

---

[35] Eg., 1 Cor. 12:4-31. For further discussion of this important issue, see the recent work by R. Banks, Paul's Idea of Community, (Sydney, 1979), 72-81, 128-137.

completed on the role of hospitality in the early church by J.B. Mathews[36] and E.A. Judge has commented briefly on Paul's patronal relations[37].

Recommendation and enmity are the subjects of two of my previous chapters and I shall adress myself to them again at length in chapters 7 and 8 in relation to the Corinthian letters. Giving and receiving is important for our understanding of the Corinthian offer to support Paul and will act as an introduction to my discussion of that.

1. Hospitality.

The act of hospitality, as I have shown previously, represents the establishment of a reciprocal relationship of friendship which can be denoted by the terms _xenia_ or _philia_. If friendship already exists, then hospitality forms part of the continuing exchange of gifts and services which constitute the relationship[38]. Though _philia_/-os do not appear in Paul's letters, he uses _xenos_[39] and _xenia_[40], together with a virtually technical vocabulary, to describe the various aspects of hospitality[41]. J.B. Mathews has argued that Greek and Roman private hospitality was in decline in the first century AD and, as evidence, points to the substantial decrease in both the number and quality of references to hospitality as a virtue in Greek and Roman authors. By way of contrast, he points to the high valuation placed upon hospitality in the literature of Judaism and early Christianity. He suggests that the 'Gentile environment of early Christianity is of no help in understanding the significance which hospitality played in the ancient church'

---

[36] Hospitality.

[37] 'The Early Christians as a Scholastic Community : Part II', JRH 2 (1961), 128-131.

[38] For details, see above 3-6, 109-111.

[39] Ro. 16:23, of Gaius : ' Who is host (_xenos_) to me and to the whole church'.

[40] Phlm. 22, where ἑτοίμαζέ μοι ξενίαν may refer to either the hospitable relations between Paul and Philemon or to the guest room. Cf. Acts 28:23; see J.B. Mathews, Hospitality, 167-168.

[41] See J.B. Mathews, Hospitality, 168-174.

and that its origin must be sought within the church itself or in its Jewish antecedents[42].

However, the hospitality extended to Paul on his missionary travels, especially in the major cities of the provinces of Macedonia and Achaia, appears to have been, as often as not, Greek in character[43]. Further, the New Testament, which provides us with one of our most coherent sets of documents for the first century for both Greeks and Jews[44], show that in the places covered by Paul and Luke, hospitality was widely practised by both Greeks and

---

[42] Hospitality, 174, 189, 193-198. Mathews has not considered Dio Chrysostom's Euboicus (Disc. 7) in which Dio commends the free rural poor who extended generous hospitality and friendship to him as a stranger in peril. The contrast he makes between the rural poor and the urban rich may be seen as a criticism of the latter's lack of virtue, though not of practice, in regard to hospitality, especially if the speech was delivered in Rome. See P.A. Brunt, 'Aspects of the Social Thought of Dio Chrysostom and the Stoics', PCPS 19 (1973), 9-34. See also Dionysius of Halicarnassus, Antiq. Rom. 1.6.5, who arrived in Rome uninvited, but expresses gratitude for the hospitality he received.

[43] There does not appear to be a marked difference in the form and structure of Greek, Roman or Jewish hospitality, and it is extremely difficult to determine on the evidence in Luke-Acts and Paul's letters what is distinctively Greek and what is Jewish. We know very little about the effect upon the social life of Greek converts to Judaism by their new-found faith or of the social position of Jews in Greek cities of the first century. See A.J. Malherbe, 'Hellenistic Moralists and the New Testament', Aufstieg und Niedergang der römischen Welt Vol. 2, pt. 3, ed. by W. Haase, (Berlin, forthcoming), 38-31 (copy of the author's typescript made available by E.A. Judge).

[44] E.A. Judge, 'St. Paul and Classical Society', 23.

Romans[45]. Significantly, the majority of the references to hospitality (and indeed, to that of friendship) are found in Luke-Acts[46], written by an author who is said to be a Gentile Christian writing for Gentiles[47]. As to the ethnic background of those who extended hospitality to Paul in Acts and Paul's letters, 'Only three are certainly Jews (Aquila, Mary, and Crispus) and two certainly are not (Lydia and Justus); the rest could be either, though it seems likely that there was a large number of Gentiles among them'[48]. Thus it is fair to say that the initial hospitality extended to Paul was not necessarily Jewish in origin, and certainly not Christian; that where Paul's hosts are Greek or Roman (and the same may be true of his Jewish hosts) their hospitality reflects the customs and ideas of their society.

The kind of hospitality to which Mathews addresses himself in the main is that which is extended to the wayfaring stranger who arrives unexpectedly. It is true that the mobility of

---

[45] Eg., Lk. 7:1-10 : Centurion, ὑπὸ τὴν στεγήν μου εἰσέλθῃς (v. 6) suggests hospitality; Acts 10:48, Cornelius, the Roman Centurion; Acts 16:15, Lydia, the Greek proselyte; 18:7, Justus, a sympathizer with Judaism; 28:2, 7, the Maltese and their leader Publius; (I have already indicated the numerous references to hospitality in Acts and Paul, see above 137, n40, 41. Against this, J.B. Mathews, Hospitality, 180-181n.2, has suggested that Cornelius and Lydia are special cases and are not prototypes of the typical Gentile. Cornelius is an exceptional man (Acts 10:2) and, in both these cases, hospitality is closely associated with reception of the gospel. He also argues that the Maltese are set off from the cultured Graeco-Roman world by the fact that they are <u>barbaroi</u> (Acts 28:2). I find this argument most unconvincing. In the cases of Cornelius and Lydia, it would have been better to have argued from the probability of the influence of Judaism upon them. Even then, it would not necessarily mean that the form of their hospitality was Jewish rather than Greek. A.J. Malherbe, Social Aspects, 66-67, suggests that Luke is interested in both the sociological and theological implications of converson. Social inequality remained between Jews and proselytes and God-fearers irrespective of the degree of adaptation to Judaism. The critical issue in both conversions was one of hospitality. The circumcision party opposed Peter's eating with Cornelius (Acts 11:3) while the litmus-test for Paul was whether he would accept Lydia's invitation to stay in her house (Acts 16:15).

[46] Cf. J.B. Mathews, Hospitality, 171-172; H.J. Cadbury, 'Lexical Notes on Luke-Acts', JNL 14 (1926), 305-322.

[47] W.G. Kümmel, Introduction to the New Testament ET (London, 1966), 104-105.

[48] So E.A. Judge, 'Scholastic Community 2', 130.

Roman society, the abundance of inns and hostels of various kinds in cities, towns and along the highways, the low cost and ready accessibility of such accommodation to the majority of travellers, led to the diminishing need for hospitality of this kind. However, people of the upper classes avoided these establishments[49], and during travel must have relied upon the hospitality of friends wherever possible, or have secured private hospitality through recommendation by a friend. Such hospitality remained one of the most important benefits in the friendship relationship and it is doubtful whether commercialised hospitality made significant inroads into the practice of hospitality in this regard and to its value as a virtue also[50]. Jews also avoided the inns and sought hospitality among their fellows who could be found in most of the cities and towns of the empire. Even though of the same race, they would be regarded and would have hospitality extended to them as itinerant strangers. Christians seem to have followed this pattern[51].

According to the author of Acts, Paul adopted a similar practice. In Philippi, he and his associates went in search of the proseuchē which is thought to be the synagogue[52], and there met Lydia, a non-Jewish synagogue worshipper[53].

---

49 There were a few good quality inns but, in general, the inns were filthy and had inferior facilities, and were frequented by prostitutes and managed by unscrupulous characters. See J.B. Mathews, Hospitality, 27-28.

50 Mathews does not examine hospitality in relation to the institution of friendship which shows no evidence of decline during the first century AD. The most frequent specific request in literary and papyrus letters of recommendation is for the recipient to extend hospitality to the recommended. Admittedly, all of the papyrus letters (none of which are Christian) which contain this request are dated in the second and third century AD. For details, see above 109-111 especially 110 n.112 and 111 n.120. See E.A. Judge, 'The Earliest Use of Monachos for 'Monk' and the Origins of Monasticism', JbAC 20 (1977), 80-81 for a group of Christian papyrus letters of recommendation.

51 J.B. Mathews, Hospitality, 200.

52 Acts 16:13-15; προσευχή as the synagogue, see E. Haenchen, The Acts of the Apostles (ET : Oxford, 1971), 494.

53 For a recent discussion of Lydia, her status and occupation, see G. Horsley, New Documents 2, 27-28, 32.

Following her conversion, she persuaded them to accept her hospitality. Similarly, Paul found Aquila in Corinth and accepted both hospitality and employment[54] and 'sought out' his fellow-Christians in Tyre in order to stay with them (Acts 21:4). Presumably Paul followed this practice in Thessalonica where Jason was his host (Acts 17:1, 5). Though in the initial contacts which Paul made in Macedonia and Achaia he was a stranger to his hosts, the relationship which developed between them, as his letters show, was much more than the temporary acquaintance between host and guest which is seen in many instances of hospitality toward the itinerant stranger. The relationships formed by him seem to have been understood by himself and his hosts in terms of friendship.

First, Paul chose to stay with his social equals or near equals in the cities where he preached[55]. Apart from the benefits this afforded his ministry, it was standard practice that one should seek friendship with one's equals, particularly with those possessing common interests[56]. Were it not for the fact that Paul's letters reveal a similar picture, the predilection that Luke seems to display toward people of some social standing in his household conversion stories[57] suggests that we should be careful about placing too much weight upon Paul's association with these people. I can find no instance after the commencement of his ministry in Macedonia where the hospitality he enjoyed was with other than people of means. For him to be accepted at this level

---

[54] Acts 18:2-3. J.B. Mathews, Hospitality, 205n.2, suggests the possibility that as Aquila is the sole object of εὑρίσκειν (and not coupled with Priscilla as is usual), it was at the synagogue that Paul found Aquila. E. Haenchen, Acts, 534, says that the clue to the meaning of εὑρίσκειν is ὁμότεχνον, 'practising the same trade'. Paul inquired in Corinth about a fellow Jewish artisan with whom he could practise his trade. He also considers, 533n.4, that Aquila and Priscilla were Christians prior to their arrival in Corinth.

[55] See E.A. Judge, 'St. Paul as a Radical Critic', 191-192.

[56] For details, see above 25-26

[57] Acts 10:1, 2, 4 : a centurion; 16:14-15 : a tradeswoman; 16:32-34 : a civil servant; 18:8 : a synagogue ruler.

must say something about his own social standing.

Second, it appears that he followed the normal practice of recommendaton, although in his own case it was that of self-commendation rather than written commendation by a third party (e.g., 2 Cor. 3:1). Third, the period of his stay normally extended beyond that which a host was obliged to extend to an itinerant stranger. The usual practice assumed three days only[58]. Fourth, the relationships he developed with his hosts were very intimate, long-lasting, and particular[59]. Fifth, guest-friendship was in this case, as usual, a reciprocal relationship which created obligations between host and guest. Paul on occasions acknowledges his debt to his hosts for the lengths to which they went in fulfilling their obligations to him as their guest[60]. He himself recommends (συνίστημι) Phoebe, who had been his patroness (προστάτις) in Cenchrea, to his associates in Rome, asking them to extend hospitality (προσδέχομαι) to her on account of his relationship with her[61]. As E.A. Judge succinctly puts it, it 'nicely illustrates the way in which he supported the system of patronage in return for the security it afforded him'[62]. Notions of reciprocity are readily apparent in Paul's recommendation of Onesimus to Philemon. Paul's appeal to Philemon is based on his relationship with him, denoted by κοινωνός (v. 17), and the fact that Philemon also owes him his own self (v. 19)[63].

---

58 J.B. Mathews, Hospitality, 51, 229-230n.3.

59 Eg., Aquila and Priscilla, Acts 18:1-3, 18; 1 Cor. 16:19; Ro. 16:3-5.

60 Eg., Ro. 16:4, Priscilla and Aquila had 'risked their necks' for Paul's life; Phil. 2:30, of Epaphroditus : 'He nearly died for the work of Christ risking his life to complete your service to me'; cf. Acts 17:5-9 : Jason was dragged from his home (v. 5) taken before the authorities (v. 6) and made to post a bond (λαβόντες τὸ ἱκανὸν) for Paul (v. 9). See above, 5-6 for the host's responsibility for his guest.

61 Ro. 16:1-2; cf. Phil. 2:29 - Epaphroditus is to be received (προσδέχομαι) by his fellow-Philippians because of his service to Paul.

62 'Scholastic Community 2', 129.

63 For the recommender's appeal to the relationship or services he has shared with the recipient see above 101-103.

Finally, the well-off and eminent converts with whom Paul stayed protected him and sponsored his activities in various localities. They provided him with an audience composed of their dependants, and a retinue of assistants. It is clear that Paul consistently relied upon and sought out their assistance[64]. It is strange then, in view of these very common elements of the friendship relationship - hospitality, equality, recommendation, intimacy, reciprocity, obligation, sponsorship - that Paul does not use the terms, philia/-os. The relationship between Paul and his hosts is conducted according to the conventions of friendship and undoubtedly was understood as such by them. We seem to be confronted with the institution in all but the name.

2. Patronal relations.

I distinguish at the outset between patronage and friendship in the patronal sense. Both relationships are kinds of friendship and have many common features. Both, generally, are unequal relationships but the status of the inferior friend differs in each. Patronage in Roman society is a relationship of trust between patron and client, between social superior and social inferior, which creates a long and often permanent obligation. Either person can initiate the relationship, but it was usually the inferior who, requiring the aid of a more powerful friend, either committed himself to his protection or received various benefits or services. In return, he was obliged to show gratitude, which consisted of rendering services and providing support in any way his patron required. The patron was morally bound to protect his client, provide for him, and render assistance to him as he had need[65].

---

[64] For details, see below 144.

[65] For a succinct summary of the various kinds of Roman patronage see E. Badian, Foreign Clientelae (264-70BC) (Oxford, 1958), 1-14. Cf. also M. Gelzer, Nobility, 70-101. For the Roman's Greek 'friends' as a relationship of patron and client see, I.E.M. Edlung, 'Invisible Bonds : Clients and Patrons through the eye of Polybios', Klio 59 (1977) 129-136. See also E.A. Judge, 'The Early Christians as a Scholastic Community', JRH 1 (1961), 6-7.

Patronal friendship had the appearance of equality between the two parties but in reality it was an unequal relationship. Aristotle makes the distinction between friends who are on an equal footing and those who are on a footing of disparity. The exchange between unequal friends is always disproportionate as the inferior always receives more than he can return. Equality, which is regarded as essential to friendship, is achieved in a sense when the inferior responds with what he can, namely love and honour[66]. Though a client may be termed 'friend', a friend, even though an inferior, could never be called a 'client' without grave insult and damage to the relationship.

E.A. Judge identifies as many as forty persons who either sponsored Paul's activities or 'who are referred to in such a way that implies that they probably did, or would have done had occasion arisen'. They were people of means who belonged to a 'cultivated social elite'[67]. The hospitality, gifts and travel facilities which they provided for Paul and his associates 'implies not only a generous spirit but the means with which to express it'[68]. They sponsored private meetings in their households, consisting of dependants and associates, protected him and provided him with a secure platform for his preaching in the major cities. Judge remarks that it is reasonable to say that Paul's sponsors in the Greek cities were from the social point of view 'occupying positions of elevated status and conferring benefits on Paul and upon the others who came to his meetings that should have created obligations'[69]. These people not only performed the normal duties of patrons but must have conceived of their behaviour and position in terms of friendship.

I have previously pointed to the conventional notions of reciprocity and obligation which are present in Paul's

---

[66] EN 8.7.2, 11.3, 12.2, 3, 5, 13.1, 14.2; 9.2.8; Cf. Seneca, de Ben. 6.34.1-5.

[67] 'Scholastic Community 2', 128-130.

[68] Id., 'St. Paul and Classical Society', 28.

[69] 'Paul as a Radical Critic', 196; id., The Social Pattern of Christian Groups in the First Century (London, 1960), 60.

relations with his hosts. This is most apparent in his only use of the technical term, προστάτις, in reference to his patroness, Phoebe[70]. There are difficulties, though, in viewing Paul's relationship with his friends as patronal friendship, especially because of the implication of inequality in status. The absence of standard status terms in regard to patronal friendship makes it hard to assess the level or nature of his relationship with them or theirs with the household churches. Even so, patronal friendship, I suggest, provides us with the best social context in which to view these relations and from which to assess the different way that Paul construes them. I shall argue in a later chapter that it is Paul who initiates the relationship, not simply as an itinerant stranger in need of hospitality, but that he deliberately entrusts himself to people who are his social equals or superiors, seeking their assistance for his efforts.

It is not altogether clear what status, if any, was conferred upon these patrons as a result of their assistance to Paul or his churches. They appear to have assumed legal responsibility for these groups and undoubtedly were regarded as the leaders of them by government officials[71]. The churches under their 'leadership' retained the normal social character of the household[72], a structure which Paul fully supported[73] and in which the conventional hierarchical levels were maintained. However, there is no notion or theory of leadership in Paul's letters, either in regard to himself or the patrons. What is clear is that Paul has introduced his own vocabulary to describe his relations with them and their responsibility to the churches. They, like his itinerant associates, are his fellow-labourers and co-slaves, as well as slaves and ministers of the churches[74]. While they appear

---

[70] See above 143-144.

[71] Acts 17:3-9. Cf. A.J. Malherbe, 'The Inhospitality of Diotrephes', God's Christ and His People : Studies in Honour of Nils Alstrup Dahl, J. Jervell and W.A. Meeks, ed. (Oslo, 1977), 224.

[72] For details see above 135-136.

[73] Eg., Eph. 5:21 - 6:9; Col. 3:18 - 4:1.

[74] For details, see above 133.

to be the leaders of these churches, it is their 'labour' (kopos) and 'work' (ergos) on their behalf to which Paul draws attention and which forms the basis of Christians' deference to them[75].

Though these terms are not unique in Paul and appear frequently in Greek authors and other New Testament authors[76], the way he uses them is. We need to watch most carefully the status of the people to whom these terms apply in Paul, the standard terms which they are displacing, and try to assess the impression such use would have made upon people of status in his society. As E.A. Judge comments, the effect would have been startling to say the least as these terms were drawn 'from the language of servitude and subordination, and not from the language of patronage or leadership or friendship in the patronal sense'[77].

There does appear to be a discernible pattern in Paul's understanding of friendship and patronal relations which centres on questions of status. It might be described as a reaction to traditional status values, but it does not make honourable that which is shameful. Though it is a deliberate reaction against traditional notions of status distinction, it does not try to enhance servility for its own sake. This pattern will be the subject of a discussion in chapter 9, but it is important that we note it now because of the implications it has for Paul in his conflict with his enemies

---

75 Cf. 1 Thess. 5:12-13 (though προΐστημι here is not a technical term of office; cf. Ro. 12:8 and see A.J. Malherbe, 'Inhospitality', 224.); 1 Cor. 16:15-16.

76 Eg., koinōnos kai synergos : Plutarch, Mor. 45E; 819C; koinōnos : Plato, Rep. 333B; Phdr. 239C; Aristotle, EN 5.5.12; synergos : Euripides, Or. 1446; Med. 396; Demosthenes 19:144; Plutarch, Lives 'Per', 169.2; cf. 3 Jo. 8; syzygos : Euripides, I.T. 250; Aristophanes, Pl. 945; syndoulos (only of slaves), Euripides, Ion 1109; Aristophanes, Pax 745; Lysias, Fr. 331S.

77 E.A. Judge, 'Paul as a Radical Critic', 196-197. There are no conventional terms of theory of leadership in Paul's letters as in Greek and Roman authors. E.E. Ellis, 'Paul and His Co-workers', NTS 17 (1970-71), 440, points to the noticeable absence of terms which were later 'to become traditional for leaders in the church' and also of terms 'identified with the spiritual or charisms specified by Paul'. E. Schweizer, Church Order in the New Testament (London, 1961), on 'Offices'.

in Corinth. Also, important for this conflict, in view of Paul's refusal of aid in Corinth, is the fact that he probably had more sponsors in Corinth than in any other city[78]. This point has not been sufficiently considered before.

3. Recommendation.

Chan-Hie Kim identifies seven letters or passages of recommendation in Paul's writings in which Paul recommends individuals or groups of people[79]. They are genuinely Pauline compositions for they do not follow the form or structure of the papyrus letters of recommendation though similar phraseology and structural elements appear[80]. Philemon is the only extant independent letter of recommendation of Paul's and it exhibits 'most of the forms and structures found in the Pauline commendation formula'[81]. By assessing the common elements in Philemon and Greek and Roman letters of recommendation we can see that a reciprocal relationship of the friendship kind existed between the two men.

First, Paul recommends Onesimus in reference to himself and the degree of intimacy which exists between them (vv. 10, 12, 16), and the valuable service he has rendered to Paul (v. 11)[82]. Second, his relationship with Paul has more weight

---

[78] Eg., Priscilla and Aquila, Acts 18:2; Justus, 18:17; Crispus 18:8, 1 Cor. 1:14; Gaius, 1 Cor. 1:14, Ro. 16:23; Erastus, Ro. 16:23; Quartus, Ro. 16:23; Stephanas, 1 Cor. 1:16, 16:15; (possibly in this category, Fortunatus and Achaicus 1 Cor. 16:18; Chloe, 1 Cor. 1:11).

[79] Familiar Greek Letter, 120 : Ro. 16:1-2; 1 Cor. 16:15-16, 17-18; Phil. 2:29-30; 4:2-3; 1 Thess. 5:12-13a; Philemon (the only complete letter). He suggests that the series of greetings in Ro. 16:3-16 are 'oblique commendations', as they follow the language, form and structure of the recommendation passages, ibid., 135-142. Only two other minor passages appear in the New Testament, Heb. 13:17 and 3 Jo. 12 (see A.J. Malherbe, 'Inhospitality', 227, who sees 3 John as at once a commendation of Gaius, vv. 5-8, and a recommendation of Demetrius, vv. 11-12) though the practice of writing letters of recommendation is referred to in Acts 9:2; 18:27; 22:5; 1 Cor. 16:3; 2 Cor. 3:1-2.

[80] Familiar Greek Letter, 124-125.

[81] Ibid., 123.

[82] For details see above 98-99.

or value than his own credentials[83]. Third, Paul bases his appeal on his own relationship with Philemon (denoted by koinōnos, v.17) and on the undefined benefits or services which Philemon owes him (vv. 19, 20)[84]. Fourth, he requires Philemon to accept Onesimus as if Paul himself were the recommended (v. 17)[85]. Fifth, he regards the action to be taken by Philemon on his behalf as a benefit (denoted by the verb, ὀνίνημι) which will refresh him (v. 20)[86]. Sixth, he stresses Onesimus' worth (euchrēstos) to Philemon (v. 11)[87]. Seventh, he asks Philemon to consider his relationship with Onesimus as to a beloved brother (v. 16) and not as to a slave[88]. Finally, he is confident that Philemon would do more for him than he has requested (v. 21)[89].

On the evidence present in this most private of Paul's letters, it is hard to escape the impression that Paul and Philemon both understand and conduct their relationship within the obligations of friendship. It is particularly noteworthy that while Paul might have commanded (ἐπιτάσσω) Philemon to do as he requests, he decides to appeal (παρακαλῶ) to him (διὰ τὴν ἀγαπήν) (vv. 8-9). Epitassein may simply imply the authority of an apostle over his convert or indicate a patronal relationship between them, depending on how we interpret the reciprocal nuances in the clause ὅτι καὶ σεαυτόν μοι προσοφείλεις (v. 19). The most popular view among scholars is that Philemon owes his life as a Christian

---

[83] Ibid., 99-100, 106-107.

[84] Ibid., 101-103.

[85] Ibid., 103.

[86] Ibid., 103-104.

[87] Ibid., 113-114.

[88] Ibid., 107-108.

[89] Ibid., 102-105; cf. Chan-Hie Kim, Familiar Greek Letter, 127-128; ἔγραφα σοι, εἰδώς ... - cf. P. Oxy. 1064; PSI 96 for the phrase γράφω εἰδώς which explicitly states the writer's confidence in the sincerity of the recipient in helping the recommended.

to Paul's preaching[90]. The clause though is very similar to other clauses used in friendship relationships to express the debt owed by one friend to another and it is probable that it is one form of a common Greek proverb[91]. Philemon's debt to Paul could be either material or spiritual, we have no way of knowing. What is certain is that Philemon is obliged to respond to this very conventional request for gratitude, though Paul softens his request by suggesting that Philemon would follow his recommendation of his own choice (ἑκών) rather than by compulsion (ἀνάγκη) (v. 14), a necessary element in friendship and in a man's self-esteem.

It is clear that Paul regards the recommendation and Philemon's response to it as forming part of the mutual interchange of services and affection between them. I have already suggested that Paul's recommendation of Phoebe is part of their reciprocal personal relationship. All of Paul's recommendations (with the possible exception of 1 Thess. 5:12-13a) appear to be of this kind. The recommended have all aided Paul in some particular way and he singles it out as

---

90 Eg., E. Lohse, Colossians and Philemon ET (Philadelphia, 1971), 204-205; C.F.D. Moule, The Epistle of Paul the Apostle to the Colossians and Philemon (Cambridge, 1968), 20; R.P. Martin, Colossians and Philemon (London, 1974), 167; N.A. Dahl, 'Paul and Possessions', Studies in Paul (Minneapolis, 1977), 29.

91 Aelius Donatus, commentator on Terence and Virgil in the 4th Cent. AD says of the Latin phrase animam debere, in Terence, Phormio 661, 'Quid si animam debet Graecum prouerbium spreuit " εἰ δὲ ὤφειλε τὰς χεῖρας" '; or alt. "τι δε ει την ψυχην οφειλει". See P. Wessner (ed.) Donatus (Aeli Donati Commentum Terenti II) (Leipzig, 1905), 466.
Cf. also the similar phrases in two of the sample letters of Pseudo-Demetrius, V. Weichert, Demetrii et Libanii : (1) Letter 4 δι᾽ ἡμᾶς ἔχων τὸ πνεῦμα (you 'owe your life to us'). This forms part of a typical letter of reproach addressed to an ungrateful recipient of a benefit. It refers to the moral obligation or debt for benefits or services which the recipient owes his benefactor. (2) Letter 21; cf. the expression of the recipient in the thankful type of letter which calls to mind the gratitude owed to a benefactor. It reads in part : 'for even if I gave my life for you (οὐδὲ γὰρ τὸν βίον ὑπέρ δου) I would still not be giving adequate thanks for the benefits I have received. If you wish anything that is mine, do not write and request it, but demand a return. For I am in your debt (ὀφείλω γάρ) . (Translation from A.J. Malherbe, 'Ancient Epistolary Theorists', Ohio Jnl. of Relig. Stud. Vol. 5 No. 2 (1977), 39.).

the reason for his recommendation of them[92].

As I have shown, the friendship relationship underlies most of the extant Greek and Latin private letters of recommendation and the various elements in them can only be understood in this context. They are private letters between persons who are intimately related with the intention of either establishing, extending or maintaining friendship between recommender, recommended and recipient[93]. Letters of recommendation were written for a variety of other reasons[94] and some could be categorised as 'official' rather than private; that is, recommendations carried by representatives of governments and various organisations. I am inclined to think that some of the allusions to recommendation in the New Testament are to recommendations of this kind[95]. I suggest, though, that Paul's recommendations belong to the general framework of private letters. Those he recommended were his intimates. Apart from Phoebe's recommendation, all of the recommended were known to the recipients. His recommendations, in these instances, were intended to strengthen the relationship between the recommended and the recipients and, in three of them in particular, to declare his support for his associates and to establish them in positions of authority[96]. This action by Paul in Corinth, as we shall see in chapter 7, had serious implications in his conflict with his enemies and does not appear to have met with success.

As with his patronal relations, the language Paul uses to describe either the recommended or the recipient is drawn from

---

[92] Eg., 1 Cor. 16:18; Phlm. 7, 20 - ἀναπαύειν 'to give rest, to refresh', is occasionally found in contexts of hospitality and denotes either the specific outcome of the act itself, or the refreshment of the guest by the hospitality of his host (so Phlm. 7). See J.B. Mathews, Hospitality, 173-174. It may indicate in 1 Cor. 16:18 material assistance brought personally by Stephanas and his associates or their companionship as friends. In Phlm. 20 it implies that Paul will in some way be benefited by Philemon's following his recommendation.

[93] For details, see above 92.

[94] Ibid., 93.

[95] Eg., Acts 9:2; 22:5; 1 Cor. 16:3.

[96] 1 Cor. 16:15-16, 17-18; 1 Thess. 5:12-13a.

the vocabulary of work[97], and it is their 'work' which he singles out for praise and because of which he urges the recipients to follow his recommendation[98]. This is characteristically Pauline. Apart from the recommendation in 3 John, in which the recipient and recommended become 'fellow-workers in the truth' (συνεργοὶ τῇ ἀληθείᾳ v. 8) through the extension of hospitality (here denoted by ἐργάζομαι v.5) to the recommended[99], I can find no other letter of recommendation which resorts to such terminology[100]. He also uses common familial terms - brother, sister - but there are none of the standard terms of intimacy which occur in the Greek and Latin private letters of recommendation[101].

4. Enmity.

As I have previously shown, echthra (and its Latin equivalent inimicitia) denotes a hostile relationship and, together with echthros forms the traditional antithesis to philia and philos[102]. We have seen that, although the idea of friendship is present, the terms philia and philos do not appear in Paul's letters. By comparison, Paul uses echthra and echthros on a number of occasions[103], and it is the enmity relationship against which many of his ethical injunctions are directed[104].

---

97 Eg., recommended : hoi kopiōntes, 1 Thess. 5:12; hoi synergountes kai kopiōntes, 1 Cor. 16:15; synergos, Phil. 2:29 (cf. hoi loipoi synergoi, Phil. 4:3); recipient : syzygos, Phil. 4:3 (though it could be a proper noun); synergos, Phlm. 1.

98 Eg., 1 Thess. 5:13; 1 Cor. 16:15; Phil. 2:29; Phil. 4:3; Ro. 16:2; Phlm. 11.

99 See A.J. Malherbe, 'Inhospitality', 225-229.

100 For Christian letters of recommendation, see Chan-Hie Kim, Familiar Greek Letter, 99-118; K. Treu, 'Christliche Emfehlungs-Schemabriefe auf Papyrus', Zetesis Festschrift E. de Strijcker (Antwerp/Utrecht, 1973), 631-632.

101 For details, see above 99 n.45, 102 nn.63, 64, 65.

102 For details, see above 35-37

103 Eg., echthra : Ro. 8:7; Gal. 5:12; echthros : Ro. 5:10; 12:20; 1 Cor. 15:25, 26; Gal. 4:16; Phil. 3:18; Col. 1:21.

104 Eg., Ro. 12:14, 17, 19-21; 1 Thess. 5:15. Cf. J.N. Sevenster, Paul and Seneca, 180-185.

Like many Greek and Roman authors, he shows a distinct distaste for relations of this kind which constantly dogged him in his work as an apostle[105] and his lists of vices consist mainly of the social evils commonly associated with enmity[106].

In two passages, Paul uses ἐχθρός of himself (Gal. 4:16) and of others (2 Thess. 3:15) in a manner which can only be understood in terms of the friendship-enmity institution. First, in Gal. 4:16, Paul asks : 'Have I become your enemy by telling you the truth ?' (ὥστε ἐχθρός ὑμῶν γέγονα ἀληθεύων ὑμῖν) [107]. The association of ἐχθρός and παρρησία, 'freedom or boldness of speech', and ἀλήθεια, 'truth', is common in Greek discussions[108]. In my study of the flatterer, I outlined the claim of the Cynics to speak the truth on all occasions to their hearers. To do so, they characteristically assumed the role of an enemy (rather than a friend) whose acid tongue would quickly reveal the true nature of an opponent's faults. Thus, by censure and reproach, they endeavoured to educate and improve their hearers. Further, I mentioned briefly, as one of the important topoi of friendship, the question of how frank a person should be with a friend. Many thought that parrēsia was evidence of an enemy rather than a friend and doubted friendship's capacity to withstand reproach from that quarter. Censure was never

---

105 Eg., Gal. 4:12-20; Phil. 1:15, 17; 1 Cor. 1:10-12; 11:18-19; 2 Cor. 12:20 and generally throughout chapters 10 - 12. See also above 44-45 for ἔχθρα as a concomitant of public life in Paul's society.

106 Eg., Gal. 5:20; Col. 3:8; cf. also 2 Cor. 12:20; Ro. 1:28-31; see above 51.

107 There is some doubt as to the punctuation here. The sentence is introduced by ὥστε and could be rendered, 'So I have become your enemy!' See D. Guthrie, Galatians (London, 1974), 120.

108 H.D. Betz in his recent and excellent commentary, Galatians (Philadelphia, 1979), 220-237, also recognizes the conventions of friendship and enmity in Gal. 4:12-20. He correctly detects the topoi of true and false friendship and of the flatterer or false friend. He considers, though, that Paul's remark, 'Become as I am, for I also have become as you are' (v. 12), refers to the commonness or equality required in friendship rather than that of the accommodation of the flatterer. Thus he dissociates it from Paul's 'all things to all men' (1 Cor. 9:23). I argue in Ch. 8 that the figure of the flatterer underlies both these passages.

far from insult in Greek society[109]. I suggest the latter provides the context for viewing Paul's question, which is not simply rhetorical, but points to a serious breakdown in his relations with the Galatians. It is a breakdown not altogether dissimilar to that in Corinth.

The Galatians had accepted him initially, says Paul, despite what must have been regarded by them as a socially debilitating disease. Paul appears to be very conscious at this juncture of the cultural significance of physical illness and especially of disfiguring illness. The Greeks highly esteemed physical qualities such as beauty, stature, agility and health, and their contraries were made the subject of laughter and ridicule[110]. In view of his emphasis upon their noble acceptance of him and the association of the terms πειρασμός, ἐξουθενεῖν, and ἐκπτύειν (v. 14), with ἀσθένεια (v. 12), I suggest that ἀσθένεια does not simply signify his physical weakness but alludes to his status also. The issue here is one of social judgment, by himself and others, on his worth and status according to popular convention[111]. Against normally held values, rather than wrong (ἀδικεῖν) (v. 12) him, they received (δέχεσθαι) him 'as an angel of God, as Christ Jesus' (v. 14). They would have plucked out

---

109 For details, see above 78-80; A.J. Malherbe, 'Hellenistic Moralists', 24-30, and 'Gentle as a Nurse : the Cynic background to 1 Thess. 2', Nov. Test. 12 (1970), 208-214, for the type of philosopher who confused parrhesia with loidoria.

110 For details, see above 53-55, 64-66. Sickness or affliction is linked in a derogatory fashion to a man's intelligence; cf. Plutarch, Lives 'Solon' 21.3, πόνος and λογισμός; C. Segal, 'Lucretius, Epilepsy, and the Hippocratic Oath on Breaths', CP (1970), 180-182. See also, C. Forbes, 'Strength' and 'Weakness', 74n.4.

111 See C. Forbes, 'Strength' and 'Weakness', 74-75. Cf. Plutarch, Mor. 633D, where Pasiades ridiculed Leon of Byzantium for the weakness of his eyes. Leon responded in part : 'You reproach me for a bodily infirmity (ἀσθένεια).' Cf. ibid., 633C - while Antigonus could not stand another insulting him, he himself made fun of his one eye. When he received a petition written in large letters (μεγάλοις γράμμασι γεγραμμένον) he remarked (633C), 'This is clear even to a blind man'. It is possible, in view of Gal. 4:12-16, that the words, ἴδετε πηλίκοις ὑμῖν γράμμασιν ἔγραψα τῇ ἐμῇ χειρί (6:11), are an attempt at humour or ridicule at his own expense. For the adverse effect upon an audience caused by physical disability, cf. Homer, Il. 2.212, 216-219; Lucian, Ind. 21, 23.

their eyes and given them to him (v. 15) and deemed themselves favoured (μακαρισμός) (v. 14) to be associated with him. We have evidence then of a relationship of warmth and quality in which the usual conventions of acceptance have been put aside.

This intimate relationship had subsequently and rapidly given place to another (1:6). The cause of the cessation of friendship appears to be twofold. First, Paul's opponents, according to him, have set out to win the support of the Galatians for themselves and to cause them to withdraw (ἐκκλείειν) their affection from him (v. 17)[112]. It appears that they have pointed to a serious defect in Paul's character. He is an inconstant person. He seeks to please men (ἤ ζητῶ ἀνθρώποις ἀρέσκειν) (1:10) and is inconsistent in his teaching and practice of circumcision[113]. He cannot therefore be trusted. As I have shown, this is a most damaging charge, for constancy and trust were regarded as the essence of friendship[114]. In addition, they have advanced their own gospel (1:6-9) and possibly ridiculed Paul's physical disabilities and more than favourably compared themselves with him. The Galatians proved susceptible to this persuasion. Their defection was complete from Paul and his gospel (1:6-9; 3:1-5), and it left him astonished (1:6), disappointed (4:11) and perplexed (4:20).

Second, there is no direct evidence that the Galatians now considered Paul as their enemy; only of the sudden withdrawal of their affection and support from him and the transfer of their allegiance to his enemies. But given the nature of such relationships as friendship and enmity in their society, their new alliance with those who were opposed to Paul would have involved them in enmities[115]. The eight

---

112 ἐκκλείειν, 'shut out, exclude' and here with reference to withdrawal of friendship. Cf. Herodotus, 1.144; Aeschines, 2.85; 3.74; Demosthenes, 19.26. Contrast the view of M. Hitchcock, 'The Meaning of ΕΚΚΛΕΙΕΙΝ in Galatians IV.17', JTS 40 (1939), 149-151.

113 For details, see below 316.

114 For details, see above 21-23, 76, 78, 81-82.

115 For details, see above 43-45.

social vices in 5:20-21 may reflect their attitude towards him and others in the congregation who still supported him. I suggest that Paul's question about becoming their enemy should be seen as evidence that he is aware of the conventions of the friendship-enmity relationship and that their relationship with his enemies is one of friendship. Censure on his part may then be regarded by them as a declaration of open hostility[116]. Caution was needed but too much was at stake for Paul. He dealt harshly with his unnamed opponents, indirectly denouncing them and their motives in a conventional periphrastic manner, sometimes vehemently, sometimes crudely[117]. It is to be noted, though, that the naming of an opponent could be construed as a declaration of enmity[118]. Paul avoids such a possibility. To the Galatians he says that, while he wanted to be with them and to change his tone (v. 20), he had no alternative but to reproach them[119]. Apart from a note of optimism on the part of Paul as to their future acceptance of him, we do not know if Paul ever successfully resolved the dispute.

I have mentioned that the formal conduct of the conflict in Galatians bears a marked resemblance to that in Corinthians. The enmity relationship, the nuance of status in relation to Paul's disabilities, the accusation of inconstancy, the susceptibility to conventional forms of persuasion, the frankness of speech and the tone of voice, the periphrastic response - all are present in the conflict in Corinth. I am not suggesting that from these similarities we can draw a connection between Paul's enemies in each situation. Rather, that Paul's appearance, mannerisms,

---

[116] Cf. Plutarch, Mor. 56A, B : 'those guilty of mistakes ... the man who by chiding and blaming implants the sting of repentance (μετάνοια) is taken to be an enemy and an accuser (ἐχθρός καὶ κατήγορος). Whereas they welcome the man who praises and extols what they have done and regard him as kind and friendly'; Cicero, de Amic. 24.89, quoting from Terence (Andria 1.1.41) : 'complaisance gets us friends, plain speaking, hate', and comments, 'a troublesome thing is truth if it is indeed the source of hate which poisons friendship'.

[117] Eg., 1:7, 9; 2:4; 3:1, 10; 4:17; 5:7, 10, 12; 6:12, 13.

[118] See my discussion in Ch. 9.

[119] Eg., 3:1-5; 4:8-11.

attitudes, and style left him open to ridicule and invidious comparison by those who wished to exploit the accepted conventions against him. We may have a slender but important clue in Galatians as to one of the major focal points of attack against Paul in Corinth. He asks the Galatians : 'Become as I am, for I also have become as you are' (γίνεσθε ὡς ἐγώ, ὅτι κἀγὼ ὡς ὑμεῖς) (4:12). It is this characteristic of Paul's behaviour, his inconsistency by Greek and Roman standards in the face of accepted conventions, of both social and religious custom, which led to so much misunderstanding and was at the centre of the accusation against him in Corinth, that he was 'all things to all men'.

It is important to note in this brief treatment of the friendship relationship in Galatians that the preacher and his gospel are integrally linked and that his status is important to the understanding and reception of his gospel by his hearers. This applies to the acceptance of Paul and his rivals and to their estimation of themselves. What we need to understand more fully are those socially accepted values by which some of Paul's converts evaluated an apostle, and by which they transferred their allegiance to those who adopted a more presentable position.

In the second of the two passages, Paul uses echthros not of himself but of others. In 2 Thess. 3:14-15, Paul warns : 'If any one refuses to obey what we say in this letter, note that man and have nothing to do with him, that he may be ashamed. Do not look on him as an echthros, but warn him as an adelphos'. Paul's command not to associate is directed against a group of Christians he describes as behaving idly or disorderly (ἀτάκτως) (3:6, 11). The verb συναναμίγνυσθαι, 'to associate', is also used in 1 Cor. 5:11 in relation to a brother guilty of immorality or idolatry. There the prohibition also excludes eating (συνεσθίειν) with him. J.B. Mathews suggests that both these terms are related to the act of hospitality which is precluded in these instances[120].

---

[120] Hospitality, 330-335.

To renounce hospitality to a person who is already an associate is a cessation of friendship. It could only be understood by either party in the normal course of events as a hostile act and it may initiate serious enmity. As I have outlined previously, there were set conventions as to how one should act toward a former friend[121] which, in the event of a dissociation of this kind, would properly be followed. There is no reason to suggest the Thessalonians would have behaved differently. One can envisage Cicero's counsel at this point : 'Ties of friendship should be sundered by a gradual relaxation of intimacy' for otherwise it will seem that 'open hostility has been aroused'[122]. Paul's advice is more positive : he is to be warned as a brother. Without Paul's explanation at this point, I suggest that the Thessalonians would have understood Paul's prohibition in terms of enmity[123]. The express purpose of the exclusion of the idlers is that they may be ashamed. Denial of hospitality, then, is to be construed as an act of brotherly love, not enmity.

5. Giving and receiving.

In Phil. 4:15, Paul tells the Philippians that after he left Macedonia they were the only church which 'entered into partnership with me in giving and receiving' (μοι ... ἐκοινώνησεν εἰς λόγον δόσεως καὶ λήμψεως). It is difficult to capture the various nuances present in this phrase. It is clear that it refers directly to gifts which Paul had received from the Philippians in the past (v. 15) and includes the recent gift brought by Epaphroditus (v. 17; cf. 2:25-30).

---

121 For details, see above 35-38, 51 n.117.

122 de Amic. 21.76-78; for the themes of cessation of friendship and of a friend becoming an enemy, see above 18-21, 39-42.

123 Cf. 2 Cor. 2:5-11 where I consider similar nuances are present. J.B. Mathews, Hospitality, 329-330, parallels the use of <u>echthros</u> here to Judaism's denial of hospitality to idolaters or law-breakers as enemies of God. They would not associate with them and would show open enmity towards them. Cf. 2 Jo. 10-11 : μὴ λαμβάνετε αὐτὸν εἰς οἰκίαν ; 3 Jo. 10 : ἐκ τῆς ἐκκλησίας ἐκβάλλει, and see A. J. Malherbe, 'Inhospitality', 228-229.

Does the phrase refer simply to the passing of money between the Philippians and Paul, or does it indicate some other kind of relationship between them as well ? Should it be interpreted only literally or is it a metaphorical expression ?

Scholars have drawn attention to the commercial background of the phrase and of other terminology in the ensuing verses. The technical nature of this terminology is expressed in the New English Bible : 'my partners in payments and receipts', and more literally by F.W. Beare : 'partnership with me in an accounting of receipts and expenditures'[124]. It has led one scholar to speculate that Paul had a banking arrangement with a wealthy Philippian and had received several loans[125]. Some recent commentators follow C.H. Dodd's psychological interpretation. After inferring from 1 Cor. 9:15-18 that Paul hates money, he pictures him as a well-to-do bourgeois who had never come to grips with money. To the Philippians, 'he can scarcely bring himself to acknowledge that money was welcome to him' and he 'covers up his embarrassment by piling up technical terms of trade, as if to give the transaction a severely "business" aspect'[126]. Dodd's inference from 1 Cor. 9 is wrong. As I will show later, Paul's argument in that chapter has nothing to do with his inner conflict about money but, rather, with his right and power to act as he chooses[127]. We must also look for an alternative explanation to Dodd's, to account for the commercial language in our passage. The terms in this phrase appear frequently in Greek authors in relation to money matters. εἰς λόγον, a technical or commercial term, means 'to the account of' and

---

[124] F.W. Beare, The Epistle to the Philippians (London, 1959), 151.

[125] B.H.D. Hermesdorf, 'De Apostel Paulus in lopende Rekening met de gemeente te Filippi', Tijdschrift voor Theologie 1 (1961), 252-256 (non vidi); cited by D.L. Dungan, The Sayings of Jesus, 29.

[126] C.H. Dodd, 'The Mind of Paul : I', New Testament Studies (Manchester, 1953), 67-82, espec. 71-72. Cf. F.W. Beare, Philippians, 151-152; R.P. Martin, The Epistle of Paul to the Philippians (London, 1959), 174, who describes Paul's attitude as 'a natural idiosyncrasy which other servants of God have shared'.

[127] For details, see below 240.

is used of business transactions in Greek literature and papyrus[128]. Most translators interpret Paul's second use of the phrase, εἰς λόγον, (v. 17) in this way. The associated terms, καρπός and πλεονάζειν, are also said to contain commercial nuances. καρπός, literally, 'fruit', is often used of the profit to be gained in a business transaction, and πλεονάζειν, 'to increase', is a regular banking term for financial growth. As a present participle, 'continuing to multiply or increase', πλεονάζων suggests the figure of compound interest[129]. The terms δόσις and λῆμψις, 'giving and receiving', refer to the pecuniary transactions derived from two sides of the ledger[130]. Finally, κοινωνεῖν can refer to a joint undertaking in business[131] and in view of its association with the terminology just mentioned, in this passage it seems to denote 'financial sharing'[132]. It has a wide range of applications, however, and is used of friends sharing together in the good things of life or in social intimacies[133]. Paul's use of commercial language seems to be quite deliberate and sustained and it is possible that he is viewing the gifts which he has received in terms of an investment by the Philippians upon which God will pay interest.

---

[128] Eg., P. Oxy. 275.19, 21; Thucydides 3.46; Polybius 11.28.8. Cf. λόγος, 'settlement' (of an account), Demosthenes 8.47; 30.15; Herodotus 3.142, 143.

[129] So F.W. Beare, Phil., 155. It has been suggested that the phrase ἐπιζήτω τὸ δόμα (v. 17) may be technical terminology for the demand of payment of interest and the verb ἀπέχειν, from its use in non-literary papyri, may be a technical term used for drawing up a receipt for payment in full in discharge of a bill. So, R.P. Martin, Phil (NCB), 167.

[130] Eg., Ecclus. 42.7 (cf. 42.3) : καὶ δόσις καὶ λῆμψις πάντα ἐν γραφῇ.

[131] Eg., Aristotle, EN 8.9.1.

[132] For koinōnein implying sharing in one's money or property, see Ro. 15:27, Gal. 6:6, and its near equivalent metechein, 1 Cor. 9:12a.

[133] Aristotle, EE 7.12.10; EN 9.12.2-3; cf. EN. 9.12.1 : κοινωνία γὰρ ἡ φιλία. See J.P. Sampley, 'Societas Christi : Roman Law and Paul's Conception of the Christian Community', God's Christ and His People, J. Jervell and W.A. Meeks, eds. (Oslo, 1977) 167, who understands koinōnia in the sense of a Latin equivalent, societas, 'partnership' as evidence of a consensual reciprocal relationship between Paul and the Philippians.

The terms, and indeed the phrase, εἰς λόγον δόσεως καὶ λήμψεως, can be used for other than financial matters, though the original application to money matters is more or less in view. In Plutarch, the phrase λόγον δοῦναι καὶ λαβεῖν denotes engaging in mutual discourse or discussion[134]. Scholars have long noticed an exact latin equivalent to the phrase in Cicero, ratio acceptorum et datorum[135]. What has not been mentioned is that it forms part of his discussion on friendship and is put forward by Cicero (though in a derogatory fashion) as an analogy of a popular view of friendship which likens it to an equal interchange of services and feelings (paribus officiis ac voluntatibus). This is the most common form of friendship, for utility or advantage[136]. What is important for our discussion of v. 15 is that phrases of this kind occur frequently in relation to friendship, and often with a positive sense[137]. As I have shown in my chapter on friendship, the mutual exchange of gifts and services, i.e. of giving and receiving was regarded as essential to friendship[138] and the recipient was morally bound

---

[134] Mor. 11B; cf. Epictetus ?.9.12 : λήψεις καὶ δόσεις with reference to character.

[135] de Amic. 16.58. Cf. J.J. Wettstein, Novum Testamentum graecum ... cum lectionibus variantibus II (Amsterdam, 1752), 280; J.B. Lightfoot, St. Paul's Epistle to the Philippians (repr. Grand Rapids, 1953), 165.

[136] For details, see above 27-30.

[137] Eg., Cicero, de Off. 1.18.59 : '... in order to become good calculators of duty (boni ratiocinatores officiorum), able by adding and subtracting to strike a balance correctly and find out just how much is due to each individual'; Seneca, de Ben. 2.16.1-2, on the advantages of a benefit : ' ... without which there can be no true reckoning of the value of the deed (sine quibus facti ratio non constabit)'; de Ben. 6.4.5 : 'So, too, a balance is struck between benefits and injuries' (inter beneficia quoque et iniurias ratio confertur); Ep. 81:18 : 'Therefore interest should be allowed for, when you compare your receipts and expenses' (itaque huius quoque rei habebitur ratio, cum conferentur accepta et expensa). For the idea of the ledger in striking a balance in giving and receiving, see Seneca, Ep. 81.6 (calculus); 81.17; Cicero, de Amic. 16.58 (calculus).

[138] Eg., Cicero, de Off. 1.17.56; de Amic. 8.26; Aristotle, ep. 3; Seneca, de Ben. 1.4.2.

[139] For details, see above 9-12.

to return the equivalent or more than he had received[139]. What Greek and Roman authors detested, as we have seen in Cicero, was the popular view of friendship which regarded giving and receiving as a commercial transaction. Aristotle refers to this kind of friendship as one of τὸ χρήσιμον, 'utility', and recommends, sometimes derogatorily, at other times pragmatically, that those who engaged in such friendships ought to conduct them as a business partnership[140].

Despite this distaste for merchandised relationships, these authors constantly resort to commercial language and ideas to describe friendships of all kinds. Seneca's de Beneficiis is a treatment of the morality of giving and receiving and commercial concepts abound throughout. Benefactors are called 'creditors' and the benefit a 'loan', a 'deposit' or an 'investment'. Recipients are 'debtors' and the gift is a 'debt' which is 'owed' and must be 'repaid' with 'interest'[141]. Comparisons and contrasts are numerous, though at times Seneca has misgivings about the adequacy and propriety of using commercial language, especially for ideal or perfect friendship[142]. I have also shown the rich use of this kind of language which Cicero makes in his letters of recommendation. In particular there is the conventional promise that the recipient's acceptance of the recommendation will be a 'sound' or 'brilliant investment' which will be a source of 'immense profit'[143]. The appearance of such terminology in discussions of friendship ought not to

---

140 EN 8.14.1; 9.1.8-9; 9.7.1; for the motive of profit (ὠφέλιμον) or advantage (συμφέρον) see EN 8.3.4; 8.13.4, 8, 11; and refer to my discussion above 27-30.

141 'Creditor' (creditor), 2.18.5; 3.12.3; 3.19.1; 'loan' (creditum), 4.12.1; 'deposit' (depositum), 4.10.1; 'investment' (faenerare) 1.1.9; 2.10.2; cf. Cicero, de Amic. 9.31; 'debtor' (debitor), 2.10.3; 4.40.5; 5.19.6; 'debt' (debitum), 2.35.4; 'to owe a debt' (debere), 1.5.1; 5.4.1; 6.4.1; Ep. 81.8; 'to repay' (reddere), 1.4.3; 2.35.1, 5; 3.10.1; Ep. 81.31; (solvere), 2.22.1; 2.35.5; Ep. 81.3; 'interest' (usura), Ep. 81.18.

142 Eg., Ep. 81. 9-10; de Ben. 2.34.1; 3.10.1; cf. ibid., 2.17.7; 3.8.3-4; 3.15.1-4; 5.21.3; 6.4.4-5.

143 For details see above 113-114 espec. 113 nn.126-128.

surprise us. A.R. Hands has shown that in the 'case of early Greece and Rome, language itself points to the original significance of giving and countergiving as doing duty for purchase and sale'[144]. For instance, the common Greek word which we translate 'to sell' is ἀποδίδοσθαι 'to give away of one's own accord'. Similarly, the Latin parallel is a phrase based upon the verb 'to give', venum dare, (to give for sale), while emere, commonly translated 'to buy' means basically no more than 'to take'[145]. In the later cash economies of Greece and Rome, among people of rank, reciprocal relationships continued to embrace the function of buying and selling. Giving and receiving encompassed a wide range of gifts and services and it was to his friends that a person turned to meet many of his needs[146]. The original commercial nature of friendship continued to be a significant factor in these relationships even though the idea of friendship underwent constant refinement. The frequent denigration of such friendships by Aristotle, Cicero and Seneca can be seen as attempts to transcend what was and continued to be the popular understanding of friendship.

In Greek discussions of friendship the verbal nouns δόσις and λῆμψις, separately, denote two of the three obligations of friendship, that of the obligations to give and to receive. While often used in this way of the activity of the benefactor or recipient, combined they appear at times to have become an idiom expressing the mutual interchange of gifts and services of which friendship consists. The phrase occurs in Aristotle's discussion of liberality (ἐλευθεριότης) as a social virtue. Liberality consists of right giving and receiving (δόσις καὶ λῆψις - λῆψις can also mean 'getting' or 'taking' depending on the context), i.e. giving and

---

[144] Charities, 27.

[145] For other examples, Ibid., 27-28.

[146] For details, see above 31-32.

receiving according to the mean in relation to wealth[147]. As I have shown, the liberal man (ἐλευθέριος) uses his wealth to obtain friends. His generosity, his giving and receiving, is generally directed towards friendship, even though it may involve him at times in friendship with unequals who can only return honour[148].

The coupling of δόσις καὶ λῆμψις with the technical terminology εἰς λόγον, in our passage suggests that the commercial nuances must prevail. But given the financial basis of the majority of friendships and the common use of commercial language and ideas in describing them, it is fair to suggest that the entire phrase, κοινωνεῖν εἰς λόγον δόσεως καὶ λήμψεως, is an idiomatic expression indicating friendship. We must not simply focus upon the gift and services nor, as some have, see in the phrase a simple two-way transaction[149]. Gifts and services, while of great importance in the initiating and maintaining of a reciprocal relationship, are one part of the total nexus of relations involved in giving and receiving.

Paul then is drawing upon familiar notions of friendship to acknowledge the recent gift and to express his gratitude. Rather than pointing to tension or embarrassment on Paul's part over the gift, the language implies the opposite. It reflects a warm and lasting relationship. He not only receives the gift gladly as a sign of their continuing

---

147 δόσις καὶ λῆψις : Aristotle, EN. 2.7.4; 4.1.1,24,29; and see his entire discussion, EN 4.1.1-45. Cf. Ecclus. 41.21 : ἀπὸ σκορπισμοῦ λήμψεως καὶ δόσεως ; Cicero, de Amic. 8.26 : ut dandis recipiendisque meritis; Seneca, de Ben. 1.1.1; quam quod beneficia nec dare scimus dec accipere. See also the similar idea φιλεῖν καὶ φιλεῖσθαι : Aristotle, EN 8.8.1,3; EE 7.4.9 (cf. 7.8.1).

148 Cf. Aristotle, EN 8.1.1; and see my discussion above 32-34. Liberality in the sense of right giving and receiving of gifts and services takes this form in both Cicero, de Off. 2.15.52-20.71 (cf. 1.15.48; 1.18.59), and Seneca, de Ben. 2.15.1 - 16.2.

149 Eg., R.P. Martin, Phil. (NCB), 166 : 'The Philippians gave and they also received, presumably spiritual good, from Paul'. This explanation is given by St. Chrysostom, so J.B. Lightfoot, St. Paul's Epistle to the Philippians (Grand Rapids, 1953), 165-166.

concern[150], but also recalls the mutual exchange of services and affection which they had shared in the past. Though he himself cannot reciprocate in kind, he is confident that God would more than make good the gift out of, and in a manner befitting, his boundless wealth in Christ Jesus (v.19)[151].

c. Summary.

We have seen that a number of aspects of the conventions of friendship and enmity appear in Paul's letters. I have argued that Paul himself conducts his relations with his churches according to these familiar social conventions[152]. At the same time we have become aware that on certain status-related issues Paul is willing to diverge from the norm and follow what he considers are the dictates of the gospel. Our understanding of friendship has shed new light upon Paul's relations with the Philippians and has provided us with a background to the conflict between Paul and the Corinthians.

---

150 They had always cared but circumstances prevented their sending aid till now. Paul's use of the imperfect tense, ἐφρονεῖτε, ἠκαιρεῖσθε shows the habitual state of their feelings. So, H.A.A. Kennedy, The Epistle to the Philippians, The Expositors Greek Testament III (Grand Rapids, 1967), 469; R.P. Martin, Phil. 175.

151 The phrase, πληρώσει πᾶσαν χρείαν ὑμῶν (v. 19), refers primarily in the context to the meeting of material needs (although we do not know the state of the Philippians' economic status, ἠκαιρεῖσθε (v. 10) may imply a lack of finance) although the provision of their spiritual needs and ultimate reward cannot be excluded from the scope of reciprocity. For the divine recompense of the benefactor or host according to the principle of reciprocity, see J.B. Mathews, Hospitality, 155-160, 275-276. Cf. the papyrus letter of recommendation, SB 7438 (6th Cent. AD) : ὥστε κα'μὲ χρήσιμον ἀυτῷ φανῆναι καὶ ὑμᾶς πολλῷ πλείονα τὸν ἀπὸ τὸυ δεσπότου θεοῦ μισθὸν ἀπολαβεῖν.

152 For other ideas of social relations between Paul and his churches, see R. Banks, Paul's Idea of Community, 61-71 : familial language; J.P. Sampley, 'Societas Christi', 158-174 : the Roman consensual contract.

Chapter 6

THE CORINTHIAN OFFER OF AID AS AN OFFER OF FRIENDSHIP

The nature of Paul's relationship with the Philippians is of great importance for our understanding of the conflict between Paul and his enemies in Corinth. It is not simply the gift or gifts which Paul received but the relationship which his acceptance of them indicated which is critical for our study. It is against this background that acceptance or refusal of aid must be viewed and that the nature of the conflict in Corinth can be understood.

a. Paul's sources of income.

In this section I will examine briefly Paul's sources of income, which I take to include the various kinds of assistance he received and his personal income derived from his work as a skilled artisan. I will restrict my analysis to the Philippian, Thessalonian and Corinthian letters and draw upon Acts where it relates specifically to the topic. The churches to whom these letters were sent were founded within a relatively short time of each other and provide almost all of the information on his means of livelihood.

The church at Philippi is the only one with whom Paul discusses acceptance of continuous aid. From the moment his work began there and subsequent to his leaving, no other church entered into a relationship with him of giving and receiving (4:15)[1]. Apart from the gift he received while in prison (2:25-30), the Philippians sent aid to him more than once (v. 16) while he was at Thessalonica and elsewhere[2], and Paul draws attention to their continued support for him in Corinth (2 Cor. 11:8-9). From Acts 16:14-15, 40, we know that he was privately assisted by Lydia during his stay in Philippi, which would possibly have been understood as patronal friendship. He may have worked at his trade while there, but this is not explicitly stated.

The Thessalonian letters provide us with an entirely

---

[1] It is difficult to know precisely to what period of time the phrase ἐν ἀρχῇ and the ὅτε clause refer. They could mean (1) the exclusive relationship of giving and receiving between Paul and the Philippians following his departure from Philippi; (2) that it was the first relationship of its kind and that no church had supported him previously; (3) that Philippi marked a decisive turning point in his ministry into the great cities of the provinces of Macedonia and Achaia. In favour of (1) is the unprecedented stress upon financial matters in the Thessalonian and Corinthian letters which suggests a particular sensitivity on Paul's part to these and to associated problems occurring after he left Philippi. It is possible that the scars of the conflict in Corinth are still with Paul; a conflict of which the Philippians were undoubtedly aware through the visits of their representatives to Corinth with aid and the subsequent visits of Paul and his associates to Philippi during the conflict.

[2] Cf. L. Morris, 'ΚΑΙ ἍΠΑΞ ΚΑΙ ΔΙΣ' Nov. Test. 1 (1956), 205-208, who shows on philological grounds that the phrase means 'Both (when I was) in Thessalonica and more than once (in other places)'. See also, F.W. Beare, Phil. 155 : 'more than once' in Thessalonica. This emphasis is too strong; J.E. Frame, A Critical and Exegetical Commentary on the Epistles of St. Paul to the Thessalonians (Edinburgh, 1912), 120-121 : 'for both (when I was) in Thessalonica and (καὶ) repeatedly (ἅπαξ καὶ δὶς) (when I was in other places) you ...'.

different situation[3]. Immediately on leaving Philippi, he went to Thessalonica and apparently took up employment there for the duration of his stay. He worked night and day to support himself (1 Thess. 2:9; 2 Thess. 3:8) and there is no mention of offers of assistance from the Thessalonians nor of the Philippian gifts. Though he had the right to be assisted by them (2 Thess. 3:9), he reminds them that he worked at his trade rather than be a burden to them. From Acts 17:1-10, we learn that Paul stayed in the house of Jason (whether immediately on his arrival of after the three weeks of dialogue in the synagogue is uncertain). Besides Jews and Gentile God-fearers, a number of women of high status (v. 4b) were converted.

The Corinthian letters only allude to Paul's working for wages. (a) It appears as a shame element in a peristasis catalogue in which he contrasts his apostleship with the position of his opponents (1 Cor. 4:12). (b) Paul refers to it as a right which he is free to exercise as he chooses (9:6). (c) There is a possible allusion to it in his use of μισθός in 9:17. He mentions specifically that he received assistance from other churches (presumably Philippa is intended) which was brought to him in Corinth by brethren from Macedonia (2 Cor. 11:8-9). Certain Corinthians offered to support him but he consistently refused their offers (1 Cor. 9:12, 15, 18; 2 Cor. 11:9; 12:14). As in Thessalonica, it was not because he lacked the right, but because he did not wish to burden them (1 Cor. 9:7-18; 2 Cor. 11:7-11; 12:13-14). Luke relates (Acts 18:1-3) how Paul enquired about a master tradesman with whom he could practise his trade and was directed to Aquila who, with

---

[3] I am assuming for the purposes of this study that both letters were written by Paul in the order and form that we have received them, the second letter written shortly after the first. See the discussion, W.G. Kümmel, Introduction NT, 181-190; E. Best, The First and Second Epistles to the Thessalonians (London, 1972), 42-58. Contra : see J.A. Bailey, 'Who wrote II Thessalonians ?', NTS 25 (1979), 131-145, for an excellent survey of scholarly opinion and his conclusion that 2 Thessalonians is a pseudoepigraphical work.

his wife Priscilla, had recently set up business there. As they were of the same trade (homotechnon) as himself, a leatherworker (σκηνοποιός), he accepted both employment and accommodation.

Although there are no direct references to this employment in his letters to the Corinthians, there seems to be no doubt that, as in Thessalonica, Paul worked to support himself. After the arrival of Silas and Timothy from Macedonia, Paul went over entirely to preaching (Acts 18:5a). The suggestion has been made that they took over the role of money-winners while Paul concentrated on preaching[4] although it is more likely that they brought with them a gift from Philippi and thus eased Paul's financial situation for the time being[5]. Apart from Priscilla and Aquila, he appears to have enjoyed the hospitality of Justus (v. 7) and, as I have mentioned, his letters to the Corinthians suggest that he sought the patronage of a number of wealthy people there[6].

There are, at first sight, a number of parallels between Paul's sources of income in Thessalonica and Corinth - working for wages; Philippian gifts; hospitality; the matter of his right; his wish not to burden anyone. Clearly, these matters are important for his understanding of his apostleship. But pointing to the similarities is insufficient for, as we shall see, the issues and emphases differ. Though the Thessalonian letters provide a basic background to our understanding of Paul as a working apostle, the Philippian letter provides us with the key to the conflict over the offer of aid in Corinth.

Paul's reference to his work in 1 Thess. 2:9 forms part of a paraenesis (1:5b - 2:12) in which he reminds the Thessalonians, in a negative and antithetic form, of his exemplary behaviour which they had already emulated. A.J. Malherbe has ably shown that this passage, along with

---

[4] E. Haenchen, Acts, 534, who cites this suggestion from The Beginnings of Christianity IV ET, K. Lake and H.J. Cadbury, eds. (London, 1933), 224.

[5] Ibid., 534.

[6] For details, see above 144-147.

others in this letter, exhibit numerous paraenetic characteristics and that Paul understood his apostleship in terms of the important issues being debated by Cynic philosophers. On the basis of formal and verbal parallels between Paul and Dio Chrysostom and between Paul and the Cynic tradition in general, he suggests that Paul views himself as the gentle philosopher and dissociates himself from the harsh charlatan[7]. In this context, Paul reminds the Thessalonians of his labour and toil. He worked night and day while he preached the gospel to them, both so as not to burden them (ἐπιβαρεῖν) (v. 9) through being harsh and demanding (ἐν βάρει εἶναι) (v. 7), and as an expression of his love for them (v. 8). His work and the rest of his conduct is linked with the nature of his call to be an apostle. He had been approved by God to be entrusted with the gospel (v. 4).

Following on the work of Malherbe, R.F. Hock has demonstrated that the connection between Paul's work and his preaching, his work and his love, and his work and his apostolic commission, can best be understood in the context of the Cynic discussion of the working philosopher and particularly that of the harsh-gentle debate[8]. He draws a picture of the ideal or model Cynic who is characterised by a love of mankind and gentleness. Coupled with this was his refusal to accept or ask for anything from anyone and his working at menial tasks to support himself. The antithesis of the gentle Cynic was the harsh Cynic whose superficial philosophy was covered up by his scolding or abusing his hearers. He taught for fees or begged for support and was

---

[7] See A.J. Malherbe, 'Gentle as a Nurse', 203-217; 'Hellenistic Moralists', 22-27; 'Exhortation in First Thessalonians' NT 25 (1983) 238-256.

[8] The Working Apostle : an Examination of Paul's Means of Livelihood, Ph.D. dissertation, Yale University, 1974; Xerox University Microfilms, (Ann Arbor) 90, 94-96.

regarded by his opponents as a mercenary fraud[9]. Hock concludes : 'Paul's inclusion of his work in a discussion of his apostolic conduct and his relating it to his decision to be as gentle as a nurse are not fortuitous. In both ways Paul was dissociating himself from frauds. In fact, by staying at his trade rather than exercising his rights to congregational support Paul would have distanced himself from the artisans-turned-philosophers. In fact, as a serious-minded preacher he had no other choice'[10].

The association, then, between Paul's working and preaching in 1 Thessalonians is quite evident. His work and his other conduct formed part of the gospel he preached and had a pragmatic function. On the basis of his understanding of his work, he gave instructions to the Thessalonians to follow his example (4:11; 2 Thess. 3:6, 10). He met with some measure of success for most of the Thessalonians emulated him (1:6). It is generally considered that his emphasis upon work in his first letter is due to the possibility or presence of a major problem in the young church, the one presented by the idlers (ἄτακτοι) (5:14; 2 Thess. 3:6; 11). The second letter shows these people to be Christians who have refused to work and were interfering in the affairs of others.

Opinion is divided as to whether Paul's instruction, that they should work with their hands, in 4:12, refers to an actual or potential problem of idleness[11]. But most scholars agree that the ataktoi are those who have become excessively future-oriented as a result of Paul's preaching of the nearness

---

[9] Ibid., 91-94; many of these were artisans who forsook their workbenches for the easier rewards possible as a philosopher. For a more detailed and recent study of the austere and mild Cynics see A.J. Malherbe 'Self-Definition among Epicureans and Cynics', Jewish and Christian Self-Definition : Self-Definition in the Greco-Roman World Vol. 3 edd. B. F. Meyer and E.P. Sanders (Philadelphia, 1983) 46-59.

[10] The Working Apostle, 94.

[11] Actual : J.E. Frame, Thess. 160-161 - the instruction in 4:12 and the reference to the ataktoi in 5:14 indicate the beginnings of a problem which finally emerges in 2 Thess. 3:6-15. Potential : M. Dibelius, An die Thessalonicher I, II, An die Philipper (Tübingen, 1923) 19-23, the instruction belongs to Paul's original paraenesis and was to guard against the possibility of idleness implicit in an eschatological message.

of the Parousia[12]. This view cannot be substantiated from the text[13]. Against the general view, Hock argues that the various elements in 4:9-12 - brotherly love (v. 9); retirement from public affairs (v. 11); working (v. 11) - together belong to Paul's original missionary instruction and reflect his concern for the opinion of outsiders. The Thessalonians are to do these things so that they may walk in a fitting manner before them (v. 12) and not be dependent upon anyone (v. 12). Thus his advice is socially and externally oriented. Further, Hock has shown that the themes of philia, retirement (ἡσυχία) and living off the land, and the associated ideas of seemliness and procuring of one's own needs, form a traditional combination and represent a social ideal recommended in the writings of Cynics like Philostratus, Musonius and Dio Chrysostom. The emphasis upon work, he

---

[12] The basic formula is old and unchanged : preaching of a particular kind which leads to enthusiasm and cessation of mundane activities, mainly work, and a preoccupation with higher interests. Cf. M. Dibelius, Thess. I, II, 19-23; L. Morris, The First and Second Epistle to the Thessalonians (Grand Rapids, 1959), 132-134, 251-252; W. Hendriksen, I and II Thessalonians, (Grand Rapids, 1955), 105-106, 199; E. Best, 1 & 2 Thess., 175-176, 333; J. Lightfoot, Notes on Epistles of St. Paul (London, 1895), 60-61; W. Kümmel, Introduction NT, 184, 187; E. von Dobschütz, Die Thessalonicherbriefe (Göttingen, 1909), 182-183; J. Moffatt, The First and Second Epistle to Thessalonians, The Expositor's Greek Testament (repr. Grand Rapids, 1967) Vol. 4, 36, 53.

[13] The idea is imported, generally with reference to parallels in later Christian communities, seized by the belief that the end was near. Eg., E. Best, 1 & 2 Thess., 175. We could argue from the context that if such an over-emphasis or misunderstanding about the end existed in Thessalonica, it arose from the intense persecution of the Christians there. There is evidence that Paul's teaching of the return of Christ is closely associated with the Thessalonian suffering : eg., 1 Thess. 1:6-10; 2:13-20; 3:1-13; 2 Thess. 1-2 (cf. θλῖψις, 2 Cor. 8:2). It also forms the basis of ethical paraenesis in 1 Thess. 5:1-11 where the Thessalonians are reminded to live according to their new existence in Christ in view of the certainty and significance of his return and to maintain their discontinuity with certain forms of their past behaviour (4:1-12). The view of W. Schmithals, Paul and the Gnostics ET (Nashville, 1972), 159 - 176, of Christians stirred to pneumatic excitement by the enthusiasm of gnostic missionaries and marked by an indifference to the parousia and a belief that perfection was a present possiblity, is similarly imported from later heretical gnostic circles and cannot constitute proof as to the cause and identity of the ataktoi.

suggests, 'is not surprising in light of the pervasive disesteem of labor in Hellenistic Society'[14].

The evidence of idleness as constituting an actual internal problem in the church appears only in the second letter. It cannot be established from 1 Thessalonians. In 2 Thess. 3:6-15, it is presented as a serious problem which had arisen in the community subsequent to, and probably as a direct reaction against, Paul's original instructions (presumably those in 1 Thessalonians)[15]. I suggest that these people had taken advantage of the generosity and hospitality of their fellow-Christians[16] and that their attitude reflects accurately the social disdain which many Greeks had for manual labour. Neither their conversion nor the apostle's instruction had changed them in this regard. Paul's prohibition not to associate (συναναμίγνυσθαι) with them (v. 14) should be understood as an act of renunciation of this hospitality and as a direct counter to the problem. Left to their own devices, they may yet learn to 'work with their hands'.

---

[14] The Working Apostle, 106 and 101-107 generally; see also 22-23.

[15] Hock, ibid., 145-152, regards 2 Thessalonians as Deutero-Pauline and in 3:7-9 in particular as so close to 1 Thess. 2:8-9 as 'to allow for a Synoptic-style redaction critical comparison'. He concedes that the writer has grasped the logic and language of Paul's view of work but that there is evidence of a significant shift. The paradigmatic character is retained but the basic theological relation between gospel and work and work and love is missing. In addition, the concern for outsiders is absent. Certainly, the paradigmatic aspect of Paul's work dominates his discussion and it appears to consist of popular ethical maxims. But the notion of brotherly love is not altogether lacking; it is found in the radical alternative to the renunciation of hospitality (3:15), i.e., brotherly love instead of enmity relations. Second, the problem of the ataktoi is actual and internal in 2 Thessalonians and it may have called for a different tone or onesided emphasis. Third, given the pervasive disesteem of work amongst the Greeks of which Hock speaks, an attitude characteristic even among the urban free poor, and the fact that Paul's emphasis was due to this attitude, it is most unlikely that Paul did not envisage this problem emerging. It is Hock's view that Paul's opponents in Corinth openly resented his working with his hands (Ibid., 140) and I see no reason why this could not be argued for Thessalonians also. Finally, it raises the overdue question as to whether a 'deutero-Pauline' letter such as 2 Thessalonians is addressed to an actual situation or is simply a literary creation.

[16] A.L. Moore, 1 and 2 Thessalonians, (London, 1969), 114-115.

b. The offer of aid in Corinth.

Hock's study is both refreshing and valuable and he has done a great service in pointing out the way in which Paul views his work in the context of the working philosopher. It is feasible to suggest that Paul came to Corinth with the same views on work and preaching, and that the Acts record of his early days in Corinth, of steady employment and Sabbath preaching, is evidence of this. It is clear that Paul was involved in a lengthy dispute over support with certain of the Corinthians which had serious repercussions for his relations with the church in Corinth (1 Cor. 9:1-12; 2 Cor. 11:7-15; 12:13-18) and that, in the context of this conflict, Paul uses language and logic which appears in the Thessalonian letters.

Because of this, Hock contends that the dispute in Corinth should be understood in the context of debates within the Cynic school over the ideal of the working philosopher, though here Paul's work has an apologetic function rather than a paraenetic one[17]. Hock is the only scholar to have advanced this point of view, and while I substantially agree with his analysis of the Thessalonian situation, I will argue against his thesis in relation to the Corinthian conflict. Rather than Paul's work, as I have previously indicated, it is Paul's mutual obligations with the Philippians, implied by giving and receiving, which is central for our understanding of the cause and nature of the dispute. Five topics need to be discussed to adequately cover the issues involved : 1. the issue in Corinth; 2. the status and conduct of his opponents; 3. the nature of the offer; 4. the nature of the refusal; 5. variance in Paul's practice.

1. The issue in Corinth.

The conflict between Paul and his enemies over aid is directly referred to in three passages - 1 Cor. 9:1-23; 2 Cor. 11:7-15; 12:13-18. In each passage the point of

---

[17] The Working Apostle, 140, 164-165; see also id., 'Paul's Tentmaking and the Problem of his Social Class', JBL 97 (1978), 558-562.

contention is identical - Paul's refusal of support when he was in Corinth. Paul refers to his employment in only one of these passages where it is listed as one of the three apostolic rights (1 Cor. 9:6)[18]. Hock describes 1 Cor. 9:6-18 as Paul's most detailed explanation of why he adopted this policy of self-support[19] and as constituting a defence of this practice in the face of criticism[20]. In vv. 6-14, he suggests that Paul asserts his right as an apostle to congregational support and provides arguments to justify it. Vv. 15-18 explain why he nevertheless decided to support himself by working with his hands[21]. In support of his contention, Hock refers to Paul's work (v. 6), to the notions of burden and right in the work passages in 1 Thessalonians and to sophistic reasoning and other terms which occur in discussions of the working philosopher in Greek authors[22].

In Chapter 8, I shall argue against these points of view in detail. For the moment I concern myself solely with the question of the issue in chapter 9, i.e. Paul's refusal. It is implied in statements to the effect that he did not make use of his right (vv. 12b, 15, 18). This claim only makes sense in the context of chapter 9 if he had received an offer or offers and refused to accept them. His argument in vv. 4-14 is a defence of his right to refuse or to accept aid at his own discretion, given the right of apostles to such aid. In vv. 15-18, he resorts to servile terminology to explain why he refrained from exercising his right in

---

[18] As I have said, misthos in 1 Cor. 9:17 may be an allusion to his work (though see my argument against this, below 223-225, 301-305. The only other instance is his reference in 1 Cor. 4:12, κοπιῶμεν ἐργαζόμενοι ταῖς ἰδίαις χερσίν where it is one element in a peristasis catalogue and I shall discuss this reference in its context in the next section. Manual labour may be connoted also by κόπος (2 Cor. 6:5) and κόπος καὶ μόχθος (2 Cor. 11:27) where again they form part of peristasis catalogues.

[19] The Working Apostle, 120.

[20] Ibid., 126, though he accepts the primary function of Chapter 9 as being pedagogical in relation to Chapters 9 and 10.

[21] Ibid., 127.

[22] Ibid., 127-131.

Corinth[23]. We may postulate that his work placed him in a position whereby he could refuse aid (though not entirely, for he relied upon the Philippian gifts). But nowhere in this chapter does he proffer his work as a justification for his refusal. We cannot assume that the concomitant of his refusal was his working for wages, nor that the defence of his freedom to refuse is identical with a defence of his self-support. Neither do the notions of burden and right, though found in 1 Thessalonians, necessarily mean that the same kind of issue is involved in both instances. It is Paul's refusal which is the critical issue between Paul and his enemies. More precisely, it is his decision to refuse an offer made to him in Corinth while accepting assistance from elsewhere.

Scholars have shown that the question of support was a crucial issue in the hostility between Paul and his rivals as seen in 2 Cor. 11:7-15[24]. Hock notes several 'reminiscences' in this passage of earlier statements in 1 Corinthians and 1 Thessalonians and these lead him to see the passage as a defence of Paul's self-support. There is the same irony and sarcasm (v. 7 and 1 Cor. 4:8-10) so typical in discusisons of support in the Socratic epistles and a similar emphasis upon servility, ταπεινοῦν (v. 7) and δουλοῦν (1 Cor. 9:19), which terms can be used in a pejorative sense to denote the lowly status of workers[25]. There is the same emphasis upon his preaching the gospel without cost (v. 7; cf. 1 Cor. 9:18); his wish not to be a burden or to be burdensome to anyone (v. 10; 1 Cor.9:15-16); and his love (v. 11); 1 Thess. 2:8)[26]. Further, in vv. 12-15 he sees Paul contrasting his practice of financial independence with that of his rivals who have accepted

---

23 For details, see below 292-306.

24 Eg., Käsemann, Die Legitimität des Apostels (Darmstadt, 1964), 36, 45, 48; D. Georgi, Die Gegner des Paulus im 2. Korintherbrief (Neukirchen-Vluyn, 1964), 234-241; H.D. Betz, Der Apostel Paulus und die Sokratische Tradition (Tübingen, 1972), 100-117.

25 For my discussion of δουλοῦν and ταπεινοῦν in these passages see below 312-316, 323-325.

26 The Working Apostle, 136-139.

support from the Corinthians. If these people will not conform to his practice, Paul deems them to be frauds and deceivers (v. 13). This contrast, Hock suggests, is the same as that in 2 Cor. 2:17 where Paul contrasts himself with 'the many who hawked (καπηλεύοντες) the word of God'. This description 'clearly places the dispute at Corinth in the context of discussions of support among philosophers and sophists'[27].

In 2 Cor. 11:7-15 though, as Hock himself admits, there is no mention of Paul's working with his hands[28]. The only reason he gives for his refusal of the Corinthian offer is his acceptance of aid from other churches. He has kept himself from being a burden to them and would continue to refrain from burdening them. It is significant that in this passage Paul's refusal is opposed to his acceptance of aid from 'other churches' while in Corinth (vv. 8-9). Implied also is the acceptance of aid by Paul's rivals from his critics (v. 12). Hock does not take these opposing notions into consideration. If the point at issue is the one between two opposing ideals of livelihood, how could Paul, on the one hand, ask his opponents to imitate him as a working philosopher and refuse aid in Corinth, while on the other, concede openly that he has been able to refuse support because he has accepted assistance from other churches ? It is not sufficient to say, as Hock does, that Paul did not accept assistance from the people he was converting[29]. Corinth, like Philippi, was long established by this time and, as in the first letter, he states not only that he has never accepted but that he never will accept their aid. As we have seen earlier, Paul strongly asserted in 1 Cor. 9:4-14 his right as an apostle to be supported by the congregation. His refusal can now be seen

---

[27] Ibid., 139-140. For the connection between 11:13 and 2:17 see C.K. Barrett, 'ΨΕΥΔΑΠΟΣΤΟΛΟΙ (2 Cor. 11:13)', Mélanges Bibliques en hommage au R.P. Beda Rigaux, edd. A. Descamps and A. de Halleux (Gembloux, 1970), 383-385. See also H. Windisch, 'καπηλεύω', TDNT 3, 605.

[28] The Working Apostle, 132.

[29] Ibid., 133.

in the light of his simultaneous acceptance of aid from other churches. It is this variance in his practice which lies at the heart of his dispute with his enemies. In the wider context of boasting and comparison in chapters 10 and 11, his refusal of their offer and his acceptance of the Philippian assistance have been used against him by his critics. They have compared him unfavourably with his rivals who have accepted their offers.

This form of argument occurs also in our third passage, 12:13-18. It reads in part : 'For in what were you less favoured (ἡττᾶσθαι) than the rest of the churches, except that I myself did not burden you ? Forgive me this wrong! Here for the third time I am ready to come to you. And I will not be a burden ... ' (vv. 13-14a). The issue, again, is his refusal in the face of his acceptance from others. But a new note is introduced which shows more clearly how the Corinthians view refusal and acceptance of offers. The use of ἡττᾶσθαι in relation to the refusal/acceptance antithesis suggests that Paul's enemies have been able to persuade the Corinthians that Paul had refused their offer because he regarded them as inferior to other churches. The rival apostles' acceptance of Corinthian aid, by contrast, showed their affection and concern. Paul in an ironical or sarcastic fashion terms his conduct an adikia. His response to the charge is found in his appeal to a familiar analogy found in many discussions of friendship, that of the unequal bonds that united father and child. By means of this, he hoped to explain the nature of his refusal and good intention towards them (vv. 14b-18). I shall return to this analogy later in this chapter. The affront which the Corinthians consider Paul has done them, I suggest, reflects the nature of their offer to him. It constituted an offer of a relationship of the same kind which his acceptance of the Philippian gift indicated he had with that church. Thus, Paul, by his refusal, had shamed and dishonoured them and was held to be responsible for the hostilities which followed.

2. The status and conduct of his opponents.

I shall argue here that the passage 1 Cor. 4:6-21 indicates to us the status of Paul's opposition and the nature of their conduct and attitude towards him. It provides us with the key to understanding Paul's refusal of support and with a context in which to view his defence in chapters 8-10. In regard to our passage, N.A. Dahl concludes that :

(a) the section, 1 Cor. 1:10 - 4:21 served as an apology for Paul's apostolic ministry;

(b) the division in Corinth (1:10-14) was mainly due to the opposition against Paul;

(c) the division was 'occasioned' or 'actualised' as a result of appeals to Paul for counsel;

(d) the section had a preparatory function for the remainder of the letter[30].

Dahl draws out of this section what he refers to as the only unambiguous if meagre facts about the situation in Corinth. First, the fact that there were quarrels. Second, that some of the persons involved were arrogant due to their assumption that Paul would not return to Corinth (4:18-19) 'Thus we get an indication that Paul is aware of the existence of some centre of opposition against him within the church'[31]. Dahl says that Paul appears to be addressing his remarks to the church at Corinth as a whole in an attempt to win the Corinthians' loyalty to Christ and to establish his authority as its apostle and 'father' (4:14-17). Thus he hoped to provide a platform from which to deal with the various facets of the division in Corinth (Chapters 5-16) without worsening the situation. However, concurrently with this there appears to be a response to criticisms which have been voiced against him. These criticisms included : Paul's lack of wisdom (1:17, 2:1, 4, 3:2); his absence from Corinth

---

30 'Paul and the Church at Corinth in 1 Cor. 1:10 - 4:21', Christian History and Interpretation : Studies Presented to J. Knox, W. R. Farmer, C.F.D. Moule and R.R. Niebuhr edd. (Cambridge, 1967), 329.

31 Ibid., 318-319.

(4:18); his working for wages (4:12). Dahl sees the elements contained in the peristasis catalogue in 4:11-13 as providing us with an insight into the nature of the criticisms against Paul. 'He is said to be an apostle who lacks stability (v. 11) and who shamefully works with his hands (v. 12).' He concludes : 'since this section contains an apology for Paul, and the strife at Corinth was linked with opposition against him, it becomes fairly easy to interpret the slogans reported in 1:12' as declarations of loyalty to or of independence from Paul[32].

Scholars have constructed a number of frameworks in an attempt to explain the source and nature of the opposition to Paul. W. Schmithals suggested gnosticism[33] and others a gnostic kind of piety[34]. In relation to 4:6-13 and v. 8 in particular, the Corinthians have been portrayed as religious enthusiasts, proponents of a realised eschatology[35]. Recently, within the pneumatic-psychic framework but against the trend of modern scholarship, we have become acquainted with the gnostic Paul, the pneumatic apostle who teaches wisdom to gnostic initiates but voluntarily humbles himself for the sake of the psychics, to preach at their level[36]. J.C. Hurd excludes extraneous influences and attributes the problems to Paul's change of mind in the interval between a previous letter (5:9-11) and his original ministry[37].

---

32 Ibid., 320-323.

33 Gnosticism in Corinth : An Investigation of the Letters to the Corinthians ET (Nashville, 1971), passim.

34 Eg., H. Conzelmann, 1 Cor., 16 : pneumatics, for whom 'freedom' allied with 'wisdom' and 'knowledge' is a speculative principle which leads to their detachment from the world; 'protognosticism', ibid., 15. Their ideas and language are said to be closely related to those which were later taken over and developed by later Gnosticism. Cf. F.F. Bruce, Apostle of the Free Spirit (Exeter, 1977), 261 - 'incipient Gnosticism'; C.K. Barrett, 1 Cor. 144-145 - 'quasi-gnostic'.

35 Eg., C.K. Barrett, 1 Cor. 108-109; N.A. Dahl, 'Paul and the Church', 332; H. Conzelmann, 1 Cor. 87-88.

36 E.H. Pagels, The Gnostic Paul (Philadelphia, 1975), 1-12.

37 The Origins of 1 Corinthians (London, 1965), 273-288.

The Greek background of 4:6-13 has long been recognized. The diatribal features such as the rhetorical questions (v. 7), irony (vv. 8, 9, 10), and the peristasis catalogue, have been well documented by R. Bultmann[38]. J. Munck proposed that the Greek character of the Corinthians led to their misunderstanding of Paul, his gospel and themselves in terms of popular philosophy and sophistry. Paul and others were conceived of as teachers of wisdom, themselves as wise, and all this the cause for boasting[39].

Recently, R. F. Hock suggested that Paul understands his apostleship in terms of the Hellenistic traditions of the true philosopher. The kind of problem which Munck thought existed between the Corinthians and Paul is seen by Hock as being similar to the one he sees between Epictetus and his students. The students were confusing sophistry with philosophy, deeming it to consist of composing speeches for display alone. In response, Epictetus put forward the qualifications of a true philosopher - one who was known not by his speech but by his conduct in the face of various hardships and sufferings[40]. He notes the same boasting by the students as by the Corinthians in their ability to interpret philosophy or scripture independently. In reply, both Paul and Epictetus use the same kind of rebuking questions, the same ironic tone, and even some of the same language[41]. Though Epictetus 'was not in principle opposed to the study of rhetoric', because of his students' delusion about the real nature of philosophy, he 'was willing to denounce such study and to be recognized as a nobody and

---

[38] Der Stil der paulinischen Predigt und die kynisch-stoische Diatribe (Göttingen, 1910), 10-19, 85-106. Cf. H. Conzelmann, 1 Cor. 86-87; R.F. Hock, The Working Apostle, 115n.16.

[39] 'The Church Without Faction', Paul and the Salvation of Mankind ET (London, 1959), 152.

[40] R.F. Hock, The Working Apostle, 115-120.

[41] Ibid., 117-118. Hock considers, wrongly in my opinion, 4:6-7 to be a reference to the interpretation of scripture and compares it with Epictetus 1.17.13-14, 1.4.9.

a know-nothing' (cf. Epict. 1.4.9 : μηδεὶς εἶναι ... εἰδέναι μηδέν). Similarly, Paul did not reject Greek wisdom in its entirety but selected some traditions and rejected others. He characterised himself as a preacher without eloquence and wisdom (2:1; cf. 1:17, 2:4) and he denied that he (and Apollos) was anything (3:7). Rather he was known by his suffering and hardship (4:9-13). These were his apostolic qualifications. They were intended to shame but, at the same time, to set an example to the Corinthians of what they themselves should be like[42].

Hock is correct in emphasising that the notions of shame, and of hardship and suffering, constituted an important part of Paul's self-understanding as an apostle and that they are representative of certain of the Corinthians' objections against him. However, I question both the adequacy of Munck's background to which Hock resorts and the Hellenistic traditions which Hock proposes, to account for the terminology, nuances and ideas which are present in 4:6-13. I suggest that the key to understanding the antithetical comparison and peristasis catalogue in vv. 9-13 lies in the meaning of vv. 6-8. Hock's understanding of vv. 7-8 as independent interpretation of scripture and his general comparison with Epictetus does not do justice to the complex range of ideas expressed by Paul.

I agree that Hellenistic traditions and conventions underlie Paul's thought and that there is a clear process of selection discernible in it. But the traditional antithesis of notions of honour and shame and associated ideas present here and throughout 1:10 - 4:21 refer primarily to social status, and indicate the attitudes and behaviour of certain upper class Christians toward Paul and toward Corinthians of lowly status. Since in this Paul alludes to the familiar notion of ὕβρις or to ideas of excess to describe this behaviour, I shall now outline the notion as it appears in Greek authors.

---

42 Ibid., 116, 118-120.

i. The idea of ὕβρις in Greek authors.

Hybris is one of the most basic Greek ethical notions and it has been the subject of much discussion by classical scholars. My study of it is indebted to two recent articles by D.M.MacDowell[43] and N.R.E. Fisher[44] though I have consulted a number of works by other scholars[45]. Hybris is generally translated as 'pride' or 'arrogance' but pride involves only one aspect of what is meant by the term. It is a complex notion which denotes a wide range of activities, the state of mind of the agent, and the effects of shame on the victim and his feelings of outrage.

MacDowell summarises several characteristic causes and results from his study of it : 'The characteristic causes are youthfulness, having plenty to eat and drink, and wealth. The characteristic results are further eating and drinking, sexual activity, larking about, hitting and killing, taking other people's property and privileges, jeering at people, and disobeying authority both human and divine. The causes are ones which produce energy or make a person, as we say, "full of himself", and inclined to indulge his own desires and wishes without respecting the wishes, rights, and commands of other people. The results are actions which are, at the best, useless, and in most cases definitely wrong. Hybris is therefore having energy or power and misusing it self-indulgently'[46]. To this he adds five further points to make its meaning more precise :

---

43 'Hybris in Athens', G & R 23 (1976), 14-31.

44 'Hybris and Dishonour : I', G & R 23 (1976), 177-193.

45 Eg., J.J. Fraenkel, 'Hybris' (Utrecht, 1941); R. Lattimore, Story Patterns in Greek Tragedy (Ann Arbor, 1969), 24-25; M. Gagarin, 'Socrates, Hybris and Alciabes' Failure', Phoenix 31 (1977), 22-37; W.C. Greene, Moira : Fate, Good, Evil (Cambridge, Mass., 1944); H. North, Sophrosyne : Self-knowledge and Self-restraint in Greek Literature (Ithaca/New York, 1966); H.G. Robertson, 'The Hybristes in Aeschylus', TAPA 98 (1967) 373-382; A. Michelini, ' ὝΒΡΙΣ and Plants', HSCP 82 (1978), 35-44, for hybris in a botanical context referring to excessive growth in plants.

46 'Hybris in Athens', 21 and 15-21 generally.

a. *Hybris* is always bad;
b. it is always voluntary;
c. it is most frequently the result of such things as youth, wealth, excess of food and drink;
d. it is not as a rule religious;
e. it often involves a victim, and is more serious when it does[47].

Hybris as a term denoting excessive behaviour already appears in the earliest Greek literature, eg., in Homer's Odyssey. In Odysseus' absence, the suitors are accused of feasting ὑβρίζοντες and ὑπερφίαλοι, 'arrogantly', in his house[48]. More than overeating is denoted by the term. It is applied nineteen times to the suitors throughout the poem and 'forms a significant part in the indictment against them; it indicates clearly the enjoyment they take in refusing to pay the proper respect and honour to anyone them come into contact with, and in particular to destroying the wealth and honour of the house of Odysseus[49].

Hybris is traditionally and closely associated with the term κόρος, 'fulness', 'satiety' or 'having too much', and the verb κορέννυμι (passive or middle), 'to be sated or glutted with a thing', 'having one's fill of a thing'. They are virtually equivalent in meaning being used interchangeably in many instances. Both notions are frequently joined with *ploutos* and *hybris* is said to either produce *koros* or *ploutos*, or to be produced by them[50]. Overindulgence

---

[47] Ibid., 21-23.

[48] Od., 1.224-229; see also D.M. MacDowell, 'Hybris in Athens', 16.

[49] N.R.E. Fisher, 'Hybris and Dishonour : I', 186. Cf. Homer, Od. 3.207.

[50] See D.M. MacDowell, 'Hybris in Athens', 16. Cf. *koros* begets *hybris* : Solon (West, IEG) 6; Theognis 153 (*tiktei toi kopos hybrin*), *hybrin korou matera* : Pindar 0.13.10; *koron hybrios huion* : Herodotus 8.77; 'incontinence, the mother of hybris' : Stobaeus 4.7.65; cf. Xenophon 01.13.9. Cf. 'wealth begets hybris' : Euripides, Fr. 438; *ploutou* ... *koron* : Pindar, I. 3.2; *ploutou pros koron* : Aeschylus, Ag. 382 (ibid., 374-380, *koros/hybris*); 'It is characteristic of wealth to be hybristic' : Aristophanes, Wealth 563f; *hybrizei ploutō kekorēmenos* : Theognis 751; *plousios* and *hybris* : Dio Chrysostom, Disc. 76.7; *hybri kekorēmenos* : Herodotus 3.80; *hyperphialousin* ... *koresaiato* : Homer, Od. 14.28' hybrizontes hyperphialōs : ibid., 1.227. For further examples, see R. R. Doyle, ' Ὄλβας, ΚΟΡΟΣ, ῞ΥΒΡΙΣ and ἌΤΗ from Hesiod to Aeschylus', Traditio 26 (1970), 293-303.

or wealth caused a person to become a *hybristēs* or he may be said to indulge further because he is *hybristēs*. Wealth is implicit in behaviour of the *hybris* kind. As 'the possibility of eating excessively seldom arose' for many Greeks, it is 'not surprising that we find *hybris* associated with wealth and riches, with having not just plenty of food but plenty of everything'[51]. The association between *hybris* and *ploutos* is most evident in Aristotle as we shall see later.

Fisher's concern is with the 'effect produced by the action on its victim, and on the mentality of the agent who wishes to produce that effect' and in particular with the ideas of shame and honour in Aristotle's definition of *hybris*[52]. Aristotle appears to regard *hybris* as the worst kind of slight (ὀλιγωρία) : 'He who insults another (ὁ ὑβρίζων) also slights him; for *hybris* consists in causing injury or annoyance whereby the sufferer is disgraced (αἰσχύνη ἐστὶ τῷ πασχόντι), not to obtain any other advantage for oneself besides the performance of the act, but for one's own pleasure; for retaliation is not insult, but punishment.

The cause of the pleasure felt by those who insult (*tois hybrizousin*) is the idea that, in ill-treating others, they are more fully showing superiority (ὑπερέχειν). That is why the young and wealthy (*hoi plousioi*) are given to insults; for they think that, in committing them, they are showing their superiority. Dishonour is characteristic of insult; and one who dishonours another slights him (*hybreōs de atimia, ho d'atimāzon oligōrei*); for that which is worthless has no value, either as good or evil. Hence Achilles in his wrath exclaims : "He has dishonoured me (*atimoun*), since he keeps the prize he has taken for himself", and "(has treated me) like a dishonoured (*atimētos*) vagrant", as if being wrath for these reasons'[53].

---

[51] D.M. MacDowell, 'Hybris in Athens', 16. See K.J. Dover, Greek Popular Morality, 110-111, for the association of *hybris* and *ploutos*.

[52] 'Hybris and Dishonour : I', 177.

[53] Rhet. 2.2.5-6.

Three important points emerge : the notion of dishonour (atimia); the state of mind of the hybrizōn; the notion of superiority (hyperechein). First, the effect of hybris upon the victim is to cause him dishonour and shame. It results in anger and a desire for revenge - i.e. the recovery of one's own honour - by punishing the ὑβρίζων by a legal action called the γράφη ὕβρεως[54]. Second, though, hybris does not simply refer to the effect or manifestation of it upon the victim; there must be deliberate intent to cause dishonour. Aristotle says in another passage : 'Such terms as hybris and theft further indicate purpose; for if a man has struck, it does not in all cases follow that he has committed hybris, but only if he has struck with a certain object, for instance, to bring disrepute (atimoun) upon the other or to please (ἡσθῆναι) himself'[55]. It is this state of mind which makes an act of assault into one of hybris. Thus Fisher expands MacDowell's definition to include 'the presence of an intention to insult and exult over another'[56].

Third, the idea of superiority or over-confidence is associated with the hybristic behaviour of the wealthy and powerful. Wealthy people, says Aristotle, are especially susceptible to hybris. Unlike the great-souled man who can act with restraint, the vain man (χαῦνος) cannot control his good fortune or position of superiority and becomes a hybristēs. Aristotle describes him in this way : 'It is true that even those who merely possess the goods of fortune may be haughty and insolent (ὑπερόπται καὶ ὑβρισταὶ); because without virtue it is not easy to bear good fortune becomingly, and such men, being unable to carry their

---

54 Cf. Aristotle, Rhet. 2.2.12. νόμος ὕβρεως in Athens, under which came all the more serious injuries done to a person. The injured party proceeded properly by γράφη ('indictment'). For instances of γράφη ὕβρεως see Isocrates 396A; Aeschines 3.14; Demosthenes 11.976; 18.1102; Athenaeus, Deipn. 6.266F-267A; and D.M. MacDowell, 'Hybris in Athens', 24-30.

55 Rhet. 1.13.10; cf. EN 7.6.4.

56 'Hybris and Dishonour : I', 180. Cf. Demosthenes 21.71ff.

prosperity, and thinking themselves superior (ὑπερέχειν) to the rest of mankind, despise (καταφρονεῖν) other people, although their own conduct is no better than another's. The fact is that they try to imitate the great-souled man (μεγαλόψυχος) without being really like him, and only copy him in what they can, reproducing his contempt for others but not his virtuous conduct. For the great-souled man is justified in despising other people - his estimates are correct; but most proud men have no good ground for their pride[57].

In a passage in his Rhetoric he further outlines the hybristic characteristics of the rich. Their wealth makes them <u>hybristei</u> and arrogant (ὑπερήφανοι). It becomes their standard of measurement and they consider everything can be purchased with it. Partly due to <u>hybris</u> and partly due to ἀκρασία, 'intemperance', they shame and dishonour others by unjust acts such as αἰκία, 'assault', and μοιχεία, 'adultery'[58]. As Fisher rightly describes this attitude, 'the rich treat people just as they like because they think that they are the most important people in existence, and that if anyone objects they will be able to buy off trouble, by compensation or by bribery of officials[59]. Their over-confident behaviour is further reflected in their conduct toward those in distress. They themselves have only experienced good fortune and confidently expect it to continue. Instead of showing pity, they <u>hybrizein</u>. That is, they take pleasure in insulting the disadvantaged,

---

[57] EN 4.3.21-22. Cf. ibid., 4.3.36; Rhet. 2.12.2 : 'good-fortune (εὐτυχία) includes noble birth (εὐγένεια), wealth (πλοῦτος) and power (δύναμις)'; Pol. 4.9.4-6 : ὑπερκάλον, ὑπερίσχυρον, ὑπερευγενῆ, ὑπερπλούσιον and ὕβρις; ἢ τάναντία, ὑπέρπτωχον, ὑπερασθενῆ, σφόδρα ἄτιμον; Cicero, de Off. 1.26.90.

[58] Rhet. 2.16.1-4.

[59] 'Hybris and Dishonour : I', 182.

in ridiculing and laughing at them[60]. The superiority of the hybrizōn is not limited toward his social inferiors. Many instances of hybristic behaviour occur 'within a relationship of equality when one party's claim to be superior and to treat the other as an inferior is naturally resented'[61].

Given this kind of conduct and attitude, it is easy to see why one of the most common characteristics of hybris is that denoted by στάσις, 'discord', and similar notions of division and disorder. Hybris results in either political or social factions and together with κέρδος, 'gain', is the most obvious cause of faction between the dominating classes and the disadvantaged. 'For', says Aristotle, 'when men in office show insolence and greed (ὑβριζόντων και πλεονεκτοῦντων), people rise in revolt against one another and against the constitutions that afford the opportunity for such conduct; and greed sometimes preys on private property and sometimes on common funds. It is clear also what is the power of honour and how it can cause stasis; for men form factions both when they are themselves dishonoured (atimazein) and when they see others honoured; and the distribution of honours is unjust when persons are either honoured or dishonoured against their deserts, just when it is according to desert. Excessive predominance causes faction, when some individual or body of men is greater or more powerful than is suitable to the state and the power of the government; for such are the conditions that usually result in the rise of a monarchy or dynasty'[62].

---

[60] Rhet. 2.8.2-3, 6. For the connection between hybris, loidoria and skōmma, see Xenophon, Cyr. 7.2.18; Aristotle, Rhet. 2.2.12; 2.12.16 (though educated hybris seems to remove the offensiveness from the words and it becomes a question of cleverness and humour). Plutarch Mor. 631 C.D.F.; 634 D-F. For hybris as a characteristic of the writers of Iambics who used loidoria see M.A. Grant, the Laughable, 42, 142.

[61] So N.R.E. Fisher, 'Hybris and Dishonour : I', 183.

[62] Pol. 5.2.3-4; cf. 5.3.3; 5.6.4-5. See above 59-60 for insult which leads to enmity.

Aristotle's remarks, as is self-evident, refer to political relations but the same stress on disorder and faction also occurs in reference to private social relations.

The passage, though, introduces another familiar kind of *hybris*, that associated with kingship or power[63]. It was generally considered that the danger and consequence of *hybris* were at their greatest with tyrants or with a ruling class obsessed with their power and rights. As with *koros* and *ploutos*, *hybris* is said to either produce the *tyrannos* or in turn result from his abuse of privilege[64]. Similarly, Herodotus states that advantage or power breeds *hybris*. He is concerned with the ruler who cannot be reproached by law. He asks : 'What right order is there to be found in monarchy when the ruler can do what he will; nor to be held to account for it (τῇ ἔξεστι ἀνεύθυνῳ ποιέειν τὰ βούλεται;) ? ... sated with power he will do many reckless deeds, some from insolence, some from jealousy (τὰ υὲν γὰρ ὕβρι κεκορημένος ἔρδει πολλὰ καὶ ἀτάσθαλα, τὰ δὲ φθόνῳ)'[65]. Aware of this danger also, Dio Chrysostom urges a ruler to act with restraint (σωφροσύνη), the traditional antithesis of *hybris*. He says : 'They have it in their power to do anything (ἔξεστι πάντα ποιεῖν)'; thus, 'who needs more steadfast control than he to whom anything is permissible ? (τίνι δὲ σωφροσύνης ἐγκρατεστέρας ἢ ᾧ πάντα ἔξεστι)'; [66].

Hybris in relation to unbridled power and the excessive maltreatment and contempt of subjects is a common theme in Greek authors. Abuse of power is the commonest single use of

---

[63] Cf. K.H. Waters, 'Herodotos and Politics'. G & R 19 (1972) 136-150, where Herodotos examines the affairs of some fifty tyrants in which the characteristic of *hybris* figures prominently. See also, P.A.L. Greenhalgh, 'Aristocracy and Its Advocate in Archaic Greece' G & R 19 (1972), 190-207. For the Roman tyrant and the use of libido and other terms in a similar manner to *hybris*, see J.R. Dunkle, 'The Greek Tyrant and Roman Invective', 151-171.

[64] Cf. Sophocles OT. 873.

[65] 3.80.

[66] Disc. 62.2.4; cf. Disc. 3.10 : ' ... who a keener sense of justice than he who is above the law (ἢ τῷ μείζονι τῶν νόμων;), who a more rigorous self-control than he to whom all things are lawful ? (ἢ ὅτῳ πάντα ἔξεστιν;)'

hybris in Tragedy. Aeschylus often associates it with the tyrant and the antithesis between eleutheria and tyrannis and between sōphrosynē and hybris is clearly evident. Similarly, many of the examples of hybristic conduct in Aristotle's Politics are of tyrants who indiscriminately inflict serious humiliation and dishonour upon their subjects and violate their rights[67]. As I will show later, the phrase, πάντα ἔξεστιν, not only described the total freedom of the king to do as he pleased, but represented a popular catchcry of a person of rank and amounted to an assertion of independence from his fellow man and to those who would impinge upon his freedom[68].

The terminology in the passage in Herodotus and Dio are important for it appears to be used in a similar manner by Paul in his conflict with his enemies. I simply draw attention to it now. In Herodotus, hybris is associated with korenymmi and kingship and the maxim so often related to unrestrained freedom, ποιεῖν τα βούλεται. In Dio, sōphrosynē is associated with panta exestin, basileia and tyrannis[69].

Hybris also shows itself in the form of excessive sexual activity. Euripides uses the verb hybrizō to denote adultery[70] and Demosthenes, in relation to the treatment of a free woman, uses it to mean 'to treat as he pleased'[71]. In Aeschylus' play, The Suppliants, five out of the ten uses of hybris and its derivatives refer to 'excessive male desire

---

67 Eg., Pol. 5.2.3-4; 5.4.4-5; 5.6.3-4; 5.7.12; 5.8.8-9; 5.9.13-18.

68 Hybris is very close in meaning to panta exestin and similar notions of freedom when used in this context. See M. Pohlenz, Freedom in Greek Life and Thought (ET : Dordecht, 1966), 52-56, for the desire for freedom of action as leading to hybris, an over-stepping of the bounds set by nature. See also H.F. North, 'A Period of Opposition to Sophrosyne in Greek Thought', TAPA. 78 (1946), 1-17; and my discussion below 285-288.

69 For the idea of Princeps Supra Leges, see Ch. Wirszubski, Libertas as a Political Idea at Rome During the Late Republic and Early Principate (Cambridge, 1968), 130-136.

70 El. 947; cf. Hipp. 1073; Hec. 785.

71 19.309.

for women' and can be translated as 'lust'[72]. However, it covers a wide range of sexual outrages, rapes, seductions committed against women, girls and boys, especially under constraint[73], in which the act brings shame and dishonour on the victims and their associates or family[74].

MacDowell's fourth observation is that hybris is never essentially a religious term. Only a small proportion of the instances of hybris in Greek literature and marginally more in tragedy include the gods. This only occurs where they are treated hybristically themselves or where they are concerned directly as defenders of human morality. The vast majority of uses of hybris and its derivatives and associated terminology occur in general moral and social contexts in the same way as terms such as sōphrosynē and timē[75].

Finally, hybris is regarded as behaviour which oversteps the bounds or limits or which exceeds the mean. It is traditionally opposed to the word sōphrosynē which is a moral and intellectual term that, like hybris, has a wide range of meanings. It basically means 'soundness of mind', having an unimpaired intellect[76] and is translated by such words as 'sanity', 'moderation', 'self-control' and 'prudence', depending on the context[77]. Unlike hybris, which remained relatively unchanged in meaning, sōphrosynē underwent periods of development, most notably by Plato, and acquired an extensive range of meanings. It was generally regarded as one of the four cardinal virtues - along with φρόνησις, δικαιοσύνη, ἀνδρεία - of which virtue (ἀρετή) is composed.

---

[72] So D.M. MacDowell, 'Hybris in Athens', 17. Cf. Plato, Leg. 835D; Xenophon, Mem. 2.1.30; Dio Chrysostom, Disc. 77/78. 29; Plutarch, Mor. 555C.

[73] See N.R.E. Fisher, 'Hybris and Dishonour : I', 188. Cf. Philo, de Praem et Paen. 24.139.

[74] N.R.E. Fisher, 'Hybris and Dishonour : I', 187-188.

[75] So Ibid., 178; D.M. MacDowell, 'Hybris in Athens', 22-23.

[76] H. North, Sophrosyne, 3 n.10 for etymology.

[77] I cannot, of course, do justice to the meaning and development of this concept in Greek or Roman authors. For an extensive treatment see H. North, Sophrosyne, espec. 150-153, 197, 243.

Two of the most common *topoi* of *sōphrosynē* are those expressed by the familiar maxims μηδεν ἀγαν, 'nothing too much', and γνωϑι σαυτον, 'know yourself'. These sayings were generally attributed to Chilon, one of the Seven Wise Men, and were inscribed in the late sixth century over the entrance to the Alcmaeonid Temple of Apollo[78]. The proverb, *mēden agan*, embodies a notion of restraint or measure concerned with the observance of moderation and became closely associated with the doctrine of the mean (*mesotēs*, *to meson*, *to metrion*) . In relation to *sōphrosynē*, it means the recognition of limits set by the gods or by human society[80]. *Metrios*, 'measurable, within measure', and *mesos*, 'middle', and their derivatives, *metrotēs* and *mesotēs*, are etymologically distinct but Aristotle uses both as synonyms in relation to his concept of moderation . Allied with *sōphrosynē*, they embody the traditional Greek instinct for moderation, restraint of impulse, and measure in all things. The mean is the rule of no excess, a device by which to measure excess (*hyperbolē*) or defect (*elleipsis*) and thus arrive at right conduct[82]. Implicit then in *sōphrosynē* is the observation of boundaries or limits upon human thought and behaviour. *Hybris*, as opposed to *sōphrosynē*, refers to the arrogant violation of divine or human limits. As such it is an affront to both the gods and man and the violator is open to the punishment of the gods or the sanctions imposed by society. Examples are numerous in Greek

---

[78] See H.W. Parke and D.E.W. Wormell, The Delphic Oracle (Oxford, 1956), 386-392, espec. 392 n.24.

[79] Diodorus Siculus, 9.10.1-3, renders it 'to know the measure of self'. Cf. similar sayings in Solon: *mēte lian*, 'not too much', 5.8; *en metroisi*, 'within the measure or boundaries', 4.7 (said of the proud rich); *metron gnōmosynēs*, 'the measure of judgment which knows the limits of everything', 16.1-2.

[80] It is the essence of Aeschylean *sōphrosynē*, where *sōphrosynē* and *hybris* and associated notions are consistently and strongly opposed to each other. See H. North, Sophrosyne, 33-50; M. Pohlenz, Freedom, 55-59.

[81] EN 4.3.8, 18. 4.5.1. See Pindar, Pyth. 2.34; Is. 6.71; Hesiod, Op. 692, 718.

[82] Aristotle, EN 2.2.6-7; 2.9.9.

literature and I cite just a few of them to further demonstrate interaction of the notions I have just discussed.

In Pindar, Ixion's failure to be content with his great prosperity and his desire for Hera, the wife of Zeus, exemplifies hybris and the failure to respect the metron[83]. Sophocles has Athena remind Odysseus of sōphrosynē in her warni against the danger of boastful speech against the gods, of unwarranted pride in strength or wealth and of the immutability of all mortals. Here the sōphrōn aner is approved but the arrogant kakoi, who in this context are clearly the hybristai, are abhorred[84]. Hesiod describes poverty in terms of limits in the sense that it is a gift of the gods. Thus to reproach a poor man because of his poverty and to expose him to insult and humiliation is regarded as hybris, an overstepping of the set bounds[85].

One of the more common instances of hybris relates to breach of hospitality. I have previously referred to the common Homeric usage of hybris as the arrogant violation of the rules of hospitality during the absence of the host[86]. Underlying the notion of hospitality is the belief that 'the things a man possesses are given by the gods'. Thus as a recipient himself, the host becomes an obligated giver. He must receive the itinerant stranger hospitably and fulfil his duties toward him. In return, he can expect honour and respect from his guest, and both receive blessings from the gods as a result. Failure on the part of either host or guest to observe the rules of hospitality is regarded as a display of hybris[87].

The second maxim, gnōthi sauton, acquired the greater reputation and is cited more frequently in Greek literature. Self-knowledge as an important component of sōphrosynē is first hinted at in Homer's Iliad where it is combined with

83 Pyth. 2.27-34.

84 Ajax 127-133; cf. Antig. 604-605 where Antignone's reckless pride is an example of a futile overstepping by man (ὑπερβασία ἀνδρῶν) against the power of Zeus.

85 WD. 717-718.

86 For details, see above 183.

87 See J.B. Mathews, Hospitality, 45-60, 155-160.

the appreciation of the boundary between god and man. Apollo responds to Poseidon's challenge to battle by claiming that Poseidon would not consider him to be sōphron if he were to fight him for the sake of mortals[88]. In the Archaic period, 'Know Thyself' is the advice of Apollo to mankind, and sōphrosynē has as its consequence, 'thinking mortal thoughts'[89]. Heraclitus made explicit the association implied by Homer between self-knowledge and sōphrosynē. He says : 'It is possible for all men to know themselves and sōphronein, and further, sōphronein is the greatest aretē, and sophia consists in speaking the truth and acting in accordance with nature, paying heed to it'[90]. Here sōphrosynē means 'contemplation of the human soul which is the source of human understanding' thus leading to an awareness of the laws which govern the human soul and the cosmos[91]. Herodotus develops these ideas and sōphrosynē and hybris are related in his works to 'the nothingness of man, the mutability of human affairs, the jealousy of the gods, and the danger of hybris in encroaching on boundaries set by nature or by the divine[92]. Sophocles' instances of hybris and sōphrosynē are related to gnōthi sauton rather than mēden agan and they generally refer to offences against human standards rather than an affront to the gods. Hybris results from a failure of a person to know himself perfectly or to know the truth about his circumstances[93].

Sōphrosynē in relation to self-knowledge continued to undergo development, especially in Plato[94], though the basic framework remained intact. The meaning of hybris, however, by the fifth century was largely settled and its basic framework was retained by later authors. Thus hybris is

---

88 21.462-464.

89 H. North, Sophrosyne, 4-5.

90 Fr. 116DK; 112DK.

91 So H. North, Sophrosyne, 27.

92 Ibid., 28 and 56 n. 53.

93 Eg., Ajax 779; see also H. North, Sophrosyne, 50-68.

94 H. North, Sophrosyne, 150-158.

is conceived of as arrogance or insolence borne out of an ignorance (anoētos, amathia) of one's true self. The hybristic person's failure to think mortal thoughts leads to an arrogant violation of limits, of both human and divine law. It is primarily a social concept which indicates the breach of one's assigned status and thus results in dishonour and shame. It is most commonly caused by undue pride in strength and wealth, both of which are given by the gods. The hybrist is regarded as a fool (aphrōn), a man who is not aware of his own limitations[95]; a boaster (alazōn) who pretends to possess praiseworthy qualities which he does not have or only possesses in limited measure[96]; a vain man who gives himself to hybris due to his wealth and false conception of his superiority over both his equals and inferiors. He is considered foolish (ἀνόητος); he succeeds as judged by his own standards (πρὸς ἑαυτὸν μὲν ὑπερβάλλει); the vain are deficient in self-knowledge (ἑαυτοὺς ἀγνοοῦντες). This behaviour is at times referred to as μανία, 'madness', irrational behaviour due to an error in common knowledge[98].

ii. The idea of hybris in 1 Cor. 4:6-13.

I now return to our passage, 1 Cor. 4:6-13. Though the word hybris does not appear in it[99], some of the more important vocabulary and ideas associated with it in Greek

---

95 See below 352-353.

96 ὁ ἀλαζών as excess, Aristotle EN 2.7.12; 4.7.1-17. Cf. id., EE 2.3.4 : ἀλαξονεία, 'boasting' or 'arrogance' as excess of the mean, which is αλήθεια, 'sincerity', 'truth'; Theophrastus, Char. 23, ἀλαξονεία.

97 Aristotle, EN 4.3.3, 13, 20-21, 36.

98 Cf. Xenophon, Mem. 1.1.16; 3.9.6.

99 The noun hybris (2 Cor. 12:10) and the verb hybrizein (1 Thess. 2:2) appear in Paul in relation to treatment he has received as an apostle. The meanings of these two words is the same as that found in Greek authors of 'insult' and 'to be shamefully treated'. Notice also the triad found so frequently in Greek literature : hybristēs, hyperēphanos, alazōn (Ro. 1:30).

authors are clearly present[100]. This leads me to suggest that the idea of hybris underlies the whole passage. In v. 6 Paul tells the Corinthians : 'I have applied all this to myself and Apollos for your benefit, brethren, that you may learn not to go beyond what is written (τὸ μὴ ὑπὲρ ἅ γέγραπται), that none of you may be puffed up (φυσιοῦν) of one against another.' This important phrase, τὸ μὴ ὑπὲρ ἅ γέγραπται, continues to be an enigma to scholars who have proffered three general explanations of it. First, the phrase belongs to the passage but the meaning is now obscure. Translations here vary considerably. There is no verb in the principal clause τὸ μὴ ὑπέρ and certain of the English versions insert a verb and sometimes an object to overcome the elliptical structure and make the phrase intelligible[101]. Commentators also offer a variety of explanations of ἅ γέγραπται. For some the clause is a general reference to the Old Testament which is implied by the use of as a formula for introducing quotations from scripture (eg. 1:19; 2:9; 3:19)[102]. Others refer it to the immediately preceding quotations from the Old Testament in 1:19, 31, 2:9, 3:19-20[103] though C. K. Barrett finds it difficult to see how a person could go beyond what precedes from chapter 1[104]. We shall see how this is possible, given our understanding of hybris, shortly.

M.D. Hooker suggests that Paul either coined the saying and had previously used it against those who added to the gospel he had taught them or that he is cleverly using one

---

[100] See H.G. Robertson, 'The Hybristes in Aeschylus' 373-374 for the list of synonyms, associated words and concepts which make up Aeschylus' rich and extensive vocabulary of hybris.

[101] Eg., AV - 'Not to think of men above'; RV - 'not to go beyond the things'; RSV - 'to live according to'; NEB - ' to keep within the rules'.

[102] Eg., G.G. Findlay, St. Paul's First Epistle to the Corinthians, The Expositor's Greek Testament II, 800.

[103] Eg., J.B. Lightfoot, Notes, 199; N.A. Dahl, 'Paul and the Church at Corinth', 328; M.D. Hooker, 'Beyond the Things Which are Written : an Examination of 1 Cor. IV.6' NTS 10 (1964), 129.

[104] 1 Cor. 107.

of his opponents' slogans against them[105]. A. Schlatter thought that the phrase was a slogan of the "Christ-group" who taught πάντα ἔξεστιν and was thus beyond the law and scripture[106]. He correctly stresses the connection between these two phrases but not for the right reasons or their real meaning. C. K. Barrett says that the use of the definite article το indicates that the following words are a quotation, if not from a book then from a current saying, thought not necessarily current in Corinth[107]. However, there is no evidence to suggest that the words formed a well known saying or proverb. Most scholars, while disagreeing on the meaning and application of the clause, consider it was readily known or recognized by the Corinthians. Recent commentators who accept the clause as it stands, after surveying the attempts to explain it, suggest that the results are nothing more than guesswork and that the phrase remains unintelligible[108].

Second, a few scholars who have found the words incomprehensible in their context have concluded, without any attempt to amend it, that the text is corrupt[109]. Third, there is the view that the five words are a marginal gloss and make no sense whatsoever within the passage. Without this distortion, they say, the sentence reads

---

[105] 'Beyond the Things Which are Written', 129-132; cf. F.F. Bruce, 1 and 2 Corinthians (London, 1971) 48-49; N.A. Dahl, 'Paul and the Church at Corinth', 328, who suggests that the phrase represents a rebuff to Paul : 'We need no instructions beyond what is written. As spiritual men we can interpret the Scriptures for ourselves. Why ask Paul ?'

[106] Paulus der Bote Jesu, (Stuttgart, 1962), 154.

[107] 1 Cor. 106. Cf. P. Wallis, 'Ein neuer Auslegungsversuch der Stelle 1 Kor. 4.6', ThLZ (1950), 506-508, who suggests that τό points to a recognized principle or slogan, μὴ ὑπέρ.

[108] Eg., H. Conzelmann, 1 Cor. 85-86. See also the reservation expressed by C.K. Barrett, 1 Cor. 106.

[109] J. Moffatt, 1 Cor. 46.

clearly[110]. There is no manuscript evidence, however, to support this contention. Their problem is simply one of coherence, but by deleting the phrase, they remove the lynch-pin in Paul's argument.

As an alternative to these three viewpoints and in line with my suggestion that the idea underlying the passage is that of hybris, the phrase τὸ μὴ ὑπὲρ ἃ γέγραπται is a warning against excessive behaviour of the hybris kind. The word, hyper, denotes here the excessiveness of the behaviour or self-conception of certain Corinthians. In Greek authors, ὑπέρ, either as introducing a prepositional phrase or as a compound with other words, is used frequently to express hybristic behaviour or behaviour which is beyond moderation[111]. It has been suggested in fact, though wrongly, that hybris is cognate to hyper, meaning therefore excess in the sense of lack of moderation[112].

We have seen that hyper in our passage is neither

---

110 See W.F. Howard, '1 Corinthians 4:6 Exegesis or Emendation', ET 32 (1922) 479-80, who examines the arguments of J. Weiss, J.M.S. Baljon and W. Boussett. He inclines towards Baljon's suggestion that the copyist found in his copy the μὴ in the second ἵνα clause added above the εἱς (= α) or above the α of the ἵνα and made a note of this in the margin of the copy he was making. Thus he proposed that the words should be excised as a copyist's remark. Cf. also J. Héring, The First Epistle to the Corinthians ET (London, 1962), 28-29; C.S.C. Williams, I and II Corinthians, Peakes Commentary on the Bible (London, 1962), 956; A. Legault, 'Beyond the Things which are Written (1 Cor. IV.6), NTS 18 (1972), 227-231.

111 I quote but a few examples which arise in the passages on hybris which I considered previously. Aeschylus, Pers. 820 : ouk hyperpheu ... phronein, 'not to direct his thoughts too high'; i.e. to respect the limitations; ibid., 831 : hyperkompos 'overweening boldness'; cf. Septem. 391; Sophocles, Sept. 734-739 : hyperbasia,'overstepping'; Aristotle, EN 2.8.1; 4.6.9 : hyperbolē, 'excess'; ibid., 2.7.13; 4.3.13 : hyperballein, 'to exceed'; ibid., 4.3.21; Rhet. 2.2.6: hyperechein, 'to be superior' (pejor. sense); EN 4.3.21 : hyperoptēs, 'disdainful or haughty'; Homer, Od. 1.134, 227 : hyperphialos, 'overbearing or arrogant'; Aristotle, Ath. 5.3; Theophrastus, Chr. 24 : hyperēphania, 'arrogance or pride'; Aristotle, Rhet. 2.16.1; Pinder, Pyth. 2.25-30 : hyperphanos, 'overweening, arrogant or proud'; Aristotle, Rhet. 3.2.1-3 : mēte hyper to axiōea, 'not above the dignity'.

112 So. W.C. Greene, Moira, 18n.45, 22. However, for a more likely explanation, see O. Szemerenyi, 'The Origins of the Greek Lexicon : EX ORIENTE LUX', JHS 94 (1974), 157, who sees a Hittite origin, from the verb huwap - hup meaning 'maltreat, outrage or harm'.

accompanied by a substantive nor a verb. P. Wallis suggests that it should be read as an adverb rather than a preposition and likens it to the adverbial form it takes in 2 Cor. 11:23, ὑπὲρ ἐγώ ('I more'), where it forms a predicate to the question, διάκονοι Χριστοῦ εἰσιν;[113]. This use is significant in that ὑπὲρ ἐγώ forms one element in a context in which excessive forms of behaviour and attitudes are compared (11:22-23) and it would support my contention that something similar is involved in 1 Cor. 4:6. It is difficult, though, to see how ἃ γέγραπται could follow an adverbial use of ὑπέρ. Rather I suggest that τὸ μὴ ὑπὲρ, 'the note above', should be understood as introducing a prepositional phrase which functions like an adjective or an adverb. If, as some have suggested, γέγραπται denotes a scripture quotation or scripture in general, Paul could be simply telling the Corinthians that they should learn 'not to be unscriptural' or 'not to think unscripturally'. I shall return to the significance of this interpretation in the wider context of chapters 1-4 soon. The negative μη, with a substantive adjective or adverb, is used in Greek literature either generically or without the article, either with or without a verb. In Aristophanes, ἡ μὴ 'μπειρία is translated as 'inexperience' and is equivalent to the phrase τὸ μὴ ἔχειν ἐμπειρίαν[114]. In Demosthenes, the words τὴν ἐλευθερίαν καὶ τὸ μηδέν' ἔχειν δεσπότην αὐτῶν mean 'freedom and independence'[115] and similar constructions, τὸ μὴ 'νδικον and τὸ μὴ καλὸν, occur in Sophocles[116]. This translation obviates the need to see the article τὸ as introducing a

---

[113] 'Ein neuer Auslegungsversuch der Stelle', 506-508. Cf. Phil. 3:4 for an equivalent phrase, ἐγὼ μᾶλλον, found interestingly in a passage with similar content and intent.

[114] Ec. 115.

[115] 18.296.

[116] OT 682 and Ant. 370. Cf. Aeschylus, Eu. 432 : τὰ μὴ δίκαια μὴ νικᾶν; Pr. 1012 : τῷ φρονοῦντι μὴ καλῶς; Ag. 927 : τὸ μὴ κακῶς φρονεῖν ; Ag. 349 : τὸ δ' εὖ κρατοίη μὴ διχορρόπως ἰδεῖν ; Plato, Grg. 459B : ὁ μὴ ἰατρός ; Lg. 966C, D : τὴν μὴ ἐπιτροπὴν εἶναι τὸ μηδέποτε ...

slogan or proverb.

Two other passages in Paul's letters may help us to understand the meaning of the phrase. In Rom. 12:3 Paul talks about excessive or moderate behaviour in a manner which recalls the traditional Hellenic commonplaces of self-knowledge, thinking mortal thoughts, and the associated ideas of divine endowment and measurement. He tells the Romans not to hink thoughts above what is proper (μὴ ὑπερφρονεῖν παρ' ὃ δεῖ φρονεῖν) but to think modest thoughts (φρονεῖν εἰς τὸ σωφρονεῖν) because of the great diversity of gifts given to mankind by God. This means to think according to the measure of faith (μέτρον πίστεως) which God has assigned (ἐμέρισεν) them. Paul's thought here has caused one classical scholar to describe it as almost Hellenistic in character[117]. This constellation of ideas is also present in 1 Cor. 4:6-13 and in 2 Cor. 10:12-13 as well. Paul protests : 'Not that we venture to class or compare ourselves with some of those who commend themselves. But when they measure themselves by one another, and compare themselves with one another, they are without understanding. But we will not boast beyond limit, but will keep to the limits God has appointed us, to reach even you'[118].

V. 13 in particular has been discussed in relation to Paul's apostolic authority, either in terms of a Gentile-Jew division of ministry or assigned geographical spheres. I shall argue against these views in a later chapter. For the present discussion, I draw attention to the vocabulary and ideas which Paul draws upon. In v. 12 three technical terms are used together and they are central to the nature of the conflict between Paul and his enemies - συγκρίνω 'compare', συνίστημι, 'recommend', μετρῶ, 'measure'. The first and second terms are the subjects of later chapters and here

---

117 See H. North, Sophrosyne, 317.

118 For a discussion of the textual problems, see C.K. Barrett, 2 Cor. 263ff, who favours this longer reading. For the short text see R. Bultmann, Der Stil., 194-195.

I concern myself with the meaning of metrō and related subjects in this passage. Paul accuses his rivals of ἐν ἑαυτοῖς ἑαυτοὺς μετροῦντες and thus they are οὐ συνιᾶσιν, 'without understanding'. By comparison, Paul and his associates will not εἰς τὰ ἄμετρα καυχησόμεθα, a phrase which tells us what ἐν ἑαυτοῖς ἑαυτοὺς μετροῦντες involves. His opponents have made themselves the measure or standard of assessment and have not subjected themselves to what Paul considers to be the true measure of apostleship[119]. From the larger context, and indeed implied by the terms sygkrinō and synistēmi, we can see that they consider themselves superior to Paul and that they have made invidious comparisons between themselves and him. Further, they have abused and insulted him and tried to displace him as the apostle in Corinth. Paul describes their arrogance and pretension as a lack of self-knowledge (οὐ συνιᾶσιν); they have simply failed to recognize the true standard and have overstepped the mark. Paul, however, suggests his apostleship has an external measure, ὁ θεὸς μέτρου, and says he will only boast κατὰ τὸ μέτρον τοῦ κανόνος.

Metron, as I have shown, is a technical term which expresses the Greeks' traditional inclination towards moderation in all things; an inclination which Aristotle systematized in his doctrine of the mean. In Pindar, both 'pursuing the true mean (metra) and holding to that mean in the act besides' is what commends a man to his fellows[120], and Cleobulus simply states : 'metron is best'[121]. Such behaviour reveals the measure of judgment; that is, conduct which knows the limit of everything[122] and is the opposite of the lack of understanding (ou syniasin) of which Paul accuses his enemies. Behaviour which is judged to be excessive meets with consistent disapproval. ἄμετρα often has a moral nuance and can be

---

119 Cf. the idea of aretē as a standard or measure of behaviour Aristotle, Pol. 4.9.1.

120 See Pindar, Is. 6.71; Solon 4. 7; Hesiod, WD. 694, 720.

121 DK 10.1.

122 Solon 16.1-2.

translated as 'immoderate' and does not differ greatly in meaning from hyper metron[123]. κανών can be translated metaphorically as 'standard' or 'measure' and is used in association with metron with this sense in Greek authors[124].

Aristotle's comparison of the vain man and the great-souled man contains many parallel notions to our passage and the surrounding chapters 10-12[125]. The vain man's conduct is an excess (hyperbolē) of the mean[126]. He 'exceeds as judged by his own standards' (pros heauton men hyperballein)[127], a common characteristic of excessive or hybristic behaviour[128]. He is both haughty and insolent (hyperoptēs kai hybrietēs), given to thinking himself superior (hyperchein) and despising (kataphronein) all. Unlike the megalopsychos, who is justified in his contempt for others and for his air of superiority, the vain man has no ground for pride[129]. He claims much without deserving it and is regarded as foolish (anoētos)[130] and lacking in self-knowledge (heauton agnoōn)[131]. By contrast, the great-souled man observes 'due measure' (metriōs echei) in regard to wealth, power, good and bad fortune in general'[132] and is correct in his self-assessment (doxazei alēthōs)[133].

Paul, then, in 2 Cor. 10:12-13 is drawing upon the conventional language of moderation to commend his own apostolic behaviour, and of immoderation to discredit his

---

123 Cf. Plato, Lg. 690E. Ametrōs : Xenophon, Cyr. 1.6.34; Diogenes, Epp. 46. Hyper metron : Theognis 498; Plato, Rep. 621A.

124 Cf. Epictetus 3.4.4-6, κανών as the standard of behaviour, i.e. showing others how to act; Euripides, Hec. 602 (pejorative use); El. 52. For kanōn and metron see Aristotle, EN 3.4.4-5; Demosthenes 18.296.

125 EN 4.3.1-38.

126 EN 2.7.7; 4.3.8.

127 EN 4.3.13.

128 Cf. Euripides, El. 52; Demosthenes 18.296.

129 Aristotle, EN 4.3.20-22, 36.

130 EN 4.3.3.

131 EN 4.3.36.

132 EN 4.3.18.

133 EN 4.3.22.

enemies. Their excessiveness, as seen in their boasting of their superiority and their use of a standard to make invidious comparisons with Paul in an attempt to humiliate and shame him before the Corinthians, can properly be described as hybris. It is possible that Paul alludes to this arrogant maltreatment of him by his use of ἐν ὕβρεσιν in 12:10. It has not been noticed before how pervasive the notion of hybris is in chapters 10-13 and how important it is for our understanding of the nature of the conflict and the kind of language which confronts us. I will discuss this further in chapter 9.

I suggest then, that the phrase ha gegraptai conveys the notion of limits or boundaries in the sense of moderation in much the same way as metron does in 2 Cor. 10:13. Even if gegraptai alludes to scripture, and I believe it does, the behaviour or attitudes which go beyond (hyper) are regarded by Paul, as we shall now see, in terms of the ideas and vocabulary commonly associated with hybris. Thus the phrase functions as a kind of 'mean' or conveys the idea of moderation much in the same fashion as the traditional phrase mēden agan[134]. τὸ μὴ ὑπὲρ ἃ γέγραπται, then, represents counsel for moderation, a warning against behaving excessively or overstepping the boundaries, or against being hybristēs. There is more conclusive evidence to support this interpretation within the passage and I now direct my attention to it.

The phrase forms part of a final (ἵνα) clause and is preceded by the words ἵνα ἐν ἡμῖν μάθητε. The verb μανθάνω, I suggest, introduces into the context the notion of 'self-knowledge', something that certain of the Corinthians lack. Paul has said earlier that these people have deluded themselves into thinking that they are wise (δοκεῖ σοφὸς εἶναι) (3:18), evidenced by their boasting in men (καυχάσθω ἐν ἀνθρώποις) (3:21; cf. 3:4). Rather, they should become foolish (μωρός) so that they may become wise (σοφός). I suggest further that the antithetical terms, σοφός (σοφία) and μωρός (μωρία),

---

134 For details, see above 191-192.

should be understood in the context of discussions of self-knowledge in relation to *sōphrosynē* and *hybris*. This antithesis is important for our understanding of the words, *ha gegraptai*, for on each of the four occasions the term is used in chapters 1-3 it relates to 'knowledge' in one form or another and in the other quotation without the *gegraptai* introduction a similar notion is involved[135]. In each instance, God is seen to be all wise, all knowing and independent as compared with man whose knowledge is limited and futile and the discussion in chapters 1-4 revolves around this antithesis. Paul appears to be reminding them that they are only men, a common element in *sōphrosynē* and *hybris*. I take it then that the phrase *to mē hyper ha gegraptai* picks up this discussion and is a warning against overstepping the limits of human knowledge set by God. *Ha gegraptai* then refers to the *gegraptai* quoted in the previous chapters[136] and to the concept of self-knowledge. It is not at all surprising, in my opinion, that a few Greek texts insert *phronein* after *mē* to fill out the meaning, though the variant is poorly represented[137]. Paul sums up in himself and Apollos the lessons to be learned from all this. He offers himself and Apollos as examples of true wisdom so that in them the offenders may learn *to mē hyper ha gegraptai*. This parallels very closely the idea of gaining self-knowledge in Euripides : 'That he may triumph not over my woes, and, taking of my pain, may learn sound wisdom's temperance (*sōphronein mathesetai*)'[138].

The second final clause in v. 6, ἵνα μὴ εἷς ὑπὲρ τοῦ ἑνὸς φυσιοῦσθε κατὰ τοῦ ἑτέπου, seems to have an exegetical function in relation to the first. The excessiveness implied

---

[135] Eg., 1:18 - *sophia* and *sophos*, *sunesis* and *sunetos*; 1:31 - *kauchasthai*; 2:9 - *ophthalmos* and *horaō*, *ous* and *akouein* (cf. 2 Cor. 12:6 - *blepein* and *akouein* and *akouein*; possibly *anabeinein* conveys a similar idea here); 3:19, 20 - *sophos*, *ginōskein*, *sophōn*; cf. 2:16 - *nous* and *symbibazein*.

[136] M.D. Hooker, 'Beyond the Things Which are Written', 128-130, is correct in her argument at this point.

[137] Eg., N^3, D^3, L, P, Syrr., Copt., Arm.

[138] Hipp. 730-731.

by ἵνα ... τὸ μὴ ὑπὲρ ἃ γέγραπται, which I have outlined in some measure, has given rise to the situation described in the second clause. What is implicit in the first is succinctly and explicitly stated in the second. Their immoderation, as measured by scripture, has resulted in their being puffed up (physioun) each (eis) on behalf of (hyper) one person - Paul, Apollos, Cephas - against another. Though it is better to see the reference in the ἵνα clause to Paul and Apollos rather than to the Corinthians themselves being puffed up against each other, the latter rendering is also possible. V. 7 goes on to discuss physioun in relation to distinctions between the Corinthians themselves and vv. 10-13 between the Corinthians and Paul. I suggest that the making of distinctions between apostles is closely associated with, if not, indeed caused by, their conceptions for themselves.

The word physioun - 'puff up, to be conceited, proud or arrogant' - is used almost exclusively by Paul in relation to the Corinthian's conduct[139]. It describes their attitude for or against an apostle or each other (4:6), or of Paul's enemies against him (4:18, 19). It is associated with a case of extreme sexual depravity (5:2), an overemphasis upon knowledge (8:1), or a spiritual gift (13:4). Finally, it is listed with a number of social vices which Paul expects to find present in the Corinthian church (2 Cor. 12:20). In two of these contexts, physioun is related to terminology which suggests the idea of hybris. In 5:1-9 it is linked with kauchasthai to describe the attitude or behaviour of those associated with a case of grave sexual misconduct which went beyond the bounds of accepted conventions. In 8:1-3 it is associated with the boastful assertion, πάντες γνῶσιν ἔχομεν, of those who eat meat which has been sacrificed to idols and blatantly disregard the injury done to their weaker brothers. This kind of knowledge puffs up (ἡ γνῶσις φυσιοῖ) and is contrasted to love which builds up. Such people delude themselves and lack true or perfect knowledge (εἴ τις δοκεῖ ἐγνωκέναι τι, οὔπω ἔγνω καθὼς δεῖ γνῶναι) which consists of loving God and being known by him.

---

139 See Col. 2:18 for the only other use.

In the context of 4:6-7, physioun denotes that arrogant behaviour which results from a failure in self-knowledge, a delusion in regard to sophia, which has led to the violation of accepted norms of behaviour. The notions of superiority and of overstepping the bounds are clearly stated in three questions in v. 7. The first question, τίς γάρ σε διακρίνει; has been rightly translated : 'Who concedes you any superiority?'[140]. The nature of this superiority is contained in the second and third questions : τί δὲ ἔχεις ὃ οὐκ ἔλαβες; εἰ δὲ καὶ ἔλαβες, τί καυχᾶσαι ὡς μὴ λαβών;. Underlying this second question is the idea of God as the benefactor who bestows all things upon the human race. In return, a man must recognize the gift with due gratitude. Acceptance of the gift, stressed here by the threefold use of lambanō, implies reciprocity and obligation. One received to return[141]. In classical terms that means reverencing the gods and honouring the boundaries set by them, knowing one's true self and one's limitations, and using one's possessions and rank in life with respect for one's fellows[142]. The violators in Corinth have transgressed these boundaries and this is clearly implied by Paul's third queston. They are boasting as if what they had received was not a gift but was inherently theirs. Instead of showing gratitude and humility, they are arrogant and boastful. Implicit in such language is the notion of freedom in regard to one's actions, of being unrestricted, of an independence which is tantamount to the pursuit of self-interest. As I have shown, this is characteristic of the behaviour of the wealthy and powerful in discussions of hybris and associated ideas in Greek authors[143].

Paul's description of the Corinthians reaches a climax in

---

[140] 'διακρίνω', Arndt and Gingrich, A Greek English Lexicon, 184, i.b.

[141] λαμβάνω, 'receive', 'accept' or 'take', depending on the context, is the most common Greek verb used to denote the recipient's acceptance of a benefit and is regarded as one of the three obligations of friendship.

[142] Cf. Seneca, de Ben. 2.30.1-2.

[143] For details, see above 188-189.

v. 8 in which he captures in three short sentences all the nuances contained in the preceding verses. He says : ἤδη κεκορεσμένοι ἐστέ˙ ἤδη ἐπλουτήσατε˙ χωρὶς ἡμῶν ἐβασιλεύσατε˙. Here we have three of the most common terms associated with _hybris_. _Koros_, 'fulness, satiety', and _korenymmi_, 'to be sated or glutted' (Pass. or mid.), are traditionally associated and virtually synonymous with hybris[144]. Two of the three groups of people of whom _hybris_ and _koros_ are said to be characteristic are the wealthy (_ploutos_) and rulers (_basileus_, _tyrannos_)[145]. This is convincing evidence indeed that the notion of _hybris_ underlies the passage and together with the preceding notions in vv. 6 and 7 it can be seen to form a coherent argument. Paul is accusing certain Corinthians of behaviour of the _hybris_ kind.

A similar range of ideas is present in Seneca's discussion of the attitude of the rich to their wealth and to others in his _de Beneficiis_. To the rich who show ingratitude to the gods by retaining their wealth which has been given to them instead of benefitting others, he says : 'Why do you spare your wealth as though it were your own ? You are but a steward. All these possessions that force you to swell with pride, and, exalting you above mortals, cause you to forget your own frailty (omnia ista, quae vos tumidos et supra humana elatos oblivisci cogunt vestrae fragilitatis); ... all these are not your own, they are committed to you for

---

[144] For details, see above 183-184.

[145] For details, see above 184, 188-189.

safekeeping (in depositi)'[146].

A passage in Philo's On the Virtues (30.161 - 32.176) has many of the same terminology and ideas. In it he makes only one explicit reference to hybris in the form of the proverb 'satiety begets violence' (τίκτει κόρος ὕβριν) (162) but the passage is rich in the hybris tradition.[147]

Pride and arrogance (ὑπεροψία καὶ ἀλαζονεία) are often the vices of those upon whom riches, honours and high offices (πλοῦτοι, δόξαι, ἡγεμονίαι) are bestowed and they lead to violence against slave and free alike (161-162).

Being elated and puffed up (διαιρόμενοι και φυσώμενοι) they forget that their strength (ἰσχύς) is a gift received from God (ὅτι δῶρον εἴληφε παρὰ θεοῦ) (163-165). Having become rich and received glory and honour (δόξα, τιμή)

---

[146] de Ben. 6.3.1-2; cf. ibid., 2.13.1-3; 4.5.1-6.5; 6.23.7-8; 7.10.6. Chapter 7 of de Beneficiis contains many parallel ideas and phrases to those expressed by Paul in the wider context in which 4:6-13 is set. Seneca says the greedy and powerful are like Onesicitus who pushed his arms beyond the bounds of nature (extra naturae terminos) driven by reckless greed (aviditas) whose limit is set by covetousness (cupiditas) (7.2.6); cf. 7.7.3 : no one has set limits to his own (boundary lines) (sibi nemo constituit). By comparison, the wise man (sapiens) lives within the limits set and performs his duties (7.3.27). Compare the following ideas : (1) All things belong to the wise man, though in reality he may possess nothing - de Ben. 7.6.2 : licet illius sint omnia (cf. 7.3.2 : unus est sapiens, cuius omnia sunt; 7.3.3 : Haec omnia mea sunt, therefore he covets nothing (ut nihi cupiat); 1 Cor. 3:21 : πάντα ὑμῶν ἐστιν; 3.22 : πάντα ὑμῶν. (2) All things belong to the gods (omnia deorum esse) 7.7.3; 1 Cor. 3:22 : πάντα ὑμῶν, ὑμεῖς δὲ Χριστοῦ, Χριστὸς δὲ θεοῦ. (3) 7.7.3 : the whole world is the temple of the gods (totum mundum deorum esse immortalium templum); 1 Cor. 3:16 : ὅτι ναὸς θεοῦ ἐστε. And also 7.7.1-5 and 1 Cor. 3:16-17, a person commits sacrilege by consuming and appropriating to his own use what belongs to the gods and he is subsequently punished by them. It is important to notice that de Beneficiis is a treatment of the morality of giving and receiving, of the social virtues of benefaction and gratitude. In chapter 7, giving and receiving is viewed in the context of divine benefaction and man's gratitude and of what constitutes appropriate behaviour on the part of the recipient in his social relations.

[147] For Philo's frequent use of the proverb, see e.g., Flacc. 11.91; de Prov. 2.12.

they make others poor and bring them ingloriousness and dishonour (ἀδοξία, ἀτιμία) (166).

Philo argues that as they have received (λαμβάνω) their gifts from God they should use them as God intended, for the universal benefit of others, making them rich and honoured and so on (169-170). Rather the ἀλαζών considers himself to be more than human and 'wholly divine (ὅλον δαίμονα) and claims 'to overstep the limits of human nature' (ὑπὲρ τοὺς ὅρους τῆς ἀνθρωπίνης φύσεως) (172)[148].

In conclusion, the hybrist 'considers himself superior to all in riches, estimation, beauty, strength, wisdom, temperance, justice, eloquence, knowledge; while everyone else he regards as poor, disesteemed, unhonoured, foolish, unjust, ignorant, outcast, in fact good for nothing' (174).

A comparison of the terms in this last paragraph and 1 Cor. 4:10-12 and their use indicates the close proximity of ideas in Philo and Paul.

ἐντιμότατος	ἔνδοξοι
ἰσχυρότατος	ἰσχυροί
φρονιμώτατος	φρόνιμοι
ἄτιμοι	ἄτιμοι
ἄφρονες	μωροί
καθάρματα	περικαθάρματα

Philo's clear reference to hybris leads me to suggest this tradition is the basis for understanding both passages.

Paul's words, as are those of Seneca and Philo, are typical of the hybris tradition and would have been felt

---

148 This parallels Philo's condemnation of the emperor Gaius, Leg. ad Gaium 75 : 'he claimed to remain no more within the limits of human nature but soared above them desiring to be thought a god'.

keenly by those against whom they are directed. 'Now you are sated! Now you are rich! Why, you have become kings, independently and self-indulgently!'[149]. I suggest that the nuance of status is present in the terms korennymi and plouteō and that they betray the social standing of these Corinthians. Both terms, particularly as they stand here at the pivotal point in Paul's argument, capture the idea of excessive behaviour expressed in the preceding verses. Basileuō heightens the emphasis seen in korennymi and plouteō. The koros and hybris of a king far exceed that of a wealthy man. As an absolute ruler, the Hellenistic king was above the law and independent of his subjects. Though he was subject to divine and natural laws which he embodied on earth as god's viceregent, should he be peverse and abuse the power given him, all things were permissible. He could do as he pleased[150].

In v. 8b Paul resorts to savage irony : 'And would that you did reign, so that we might share the rule with you!' It acts as an effective introduction to the antithetical comparison and peristasis catalogue in vv. 9-13. Paul commences the contrast between the hybristai and himself with a graphic metaphor drawn from the arena. It intensifies the irony in v. 8b : 'For I think that God has exhibited us as apostles last of all (eschatoi) like men sentenced to death (epithanatioi); because we have become a spectacle (theatron) to the world, to angels and to men'. It is almost a kind of mocking gladiatorial salute to the would-be kings : 'Hail, Emperor, greetings from men about to die' (Ave, Imperator, morituri te salutant). It links the notion of

---

[149] My paraphrase. Χωρὶς ἡμῶν could mean 'without our help', i.e., 'by yourselves'; cf. C.K. Barrett, 1 Cor. 110, 'apart from us (that is, without the assistance of such nonentities as Paul and Apollos)'. However, combining the idea of kingship with the nuances in the preceding verses and the antithetical comparison which follows, I take the meaning to be something akin to 'independently and for your own interests'.

[150] For details, see above 188-189. Cf. Dio Chrysostom, Disc. 62.2-4 and note the contrast with the good king who covets nothing because he has everything.

shame to the position of the apostle and Paul maintains the association throughout the following verses.

Three traditional antitheses follow in v. 10, in which Paul contrasts his shame as an apostle with the honour of the hybrists. He is mōros, asthenēs, and atimos; they are phronimoi, ischyroi and endoxoi. The first two antitheses reflect the two dominating motifs in chapters 1-3 - foolishness and wisdom[151], weakness and strength (dynamis and ischyros). The third antithesis, while already implicit in the preceding antithesis, emphatically expresses the notions of shame and honour. Paul had previously made a contrast of this kind in relation to the ou polloi sophoi, dynatoi and eugeneis in Corinth and those who were considered to be ta mōra, ta asthenē, and ta agenē; that is, the ta mē onta (1:26-28). Amazingly, Paul asserts that God has chosen the dishonourable to shame (kataischynō) the things held to be honourable. The contrast here, and I suggest in 4:10, is primarily a social one and the terms belong to the 'rhetoric of status'[152]. Paul assumes the position of someone who is socially disadvantaged or, possibly, of someone with status who has been humiliated and dishonoured. He is socially inferior; the hybrists are socially superior. Following the ideas of hybris in vv. 6-8 - of overstepping the mark, of excess, of superiority and arrogance - Paul appears to be placing himself in the position of one who is the victim of hybris. The viewpoint he expresses, then, is the traditional one in Greek authors of the sufferer whose status or rank has been violated. The hybrist not only considers himself to be superior in all respects,

---

151 Phronēsis and sophia as representing the practical and speculative wisdom respectively in Greek literature. H. Conzelmann, 1 Cor. 89, says the use of phronimoi instead of sophoi here as the antithesis of moros is 'merely a rhetorical variation without inherent meaning'.

152 See C. Forbes, 'Strength' and 'Weakness', 83. Contrasts of this kind are common in Greek authors, Ibid., 10-69, and belong to the topoi of arete or their contraries by which one either amplifies himself or depreciates his adversary before others. For details, see my discussion above 51-67. See also, for the sociological use of these terms, G. Theissen, 'Soziale Schichtung', 233-235.

especially when hybrizon, but intends that his conduct should dishonour or shame others, whether they are his equals or inferiors[153].

Both sides of Paul's antithesis are similar to the lists of the opposites which Aristotle describes as being an excess or deficient of the mean or what is moderate. His discussion is in a context in which he deals with the kind of standard or mode of life which a constitution should reflect, and the qualities or their opposites which he lists denote classes of people and the behaviour which he deems to be characteristic of them. Those who are 'exceedingly beautiful or strong or nobly born or rich' are contrasted to the 'exceedingly poor or weak or of very mean station. The former become insolent and excessively wicked and 'are not willing to be governed' and are contemptuous of their fellows; the latter are malicious, pettily wicked, too servile, and covetous[154].

Paul's description of himself as a socially and economically disadvantaged person becomes clear in vv. 11-13. The direct contrast between himself and the hybrists ceases and he singularly develops the notion of shame, the negative aspect of antithesis, in the form of a peristasis catalogue. Three distinct characters are used. First, he describes himself as a maltreated stranger : 'We hunger and thirst, we are ill-clad and buffetted and homeless'. The stranger (xenos) in need of hospitality (xenia) was liable to maltreatment at the hands of the native inhabitants. Hybrizō denoted the violation of the itinerant's rights and it involved shaming him and treating him as a person of inferior social

---

[153] For details, see above 184-187; and see also K.J. Dover, Greek Popular Morality, 147, whose definition reflects one common aspect of ὕβρις. He defines it as 'violent and contumacious treatment of a fellow-citizen as if he were a foreigner or slave'.

[154] Pol. 4.9.1-5; cf. ibid., 4.10.1-2 - terms such as eleutheria, ploutos, paideia, and eugeneia denote qualities or characteristics of those of the upper status; Rhet. 2.17.6 - ploutos, eugeneia and dynamis; and ta enantia, pevētos ('poor'), atuchos ('unfortunate'), adynatos ('weak').

class[155]. Aristotle illustrates atimia as a characteristic of hybris by an example of inhospitality of this kind. Achilles, in the Iliad, angrily protests, he 'has treated me like a dishonoured vagrant'[156].

Secondly, he refers to his work : 'and we labour, working with our hands'. Manual labour was regarded as demanding for a man of quality although fitting for a servile person. It is more than likely that Paul's work as the subject of much ridicule by the hybrists and that he includes it as a significant shame element in his peristasis for this reason[157]. Third, he speaks of himself as the object of much ridicule, abuse and violence : 'When reviled (loidopeō) we bless; when persecuted (diōkō) we endure; when slandered (dusphemeo) we try to conciliate; we have become, and are now, as the refuse (perikatharmata) of the world, the offscouring (peripsema) of all things'. Acts denoted by loidoreō, diōkō, and dysphēmeō, do not necessarily amount to, and can be considered distinct from, hybris. Hybris involves a breach of a person's status, an insult, a violent act with the intention of bringing dishonour upon the victim and pleasure to oneself[158]. The emphasis, though, throughout vv. 9-13 is upon notions of shame and I suggest these acts qualify as conduct of the hybris kind[159]. This is further emphasised by Paul's use of the almost synonomous

---

155 Xenia and hybris are distinctly opposed. See my discussion above, and see also, J.B. Mathews, Hospitality, 292-293. In the Hellenistic world resident aliens and itinerant foreigners were often regarded as socially inferior by the native inhabitants; ibid., 103n.1; and see 2 Cor. 11:27.

156 Rhet. 2.2.6.

157 R.F. Hock, The Working Apostle, 119-120, considers that Paul's inclusion of his work is made intelligible if viewed in the context of the working philosopher and that the Corinthians' criticism of his work is also understandable given the disesteem of work in this period and the objection to philosophers working. He concedes that work was not a standard element of peristasis catalogues, though it may be inferred from the common inclusion of general toils (ponoi). However, working for wages was regarded as shameful for any free Greek and does not need to be viewed against traditions of the working philosopher to retain the notion of shame and the Corinthians' disdain.

158 Eg., Aristotle, Rhet. 1.13.9; 2.2.12; Demosthenes 21.71ff.

159 Aristophanes, Ach. 479, 1117; Peace 1264; Herodotus 7.160; Pindar, Ol. 13.10; and see my discussion above 184-187.

terms, perikatharmata and peripsēma. Perikatharmata is derived from the root meaning 'to cleanse' and its use in other literature has presented scholars with a range of options. It is used in the Septuagint to signify sacrificial cleansing[160] and in Greek authors to denote an expiatory sacrifice in which a criminal, who was condemned to death, was vicariously sacrificed for the purity of the city[161]. The use of worthless men as the means of purification led to perikatharmata becoming a term of abuse[162] and it is this nuance which best fits the pattern of the socially dishonoured in our passage[163]. Peripsēma, 'that which is scraped off around' hence 'dirt or scum' removed in the process became a common term of polite self-depreciation[164]. However, it appears to be used more strongly here and must indicate what Paul has become as a result of the contempt and maltreatment of him by others. Rather than self-effacement or humility, it designates abject humiliation at the hands of others. Both terms may refer to the theme of shame throughout vv. 9-13 or simply to the preceding ladopeō, diōkō and dysphēmeō.

Paul's response to this treatment, as indicated by the words, eulogeō, anechomai and parakalō differs from the conventional response to hybris. As I have shown, the

---

160 Prov. 21:18; cf. C.K. Barrett, 1 Cor. 112-113, 'scapegoat'.

161 See H. Conzelmann, 1 Cor. 90n.49, who cites the argument in favour of this meaning.

162 Eg., Epictetus 3.22.78; cf. 'scum', Lucian, Hermot. 81; Philo, de Virt. 174 where katharma must be understood in a sociological sense. Cited by H. Conzelmann, 1 Cor. 90n.49.

163 It would be interesting to be able to show that perikatharma, (or katharma) is used here in relation to hybris as the antithesis of what H. North, Sophrosyne, 242 (see 231-242), terms the Neoplatonic association of sōphrosynē with the process of catharsis (katharsis) and the consequent assimilation of this excellence to katharotes (purity), hagneia (holiness) and other qualities related to purity. It is possible that Paul alludes to this kind of antithesis in 1 Cor. 7:14 (akatharton and hagion) and to notions of conjugal sōphrosynē. Cf. 1 Thess. 4:5-7 - pathos, epithymias and akatharsia as opposed to the unclassical hagiasmos. This association was especially prominent in Patristic literature; eg., Gregory of Nyssa and Gregory of Nazianus in which sophrosyne allied with katharotēs and hagneia are key values in the ascetic life which lead to the soul of God. So ibid., 31, 339-353.

164 Cf. Eusebius, Hist. Eccl. 7.22.7; Ignatius, Eph. 8.1, 18.1.

humiliation suffered normally led to anger which is defined as a desire for revenge accompanied by pain, and the recovery of one's own time by punishing the hybrizōn by recourse to the courts[165]. There is no such response by Paul. Rather, he blesses, endures and conciliates. On the other hand, Paul's warning against the arrogant in vv. 18-19 is similar to the response by the slighted in Aristotle's Rhetoric. Aristotle reasons that the young and wealthy, overconfident because of their power and wealth, engage in insulting and damaging behaviour to indulge their desire to be thought superior to others. They think they are superior when hybrizontes. But they often miscalculate their own and their victim's power with disastrous results and suffer the consequence of the retaliation of a superior person[166]. We have seen that Paul emphasises non-retaliation. In v. 14 he tells the Corinthians in general that he does not wish to shame (entrepō) them[167] (though the imagery and contrast in vv. 6-13 would undoubtedly have caused them some consternation and discomfort) but to see that they were soundly instructed in his gospel (vv. 14-17). But the hybrists who were behaving arrogantly (physioō) in his absence would be tested when he came (vv. 18-19). The contrast at this point is between the power (dynamis) of the kingdom of God with which Paul would come (presumably, through his weakness 2:3-4) and the power of his opponents which he suggests has only been displayed in words of eloquence (logos).

I now return to the question with which I commenced this study of hybris : the status of the opponents. Who are these hybrists and what is their relationship to Paul ? What connection is there between them and Paul's defence of his refusal ? A number of general considerations already outlined suggest that they belong to the upper class in Corinth and constitute the major threat to Paul's apostolic

---

165 See my discussion above 185.

166 2.2.5-8.

167 Cf. the social sense at 2 Thess. 3:14, and see above 156-157.

authority in Corinth. First, G. Theissen contends that Paul's arguments in Corinth were directed against Christians from the upper social strata; practices such as going to court, eating of meat at cultic meals, the financial support of missionaries, confirms their high social and economic status[168]. Second, I have shown that the notion of *hybris* and associated ideas are used in the majority of instances to describe the behaviour of the wealthy and powerful. While much of the language in 4:6-13 is rhetorical, I suggest that the terms *korennymi*, *plouteō* and *basileuō*, associated as they are with the *phronimoi*, *ischyroi* and *endoxoi*, are status terms and indicate to us that the hybrists come from the upper ranks. The language cannot describe those referred to as *ta mē onta* (1:28). Further, the excessive behaviour of the kind displayed by the hybrists in Corinth is generally not possible for people of the lower ranks of society and it is precisely people of this status with whom Paul seems to be aligning himself to oppose the hybrists.

Thirdly, I have pointed to the use of the traditional terminology of freedom, such as *eleutheria*, *panta exestin*, and χῆν ὡς βούλετια τις, by the wealthy and powerful in Greek literature as a means of justifying hybristic behaviour. It is also used by philosophers in their attacks against abuse of power and privilege by these people. Such notions are implicit in the language and ideas which Paul uses in 4:6-13 and are explicit in the catchcry and related terminology associated with the sexual activity and eating of idol meat in chapters 6, 8 and 10[169]. Such claims only make sense if one has the power and means to fulfil them. I have also mentioned what I consider are forms of hybristic behaviour in 5:1-8 and 8:1-3, of excessive sexual behaviour which contravenes accepted standards of morality, and abuses which occur due to a lack of self-knowledge. Thus I believe that there is a close connection between the hybrists in 4:6-13

---

[168] For details, see above 2.

[169] Cf. 6:12 and 10:23 - πάντα μοι ἔξεστιν;8:9 - ἐξουσία; 10:29 - ἐλευθερία.

and the excessive kinds of conduct in chapters 5, 6, 8 and 10. This relationship is important for our understanding of the context of Paul's refusal in chapter 9. I will argue in chapter 8 that eleutheria and associated notions came to signify the interests of those in positions of wealth and power and that the catchcry, panta exestin, in Corinth represents the attempt by upper class Christians to protect their vested interests and to pursue their own ends. Further, that the eleutheria/douleia theme running through chapters 8, 9 and 10 indicates that the same people are involved in the conflict with Paul over his refusal. In both 4:6-13 and chapters 8-10, Paul responds in a similar fashion; he sides with those of lowly status and himself assumes the position of a socially disadvantaged person to shame the hybrists.

Fourthly, most instances of the ὕβρις kind occur in social or moral contexts rather than a religious one[170]. This is true of hybristic behaviour in Corinth where the disorder and division, so typical of hybris (in chapters 1-3, in the matter of the Lord's meal (11:17-22) and as a result of eating idol meat), reflect the social structure of the church and the relations between upper and lower class Christians. However, Paul, like so many of the Greek authors, consistently reminds the hybrists of the religious significance of their acts. In relation to their disregard of their weaker brothers, he tells them that to wrong (hamartanō) - hamartia and adikia are frequently used to describe the immorality of acts of hybris - is to commit an offence against Christ (8:12)[171]. Paul's reminder to the hybrists in 4:6-7 of limits and divine benefaction are also of this kind.

Fifthly, Paul's argument in chapters 1-3 appears to be addressed to the Corinthians in general. It is extremely difficult to gauge how inclusive or particular Paul's remarks are at times and I suspect that he resorted to a number of

---

[170] For details, see above 190.

[171] Cf. also 10:22; 11:27-32.

familiar rhetorical devices to indicate immediately to his addressees the people to whom his remarks were intended[172]. There are, as I have just outlined,reasonable grounds for narrowing Paul's remarks to people from the upper class. But also we know that not all the people from this strata were opposed to Paul. Many of them were among his supporters and at the end of his first letter he acknowledges them by name, declares his support for them by recommendation, and asks the Corinthians to recognize and submit to them. It is clear that throughout 1:10 - 4:21 Paul is defending himself in an endeavour to re-establish his apostolic authority in Corinth and that the divisions in Corinth were related to criticisms that some had made against Paul's conduct as an apostle[173].

Paul refers to this critical attitude in general in 4:1-5. There appear to be specific objections to his lack of status and eloquence (1:17, 2:1-4, his working for wages (4:12), his absence from Corinth (4:18), and possibly his intimacy with certain of the Corinthians (1:14, 16). But it is his refusal of financial assistance (9:1-23) that is the major issue on which he conducts his defence in 1 Corinthians. Paul narrows down his opposition specifically in 4:18-19 to the arrogant few. His periphrastic response - he does not name them but refers to them as ἐφυσιώθησάν τινες and τὸν λόγον τῶν πεφυσιωμένων - enables him both to identify them and to disparage them before the Corinthians[174]. In doing so, Paul provides a fitting introduction to the contest of power (dynamis) which he envisages having with the hybrists in the future.

In conclusion, 4:6-13 indicates to us the status and nature of the opposition to Paul and its view of him. Members of it consider themselves to be superior both to their fellow-Christians and Paul and are behaving in a hybristic manner

---

172 I shall refer to these conventional means of response in chapter 9 e.

173 See N.A. Dahl, 'Paul and the Church at Corinth', 318-326, though he relates the quarrels to the decision to seek Paul's counsel on matters of difference.

174 For the advice of non-naming, see below chapter 9 e.

towards them. In particular, they are attempting to place Paul in Corinth and have made him the object of insults and abuse in an attempt to humiliate and shame him. The section 4:6-21 appears to act as a pivot between chapters 1-3 in which Paul outlines in general the nature of the hybristic behaviour and the ensuing chapters in which the various aspects of it are identified and discussed.

In this discussion of hybris in Greek literature and its consequences for 1 and 2 Corinthians, I have concentrated upon the social aspects of hybris. To do full justice to the matter, the religious and philosophical dimensions would need to be investigated as well. The notion of hybris and related ideas could also be applied to other passages which have commonly been thought to show gnostic tendencies. But already, the material I have explored shows that reference to hybris rather than gnosis provides a satisfactory explanation of the attitudes and conduct of the Corinthians.

3. The nature of the offer.

Scholars have long argued for the existence in the early church of a paid or salaried class of workers consisting of either part-time or full-time, resident or itinerant preachers and teachers[175]. Many passages are adduced to support this view[176] and it is generally accepted that the practice stemmed from a saying of the Lord similar to those preserved in the gospels[177]. It has been suggested that it was a widely recognized practice which was both highly valued and binding on the community and the worker[178]. Recent work by scholars such as J. A. Kirk, G. Theissen, and J.B. Mathews

[175] Eg., E. E. Ellis, 'Paul and His Co-workers', NTS 17 (1971), 440-445.

[176] Eg., 1 Cor. 9:4-5, 11-12, 13, 14, 15-17; 2 Cor. 11:7-10; 12:13; 1 Thess. 2:5-6, 9; 5:12; 2 Thess. 3:7-9; Phil. 4:15-19; Gal. 6:8; 1 Tim. 5:17-18; and what appears to be the practice of false teachers : Ro.16:17-18; 2 Cor. 2:17; 11:12; Phil. 3:19; Titus 1:11; 1 Pet. 5:2.

[177] Eg., Mt. 10:10; Lk. 10:7; cf. 1 Cor. 9:14; 1 Tim. 5:17.

[178] Eg., E.E. Ellis, 'Paul and his Co-workers', 443-444; D. L. Dungan, The Sayings of Jesus, 3, 11, 39-40.

has shown that a. distinctions must be made on the basis of the different situations on view in these passages; b. the practice of hospitality played the major role in supporting itinerant workers; c. the number of passages upon which a case for paid, resident, full-time leaders is small (eg. 2 Thess. 3:6ff; Gal. 6:6; 1 Tim. 5:17-18) and that these passages are open to alternative explanations[179]. Much reappraisal needs to be done in the light of their studies. My concern is for those passages which deal with Paul's sources of income, and, in particular, the nature of the support.

In Paul's letters we have only one clear instance of his acceptance of aid. He received a gift (doma) from the Philippians, which, I have argued, was part of a lasting reciprocal relationship denoted by the phrase koinōnein eis logon doseōs kai lēmpseōs (4:15-17). He also alludes to

---

179 In a recent article, J. A. Kirk, 'Did Officials in the New Testament Receive a Salary'. ExpT. 84 (1973), 105-108, has argued convincingly against what he considers to be the importation of the later practice of formal and regular remuneration. He correctly points out that not enough attention has been given to the different kinds of situation on view in these passages. He draws a distinction between itinerant ministries, where the worker had the right to expect support in the form of hospitality or possibly a regular income, 105-106 (eg., 1 Cor. 9:4-5, 11-12, 13, 15-17; 2 Cor. 11:7-10; 1 Thess. 2:5-6, 9) and local ministries, where the elders should receive a free-will offering from the community as an expression of thanksgiving for their oversight, 106-108 (eg., 1 Tim. 5:17-18). The differences, though, are more complex than this. G. Theissen's article, 'Wanderradikalismus', 245-271, is valuable in illustrating the different sociocultural and economic factors which influenced the retention of 'support' traditions concerning the itinerant ministry in the gospels and those relating to the itinerant artisans, like Paul and Barnabas, who spent time in the large Hellenistic cities. He emphasises the extremely hazardous nature of the itinerant preacher's existence as portrayed in the gospels, the harshness of the sayings and the dependence of the itinerants on hospitality of those who themselves were on the margin of society. In relation to Paul, I suggest that : a. a further distinction needs to be made before and after he moved into the large Greek cities of the provinces of Asia, Macedonia and Achaia; b. attention needs to be given to the emphasis Paul places on himself as a maltreated stranger in the peristasis catalogues (1 Cor. 4:11-13; 2 Cor. 6:8-10; 11:23-27, 32-33). Kirk, Theissen and Mathews all emphasise the importance of hospitality for the preacher of the gospel in the early church. In this regard, see J. B. Mathews, Hospitality, 166-174, 198-228.

this aid in 2 Cor. 11:7-9 as opsōnion received from other churches (v. 8) or, more expressly, from brothers from Macedonia. There is only one clear instance of his refusal of assistance where he, unlike others, refused to exercise his right to support in Corinth (1 Cor. 9:3-18; 2 Cor. 11:7-12; 12:13-18). We do not know whether an offer was made in Thessalonica or not. He expressly states that he did not exercise his prerogative but worked at his trade to set an example to them and to pay his own way (1 Thess. 2:7, 9; 2 Thess. 3:6-15)[180].

It is unquestionable that Paul accepted the right of apostles, including himself, to be supported by the communities in which they worked. This is the substance of his argument in 1 Cor. 9:7-14[181]. He argues in part : 'If we have sown spiritual good among you, is it too much if we reap your material benefits ? If others share this rightful claim (εἰ ἄλλοι τῆς ὑμῶν ἐξουσίας μετέχουσιν),

---

[180] Some commentators have understood οὐδὲ δωρεὰν ἄρτον ἐφάγομεν παρά τινος (2 Thess. 3:8) to mean that Paul paid for his whole board and lodgings (presumably to his host, Jason) out of his hard earned cash, as against the freeloading of the ataktoi. Eg., A. L. Moore, 1 & 2 Thess. 117; J. E. Frame, Thess. 301-302. Such a meaning is unlikely. The payment of cash in return for private hospitality or any other gift or service was a shocking and dishonourable act for it implied that the benefactor was a dependant, a hired hand receiving wages. Thus it was unacceptable and was regarded as an insult. However, it was common for gifts to be exchanged before departure as a symbol of friendship. For religious reasons for not offering payment to a host, see J.B. Mathews, Hospitality, 158-160, espec. 158n.4. It is better to translate δωρεάν as 'freely' rather than 'without paying'. Paul did not rely solely upon the generosity of others, as he had the right, but worked to support himself. In 2 Cor. 11:7, δωρεάν is translated as 'free of charge' or 'without cost' and it appears to be restricted to his non-acceptance of financial assistance from the Corinthians. It does not exclude hospitality which he and his associates received over a long period of time in Corinth. It is possible that the idea expressed by Paul reflects similar kinds of sentiments found in popular sayings in Antiquity such as 'and if a man wishes to settle among you and has a craft, first let him work for his bread' (Did. 12.3f). So R. F. Hock, The Working Apostle, 150-151.

[181] For details, see below 292-295.

do not we still more ?' (vv. 11-12a)[182]. The context suggests that financial support is being referred to, though it is not necessarily implied by exousia. In support of this exousia he draws upon a wide range of occupations to substantiate his argument - the soldier and his wage; the vigneron and shepherd and their produce; the ox and the grain; the priest and sacrificial gifts. The emphasis is upon the exousia itself, rather than the content or form it takes. His citation of what the Lord commanded (v. 14) further indicates this. If this saying belongs to the same tradition as those in Mat. 10:10 and Lk. 10:7, then the exousia of the apostles must include the extension of hospitality to them. This is, in fact, the only context of the sayings and others like them in the gospels[183]. But, as I have said, the point of contention in Corinth seems to be more specific. While Paul consistently refused to accept the offer or offers which had been made to him, he received and expected to receive a wide range of assistance from his Corinthian friends in the form of hospitality and sponsorship[184]. It is most likely then that Paul is referring

---

182 There is a difficulty in determining to whom the genitival phrase ὑμῶν (τῆς ὑμῶν ἐξουσίας) refers. A. J. Malherbe drew my attention to the similar construction ἡ ἐξουσία ὑμῶν in 8:9 where the reference is clearly to the right of the Corinthians to eat idol-meat. If Paul is alluding to this issue again then the clause εἰ ἄλλοι τῆς ὑμῶν ἐξουσίας μετέχουσιν should be translated, 'if others share in the right of yours'. The primary reference of ἐξουσια would then be to the idol-meat question. It is clear from Ch. 8 that Paul has the right to eat meat but forgoes it. But his claim to have a greater right (οὐ μᾶλλον ἡμεῖς) (9:12) to share in it than others (ἄλλοι) would not be clear. The comparison, rather, appears to be governed by the previous sentence ... μέγα εἰ ἡμεῖς ὑμῶν τὰ σαρκικὰ θερίσομεν, and the meaning of ἐξουσία to that of the apostles' right to aid from the Corinthians. See H. Conzelmann, 1 Cor., 155 ὑμῶν - 'over you'.

183 See J. B. Mathews, Hospitality, 293-294 and more widely, 187ff.

184 Eg., 1 Cor. 16:5-7, 10-11; 2 Cor. 1:16 - προπέμπειν. See also J. B. Mathews, Hospitality, 230-234. Mathews' belief that Paul's acceptance of money in Philippi was a unique exception leads him to preclude προπέμπειν as implying monetary assistance. However, as we have seen, such a view of Paul's relationship with the Philippians is too narrow. προπέμπειν is used in the New Testament only of sending a departing traveller on his way. It could involve providing him with an escort or servants for a short distance (Acts 20:38, 21:5) or, mostly, equipping him with the necessary provisions for his journey (cf. Ro. 15:24; Tit. 3:13; 3 Jo. 6).

to an offer of money, but whether it is in the nature of a salary, as D. L. Dungan suggests, cannot be determined on the evidence viewed so far[185]. The meaning of μισθός, 'reward, salary, or fee' (1 Cor. 9:17, 18), in the context of his refusal, has been the subject of much discussion[186]. Its use with other technical terms in vv. 16-18 - ἀνάγκη, ἄκων, οἰκονομία πεπίστευμαι, and the antithesis, ἑκών, μισθός - suggests that it should be rendered as 'wage' or 'salary'. But I doubt that such a meaning here can be deduced as evidence that the offer constituted a salary, or that other visitors to Corinth were paid one. As I shall argue later, in vv. 16-18 Paul is giving an explanation of why he exercised his right as a refusal in Corinth and μισθός acts as a foil to the servile notions contained in them[187]. The most that we can conclude from 1 Cor. 9 is that Paul is defending his right to refuse an offer of financial assistance of some kind.

Scholars generally have made a distinction between Paul's refusal of the Corinthian offer of aid and his acceptance of the Philippian δόματα. The former is said to be his usual practice, as evidenced in Thessalonians, the latter a 'unique exception'[188]. Others make a distinction between the 'salary', implied by exousia and misthos, in Corinth and the Philippian 'gift' (δόμα)[189]. There are a number of factors that should make us wary about drawing too fine a distinction between these two situations, or labelling one as 'normal' and the other as unique. First, Paul's use of οὐδεμία and εἰ μὴ ὑμεῖς μόνοι in Phil. 4:15 indicates that he had only one relationship of giving and receiving with a church. We need, though, to take into account Paul's references in 2 Cor. 11:8 (allai ekklēsiai) and 12:13 (hai loipai ekklēsiai). While the references appear to refer to the Philippian gifts in

---

185 The Sayings of Jesus, 28.

186 Ibid., 23-24n.1.

187 For details, see below 301-304.

188 J. B. Mathews, Hospitality, 233.

189 R. F. Hock, The Working Apostle, 126n.40.

in contrast to his refusal of the Corinthian offers, some scholars have suggested that the plural form indicates a wider practice of acceptance than just of the Philippian offer is intended[190]. Given the restriction of 'the brothers from Macedonia' (11:9)[191], and the rhetorical forms Paul is using in chapters 10-12, it seems more likely that the very definite οὐδεμία ... εἰ μὴ ὑμεῖς μόνοι must prevail. However the passages in 2 Corinthians should introduce a note of caution into our analysis of Phil. 4:15-17. Further, as I have said before, we must draw a distinction between Paul's example of work in Thessalonica and his refusal of assistance in Corinth. Each is unique though there may be some common factors[192].

Second, misthos and doma are different in meaning and should not be confused. D. L. Dungan wrongly assumes on the evidence of Phil. 4:15-17 that the Philippian gifts, amounting to several payments, could be termed a salary[193]. R. F. Hock draws attention to this error and points to the difference in meaning between misthos and doma and suggests that Dungan has overemphasised the significance of the Philippian gifts to Paul in relation to the Corinthian problem[194]. Later I will argue that Dungan's general estimation of variance in Paul's practice is correct but for the moment I will confine myself to the meaning of misthos and doma. Misthos, in the sense of 'fee' or 'salary', refers to the payment of cash in return for services rendered while doma includes a wide range of gifts and services given freely or for return. Doma is often used in connection with friendship or an offer

---

190 Eg., D.L. Dungan, The Sayings of Jesus, 38 - 2 Cor. 11:7-9 : 'several congregations helped him out'; 12:13 : 'all other congregations except the Corinthians'. Though he suggests that Paul's anger should preclude too precise an interpretation of these words. See also R.P. Martin, Phil. 180.

191 See R. Bultmann, 2 Kor. 208 : the adelphoi are possibly Philippian messengers or Silas and Timothy who brought the first gifts to Paul in Corinth.

192 For details, see above 173-176.

193 The Sayings of Jesus, 29 n.105.

194 The Working Apostle, 126n.4.

of friendship and this appears to be the sense in Phil. 4:15-17 where Paul's relationship with the Philippians is denoted by the phrase koinōnein eis logon doseōs kai lēmpseōs[195]. Only crass ignorance or blatant ingratitude could lead a recipient to insult his benefactor by referring to his doma as a payment, even where, as is the case with the Philippian gifts, it consisted of money. Though misthos and doma are different in meaning, I do not consider that Paul's use of misthos in 1 Cor. 9:17-18 should be used to make a distinction between the situation in Corinth and Philippi. Neither does there appear to be any good reason for excluding the notion of gift from the Corinthian offer of aid.

Third, Paul's use of ὀψώνιον, when he refers to the gifts or aid he received from other churches in 2 Cor. 11:8, must at least include the Philippian gifts. opsōnion is a technical term used specifically of the 'pay' or 'allowance' of the soldier[196]; metaphorically, it has the sense of 'provision' or 'support'[197]; and generally, it can mean 'wages', 'pay', 'salary' or 'allowance'[198]. It is never used of a gift. Paul could be using it in a general sense and thus too much weight should not be put upon it[199]. However, the point at issue is very critical for Paul as the sarcasm and irony in his use of ἁμαρτία and ταπεινοῦν (v. 7) shows. He may then be using it provocatively in view of the comparison that has been made between his conduct and his rivals in regard to offers of aid. He 'robbed' other churches

---

[195] For details, see above 157-164. See also Diogenes, Ep.38 where the gifts accepted in return for teaching include money, things worth money (including barley meal) and hospitality (invitations to dinner).

[196] Eg., 1 Cor. 9:7; Lk. 3:14; Polybius 3.25.4; 5.30.5; 6.39.12.

[197] Eg., P.Oxy.531.21.

[198] Eg., P.Oxy.731.10.

[199] So H.W. Heidland, 'ὀψώνιον' TDNT 5, 591-592; who says that Paul here uses the word 'comprehensively for any support in cash or kind', though the legal claim implicit in the word is also emphasised. See also more recently G.H.R. Horsley, New Documents 2, 93. An allowance paid normally in coin but on two occasions in kind (wood, and a chiton), and a wage for child-care and military service.

of wages to show the Corinthians that he loved them and did not wish to burden them. His rivals, who boast that they are like Paul (v. 12), albeit superior, are in reality unprincipled wage-earners who care only for themselves (cf. 2 Cor. 2:17 οἱ πολλοὶ καπηλεύοντες˙ 11:13 ἐργάται δόλιοι; 11:20 εἴ τις λαμβάνει)[200]. The Corinthians see the reverse as being true. They made offers to Paul and have found something lacking in his attitude towards them because of his refusal. His rivals' acceptance counts in their favour.

It is also possible that Paul chose the word deliberately to offset the relational nuances in terms such as doma. The comparison is not simply between acceptance and refusal but the quality of Paul's and his rivals' relationship with the Corinthians as indicated by refusal or acceptance. Paul's question, 'For in what were you less favoured than the rest of the churches, except that I did not burden you', followed by the sarcastic plea, 'Forgive me this wrong!' (12:13), implies that his opponents have made his acceptance of gifts from others and his constant refusal of the Corinthian offers the test of his affection for the Corinthians. Paul does not love them (11:11; 12:15b)[201]. It is this aspect of the Corinthian offer to which I wish to draw attention. While I doubt that on the evidence of terminology alone we can draw conclusions as to whether the Corinthian offer was in the form of a salary or gift, it is clear that Paul's refusal has in some way reflected upon the Corinthians and resulted in a deterioration of his original relationship with them.

We need to look closely at the relationship between Paul and the Corinthians, and indeed between that of his rivals and their friends in Corinth. Why, for instance, should the refusal of their offers evoke such hostility and mistrust ? Why should it become the continuing focus of criticism

---

[200] Though the connection is made between 2 Cor. 11:12 and 2:17 by a number of scholars, Paul does not make this an issue in chapters 10-12.

[201] Cf. C.K. Barrett, 2 Cor. 284; F.F. Bruce, 1 & 2 Cor. 238; R.F. Hock, The Working Apostle, 138; H. Windisch, 2 Kor. 334.

of Paul and the point of invidious comparison of him by his enemies ? Why has it led to invective of the kind which is present in 2 Cor. 10-12 and what does it indicate about his opponents ? What does his refusal suggest about the nature of the purpose behind the offers ? Why does he continue to refuse despite the mounting distrust of him ?

Hock's study of the philosopher's practice of charging fees centres entirely upon the morality of their right to charge or waive fees[202]. On the one hand, sophists espoused the more popular option of charging fees and their practice was followed by many post-Socratic philosophers. Aristotle accepted this practice in principle and Aristotelian and Stoic philosophers accepted fees or gifts from their students[203]. Epicurus rather sought modest and voluntary contributions (syntaxis) or offerings (aparchai) from his followers[204]. People generally were willing to give money to philosophers, whether they were begging-Cynics or friends[205], and to pay fees and this appears to be the normal and accepted practice. On the other hand, Socrates, followed by the true Cynic philosopher, refused to accept dōra or bequests or to charge fees and was critical of those who did. For Socrates, the acceptance of a fee or gift was a form of servile dependence; he would have been under compulsion (anagkē) to teach anyone who had the money. By refusing, he retained his freedom and demonstrated his self-sufficiency which allowed him to speak to anyone he chose[206]. Hock does not consider,

---

202 The Working Apostle, 49-78.

203 Ibid., 69-70.

204 Ibid., 70-71. However, it must be remembered that the Epicureans generally regarded their relationships in terms of friendship and the absence of terms such as misthos may be accounted for by this. The kind of friendship which Epicurus proposed and for which he was roundly criticized was based on utility. The popular anti-Epicurean polemic reflected this as it suggested that Epicureans were flatterers, forming friendships for advantage, and seekers of patronage. For details, see above 30,76.

205 The Working Apostle, 76n.226, 77; the practice was widely followed in the time of Dio Chrysostom and especially in the Second Sophistic.

206 Ibid., 57-66.

however, the moral obligation placed upon the recipient to return the benefit he has received from his teacher, nor the nature of the relationship between teacher and student.

The situation is more complex than the dichotomy of charging or non-charging teachers put forward by Hock. Aristotle, as has been said, accepted in principle the charging of fees. However, he distinguishes between two kinds of teacher-pupil relationships : the commercial kind as opposed to one of true friendship. He asks : 'Which party's business is it to decide the amount of the return due ? Should it be assessed by the one who proffers the initial service ? Or rather by the one who receives it, since the one proffering it seems to leave the matter to him ?' In the commercial kind of relationship, teaching is offered with a view to recompense and appears, says Aristotle, to operate according to Hesiod's principle, 'Let the wage (misthos) stated to a friend stand'[207]. Thus both parties agree to the amount due beforehand. This relationship is akin to Aristotle's friendship for utility, the lowest kind of social relationship which he thoroughly disapproves of throughout his treatise on friendship.

By contrast, where no such agreement is made, the teacher's service is regarded as disinterested, proffered in love with an intention only to benefit the recipient. The pupil reciprocates according to the value that he himself places upon the knowledge he has gained. This is the highest form of friendship based on virtue. Aristotle concludes : 'the return made should be in proportion to the intention of the benefactor, since intention is the measure of a friend, and of virtue. This is the principle on which it would seem that payment ought to be made to those who have imparted instruction in philosophy; for the value of their service is not measureable in money, and no honour paid them could be an equivalent, but no doubt all that can be expected is that to them, as to the gods and to our parents, we should make such return as is in our power'[208]. A teacher with propriety cannot ask for a return.

---

207 WD 370.

208 EN 9.1.5-8; cf. 8.13.2.

But because of the binding obligation on the recipient to return a gift or service, he can confidently expect it. It is important to notice that Aristotle regards the relationship between teacher and pupil as 'friendship' of one kind or another in which the normal conventions of giving and receiving apply. The service rendered by the teacher is called a dosis which places the recipient under a moral obligation to respond. What appears to determine whether the return is in the form of a gift or payment of a fee is the kind of relationship which exists between the two parties.

Seneca also discusses the relationship of teacher and student (and physician and patient) in his de Beneficiis in terms of friendship, makes the same distinctions, and draws upon the same conventions of giving and receiving as Aristotle. He distinguishes between the commercially-minded teacher who simply demands his professional service from his pupil and does not consider him worthy of any particular consideration, and the teacher who devotes himself to the well-being of his student and thus places him under an obligation, not as a teacher but as a friend (amici). About the relationship of friendship between student and teacher, he asks : 'Why is it that I owe something to my physician and my teacher, and yet do not complete the payment of what is due to them ? Because from being physician and teacher they pass into friends, and we being under obligation to them, not because of their skill, which they sell, but because of their kindly and friendly good-will'. And again : 'If I do not owe such a man all the love that I give to those to whom I am bound by the most grateful ties, I am indeed ungrateful'[209].

The kind of friendship between teacher and student is not the only aspect of this kind of relationship which determines whether the return for services is termed a gift. As I have shown earlier in the chapter on friendship, the terms philia and amicitia encompassed a wide range of relations based on

---

209 de Ben. 6.16.1-7; 17.1-2. Cf. Ep. 64.9; 73.4.

conscious reciprocity and goodwill and consisted of a vast complex of mutual services[210]. I largely restricted myself to friendships between equals (though the conventions of giving and receiving apply to unequal and other grades of friendship) where giving and receiving was indicative of the behaviour of the rich and powerful[211]. When in need of the services of a lawyer or a physician, of a loan or security, a person of quality turned to those friends whom he had secured through past services. He used his wealth to secure friends, never to respond directly to a benefit he had received. Payment in cash for these services implied that the benefactor was an employee of the other party and was regarded as an insult to his honour[212].

Given this kind of exchange between people of rank, A. R. Hands suggests that the nature of payments between patients and doctors 'may have been regarded officially as gifts rather than fees'. In the case where doctors of the social and cultural standing of a skilled physician attended citizens of similar standing to themselves, 'it would be entirely in keeping with what we have said of relationships within their class for the reward for their service to be offered (and expected) as a 'gift' rather than be demanded as a fee'[213]. In reality both were payments for services rendered, but propriety determined that it should be in the nature of a gift. This is certainly true of a lawyer-client relationship[214] and, as we have seen, of the philosopher-pupil

---

[210] For details, see above 24-25, 43.

[211] Ibid., 12.

[212] Ibid., 32-34.

[213] Charities, 137. His chapters on 'Education and Culture', 116-130, and 'Health and Hygiene', 131-145, are particularly helpful in setting out the varying attitudes of teachers and doctors in regard to the charging or waiving of fees to the wealthy or poor.

[214] Eg., Cicero, de Off. 2.9.32; 2.9.65-68. Though under Roman law a lawyer could not accept a fee, his services were construed as 'acts of kindness' or 'kind services' which bound the recipient to him for future services and the relationship between them was one of friendship. Cf. ibid., Fam. 7.1.4. Cf. Quintilian 12.7.8-12 & esp. 12.7.12 : '...he will not regard his payment as a fee, but rather as the expression of the principle that one good turn deserves another ... gratitude is primarily the business of the debtor.'

relationship among people of rank[215]

---

215 More attention must be given to questions of status and relationship in the sophist-philosopher debate over fees and gifts. In particular to the various practices of charging or waiving of fees in relation to the different socio-economic standing of the students, and to the effect of subsidised education, by public monies or wealthy donors, upon the practices Hock presents us with one common view of Socrates' practice : Socrates' denigration of making money from philosophy includes both the receiving of gifts from friends or those of high status and the charging of fees. (Eg., gifts : Xenophon, Apol. 16; D.L. 2.31, 65, 74; fees : Plato, Apol. 19D-E, 31B-C, 33A-B; Xenophon, Mem. 1.2.6-7, 61, 6.1-5, 11-14; Apol. 16.26; D.L. 2.27. All references cited by R.F. Hock, The Working Apostle, 53n.148, and see 60-61, 62). For him, acceptance of both gifts and fees created an obligation in which the nuance of servility was always present. This picture of Socrates fits what we know of him in the traditional accounts in Aristotle and Seneca of his refusal of Archelaus' invitation (see above -3-34). Cf. also Philo, de Prov. 2.31. However, Socrates' refusal must be seen together with evidence of his acceptance of gifts from his students and his understanding of friendship. Socrates' refusal is surprising in view of Xenophon's opinion that Socrates considered friendship only in utilitarian terms, as a relationship of choice formed by services rendered and existing by the continuation of mutual service (eg., Mem. 1.2.52-55; 2.6.4-55; 2.6.4-5, 22-28; cf. Cyr. 8.7.13). Further, Seneca, de Ben. 1.8.1-3, relates an occasion in which Socrates is said to have received many gifts from his pupils, each giving according to his means, some substantial, some little, in response to the services he had rendered them. Quintilian 12.7.9, 12 also justifies acceptance of payment in the sense of gratitude for services rendered, 'since collections were made even on behalf of Socrates, and Zeno. Cleanthes and Chrysippos took fees from their pupils. However, he will not take it as a fee but as an act of reciprocal kindness (mutua benevolentia).' Cf. also R.F. Hock, The Working Apostle, 74-75. The refusal of a gift or waiving of a fee in itself does not remove the obligation to reciprocate on the part of the recipient. A popular <u>topos</u> of giving and receiving concerned the question of when a benefit was not a benefit and no obligation incurred. Seneca suggests that it depended on the disposition of the benefactor (de Ben. 6.4.6), the absence of good-will, an unintentional service, or a service which was intended as an injury (Ibid., 6.9.3). Socrates intended his teaching as a gift, and though it is said in some sources that he would accept not material return, the return of honour and esteem (usually in the form of social and political support) was both expected and accepted, especially from those who did not possess the means. (For this moral obligation in friendship, see Aristotle, EN 8.14.13 : τίμην ἀνταποδοτέον, where <u>timē</u> refers to the social and political support the recipient owes a superior benefactor). The Cynic letters preserve Cynic tradition and reveal a diversity of opinion and practice in relation to giving and receiving. Eg., see Diogenes, Ep. 38, where the author indicates Diogenes received money, other gifts and hospitality, in return for his teaching from moderate people or from those who were benefited by it. He refused from worthless people and those who received nothing from his teaching. From those who were grateful toward him for accepting he would accept gifts again. The Cynic Letters Socrates Epp. 1, 2, 6, should be included in the discussion. In Ep. 2 the writer has Socrates seeking hospitality for a friend. It is a traditional recommendation letter in which reciprocity is clearly intended.

While we do not know whether it was the community or a group of individuals who made the offer to Paul, there is every indication that those who have made an issue of his refusal are people of rank. As I have shown, a. Paul's confrontation over this issue and others in 1 Corinthians is with upper class people; b. Paul's aid in the form of hospitality and sponsorship comes from people who belong to the upper classes; c. generally speaking, it was not possible for the poor lower classes to be involved in such activity, a concession that Paul makes in regard to the collection (2 Cor. 8:1-5)[216].

D. L. Dungan makes the interesting observation that the factions in 1 Cor. 1:11 may have been caused by differences of opinion over the support of apostles. Paul and his associates, unlike Peter and the brothers of the Lord (9:4-6), departed from the norm and entered into bitter controversy with some of the Corinthians as a result[217]. Dungan correctly sees Paul's refusal of aid in Corinth as being the cause of conflict there, and also observes the adverse effect his acceptance of Philippian gifts had upon the struggle. He is also sensitive to the relational aspects of the conflict caused by Paul's refusal. He notes that a. Paul 'came almost to breaking-point' in his relationship with the Corinthian congregation because of certain misunderstandings arising out of his way of handling the matter of support; b. 1 Cor. 9 is probably the 'first stages of the conflict that later reached grave proportions of bitterness and invective' as seen in 2 Cor. 10-12; c. Paul was seen to be 'spurning their legitimate right to help him' even while he was secretly helped by another congregation. Thus they drew the natural conclusion that he didn't really love them; d. he behaved in a 'curiously deceptive manner', was wide-open to 'accusations of inconsistency, deceitfulness, and confused thinking', and that a 'great wave of distrust

---

[216] The generosity of the Macedonian churches which gave out of their poverty may count against this, though in the case of the collection it was a once only event and not a characteristic practice.

[217] The Sayings of Jesus, 7-9.

suddenly arose in Corinth against Paul' in relation to it[218].

The factions undoubtedly reflect a wider range of issues and interests, but from the evidence of 2 Corinthians it is clear, as Dungan suggests, that the one continuing problem which Paul had with the Corinthians centres upon his refusal of aid and the inconsistency of his conduct. I argued in the previous section that the kind of issues raised and the terminology used in 1 Cor. 1-4, 6, 8, 10, denote the behaviour and interests of people of rank and wealth and that these people comprise Paul's opposition in Corinth[219]. Their high status is also implied, as I show later, by the content of the invective which they use against Paul and by the form of servile self-depreciation which he uses to oppose them.

Whether the leaders of one of the factions made the offer to Paul is not indicated. That similar offers were made to others (1 Cor. 9:11-12a) who accepted is known; that these recipients were made figureheads of the factions and the means of comparison and opposition to Paul is probable. While people such as Apollos and Cephas themselves may not have been directly involved, indications in 2 Corinthians are that the rival apostles to whom Paul's enemies resorted as replacements formed a relationship with them based on friendship[220]. A similar intention may have underlined their offers to Apollos and Cephas. It is possible that the offer to Paul was intended as a return for services rendered; that is, as a conventional response of obligation. But it was more likely meant as an initial offer of friendship; that is, as an attempt to get Paul over to their side and thus obligated to them. The possibilities within the context of giving and receiving and the complex nuances associated with it are numerous. What is certain is that the refusal of the offer in association with his acceptance of the Philippian gifts, was regarded by his enemies as a serious affront to their status and, because of their efforts, to the Corinthian

218 Ibid., a. 9, b. 19, c. 39, d. 22, 39, 28.

219 For details, see above 214-217.

220 Ibid., 106-109, 113-114, for recommendation as instituting friendship and the obligations binding on both parties as a result.

congregation as a whole. This makes it more probable that the offer of aid was intended to create friendship and that it was made by those whom I have called 'hybrists'.

So then the offer made to Paul was not disinterested but represented the vested interests of a group for people from the higher ranks in Corinth who wished to put Paul under obligation to them. Their subsequent alliance with the rival apostles, as seen in 2 Corinthians, has all the traditional elements of a relationship of this kind. Given this context of status and friendship, I am inclined to think that their offer was in the form of a gift rather than a fee or salary. These aspects will become clearer as we examine the nature of Paul's refusal.

4. The nature of Paul's refusal.

Paul gives three reasons for his refusal of the offer in Corinth. a. He did not wish to place an obstacle in the way of the gospel of Christ (1 Cor. 9:12b). b. He did not want to burden anyone (2 Cor. 11:9; 12:13, 14). c. He loved them (2 Cor. 11:11; 12:15). Scholars have given a number of explanations of these and I will examine some of them. Then, on the assumption that the offer either stems from an intention to form a friendship relationship or, at least, should be understood within the context of this institution, I will recall the conventional grounds for declining of such offers in Greek and Roman society and examine Paul's refusal in the light of these.

First, scholars have advanced economical, pastoral, ethical, philosophical and psychological considerations for Paul's refusal. Some also see the collection as having an important bearing on his decision. a. In economic terms, it has been suggested that the church at Corinth, as in Thessalonica, was poor, and as Paul did not wish to be a financial burden, he refused to exercise his right to support[221]. Dungan adds

---

[221] Eg., J. Weiss, 1 Kor. 238; D. L. Dungan, The Sayings of Jesus, 15, 30-31. Cf. G. Stählin, 'κοπετός', TDNT 3, 857, who suggests that the poor might have been frightened from entry into the community if they had to make a contribution.

to this general view : if Paul had claimed his right to support in the face of their poverty, it would have provoked the comment, 'The Word of Grace comes dear these days!', and Paul would have been accused of using the gospel for base gain[222]. Although a number of the Corinthians belonged to the urban poor (1 Cor. 1:26, 11:22), it is far from certain that we should characterize the church as poor overall. Similarly, we cannot assume, as Dungan does, that Paul's acceptance of the Philippian gifts indicates that this church was relatively wealthy[223]. Paul's acceptance and refusal of aid does not seem to be motivated simply by socio-economic considerations. There is good reason to believe that the Macedonian churches were poor. Paul had not asked them to contribute to the collection but they had given generously out of desperate poverty (κατὰ βάθους πτωχεία) and economic hardship (θλῖψις)[224] (2 Cor. 8:1-5). He also personally accepts aid from these churches, which supposedly could ill afford to give (2 Cor. 11:7-9)[225]. Presumably, both Philippi and Thessalonica are included in this reference to the Macedonian churches. Yet we find no indication of poverty in any of the letters addressed to these churches. The evidence in Acts suggests that there were a number of wealthy people in them who had supported and continued to support Paul[226].

In Philippians we only find Paul's personal attitude to his socio-economic position. He emphasises that he is self-sufficient (αὐτάρκης), sustained by grace (ἐν τῷ ἐνδυναμοῦντι με) in whatever economic situation he finds himself, whether

---

[222] The Sayings of Jesus, 31.

[223] Ibid.

[224] Cf. 8:13 where Paul assures the Corinthians that he does not intend that their giving to the collection should result in economic hardship (thlipsis).

[225] συλᾶν, 'rob', may suggest this. So C. K. Barrett, 2 Cor. 283.

[226] Cf. Philippi, Acts 16:14-15; Thessalonica, Acts 17:4, 9; Beroea, Acts 17:12.

in poverty (denoted by the verb, ταπεινοῦσθαι) or plenty (περισσεύειν) (4:11-13)[227]. In Thessalonica, Paul's wish not to burden them (1 Thess. 2:9) relates to his working for wages and the avoidance of living at the expense of the community (2 Thess. 3:8). His work there, as we have seen, has an economic and paradigmatic function and most probably is directed at the social problem, the ataktoi, who have taken advantage of the generosity and hospitality of their

---

[227] Tapeinousthai as a socio-economic term, see B. Rolland, 'Saint Paul et la pauvreté : Phil. 4:12-14, 19-20', Assemb. Seign. 59 (1974) 10-15, who suggests that tapeinousthai, 'to live on little', describes the situation of the small and the poor and reflects Paul's use in the peristasis of shame, 2 Cor. 11:22-23. R. P. Martin suggests that, in addition, 'it reflects his entire outlook on and disregard of personal comforts of life (cf. 1 Cor. 4:11; 2 Cor. 6:3-10; 11:23ff)'. See Phil. (NCB), 163. I suggest that this is implied by autarkēs which denotes Paul's attitude in the extreme circumstances of life such as tapeinousthai and perisseuein. The socio-economic sense of these two words is further emphasised in the contrast which follows : tapeinousthai, peinan, ystereisthai and perisseuein, chortazesthai, perisseuein. (Cf. the noun forms, perisseuma and ysterēma, in 2 Cor. 8:14 where the Corinthians' financial contribution is to supply the want of the Jerusalem Church. Paul plays upon the socio-economic usage so that the perisseuma of the Jerusalem Christians will supply the ysterēma of the Corinthians. This at first sight appears to be an indictment against the 'spiritual' quality of the Corinthians, an unfavourable comparison. But Paul's use of ἰσότης, 'equality', 'equal proportion' appears to reflect the reciprocal nature of friendship in which a recipient should attempt to redress the benefactor, in whatever way he can if he has not the means, so that the equality or at least the appearance of equality exists. See Aristotle, EN 8.7.2 : 'Since when the affection rendered is proportionate to desert, this produces equality in a sense (πῶς ἰσότης between the parties, and equality is felt to be an essential element of friendship'). The alacrity of scholars to see Paul as a man without means is reflected in their discussions of perisseuein. In his earlier commentary on Philippians, R.P. Martin, Phil. 176-177, restricts its application to Paul's pre-Christian days (the socio-economic sense) or to his possession of spiritual wealth as an Apostle. Cf. also W. Hendriksen, Philippians (London, 1962) 205-206. In his later commentary, Phil. (NCB), 163, he calls it 'spiritual elation'. But he allows its corollary chortazesthai (together with its antithesis peinan) to refer to 'physical supply or lack', ibid., 163. Manthanein and myein indicate that both tapeinousthai and perisseuein refer to his apostolic experience and, in relation to the gift he has just received, Paul is saying that in either prosperity or adversity, wealth or poverty, whether by choice or circumstance, he is content because of the enabling strength of God. For the quality of autarkēs and its relation to reciprocal philia comprising the giving and receiving of goods and services, see A.W.H. Adkins, '"Friendship" and "Self-sufficiency"', 30-45 and espec. 43-45 where autarkēs in Aristotle characterises the megalopsuchos, a person of rank and wealth.

fellow Christians. There is no hint that μὴ ἐπιβαρεῖν is associated with Thessalonian poverty.

In regard to the economic status of the Corinthians, Paul shows no hesitancy in asking them to contribute to the collection (1 Cor. 16:1-4; 2 Cor. 8-9). Their reluctance to do so can be attributed to their growing mistrust of Paul rather than their supposed poverty[228]. We have seen previously that among Paul's friends and enemies in Corinth were a number of wealthy Christians and that he resorts to his friends for material assistance for himself and his associates when there[229]. Further, members of this church have made a practice of supporting other visitors (1 Cor. 9:12a) and his enemies, in particular, have financed Paul's rivals. His adamant refusal seems to be in the face of persistent offers. I conclude then that Paul's use of the term 'burden', though it relates to refusal of offers of financial assistance, does not mean that an economic strain would have been placed upon the Corinthians if he had accepted. Rather the offers flow out of their 'prosperity' and both his and their attitude must be understood within the popular conventions which operate at this level.

b. R. F. Hock offers the pastoral consideration that Paul, as a general policy, did not accept support from those he was converting[230]. Paul's acceptance of the Philippian aid appears to be an exception to this policy and there is no mention of his not wishing to burden them. However, Hock

---

228 Cf. 8:16-24; 9:1-5. There is good reason to believe that the language Paul uses throughout 8:8-15 and 9:5b-14 would have special significance for people of means. Some of the Corinthians may have derived their income from estates and the illustrations of profitable returns on primary products (9:6-11) may have had special appeal. Cf. Dio Chrysostom, Disc. 7, 'Euboean Oration', in which he describes and compares wealthy land owners who reside in the city and draw their wealth from their estates with the free rural poor.

229 For details, see above 147 n.78.

230 The Working Apostle, 126-127, espec. n.40, 133, 137-138. See also A. Plummer, Second Epistle to the Corinthians (Edinburgh, 1915), 305.

notes that Paul expressly states that he did not seek the latest gift, for he was self-sufficient (4:11, 17) and, citing Plummer, that Paul did not accept gifts while with the Philippians but only after he left them[231]. In fact, this support from a founded congregation enabled him to maintain his policy of not being a demanding apostle when preaching in Thessalonica and Corinth[232]. Certainly, the original offer which was made to Paul in Corinth and to which he refers in 1 Cor. 9:12b occurred during his first visit. However, Paul not only refused it then but continued to insist that under no circumstances would he accept it (1 Cor. 9:15; 2 Cor. 11:9b-10) even on his proposed third visit. This is long after the Corinthian church was founded. So there is a clear distinction between Paul's attitude towards the Philippian and Corinthian offers of aid. It may be argued, on the one hand, that the problems which arose due to his refusal were of such a nature that he had no alternative but to continue refusing. On the other, Paul may have seen in the original offer the factional interests of his would-be benefactors, the acceptance of which would have placed an obstacle in the way of the gospel then and at any time thereafter.

c. General moral or ethical grounds have been suggested by a number of scholars. Paul wished to avoid an appearance of selfishness[233]. More fully stated, this means that 'the gospel, which centred on the love and self-sacrifice of Jesus, could not fitly be presented by preachers who insisted on their rights, delighted in the exercise of authority and made what

---

231 Ibid., 126n.40, 138. And see A. Plummer, 2 Cor. 305. Cf. D.L. Dungan, The Sayings of Jesus, 31-32, who sees the significance of ὅτε ἐξῆλθον ἀπὸ Μακεδονίας (4:15) is that Paul only took money where it would advance missionary work and not simply to meet his need where he was working at the time. Cf. D. Georgi, Gegner, 236.

232 The Working Apostle, 138.

233 Eg., Lietzmann-Kümmel, Kor. 42; Robertson and Plummer, 1 Cor. 186-187; J. Weiss, 1 Kor. 238; G. Stählin, 'κοπετός', TDNT 3, 857.

profit they could out of evangelism'[234]. In a general sense, this may be true. Paul's conduct as an apostle in regard to the offer, and indeed all his behaviour, may probably be termed unselfish and undoubtedly it is motivated by his understanding of the gospel. 1 Cor. 9 is about his subjecting his right to accept or refuse to the gospel. When referring to his refusal in 2 Cor. 11:11 and 12:15, he states that it was because he loved them. However true moral considerations of this kind may be, they do little to explain the precise reasons for refusal. As a question of morality, acceptance of the offer, on the face of it, appears to be perfectly proper. Paul argues from a number of social and religious customs and a saying of the Lord that he and others had the right to accept it (1 Cor. 9:7-14). Acceptance by a preacher of the gospel is consistent with the gospel. There can be no doubt that the Corinthians considered acceptance to be perfectly moral. It is his refusal that has caused them to criticize him and his wrong lies there from their viewpoint. Others have accepted, and, while Paul may have had misgivings about the wisdom and lack of judgment shown by these recipients, he still insists that it is their right[235]. From a general ethical viewpoint we could also say that Paul's acceptance of the Philippian gifts over a period of time was unselfish and in accord with the furtherance of the gospel among them and elsewhere[236]. That is, the same ethical considerations motivate acceptance and refusal. What we need to know, in each instance, are the reasons for Paul's contrary actions.

---

234 So C. K. Barrett, 1 Cor. 207; cf. F. F. Bruce, 1 & 2 Cor. 85; N.A. Dahl, 'Paul and Possessions', 34.

235 It is difficult to avoid the strong contrast between Paul's behaviour and that of the others in 1 Cor. 9:11-12, especially in view of the ἀλλ᾽ οὐ construction strengthened by the final clause ἵνα μή τινα ἐγκοπὴν δῶμεν τῷ εὐαγγελίῳ τοῦ Χριστοῦ. Cf. H. Conzelmann, 1 Cor. 155. Paul may have considered that their acceptance has had a detrimental effect upon the progress of the gospel in the church and upon his relations with it. But there is no criticism of their right to accept.

236 Eg., Phil. 4:14. By their gift they participate in Paul's suffering. Cf. 2 Cor. 1:3-7 where to share in the apostle's suffering is to share in the comfort God gives his apostle. See also divine reciprocity, Phil. 4:17b.

d. There has been a recent trend to attribute Paul's refusal to philosophical concerns. Paul is attempting to dissociate himself from the practice of his opponents or others like him in society who accepted fees. I have referred on a number of occasions to R. F. Hock's thesis that Paul is following the Socratic-Cynic tradition of the working philosopher and is distancing himself from mercenary sophists. In 2 Cor. 11:12, he continues to refuse the offers 'to force his opponents to conform to his practice so that in what they boast (ἐν ᾧ καυχῶνται) they would be found to be like him (v. 12). Otherwise, they were false apostles and deceitful workers'[237].

Hock more extensively develops the backgound of the Socratic-sophistic debate over gifts and fees than D. Georgi and H. D. Betz[238]. Betz argues that the reasons for Paul's refusal are no longer accessible and that in fact Paul consciously withholds the real reasons for refusing the offers. Paul's appeal to Socratic traditions, he suggests, is a result of the criticisms he received over his refusal and is an attempt to discredit the status of his rivals[239]. Hock counters that Paul's defence is more fundamental than this and that it is integrally linked with his understanding of himself as a working apostle. The refusal and the traditions upon which he draws in his defence are in accordance with his general policy[240]. Against Hock and in favour of Betz' general consideration, that Paul's apology is a reaction to criticism, is the fact that Paul makes no mention of his work. As I have shown, in 2 Cor. 11:7-11 and 12:13 he refers only to the fact of his refusal in relation to his acceptance of aid from elsewhere, the practice of his opponents, and the adverse effect his refusal has had on his relations with the Corinthians.

---

[237] The Working Apostle, 139.

[238] D. Georgi, Gegner, 234-241, and see R. F. Hock, The Working Apostle, 134 and espec. n.61. H.D. Betz, Sokratische Tradition, 100-117, and id., 'Paul's Apology : II Corinthians 10-13 and the Socratic Tradition', Colloquy 2 (1970) 1-16, and espec. 12-13. For Criticism of Betz' position see E.A. Judge, 'St. Paul and Classical Society', 35; R.F. Hock, The Working Apostle, 134-135.

[239] Sokratische Tradition, 104, 115; 'Paul's Apology', 13.

[240] The Working Apostle, 136.

Against the viewpoint that Paul is attempting to discredit his rivals by an appeal to Socratic traditions, is the fact that Paul has accepted aid (opsōnion) from other churches (11:8). It is not simply because of his refusal of the offer at Corinth that criticism arises; it is his refusal in the light of his acceptance of aid from Philippi and possibly elsewhere. This inconsistency on Paul's part in his relations with his churches is implied in 1 Cor. 9:19-23 and underlines Paul's defence in 2 Cor. 11:7-12 and 12:13-18. How can it be argued that Paul is endeavouring to contrast his 'general policy' with the practice of his opponents, asking them to be like him, if it is well known that he too accepts aid from churches ? As E.A. Judge comments : 'In the case of his claim not to have accepted maintenance from his audience, it can be shown that he only refused it to make a point, that he always insisted on his right to support, and did in fact accept it in the normal way where it was not an issue'[241]. What then is the point ? I suggest that it lies in the particular nature of the offer made to Paul which Paul felt bound to refuse for the sake of the gospel in Corinth. His rivals had no such care and consideration.

e. I have referred previously to Dodd's attempt to interpret Paul's supposed 'hesitancy' or 'reluctance' in Phil. 4:10-17 and his refusal of aid in 1 Cor. 9 in psychological terms[242]. In general, it may be true that we can see in Paul's 'sensitivity to questions of status' a man who has undergone, and continues to struggle with, the severe reversals of his social rank for the sake of the gospel[243]. But in the particular instance of aid, we have ample evidence of a well-adjusted apostle. Paul enjoys a happy relationship with the Philippians and appreciated deeply the gifts and services they had given them. This is what Dungan describes

---

241 'Scholastic Community 2', 136.

242 For details, see above 158.

243 So E.A. Judge, 'St. Paul as a Radical Critic', 191-193.

as 'the positive side of Paul's attitude'[244]. The question in Philippians is not about money or wealth per se. Certainly, there are none of the pronouncements we might expect from his Greek counterparts on the subject[245]. Rather, he welcomes the gift as evidence of the concern that the Philippians have for him (4:10) and looks forward to the prospect of the divine reciprocity they would receive (4:17). In 1 Cor. 9, his argument is again positive. It concerns his freedom to accept or to refuse an offer of aid as he chooses.

f. J. C. Hurd and C. K. Barrett have suggested that the collection underlies Paul's refusal, though for different reasons. Barrett suggests that Paul wished to avoid misrepresentation in regard to the collection[246]. Hurd's proposal is quite novel to say the least. Paul's refusal is due to the fact 'that they had not offered him financial support'[247]. He concludes this on the basis of Phil. 4:15, 16, 19, where it is clear that Paul was not 'constitutionally opposed' to accepting money. He stresses correctly the caution with which Paul approaches the matter of the collection in Corinth, as if 'he wished to allay any suspicions on the part of the Corinthians that he had personal designs on the collection'. He also notes the reluctance on the part of the Corinthians to participate though they had previously agreed to do so (1 Cor. 16:1-4; 2 Cor. 9:1-5), and the clear evidence of their distrust of Paul over 'money' matters (2 Cor. 12:16-18). Thus Paul's vehement defence of his right to support and his equally vehement statement that he had never accepted anything

---

[244] The Sayings of Jesus, 29 and see n.5. Contrast R.F. Hock, 'Paul's Tentmaking' 561 who says the words, ἐμαυτὸν ταπεινῶν (2 Cor. 11:7), though primarily alluding to his working for wages, in the context must also include the gifts from Macedonia. He concludes that both working and acceptance of gifts must have been demeaning to him. However, as I argue in Chapter 8, tapeinoun refers to his contrary conduct alluded to in these verses.

[245] Cf. Dio Chrysostom, Disc. 79; Plutarch, Mor. 523C-538B; Seneca, Ep. 110, 'On True and Fake Riches'; Crates, Epp. 7, 8.

[246] 1 Cor. 207

[247] Origins, 204.

in 1 Cor. 9:16-18 is part of his attempt to clear himself of the suspicion that he intended to use the collection for his own purposes, a suspicion which may have first arisen when gifts arrived from Macedonia[248].

It is true that Paul never says in 1 Cor. 9, 'I refused your offer', but only that he has not availed himself of his right and never intends to (vv. 12b, 15a). Hurd, though, does not take into account the offers which were made to others, the ill-feeling over Paul's refusal, nor the conclusion which they draw about his lack of affection for them. He totally ignores 2 Cor. 11:7-15 and 12:11-15 and the important comparisons contained in these passages. I suggest that it is Paul's refusal of aid, compounded by his 'preferred' relations with the Philippians, which has resulted in problems about the collection and has led to the kind of suspicion we find in 2 Corinthians.

The inadequacies of many of these explanations are in measure due to the failure to see the social context of giving and receiving. None look at the moral questions relating to acceptance and refusal, nor at the kind of relationships to which either of these actions may lead. I will summarise briefly from my chapters on Friendship and Enmity the accepted grounds for refusal and the consequences of such action and then examine Paul's refusal in this context. It must be remembered, first, that the offer of a gift constituted an offer of friendship. While in theory it was voluntary and disinterested, it was intended to place the recipient under an obligation to repay. Acceptance was conditional; the recipient must respond with a counter-gift or service, immediately or at some later time, and numerous and popular conventions governed the behaviour of both benefactor and recipient[249].

Second, giving and receiving was an integral part of the status apparatus and as such was linked with the notions of honour and shame. The gift was not only intended to create a relationship of one kind or another but to enhance the

---

[248] Ibid., 200-206; cf. 70-71.

[249] For details, see above 7-12.

giver's status and to win honour and recognition from others. The acceptor, in turn, so as not to lose face, had to outdo the benefactor in generosity to regain the advantage in status. This is the 'rivalry' which Greeks and Romans of wealth and power either loved or hated[250]. Third, friendship undergirded the activity of people of high status who used their wealth not only to cater for their social and economic needs, but to form alliances, to secure power, as a form of security and protection against personal and political enemies. By their gifts and services, they obligated people from all ranks - superiors, equals, inferiors - in a network of relations based on common interests and reciprocal services[251].

Refusal is seldom discussed in Greek or Roman authors but there are, as I have outlined, proper grounds for refusal. a. Aristotle says one ought to refuse where one is unwilling to return the favour[252]. b. Seneca absolves a person where he would not have chosen to give to the offerer in the first place. That is, where the offerer is an unworthy person[253]. In both instances, these grounds for refusal are formulated from hindsight, as a result of the many conflicts and disputes known to both writers which occurred after acceptance, and the advice forms part of one of the common _topoi_ of friendship, the careful choice of friends[254]. c. I suggested earlier that Paul offered three reasons for refusal - a hindrance (1 Cor. 9:12b); a burden (2 Cor. 11:9; 12:13, 14); love (2 Cor. 11:11; 12:15). There is a fourth, freedom. Seneca maintains that where coercion through fear is absent, in most situations one is free and able to decide wisely whether to accept or refuse[255]. Socrates' much lauded refusal of Archelaus' invitation, says Seneca, was because he valued his freedom. He exercised his right to choose and remained

---

250 Ibid., 2, 6, 12, 49.

251 Ibid., 31-34, 66-69.

252 EN 8.13.9.

253 de Ben. 2.28.3-6; cf. 2.21.5-6.

254 See my discussion above 13-15.

255 de Ben. 2.18.6-7.

free of obligation. By refusing the invitation, the equivalent of refusing a gift, he declined to enter into voluntary servitude[256]. Aristotle implies as much also. To be unable to reciprocate in kind to a wealthy king would have shamed Socrates[257]. This is consistent with what we have seen in Hock's study of Socrates' practice with gifts and fees. But Hock does not emphasise enough that Socrates' refusal of a fee or gift would often have been a refusal of a binding reicprocal relationship. By refusing, Socrates remained free rather than become a dependant of those who had the fee. Paul also refuses on the grounds that he is <u>eleutheros</u> (1 Cor. 9:1) with the <u>exousia</u> (9:12, 18) to choose as he pleases. There is a vast difference, though, between Socrates and Paul's refusal, as I will later argue in ch. 8 in detail. According to a Cynic tradition, Socrates' freedom is preserved by his rejection of all gifts and fees from those he teaches[258]. Paul's freedom is exercised as a right to accept (the Philippians) or to refuse (the Corinthians) as he himself chose.

d. Seneca allows for refusal where acceptance of the offer may result in some injury, inconvenience or risk to a worthy benefactor. For example, where the service consists of defending a person in the courts, the reciprocal relationship which ensued may make him an enemy of a powerful opponent. Rather than become an imposition, Seneca suggests a person should run his own risk without him[259]. It is important to notice the binding nature of the ties which acceptance creates. Does Paul's refusal of the offer of financial assistance on the grounds that he did not wish to burden them carry with it these wider implications ? The Corinthians have seen refusal and acceptance in terms of a relationship (2 Cor. 11:11; 12:13)

Cicero, in a letter of recommendation, may express a

---

[256] Ibid., 5.6.2-7.

[257] Rhet. 2.23.8; and see above 16-17.

[258] For details, see above 226-230.

[259] de Ben. 2.21.3.

similar sentiment to Paul's although it is in the form of a request. To his friends he writes : 'Were it not so, I would observe my usual practice and avoid giving you the slightest trouble. Indeed you yourselves can best testify to the fact that, though I could make no request of you which you would not grant, it never has been my wish to impose a burden upon you'[260]. That is, though he usually avoids being a burden, within the ties of friendship he has the right, as his recommendation shows, to ask his friends to fulfil his request. In this instance he has chosen to place a weight upon them in the context of a mutual relationship. Not to be a burden of one kind or another, then, is a legitimate ground for refusal, where the obligations of the relationship could cause hardship or injury to a good benefactor or friend.

It is possible to argue that Paul conceived of his relationship with the Corinthians in terms of friendship, one of trust constituted by recommendation (2 Cor. 3:1-3). Faced with a deteriorating relationship, he consistently refused to commend himself again for they of all people had received him and knew him (2 Cor. 3:1-3, 5:11-12; 10:18; 12:11; cf. 1:12-14[261]. Paul should have been able to expect the Corinthians to accept his refusal in terms of his not being a burden to them, as a sign of his love and concern for them. But as his friends they might well have expected Paul to accept the aid they so willingly offered as evidence of his affection. They had chosen to construe his refusal otherwise in the light of his acceptance of Philippian gifts.

As I have said previously, refusal is seldom discussed by Greek and Roman authors. Their discussions of friendship almost entirely centre upon the moral obligations of giving, receiving and returning. The obligation to receive was almost

---

260 Fam. 13.76.1. Cf. also ibid., 5.9.1, for a request for a friend to accept a 'burden of service'; id., Att. 3.21, where Atticus is bearing 'several men's burdens' on Cicero's behalf.

261 See Chapter 7 for the alliance between Paul's Corinthian enemies and the rival apostles and the institution of their friendship by recommendation.

universally honoured, though often carelessly, foolishly and begrudgingly. The majority of instances these authors cite of friendship and enmity relate to the cessation of friendship and a number of grounds are provided for ending unwanted friendships[262]. On the evidence available, I doubt if refusal was generally practised. Most accepted the gifts and services despite the reservations and misgivings they may have had. It was the easier course of action.

Though the grounds may have been just, refusal or cessation of friendship often led to hostility. Though M. Mauss' observation, that refusal was the equivalent of a 'declaration of war' and 'a refusal of friendship and intercourse in which there was no middle ground[263], is not entirely true of the social or political relations of the Late Republic or Early Empire, there are many instances of hostilities being caused by refusal or violation of friendship. There was a marked reluctance to enter into hostile relationships and there would need to have been good reason for a declaration of enmity. It is clear enough that refusal of gifts and services or attempts to end a friendship could be and were construed as an act of hostility by the offended party[264]. This is particularly so in the case where a person was placed in the unenviable position of having (or appearing) to decide in favour of one friend and against another. The choice would inevitably strengthen one friendship and turn the other into enmity[265].

Paul's acceptance of the Philippian gifts does appear to have been understood by the Corinthians within the conventions of friendship and enmity. By his refusal he has insulted and dishonoured them, treated them as inferiors and showed that he did not love them. Undoubtedly they considered themselves to be in the right. Hence Paul's ironic plea : 'Forgive me this wrong' (2 Cor. 12:13; cf. 11:7). There is ample evidence of a hostile relationship between Paul and his enemies -

---

262 For details, see above 18-19.

263 The Gift, 10-11, 37-41, 79.

264 For details, see my discussion 16-21, 39-40.

265 Ibid., 40-42.

invective, comparison, conspiracy, charges - and it does appear to result from Paul's refusal, and his subsequent behaviour.

One relationship which precedes all other reciprocal relationships in both time and importance is that of parent and child. Though it is a familial relationship, it appears in the major discussions of friendship of Aristotle and Seneca as a kind of friendship, as a giving and receiving between unequals akin to that between god and man, ruler and subject, or husband and wife. This is an extremely important relationship for our study, for when Paul is attacked for favouring the Philippians and others in preference to the Corinthians, he appeals to his higher reciprocal familial relationship to further justify his refusal. He writes : 'Here for the third time I am ready to come to you. And I will not be a burden, for I seek not what is yours but you; for children ought not to lay up for their parents but parents for their children. I will most gladly spend and be spent for your souls. If I love you the more am I to be loved the less ?' (2 Cor. 12:14-15).

The parent-child relationship has priority over all other kinds of relationships[266]. A passage which contains many of the popular sentiments about this relationship and which will shed light on the ideas which Paul uses, is found in Aristotle's essay on friendship. He writes : 'Now in these unequal friendships the benefits that one party receives and is entitled to claim (ζητεῖν) from the other are not the same on either side. But the friendship between parents and children will be enduring and equitable, when the children render to the parents the services due to the authors of one's being, and the parents to the children those due to one's offspring. The affection rendered in these various unequal friendships should also be proportionate : the better of the two parties, for instance, or the more useful or otherwise superior as the case may be, should receive more affection than he bestows; since when the affection rendered is proportionate to desert,

---

[266] Eg., Aulus Gellius, 5.13.1-5.

this produces equality in a sense between the parties, and equality is felt to be an essential element of friendship'[267].

Note the important elements which are common to most types of friendship of disparity. a. Parents do and should outdo their children in benefits and services. b. These benefits and services are those which parents owe their children. c. Children can never repay in kind or in equal value. d. They must therefore repay with greater love and honour. These elements recur throughout his essay and the stress is always upon the parents as generous benefactors and the children as loving recipients. This distinction does not exclude the parent from loving or the child from providing services. Each love and give to the other above other relationships, though the parent is generally considered to bestow more love than he receives in both degree and duration[268].

This reflects the way in which Greeks and Romans viewed unequal relationships. When Aristotle says that 'the benefits which one party receives and is entitled to seek from the other are not the same on either side', he means that not only are they different in kind but that their value is unequal also. The parent is and always remains the benefactor and the child can expect this to be so. Parents give life and sustain it. The child is the recipient who, being unable to respond in the same kind or equally, still must reciprocate with what he can, namely honour and love[269]. In this way the disparity in the parent-child relationship is redressed and the relationship has the appearance of equality. Honour and love are the foremost duties of the child throughout the whole of his life.

As Seneca also observes : 'Our parents almost always outdo us'[270]. Their giving is different to other kinds, 'For to those to whom they have already given they nonetheless give, and will continue to give, benefits'[271] What they give

267 EN 8.7.2.

268 EN 8.12.2; 9.7.1-3.

269 EN 8.11.3; 8.12.2, 3, 5; 8.14.2; 9.2.8.

270 de Ben. 5.5.2.

271 Ibid., 3.11.2

are considered to be 'the greatest of all benefits'[272]. While it is no disgrace to be outdone by them, Seneca is concerned lest this popular sentiment should become an excuse or a means of discouraging a child from attempting to reciprocate in kind. Thus he urges parents and children to enter into a glorious contest to decide whether they have given to receive the greater benefits[273]. He considers, however, that 'not to love one's parents is unfilial'. That is, an ungrateful person who has forgotten the benefits his parents have bestowed upon him[274].

Paul resorts to the parent-child analogy on a number of occasions to describe his relationships with his converts, whether viewed as a community[275] or as individuals[276]. The use of this metaphor is common enough in Greek and Roman authors in a wide range of contexts. For Paul, it appears to be more than an illustration; rather it is fundamental to his understanding of his relationship with those whom he has begotten through the gospel. When he speaks as a father, it is to convey his authority and affection and care[277]. In 2 Corinthians, his parental feelings give way to expressions of hurt and indignation at not being loved despite his

---

272 Ibid., 6.24.1-2; cf. 2.11.5; Aristotle, EN 8.11.2.

273 Ibid., 3.37.1; see also 3.29.1-38.3.

274 Ibid., 3.1.5; cf. Cicero, Planc. 33.80 : 'What is filial affection, if not a benevolent gratitude towards one's parents ?'.

275 Father : 1 Cor. 4:15; 1 Thess. 2:11; mother : Gal. 4:19; parent : 2 Cor. 12:14; children : 1 Cor. 4:14; 2 Cor. 6:13; 12:14; 1 Thess. 2:11.

276 Timothy : 1 Cor. 4:17; Phil. 2.:22; Onesimus : Phlm. 10.

277 1 Cor. 4:21; 2 Cor. 6:11-13; 1 Thess. 2:11. The absolute authority and rights of a father over his family were grounded in law and sanctioned by conventions held to be sacred. Under Roman law, a son, even if he were of age, had no independent legal rights. Paul appears to refer to Roman law in regard to his metaphor of adoption (Ro. 8:15-17); Gal. 4:1-2) and it is possible that the authority of a Roman father is brought to mind by his use of familial language. This must be kept in mind when we say that Paul does not appeal to conventional notions of authority and leadership; for details, see above 45-46. For the adoption metaphor, see F. Lyall, 'Roman Law in the Writings of Paul - Adoption', JBL. 88 (1969), 458.

openheartedness[278], and his jealousy at his children's giving their affection to his rivals[279]. From the foregoing, it is plain that Paul believes his relationship with his converts should have priority over any which they may form with others : 'For though you have countless guides in Christ you do not have many fathers. For I became your father in Christ Jesus through the gospel'[280]. All this is in jeopardy. The Corinthians have become convinced that Paul does not love them and prefers others. He has refused their offers while his opponents have openly demonstrated their friendship by acceptance.

I suggest that it is against this familiar background that we should view Paul's remarks in 2 Cor. 12:14-15. Paul is appealing to his known rights and duties as a parent and patently reminding the Corinthians of theirs. The first argument of his duties as a parent reflects the first two common elements in Aristotle's passage. His refusal of their offers of financial aid was in line with his parental duties. He would not burden them. He would not seek their possessions; rather he would seek them. For children are not under an obligation to provide for their parents but parents are to their children. Thus he is well within his rights to refuse. And he would continue to spend (δαπανᾶν) and to be spent (ἐκδαπανᾶσθαι) on their behalf. The superiority in benefits must always be on his side. δαπανᾶν may recall Paul's use of ἀδάπανος, 'free of charge', in 1 Cor. 9:18[281]. However, it is used with many other commercial terms as part of the reciprocal language of

---

278 2 Cor. 6:11-13.

279 2 Cor. 11:2-4.

280 1 Cor. 4:15.

281 So R. F. Hock, The Working Apostle, 143. He argues that both δαπανᾶν and ἀδάπανος refer to Paul's working to support himself and cites instances in discussions of the philosopher's support where the student spends (δαπανᾶν) money on his teacher. Thus Paul is emphasising that he would not burden the Corinthians in this way as evidence of his love for them; love (ἀγαπᾶν) being another characteristic of the true philosopher. I suggest though that both δαπανᾶν and ἀγαπᾶν continue the parent-child metaphor and emphasise the traditional reciprocal duties of each.

friendship, of giving and receiving. Aristotle, in fact, takes spending (δαπάνη) to be included in giving (δόσις)[282]. Both δαπάνη and δόσις are characteristics of the great-souled person who uses his wealth correctly, i.e., as a means of securing friends[283]. Thus δαπανᾶν can have this reciprocal nuance denoting the generous act of the benefactor. Here, I suggest, it refers to the parent's fulfilling of his obligations in a reciprocal familial relationship.

It is not at all surprising to find, after the stress upon his parental duties, reference to the obligations of the children in the way Paul develops the metaphor. He asks them to love him in return : 'If I love you the more, am I to be loved the less ?' (εἰ περισσοτέρως ὑμᾶς ἀγαπῶ, ἧσσον ἀγαπῶμαι;) (v. 15b). This must reflect the common sentiment found in Aristotle, that children must repay their parents with greater love and honour; the superior 'should receive more affection than he bestows' (μᾶλλον φιλεῖσθαι ἢ φιλεῖν)[284]. The charges against Paul that he does not love the Corinthians[285], that he has violated the relationship by his refusal, that he holds them in less esteem (ἡττάομαι) than the other churches from whom he has accepted gifts (v. 13), are put into true perspective. He has given them every benefit that other churches had received. The only difference being that out of love he did not burden them by accepting the offers made to him. He has acted as a generous and loving parent and would continue to do so. They are behaving as ungrateful children.

5. Variance in Paul's practice.

D. L. Dungan and R. F. Hock put forward two different views of the consistency of Paul's conduct. Central to Dungan's stress upon Paul's departure from the norm is his understanding of the saying of the Lord in 1 Cor. 9:14 : 'the Lord commanded (διατάσσειν) that those who proclaim the gospel should get their living by the gospel'. Paul's citing of this

---

[282] EN 4.1.29.

[283] Ibid., 4.1.7, 23, 24; and see above 32-34.

[284] Ibid., 8.7.2.

[285] Cf. 2 Cor. 2:4, 6:11-13, 11:11, for Paul's affirmation of his love for the Corinthians.

'command' obviously implies 'that it is a regulation binding upon the Christian community. A law in the technical sense of that term'[286]. Yet he openly states his disregard for it in vv. 15-18 and adopts a practice for the entire Gentile mission 'that appears to be in flat opposition to the custom of the Jerusalem apostolate'[287]. More than this 'he dares to denounce in the most savage way certain other famous apostles (none other than Peter and the brothers of the Lord) who were proceeding in accordance with it'[288]. His refusal confused the Corinthians who, Dungan suggests, knew of the custom of support and adhered to it and deeply felt his 'spurning' of their 'legitimate right' to assist him[289].

His relationship with the Corinthians worsened when they discovered, either by comparing notes or being told by Jerusalem apostles, that Paul, despite all his previous vehement declarations 'had been secretly accepting financial support from a congregation in Macedonia'[290]. Dungan conceives of this as a most embarrassing disclosure for Paul and takes his words in 2 Cor. 11:7-11 to be in the form of a confession or admission of deception. Paul's previous explanation as to the reason for his refusal in 1 Cor. 9:19-23 is now thrown back into his face with deadly effectiveness. They accused him of inconsistency, deceitfulness, and confused thinking[291].

Dungan's analysis of the situation has a number of commendable features. He rightly sees Paul's versatility as the cause of confusion and misunderstanding and the adverse

---

[286] The Sayings of Jesus, 3.

[287] Ibid., 8.

[288] Ibid., 3, 18-19, 37. Dungan considers that the apostles in 1 Cor.9:5 and the οἱ ὑπερλίαν ἀπόστολοι of 2 Cor. 11:5 and 12:11 are the same people. Thus the conflict is one of Paul and Jerusalem, a popular view against which I will argue in a later chapter.

[289] Ibid., 6, 9, 11, 39.

[290] Ibid., 3-4, 22. He suggests that the Thessalonians, who had heard Paul's boast previously, would have been less than impressed had they known of the Philippian connection.

[291] Ibid., 37-39. He regards Paul's reaction in 2 Cor. 12:13 as not being wholly straightforward, though his anger may account for what appears to be further 'attempts at concealment'.

effect his relations with the Philippians had upon the situation. He correctly sees a firm connection between 1 Cor. 9 and 2 Cor. 11:7-11 and 12:13-18 and the deterioration of the relationship between the Corinthians and Paul over a period of time as a result of his refusal of support. However, I cannot agree with his ordering of the events, the weight he places on the saying of Christ, nor what he describes as Paul's curiously deceptive behaviour.

First, Dungan suggests that the Corinthians were aware of the custom and made their offer to Paul as a result. He refused while at the same time refrained from telling them that he was receiving gifts from Philippi. It was only much later that the Corinthians discovered the real situation and attacked him. Dungan does not explain how the Corinthians became aware of the saying. Their offer to Paul occurred during his first visit and if it was prompted by the Lord's command then Paul and his associates alone could have informed them. Apollos, possibly a recipient of aid, arrived after Paul had gone (Acts 18:24-28) and we have no indication as to when Cephas or the others referred to in 1 Cor. 9:12a arrived. All the evidence suggests that Paul received the Philippian gifts during his first visit, a situation which could hardly have been kept from the Corinthians. Thus Paul's refusal of the Corinthian offer and his acceptance of the Philippian gifts occurred before other 'apostles' appeared in Corinth. It is possible that they only learned of this practice after Paul's departure and that the saying and the relationships they formed with the new arrivals became part of their criticism and comparison of him with others.

What then prompted the original offer ? One possibility is, as we have seen, that Paul informed them of his right from the outset but then refused to accept offers which followed. Or was it the arrival of the Philippian gifts which the Corinthians wished to emulate only to be mortified by Paul's refusal ? Or was it the first beginnings of factional interests in which one group endeavoured to win Paul. If Paul did not inform them of the saying or general custom followed by other apostles, was the offer prompted by social custom within the conventions and expectations of friendship ? To refuse under these circumstances while accepting gifts from others could certainly account for the hostility against Paul, the desire for other 'recipient' figureheads, and the accusation of inconsistency which I believe is contained in the words, 'all things to all men'.

Second, I doubt that diatassein (1 Cor. 9:14) has the absolute meaning of 'regulation' or 'law' which Dungan sees in it. Such a sense leads him by necessity to describe Paul's variance as deliberate disobedience[292]. He says that Paul set aside 'a command of the Lord explicitly ordering him as well as other apostles to accept financial support' and changes the status of this obligation (opseilēma) into a discretionary privilege (exousia)[293]. He believes that the saying Paul had in mind is the one preserved in Matt. 10:10 and Lk. 10:7, but as I have argued before, the primary reference is to hospitality in these passages, not to salaries. Even if, as Dungan believes, the gospel sayings have undergone qualification due to abuses by some itinerants[294], I can not see any evidence in them of the weight that he attaches to Paul's use of it. While it seems to represent the practice of the majority of the apostles, and Paul's conduct and that of his associates is exceptional and even variable, it is too strong to say that the intention of it is to exclude the right of refusal or to debar an apostle from working for his living. The intention of the saying is to give to the preacher the right to be supported because of his work, which in the majority of cases prevented him from earning any income in the normal way. This 'right' (exousia), as Paul has previously shown in vv. 7-13, is

---

292 Ibid., 3, 39. Dungan suggests that Paul's disobedience is an argument from silence. Paul was open to such a charge but no one made use of it.

293 Ibid., 20-21, espec. 20n.3 for the distinction he makes between opseilēma and exousia.

294 Ibid., 41-80.

widely recognized in many religious and social contexts. His argument in chapter 9 is not about a breach of command but is a defence of his variable behaviour in terms of his right or freedom to accept or refuse as he chooses.

Third, I have shown that though the Corinthians knew about the Philippian gifts from the outset, it was Paul's variable conduct that led to their hostility towards him. Dungan is correct, though, in saying that the invective in 2 Corinthians largely reflects the ideas contained in 1 Cor. 9:19-23, which he takes to be Paul's explanation of his 'relativization under the Gospel'[295]. These ideas become the vehicle by which they express their mistrust and suspicion of Paul as a 'cunning swinder'[296], once his deception became known. However, Dungan does not raise the question as to whether 1 Cor. 9:19-23 contains charges relating to his variable conduct or that the words 'all things to all men' formed part of the invective against Paul. I suggest, then, that this conflict and the kind of charges that were brought against Paul arose, if not during his first stay there, not longer after his departure.

R. F. Hock argues for the consistency of Paul's conduct. Paul dissociates himself from mercenary sophists and stands within the Socratic-Cynic tradition of non-charging philosophers. The weakness in Hock's argument, as I have shown, is his failure to demonstrate that there is a difference between the Philippian gifts and the Corinthian offers of aid. The only difference the Corinthians have detected is in Paul's attitude to the Philippians and themselves: he takes from one and not the other. Paul's behaviour is more complex than what we see in the stated positions of the various Cynics. His acceptance of the Philippian gifts (even if it were unique) would have offended a Demonax or a Musonius Rufus especially as the gifts were being received by him at a time when he was refusing others. Given the context which Hock provides for Paul's work in Thessalonica, his acceptance of gifts would have been seen

---

[295] Ibid., 33-36.
[296] Ibid., 22, 38-39.

by the true Cynic to be incongruent with his declared behaviour. In Corinth, if he was endeavouring to abide by these traditions, ideal Cynics would have condemned his variable behaviour, as had his enemies. It was evidence to them of an inconstant character, not unlike the changeable, servile philosopher-flatterer described by Dio Chrysostom[297].

Scholars have noticed Paul's inconsistency and have endeavoured to explain it in terms of a 'higher consistency', of an obedience to the higher principle of the gospel. They have also noticed the dilemma which he presented to people in his churches[298]. I have already commented on this aspect of his relations with the Galatians in which I suggested that Paul's conduct left him open to misunderstanding, and to ridicule and comparison by those who wished to exploit the accepted conventions against him[299]. I shall examine his inconsistency in chapter 8. It is necessary to ask by what standard of consistency his conduct is measured and found to be offensive. It must be that of his own society. The Greeks had a very fixed view of character. What commended a man to his fellow was his uniform consistency throughout the various circumstances of his life and constancy in his relations with both his friends and his enemies. In technical terms, this meant that he should remain true to his inhereted characteristics, those imposed by nature (physis) and his acquired characteristics (ēthos). Physis and ēthos represent his total pattern of conduct from which people could make predictions about how he would behave with a certain degree of accuracy in all situations. He was expected to conform to his known character, to what people expected of him.

It was accepted that people could change due to coercion or the vicissitudes of life, and versatility in the face of the various contingencies of life was not always denigrated. But the free man who deliberately and consciously changed his behaviour to accommodate to the interests of others or

---

297 For details, see above 75, below 311.

298 Ibid., 306-309.

299 Ibid., see above 155-156.

to different circumstances, as Paul is criticized as doing, was regarded as abjectly servile and deserving of ridicule. This is particularly true of those who are inconstant in their relations with others[300]. While Paul's refusal was a serious breach of his social and moral obligation to the Corinthians and was the cause of the hostility, the kind of criticism that his enemies level against him suggests that they are focusing their invective upon his inconstancy, the variance of his conduct in relation to giving and receiving, rather than on the refusal itself. This is most evident in 2 Corinthians but, as I shall argue, is implied in the ideas and language contained in 1 Cor. 9. Such a focus enables them to include other aspects of Paul's anomalous behaviour also. This will become more evident as I examine the formation of the hostile alliance and the nature of that relationship and its opposition to Paul, and the nature of Paul's relations with the Corinthian church.

c. Summary.

I have argued in this chapter that the conventions of friendship and enmity underlie the conflict between Paul and his enemies. I suggested that the Corinthian offer of aid consisted of an offer of friendship, in the form of a gift made to Paul by certain wealthy Corinthians. His refusal of their gift was construed by them as a hostile act and a refusal of friendship and his acceptance of gifts from his Philippian friends led to the charge that he viewed the Corinthians unfavourably. This gave rise to suspicion and invective and an attempt to displace him as the apostle in Corinth with invitations being sent to other apostles. His enemies commenced to ridicule him as an inconstant person, or false friend and flatterer who accommodated to others and different circumstances to please himself and disregarded his social and moral obligations.

The analysis of the notion of hybris provided us with a new social and moral context to understand the various kinds

---

[300] Ibid., 74-76, 78-80

of excessive behaviour, the ideas and terms Paul uses, and the unpalatable remedy of moderation which he prescribes. I have suggested, as a result, that we should call Paul's enemies 'hybrists', rather than 'gnostics'. This context also gave us a basis for understanding why Paul adopted the shameful position of a socially and economically disadvantaged person in response to their attacks upon him. We saw, briefly, that Paul described the rival apostles in 2 Cor. 10:12-13 in similar language and it has enabled me to propose a connection between them and Paul's opponents in 1 Corinthians, based on a common pattern of behaviour. This link has been further hinted at in terms of friendship between these people formed by mutual recommendation, and we now proceed to examine this relationship and the conduct of enmity between Paul and the Corinthians.

Section 3

THE CONDUCT OF ENMITY BETWEEN PAUL AND THE CORINTHIANS

Chapter 7

THE ASSOCIATION OF PAUL'S ENEMIES AND THE RIVAL APOSTLES: THE INITIATION OF FRIENDSHIP BY RECOMMENDATION

a. Recommendation passages in 2 Corinthians.

2 Corinthians contains seven passages in which the verb συνίστανει or the adjective συστατικος appears (3:1-3; 4:1-6; 5:11b-13; 6:4; 7:11; 10:12-18; 12:11-13). With one exception[1], synistanai and systatikos are technical words which refer to the common practice of recommendation. The key verse is 3:1 where Paul asks: 'Αρχόμεθα πάλιν ἑαυτοὺς συνιστάνειν; ἢ μὴ χρῄζομεν ὥς τινες συστατικῶν ἐπιστολῶν πρός ὑμᾶς ἢ ἐξ ὑμῶν;. The other passages appear to reflect the various nuances present in these two questions. The passages occur at important points throughout 2 Corinthians and it is evident that recommendation is a critical issue for both Paul and his rivals' relations with the Corinthians.[2] Though Paul refers to a previous recommendation of himself to the Corinthians - implied by πάλιν (3:1) - we have no record of it in either of his letters to them. 1 Corinthians contains two of his recommendations of others (16:15-16; 17-18),[3] a reference to credentialled representatives (οὓς εἀν δοκιμάσητε, δι' ἐπιστολῶν ...) of the Corinthians with regard to the collection (16:3) and what might be described as the 'despatch of an

---

[1] 7:11, where συνίστασαι has the sense of 'prove'; cf. Ro. 3:5; 5:8; Gal.2:18.

[2] C.K. Barrett, 2 Cor. 129, has referred to it as a theme which played an important part in the affairs at Corinth.

[3] For details, see above 150.

emmisary' (16:10-11; cf. 4:17)[4]. There are, in addition, two passages in which Paul defends himself by reference to his work (κοπιῶμεν ἐργαξόμενοι ...) which may be regarded as self commendatory (4:12; 15:10) though I am of the opinion that comparison rather than self-commendation in the technical sense is involved in both instances[5].

b. The reconstruction of events between 1 and 2 Corinthians.

First, the historical reconstruction cannot be separated from the literary problems in 2 Corinthians and historical conclusions largely reflect the literary hypothesis which is adopted. I will look briefly at the problem of the integrity of 2 Corinthians in my last chapter in relation to the presence of the different tones adopted by Paul in his letter which have led many scholars to view it as a composite work. The historical reconstruction I prefer is as follows[6]:

a. Paul first planned to leave Ephesus after Pentecost and visit the Macedonian churches en route to Corinth where he intended to stay for some time (1 Cor.16:5-9). He wanted to deal with his arrogant opponents, the hybrists (as I call them), if they persisted in their opposition to him despite his letter (4:18-21) and to complete the collection (16:1-4). If he deemed it necessary, he would travel with their chosen representatives to Jerusalem.

b. He amended this plan and decided to visit Corinth before going on to Macedonia and then returning from there to Corinth, and to continue from there to Judaea with the collection (2 Cor.2:15-16). He gives only one reason for the change: that

---

4 So Chan Hie Kim, Familiar Greek Letter, 139-140; cf. 2 Cor. 8:23; 1 Thess.3:2; Phil. 2:25.

5 Ibid., 139. The verb kopiav is used almost exclusively by Paul in the context of recommendation: 1 Cor.16:16; 1 Thess.5:12; Ro.16:6, 12a, 12b; cf. Gal.4:11, Phil.2:16. See also ibid., 140, synergos in recommendation passages: Phil. 4:3; 1 Cor.16:16 (participial form); Phlm. 24; Ro.16:3, 9a; dispatch of an emissary: Phil.2:23; 2 Cor. 8:23; 1 Thess.3:2 ; only twice used elsewhere, 1 Cor. 3:9; 2 Cor. 1:24;

6 See further, C.K. Barrett, 1 Cor. 5-11, 18-21; W.G. Kümmel, N.T. Intr. 210; F.F. Bruce, 1&2 Cor, 164-166; G.D. Fee, 'ΧΑΡΙΣ in II Corinthians 1:15; Apostolic Parousia and Paul-Corinth Chronology', NTS 24 (1978), 533-538.

they might twice have the opportunity to help him along the way[7]. Fee suggests that Paul wished to give the Corinthians the chance to do something for him seeing he had refused their earlier offers of aid and that their complaints may have caused him to change his travel plans[8]. F.F. Bruce thinks that news of worse problems in Corinth (or, possibly, his affiliation in Aisa - 2 Cor. 1:8-11) threw his already modified plans into disarray and made it essential for him to visit Corinth urgently[9]. The possible reasons are numerous. I suggest that Paul wished to bring his conflict with the hybrists to a head before tending to the matter of the collection in both Macedonia and Corinth and therefore decided to visit Corinth first before making a return visit.

c. On his arrival he found that the situation had deteriorated. Things went badly for him. He was openly humiliated[10] before the Corinthians. Either Paul's enemies had won the contest of strength with him or the newly arrived apostles had shamed him before the Corinthians who apparently failed to come to his aid. He withdrew suddenly to Ephesus, presumably through Macedonia, and remained there.

d. The hybrists had won the day and the collection still remained to be completed. Assuming that his return from Macedonia would provoke wider hostilities, he decided to spare the Corinthians the promised painful confrontation with himself (1:23-2:2; 13:2). Instead he sent Titus armed with a strong letter to resolve the conflict. Titus' visit seems to have been directed solely at regaining the Corinthians' loyalty

---

7 So G.D. Fee, 'ΧΑΡΙΣ in II Cor.1:15', 533-537, who argues that χάρις is active from the perspective of the Corinthians rather than Paul with the emphasis upon the clauses δι' ὑμῶν διελθεῖν and ὑφ' ὑμῶν προπεμφθῆναι. This interpretation certainly fits into our understanding of προπέμπειν which denotes the responsibility of the host to provide for his departing guest and accords with Paul's seeking aid in his travels from the Corinthians in 1 Cor.16:6-7. Paul then in 2 Cor.1:15 is seeking hospitality rather than imparting some benefit.

8 Ibid., 536.

9 1&2 Cor. 164; see also W.G. Kümmel, N.T. Introd. 210.

10 2 Cor.2:1,5; λυπεῖν, cf., Arndt and Gingrich, XXIV, 'more than "vex" or "cause grief" but "severely humiliate"'. Cf., 12:21: μὴ πάλιν ἐλθόντος μου ταπεινώσῃ με ὁ θεός μου πρὸς ὑμᾶς.

to Paul, something Paul felt confident about achieving, and effecting their consequent withdrawal from his enemies (2:3-4; 7:12). This involved a further change of plans. How, or even whether, he returned to Corinth depended largely upon Titus' report when he met him at Troas (2:13-14).

e. Paul's extreme affliction in Asia (1:8-11) may have further disrupted his plans at this stage and delayed his arrival at Troas. For on reaching there, though he had planned to preach and indeed had met with favourable opportunities, he became most anxious when Titus did not arrive. He crossed immediately into Macedonia where he received voluntary contributions from the churches there (9:1-4) and met Titus who cheered him with the news that he brought. The problem with the Corinthians was solved and Paul could now proceed with the collection.

f. He sent Titus and two associates ahead to ensure that the collection would be completed by his arrival (8:16-24). With them he sent a letter[11] in which he explained the arrangements he had made for the collection. He also responded to the charges of inconsistency which had been made against him in relation to his conduct over his travel plans and money matters and to the unfavourable comparisons which the hybrists had made between themselves and him.

Second, it is clear from this reconstruction that Paul's relations with the Corinthians at this time were extremely fragile and were in danger of deteriorating even further in the face of a concerted attack on him by the hybrists. This, more than any other factor, caused him to alter his travel plans.

---

[11] Among scholars who accept the unity of 2 Corinthians, opinions differ as to whether the letter consisted of chapters 1-9 or 1-13. Some see an interval between the sending of chapters 1-9 and chapters 10-13, the latter being written after Paul received news of a worsening of the situation or of a new crisis developing in Corinth. So C.K. Barrett, 1 Cor. 9-10; F.F.Bruce 1&2 Cor. 169-170; J.L. Price, 'Aspects of Paul's Theology and Their Bearing on Literary Problems of Second Corinthians', Studies and Documents 29, B.L. Daniels and M.J. Suggs, Ed. (Salt Lake City, 1967), 102.

2 Corinthians reveals considerable suspicion and mistrust of Paul which could only have developed in the period between the two letters or just prior to the first being written. In 1 Corinthians there is no hint or, at least, Paul does not appear to be aware, of this attitude existing outside of his enemies, the hybrists. Besides these people, Paul names some of his more intimate supporters in Corinth.

In 2 Corinthians, Paul's enemies, in association with the rival apostles, seem to have assumed control and to have persuaded the majority of the Corinthians against Paul. None of Paul's supporters are named. Were they, too, shunned by their fellow Corinthians as his friends? What caused such sudden disaffection and why were the hybrists and their new friends so successful in winning the Corinthians over to their side? Why did Paul have to take such steps to win them back and, despite his expressions of confidence and joy, why was his relationship with them so fragile that he had to persist in his self-defence and to take such precautions over the collection? We have seen one major reason for distrust: Paul's refusal of aid in Corinth and the resultant charge of inconstancy in his relations with others. I shall return to this charge in detail in the next chapter. But as we have seen, the recommendation passages in 2 Corinthians refer to Paul's and the rival apostles' relationships with the Corinthians and I suggest that a further answer to these questions may be found in the nature of recommendation itself.

It would be a fallacy to suggest that Paul did not take sides in the rivalry but was impartial. It is true to say that he did not elevate any one of the figureheads, including himself, over the others, nor compare them unfavourably in any way. But he did oppose the hybrists and threatened to deal with them on his next visit to Corinth if they did not submit to his authority as the parent apostle of Corinth (4:14-21). He may have expected them to do so, but I suggest that the seeds of a future confrontation between the hybrists and Paul were sewn long before this. I have argued in the previous chapter that the hostilities ensued from Paul's refusal of their offer of friendship; that prior to the writing of 1 Corinthians the hybrists were already attempting to displace

Paul as the apostle in Corinth; that the divisions between the Corinthians represented declarations of loyalty to or of independence from Paul. This is to say, the claims 'I am of Paul', 'I am of Apollos' and 'I am of Cephas' indicate primarily a social rather than theological bond, and that the Corinthians were divided along the lines of friendship or enmity with Paul.

In contrast to his attitude towards the hybrists, Paul recommends his supporters (16:15-16, 17-18) and asks the Corinthians to submit to (ὑποτάσσεσθαι) and to recognize (ἐπιγινώσκειν) them because of their service (διακονία) to the church and to Paul. Recommendation as I have shown at length, is based upon the reciprocal relationships (mostly of friendship) between the recommender and recommended and the recommender and recipient[12]. The recommendation places upon the recipient a moral obligation to do as requested as proof of the relationship between himself and the recommender[13]. It is never intended to be optional and failure to respond as requested can be construed as evidence of the cessation of friendship[14]. Undoubtedly Paul is confident that the Corinthians would give due weight to his recommendation[15]. Their refusal to do so would constitute a serious affront to his status as the apostle in Corinth.

How then did the hybrists respond? 2 Corinthians reveals the presence of rival apostles who appear to be in alliance with the hybrists. This alliance seems to have the upper hand in Corinth and was sufficiently strong to humiliate Paul during his second visit and frustrate his plans. The rest of the Corinthians held the visitors in high esteem (eg., 2 Cor. 11:4, 19-20). More than neutrality is suggested by their failure to support Paul on this occasion. Their mistrust of him is clearly evident throughout 2 Corinthians. And all this in the short space of twelve months which elapsed between the

---

[12] For details, see above 92-94, 97-98.

[13] Cf. Paul and Philemon, see above 147-150.

[14] For details, see above 104-106.

[15] F.F. Bruce, 1&2 Cor. 160-161, suggests that Paul's recommendation was 'to remedy a tendency toward anarchy' among the Corinthians.

writing of 1 and 2 Corinthians[16]. I am of the opinion that the hybrists decided to invite apostles of their own to oppose Paul and his supporters and that this was accomplished by letters of recommendation exchanged between themselves and the rival apostles. It is possible that negotiations were under way before 1 Corinthians was written.

c. The recommendation passages in modern scholarship.

In 2 Cor.3:1a, Paul asks the question: ἀρχόμεθα πάλιν ἑαυτοὺς συνιστάνειν;. The negative answer, implied by μή in the following question in v.1b, is found in the similarly worded statement in 5:12: οὐ πάλιν ἑαυτοὺς συνιστάνομεν ὑμῖν. Many commentators suggest that πάλιν indicates that Paul had previously commended himself to the Corinthians, either in a letter or in person, and that a charge of self-praise had been made against him in relation to it[17]. According to this interpretation, heautous synistanein has the sense of 'self-praise' and is almost the equivalent of 'boasting' (καύχημα, καυχάομαι), which is found in a number of the recommendation passages[18]. Such an understanding leads to certain difficulties. Paul had previously claimed that he was not a boastful apostle (1 Cor.9:15-16), a claim which he restates in 2 Cor. 10:13-15. Thus with synistanein as 'praise' in mind, scholars have suggested that palin heautous synistanein means that Paul will not resort to self-praise before the Corinthians. P.E. Hughes says that παλιν does not imply that Paul was guilty of doing so on a previous occasion, only that the charge of self-praise had already been made against him[19]. Palin therefore should be understood as being ironical[20]. In

---

[16] For this estimation, see C.K. Barrett, 2 Cor. 11.

[17] Ibid., 106, possibly the sorrowful visit or when the severe letter was received; A. Plummer, 2 Cor. 77, who suggests as possible instances of self-commendation, 1 Cor.9:15; 14:18; 15:10; cf. 4:16; 7:40; 11:1; 2 Cor. 1:12. Cf. P.E. Hughes, 2 Cor. 85, F.F. Bruce, 1&2 Cor. 189; Chan Hie Kim, Familiar Greek Letter, 139, who calls 1 Cor.4:12 and 15:10, where Paul defends and esteems himself, 'passages which may be regarded as Paul's self-commendation'.

[18] Eg., 2 Cor. 5:12; 10.12-18.

[19] 2 Cor. 85

[20] Ibid.

5:12 where Paul does commend himself again, it is said to be only apparently self-commendation[21], or something which he is forced to do because of his rivals' impressive recommendation and the Corinthians' acceptance of it[22]. Even then, his self-commendation is 'commendation of the gospel as he himself represents it' and not self-praise in a bad sense[23].

Scholars have also made a distinction between acceptable and unacceptable forms of self-commendation. For some the test for self-commendation as being unacceptable self-praise or boasting depends upon the criterion for assessment. In 4:2 Paul says: 'by the open statement of the truth we would commend ourselves (synistanontes heautous) to every man's conscience in the sight of God'. C.K. Barrett says there is only a 'superficial contradiction' with other passages where Paul refuses to commend himself. 'The distinction between Paul's self-commendation and that of his rivals is that he acts in the sight of God. And he appeals to the conscience'[24]. Others have suggested that the position of heauton determines whether the self-commendation has a legitimate sense or a bad sense. Heauton synistanein (3:1; 5:12; 10:12,18), with heauton in the prominent place signifying undue egotism, has a bad sense and reflects either the charge against him or the activity of his opponents. Synistanein heauton (4:2; 6:4) is the 'legitimate commendation of himself and his message which every faithful minister will adopt'[25]. This use of heauton creates an artificial division and reflects the dilemma caused by the rendering of synistanein as 'praise' and scholars' desire to protect Paul from the possibility of self-praise.

As we shall see, self-commendation is an accepted and

---

[21] So R. Bultmann, Exegetische Probleme des Zweiten Korintherbriefes (Upsala, 1947), 14; cf., id., 2Kor. 149.

[22] So C.K. Barrett, 2 Cor. 165-166.

[23] Ibid., 165

[24] Ibid., 129.

[25] So J.H. Bernard, The Second Epistle to the Corinthians, The Expositors Greek Testament, W.R. Nicoll ed. (Grand Rapids, 1967), 53; cf. A. Plummer, 2 Cor. 77.

common convention which differs little from written commendation by third parties. Praise or complimentary phraseology is a traditional though not essential element of both third party and self-commendation and was acceptable if done inoffensively; even extravagant praise by a recommender was acceptable, especially if the recommended proved himself to be worthy of it[26]. However, the wrong emphasis upon synistanein as 'praise' causes us to miss the point which Paul is making about recommendation. He is concerned about: a. the credentials of the recommender and the criteria for apostleship which appear to be contained in the praise element of the recommendation; b. the relationship of trust which recommendation initiates between the recommended and recipient and thus his standing and credit with the Corinthians as opposed to that of his rivals.

Though heauton synistanein in 3:1 is seen as self-praise, the phrase, systatikai epistolai, is accepted unanimously as referring to letters of recommendation, and is the most commonly used terminology for such letters[27] and scholars readily regard systatikos in 3:1 as a technical term[28]. Relatively few allow the preceding heauton synistanein to have a similar technical sense. The NEB moves in that direction: 'Are we beginning all over again to produce our credentials?'[29]. C.K. Barrett does allow the comparison which Paul is making in terms of credentials, suggesting that, while his rivals produced impeccable written credentials, Paul was 'open to the charge of manufacturing his own'[30]. Even allowing for this improved rendering, scholars have not recognized the widespread custom of self-recommendation in Greek and Roman society. Therefore, none, as far as I can ascertain, note the social content of the terminology, though Paul is clearly discussing his and the rival apostles' relations, initiated by

---

[26] For details, see above 121-124.

[27] See Chan Hie Kim, Familiar Greek Letter, 119.

[28] Eg., H. Windisch, 2 Kor. 102-104; C.K. Barrett, 2 Cor. 106.

[29] Cf. Chan Hie Kim, Familiar Greek Letter, 119.

[30] 2 Cor. 105.

recommendation, with the Corinthians. They discuss <u>synistanein</u> almost exclusively as a moral rather than as a social issue. If self-praise was intended (especially in view of the other technical terms <u>metrein</u> and <u>synkrinein</u> in 2 Cor. 10:12) then we should expect the common Greek word for 'praise', ἐπαινεῖν, rather than συνιστάνειν[31].

I propose that Paul's relationship with the Corinthians was initiated by recommendation as was his rivals' and that Paul committed himself to a relationship of trust with the Corinthians; also that he was later offended by the need to commend himself a second time to the Corinthians after the breakdown of his relations with them and their acceptance of the rival apostles. Before pursuing this further, I will recall briefly the important elements of recommendation from my earlier study.

d. Recommendation in Greece and Rome: a summary:

Reciprocal relationships based on fides or πίστις were initiated by recommendation though ties of fides did not lie behind every commendation. The majority of Latin and Greek papyrus or literary letters of recommendation which we possess, and allusions to recommendation in other sources, relate to the institution of friendship and were an essential and fundamental element in the establishing, extending and maintaining of friendship of all kinds and degree[32]. In the second century A.D., Fronto commented that 'the custom of recommendation is said in the first instance to have sprung from good will, when every man wished to have his friends made known to another and rendered intimate with him'[33]. In many of the recommendations, the recommender requests the recipient

---

[31] Cf. 1 Cor. 4:5 ὁ ἔπαινος... ἀπὸ τοῦ θεοῦ; 11:17: ἐπαινεῖν. See also Plutarch, Mor. 539Aff; Aristotle Rhet. 1.3.5, 1.9.3,33. Paul never uses <u>synistanein</u> in this way, see above n.1 and I have been unable to find such a use in Greek literature or papyrus. Cf. the sample letter of recommendation of Demetrius Phalerus, V. Weichert, Demetrii et Libanii 3.2.17 - 4.2.4, in which <u>epainos</u> is distinct from <u>systatikos</u> and refers to (a) the praise included in the recommendation and (b) the recipient's praise of the recommended.

[32] For details, see above 92-98.

[33] Amic. 1.1.1; and see above 97-98.

to receive the recommended into his friendship[34]. By the use of the Latin committal, commendo tibi, or the Greek equivalents, paratithēmi soi and synistēmi soi, the writer entrusted the recommended to the care of the recipient[35], and the conduct of all parties was governed by the conventions of friendship. The recommendation placed the recipient under a moral obligation not only to receive the recommended but to esteem him as if he were the recommender himself[36]. Likewise, the recommended had to respond with due gratitude and consider himself to be bound by the strongest ties of obligation and respect[37].

In all instances of third party recommendations, the recommended's relationship with the recommender was regarded as more valuable than the recommended's own credentials. Friendship with the recipient depended upon friendship with the writer[38]. However, character praise was an important element in recommendation. Character, status, background, ability and pursuits not only enhanced the reputation and prospects of the recommended but enabled the recipient to calculate the reciprocal services and benefits he could expect in return. It was commonly held that the character of a good or outstanding man commended itself and this maxim was on occasions included as a formal element in written recommendations, usually as an addition to the normal praise element. Other facts of a person's career or background could obviate the need for third party recommendation, such as noble birth, office, achievements and the rights and merits of certain nationalities[39]. Inevitably, these also were mentioned in praise of character in written recommendations.

Self-commendation was a common form of recommendation in which a person committed himself to another, with or without

---

34 For details, see above 106-109.

35 Ibid., 109 n.110

36 Ibid., 102-103.

37 Ibid., 113-114.

38 Ibid., 78-79, 86-87.

39 Ibid., 120-123.

the aid of mutual connections, with the intention of forming a reciprocal relationship based on trust. It was also a common practice between existing friends. The notion of trust is implicit in the use of commendo or synistēmi and it was often strengthened by the use of other 'trust' words. The common Latin phrase for the act of self-entrustment was commendo me in fidem alicuius, though fides was occasionally accompanied or replaced by other relational terms such as amicitia, amor, necessitudo and clientela. There does not appear to be any Greek equivalent to this peculiarly Latin stock phrase, though Plutarch's ἐκείνῳ πιστεύοντες αὐτοὺς has the same sense and varies little, if at all, in meaning from Paul's synistanein heauton. Though initiated by a third party, commendo tibi and synistēmi soi indicate the same act of entrustment as in self-commendation[40].

There appears to be very little difference between third party and first person recommendations. Both could be written or made in person. The same range of things could be committed to the recipient. While the praise element was less common and certainly less extravagant in self-recommendation, it was still evident and could take the form of the self-recommender reminding the recipient of past services he had done for him or of giving an outline of one's background, ties or worth to the recipient. Extravagant self-praise would be regarded as inappropriate; certainly where a person, if disadvantaged or of inferior status, could only entrust himself to the fides of the second party. With known friends it was regarded as unnecessary[41].

Finally, as we have seen, commendare and synistanai, in the majority of letters of recommendation, mean much more than 'introduce'; they indicate the intention to create friendship. Moreover, a considerable number of recommendations strengthened and extended existing friendships between all the parties concerned. The recommended was already the friend of both the recommender and recipient. Here there can be no sense of introduction. A second or series of recommendations

---

[40] Ibid., 123-127.

[41] Ibid., 126-129.

could be sent on behalf of the one person to the recipient to foster and encourage the development of the friendship initiated by the first letter. On occasions a number of people wrote recommendations on behalf of the one person[42]. Letters were exchanged between the recommender and recommended and recipient prior to and subsequent to recommendation. Negotiations between the recommender and recommended and the recommender and recipient could precede the recommendation itself and essentials could be worked out and agreed upon. Inquiries were made and reports sought and given on the progress of the relationship. Such interchange of letters was an important element in Cicero's recommendations in particular and was regarded as a mark of the friendship[43].

e. Recommendation as a relational notion in 2 Corinthians.

I suggest that heauton synistanein in 2 Cor.3:1 and 5:12 is technical terminology and is the equivalent of the Roman committal, commendo me in fidem. Together with πάλιν it indicates that Paul on his arrival in Corinth entrusted himself to his first converts or Christian contacts. Though we have no instance of self-commendation in his other letters, we know that he sought the hospitality of people of rank in the major cities who subsequently became his sponsors[44]. Hospitality appears as the most frequent specific request in the papyrus letters of recommendation and to extend hospitality to a person was the first step in initiating a reciprocal relationship[45]. Paul recommended Phoebe to the Roman (or Ephesian) Christians in this manner as his patroness and, as we have seen, hospitality was important to Paul in the carrying out of his mission. The technical use of heauton synistanein in Corinthians may indicate to us that Paul followed the normal convention of self-commendation as he sought out his first hosts in the various localities he visited and that he and his hosts and the churches in their

---

42 Ibid., 115-120.

43 Ibid., 95-96, 119-120.

44 Ibid., 144.

45 Ibid., 109-111.

households may have understood their ensuing relationship to be bound by conventional notions of trust. It is almost certain that he entrusted himself to them in person rather than by written commendation, as the contrast in 2 Cor.3:1 with the systatikai epistolai of the rival apostles indicates.

πάλιν also implies that the original relationship between Paul and the Corinthians has been broken and that, as we have seen, Paul has been held responsible for the breach. The Corinthians had strong misgivings about Paul which were fostered by the hybrists. They said he was an inconstant person who could not be trusted in his relations with others. Inconstancy in friendship, as the antithesis of pistis or fides, was abhorred by Greeks and Romans and undoubtedly also by the Corinthians[46]. Three of the recommendation passages show that Paul's character is being questioned (3:1; 4:2; 5:12) and four others indicate that the Corinthians' acceptance of his rivals' recommendation is associated with their withdrawal of affection from Paul (3:1; 5:12; 10:12-18; 12:11). He was considerably troubled that the Corinthians did not understand him and made numerous attempts to clear himself before them and reestablish his relationship with them. In doing so, he appealed to the original relationship of trust established between them by recommendation. They trusted him in the past and they of all people ought to know him (5:11).

Paul's defence at this point is similar to the popular notion that a good man's character and record commend themselves. He told the Corinthians that he had always acted with sincerity and simplicity toward them (1:12), that he was neither fickle (1:17-18) nor guilty of deception of any kind (4:2; 12:16-18). He did not deserve their mistrust nor the restriction of their affection (6:12). Accordingly, he refused to recommend himself to them a second time - not that they would have asked him to do this. To do so under the

---

46 For Paul's inconstancy and the passages related to it, see below 306-325 and above 251-257. See also C.J.A. Hickling, 'The Sequence of Thought in II Corinthians Chapter Three', NTS 21 (1975), 382, who correctly sees the relational aspects implicit in heautous synistanein and further suggests that due to Paul's conduct, the Corinthians had come to regret the initial introduction.

circumstances could be understood as an admission of guilt on his part. In fact, he argued that he had sufficient credit with them. They were his letter of recommendation written on his heart for all to read (3:2-3). Rather than recommend himself again to them, they should have recommended him as their parent apostle who had fulfilled all the requirements of an apostle among them (12:11). It is interesting to note that where Paul commends himself in 2 Corinthians, he either rebuts charges of inconstancy or does it in conjunction with notions of shame. In the peristasis catalogue in 6:4-10 he commends himself in both these ways. In the peristasis in chapter 11, while he could resort to the usual praise elements of birth and rank (vv.21b-23a), he compares himself with his enemies by an extensive listing of marks of shame (vv.23b-33). He follows this with unusual restraint with regard to the 'abundance of revelations' which had been given him (12:1-7a). Paul is forced to self-commendation, even if it should be in such uncomplimentary phraseology and comparison, by their failure to commend him (12:11).

Paul's ultimate credential for his apostleship in Corinth is God. His ministry (diakonia - 4:1; cf. diakonia/diakonos - 6:3-4) was from God, and his being an accredited and approved (dokimos) apostle is from him (10:18). Thus he seeks to answer firstly to his divine recommender and thereby to every man (5:11; cf. 4:2). Even though the Corinthians had allied them themselves with his rivals and failed to recommend him, God's recommendation of him was indelibly written by the Spirit and, with regard to them, could not be withdrawn (3:3)[47].

The rival apostles came to Corinth with letters of recommendation and they were readily received by the Corinthians. Paul implies as much in the contrasts he makes between his self-commendation and the rival apostles' written commendation (3:1; 5:11) and states it explicitly elsewhere (11:4; 19-20). The readiness with which the Corinthians received them has led most scholars to assume that a powerful centre, namely Jerusalem, recommended them; an assumption which is allied to

[47] For the withdrawal of a letter of recommendation by the recommender, see above 120-121.

the Paul-Jerusalem problem which many of them believe underlies the conflict here[48]. There is no hard evidence to support this. Paul does not give details of the writer's credentials or the identity of the recommended[49]. Rather he concentrates on various aspects of his rivals' character which may have come from the praise section of their recommendation.

Paul accuses them of recommending themselves by their standards (en heautois) (10:12), of boasting of their superiority[50] over him by using their standard as a basis of their unfavourable comparison of him with themselves. C.K. Barrett suggests that their praise may have included such things as their contact with the earthly Jesus (5:16) their visions, achievements which were not really their own, and their personal qualities (chapters 10-12), together with their official recommendation[51]. I shall examine the various elements in my study of the rhetorical notion of sygkrisis, 'comparison', in my next chapter. However, I suggest that the content of the comparison reflects cultural conventions, especially those by which a person causes shame and dishonour to others. As I have mentioned previously, when Paul commends his apostleship in 2 Cor.10-12 and the Corinthian letters generally, he mainly draws upon conventional notions of shame rather than of honour, and upon terms which denote inferior rather than superior status.

It is clear that Paul does not oppose recommendation either by a third party or by one-self. He practises both. Rather he is concerned with the basis on which the hybrists and the rival apostles have assessed apostleship and the compliance of the Corinthians in this regard. This is described as en heautois in 10:12 and was previously termed ... en prosōpō ...

---

[48] Eg., E. Käsemann, Die Legitimität des Apostels, 23-26; J. Schoeps, Paul, The Theology of the Apostle in the Light of Jewish Religious History, ET (Lutterworth, 1961), 76; J.J. Gunther, St. Paul's Opponents and Their Background, Supplement to Nov. Test. 35 (Leiden, 1973), 299, 302; F.F.Bruce, 1&2 Cor. 174, 189.

[49] See, C.J.A. Hickling, 'Sequence of Thought, 2 Cor.3', 181-182.

[50] As suggested also by the use of other technical terms, metrein and sygkrinein. For metrein, see above 198ff; for sygkrinein, see chapter 8.c. and chapter 9.b.

[51] 2 Cor. 165-166.

kai mē en kardia, i.e., apostleship which has appearance rather than the heart as its criterion (5:12). Rather than standards of this kind, Paul judges his apostleship according to the measure (*metron*) which God assigned (*emerizein*) him (10:13) and seeks only God's commendation (10:18) as he speaks and acts openly and truthfully before all (4:2; 6:6-7). The absence of third party credentials and of what may be termed the more 'traditional' criteria for apostleship[52] and the emphasis upon the elements of character praise, may suggest that the rival apostles recommended themselves. While 3:1 refers to written commendations (*systatikai epistolai*) without any indication as to the recommender, 10:12 indicates that the rival apostles have commended themselves (τισιν τῶν ἑαυτοὺς συνιστανόντων). Are they then the authors of their own recommendation?

The phrases, πρὸς ὑμᾶς and ἐξ ὑμῶν, are usually understood to mean that the rival apostles came with letters from recognized authorities to the Corinthians and, on their departure, sought letters from the Corinthians to continue their

---

[52] The attacks made on Paul's apostleship are of an extremely personal nature. We look in vain for the principle of tradition of apostleship which E. Käsemann suggests underlies these attacks. He envisages a legitimizing principle for apostleship which is based on a Jerusalem model, but his conclusion is derived from his identification of Paul's rivals as representatives of Palestinian Jewish Christianity who claimed to draw authority from the Jerusalem apostles. See Legitimität des Apostels, 12-36, 43ff. Cf. J.D.G. Dunn, Jesus and the Spirit (London, 1975), 274-275, who is hardly correct in inferring from Paul's reference to 'visions and revelations' (2 Cor.12:1) that the ἀπόστολοι χριστοῦ (11:13) laid claim to a resurrection appearance and commission from the risen Christ which Paul judged to be of a different order (and thus false) to his own. Neither is it probable, as F.F. Bruce thinks, 1&2 Cor. 231,237, that Paul's opponents laid claim to a superior authority for themselves and the super-apostles (11:5) because they had seen the earthly Jesus. If criticisms of this kind were made, then, I presume, they would have constituted a serious and fundamental challenge to Paul. Yet he makes no mention of them. Rather he justifies his apostleship almost entirely from his conduct as an apostle. The traditional concepts of apostleship are wrongly imported into the conflict. Even Paul's specific references and allusions to his Damascus experience (1 Cor.9:1 ἑώρακα; 15:8 - ὤφθη; 2 Cor. 4:6 - ἔλαμψεν) are used by him to describe the kind of apostle he is under the gospel. His conduct rather than his call is being questioned. There is nothing to suggest that his detractors based their claim for apostleship on a superior seeing of Jesus or that they questioned his ἑώρακα experience. Nor is there any evidence in Corinthians of what might be termed a Jerusalem criterion for apostleship.

work elsewhere[53]. Though recipients on occasions were asked to recommend the person by letter or in person to others[54], it is difficult to understand why the rival apostles would seek credentials from a lesser church (ex hymōn) if they had arrived in Corinth (presumably from a number of other localities) with letters from the Jerusalem church. Surely no further credentials would be required. Further, the evidence points to the rival apostles as still being in Corinth[55]. Paul's responses and his polemic indicate this is the case. It is entirely possible that pros hymas and ex hymōn refer to an interchange of correspondence between the hybrists and the rival apostles prior to the latters' arrival in which they were invited by the hybrists to Corinth. This would help to explain the acceptance they received from the Corinthians.

There is no need to suppose that the Corinthian acceptance of the rival apostles was due to their having better credentials or to the superior quality of their apostleship. Their acceptance must be seen against the background of the church's growing disenchantment with Paul which led to a breakdown in its relations with him. The hybrists appear to have been successful in persuading the Corinthians that Paul was not to be trusted. He had refused their gifts while accepting them from others. He had behaved inconsistently in a number of matters; most recently, in the many changes that he had made to his travel plans. In addition, he had been absent from Corinth for a considerable period of time, a matter about which Paul is particularly sensitive. By contrast, the rival apostles received their gifts and seemed to fulfil all the expectations of the Corinthians for apostleship. An important aspect of this friendship, though, as we shall see in the following chapters, is that the rival apostles more closely represented the social and cultural interests of the Corinthians than Paul and that they were able to use this as

---

53 Cf. C. K. Barrett, 2 Cor. 106; A. Plummer, 2 Cor. 78; P.E. Hughes, 2 Cor. 85, who comments that they were 'largely dependent on these bills of clearance'; J.H. Schütz, Apostolic Authority, 171.

54 For details, see above 120 n.171.

55 So C.K. Barrett, 2 Cor. 267

an effective platform from which to persuade the Corinthians against him.

Recognizing the social significance of the practice of recommendation helps us to see the seriousness of the breakdown between Paul and the Corinthians. A relationship formed by recommendation, whether by self-committal or by a third party, was equally binding on the recipient and the recommended and, given the nature of a reciprocal relationship in Greek and Roman society, it would have required serious grounds for terminating it. Inconstancy, such as Paul was accused of, was one of the chief causes for ending friendship and hostility or enmity usually followed. Whether the Corinthians could be said to have regarded Paul as their enemy depends largely upon whether their acceptance of the rival apostles should be understood in terms of friendship. A number of factors suggests that this was indeed the case. Paul implies as much by the contrast he makes between the Corinthians' attitude towards them and himself (3:1; 5:11) and says more explicitly: 'For you bear it if a man makes slaves of you, or preys upon you, or takes advantage of you, or puts on airs, or strikes you in the face' (11:20). Further, the withdrawal of their affection from him, their silence when he was humiliated, the accusations against him which they have accepted, his expressions of hurt and harsh rejoinders, and his hurtful letter, are evidence of the deep rift between them. Their obligations to the rival apostles would have involved them, to one degree or another, in the hostilities against Paul and may explain why he found it so difficult to reestablish his relations with them and account for their lingering doubts about him.

Chapter 8

THE ENMITY RELATIONSHIP: THE HOSTILE ALLIANCE

a. The enmity relationship in Greece and Rome: a summary.

I have argued in the two previous chapters that Paul has been held responsible for the turning of a relationship of friendship into one of enmity. We have clear evidence in 2 Corinthians of the hostile relationship between Paul and some of the Corinthians. These people have formed an alliance with the rival apostles against Paul. Though scholars have long commented on the bitterness of these hostilities, none, so far as I can ascertain, has endeavoured to understand them in the context of the enmity relationship. I will summarise the salient features of enmity from chapter 2.

The term echthra and inimicitia denote the reciprocal relationship of enmity, a relationship as ancient and as commonplace in Greek and Roman society as its more widely recognized antithesis of friendship (philia, amicitia). Popular maxims such as 'to help a friend and harm an enemy' determined and justified behaviour and were used as a form of high commendation of those who excelled in the performance of this duty. A person could draw a clear line between his friends and his enemies and knew what was the appropriate conduct towards each, his actions being sanctioned as just, noble and honourable by social practice and literature[1]. Enemies were not only inherited but ensued from friendship; a friend's enemies became one's own. There was a marked reluctance to create new enemies. Relationships were not stable and there was genuine concern over the possibility of a friend becoming an enemy. Writers on friendship offered advice on how to avoid creating hostilities. This was particularly evident where a person was faced with the conflicting obligations of choosing between two friends. He could hardly avoid binding

[1] For details, see above 35-38.

[2] Ibid., 39-43.

one to himself more intimately and making an enemy of the other. The question of having to accept an enemy as a friend was also discussed and the experience was a reality of life in political and public circles, especially of the Late Republic. Greeks and Romans alike preferred to endure unwanted friendship rather than end them, for they regarded broken friendships as the source of the most serious enmities and of their concomitants, disputes, abuse and invective. This social situation may be reflected in the wide range of relationships encompassed by the terms philia and amicitia as against what appears to be the more specific terms, echthra and inimicitia[2].

Enmity was as inseparable from public and social life as friendship. Philia presupposed echthra and Greek and Roman authors reflect a genuine fear of hostilities and the injurious intentions of an enemy[3]. This can be seen in a common corollary of the popular convention, 'to help a friend and harm an enemy', which says 'friends share one's joys while enemies gloat over one's misfortunes'. Implicit in this is the frequently mentioned shame and dishonour a person feels before a triumphing enemy, before his laughter and ridicule. It has as its counterpart the common idea that a person should do everything to conceal his misfortune and thus guard against this eventuality. Few emulated Socrates who cried 'Let them mock'[4]. The phrase kakōs poiein summed up one's duty towards an enemy. Seneca succinctly expresses the reciprocal nature of these obligations: 'thanks in return for a benefit and retribution for an injury'. Success led to great honour, pride and pleasure. Failure brought distress and dishonour[5].

Invective provided one of the most common forms of shaming an enemy publicly. The intention was twofold - (a) to place oneself in a more favourable light than one's enemy; (b) to ensure his humiliation and disgrace. Rhetoric was regarded by the Greeks and Romans as the art of persuasion. There were numerous techniques by which a speaker could win praise for

---

[3] Ibid., 43-46.

[4] Ibid., 46-48.

[5] Ibid., 48-49.

himself and the censure of his enemy. By arousing the emotions (pathos) of his hearers and casting his own character (ēthos) in a good light, he endeavoured to dispose them favourably towards himself.

Lists of popular topics and physiognomic traditions provided a framework of values and characters by which a person praised himself as a good man and, by their opposites, blamed his enemy as an unworthy person. It follows that, while invective contained elements of truth, much of it was exaggerated or invented. It was not necessary for it to be true at all. Rather the aim was to amplify or to depreciate according to the economiastic topics. Defamatory conjecture was as good as historical fact; where an enemy was blameless, a speaker could resort to deliberate fabrication. There were standards or rules of rhetoric which a speaker had to observe which determined whether invective was legitimate or malicious, whether laughter was good-natured or ill. Against an enemy such precepts could be properly disregarded, though a person could enhance his reputation by choosing to abide by them. Our unfamiliarity with these conventions makes it difficult for us to separate fact from fiction. Gelzer suggests that much can be discarded where we can control such testimony. Long familiarity with invective, its conventional nature, its respectability and acceptance as a rhetorical device, meant that much of it could be disregarded by victim and audience alike. However personal insult or abuse, injury to a man's status or dignity which shamed and dishonoured him, would lead immediately to enmity[6].

Kakōs poiein went beyond ridicule. One endeavoured to deprive an enemy of his friends and other possessions, to secure his public humiliation and disgrace, and to win over his friends. Withdrawal of friendship or the transfer of allegiance was more deeply feared than the loss of wealth for it deprived a person of those services and benefits which were indispensable to a man of quality. Without friends a person

---

[6] Ibid., 52-65.

was helpless before a powerful enemy[7]. There was no middle ground in an enmity relationship. Failure almost always meant the destruction of a man's status and reputation in public estimation, often permanently[8].

To return to the situation in Corinthians, Paul's enemies have made numerous and serious charges against him. Their accusations appear to take two forms: a. of inconstancy in his conduct and relationships; b. of unfavourable comparisons according to accepted social and cultural values. The charges of inconstancy, I suggest, are drawn from the familiar character of the servile flatterer and the comparisons reflect the economiastic topics of rhetorical convention. Most of the instances of both forms of invective occur in 2 Corinthians though they are anticipated in 1 Corinthians. I have argued that the invective is the concomitant of the hostilities which arose over Paul's refusal of a gift from a powerful group of Corinthians. These people have been responsible for the withdrawal of the friendship of the Corinthians from Paul and for the coming of the rival apostles. I shall examine first, the charges of inconstancy against Paul and, secondly, the dispraise, before seeking to discover what picture the invective gives us of Paul and his enemies and the effect of their persuasion upon the Corinthians.

b. The character of the flatterer as a device of invective.

In this section, I direct my attention to the charges of inconsistency made against Paul by his enemies. I concentrate on 1 Cor.9 in its context and the conflict over financial support and then follow its outcome and related hostilities in 2 Cor. In doing so, I examine the regular use of terms which denote free and servile status, the breakdown in relations between Paul and the Corinthians and its concomitants of mistrust, suspicion and deception. I argue that the familiar character of the flatterer provides the social and literary background against which these charges are to be viewed and, in

7 Ibid., 66ff; for the necessity of friendship and its relation to wealth, see above 32-34.

8 Ibid., 69.

particular, that we are dealing with the use of the stock character of the flatterer as a focus for invective.

(1) 1 Cor.9 in context.

The apparent abrupt transition between chapters 8 and 9, and also 9 and 10, has led to a variety of suggestions by scholars. Some argue for the full unity of the chapters[9] while others propose secondary redaction[10]. Again, some see chapter 9 as an excursus[11]. From this viewpoint, H. Conzelmann suggests that Paul surprisingly introduces a new theme: his apostleship. He sees the chapter as Paul's apologia directed against opponents who have questioned his apostleship over his refusal to accept support. Though the theme of freedom underlies both chapters, the sense is different and its meaning in chapter 9 can only be determined by exegesis of the chapter itself[12]. This emphasis upon the apologetic function tends to isolate chapter 9 from its context. C.K. Barrett points to digression as a characteristic of Paul's letters and says that here we have evidence of a mind that was ready to digress. Though two different issues are involved, he sees the same sort of complaint underlying both - the restriction of Christian liberty, which the strong refuse to accept, criticizing an apostle who allows himself to be restricted in this way[13]. Chapter 9 is strongly joined to its context.

Others who have argued for the close association of the chapters, have attributed a pedagogical function to chapter 9[14]. D.L. Dungan calls it an explanatory digression. Paul offers his own behaviour in refusing his right to financial support as an example to the strong in relation to the idol-

---

[9] Eg., F.W. Grosheide, Commentary on the First Epistle to the Corinthians (Grand Rapids, 1968) 200-201.

[10] Eg., J. Hëring, 1 Cor. XIII-XIV.

[11] Eg., H. Lietzmann and W.G. Kümmel, An die Korinther 1, 2 (Tübingen, 1949) 43.

[12] 1 Cor. 151-153.

[13] 1 Cor. 200.

[14] Eg., H. von Campenhausen, Die Begründung Kirchlicher Entscheidungen beim Apostel Paulus (Heidelberg, 1957), 11. J. Jeremias, 'Chiasmus in den Paulusbriefen', ZNW 49(1958), 156, who sees ch.9 functioning in a similar manner to ch.13 between chapters 12 and 14.

meat problem. While the apologetic note is important, it is subordinate to the pedagogical intention[15]. Recently R. Hock added his support to this point of view and provided two additional arguments. First, Paul's work (which he understands to be the point at issue in chapter 9) has a similar paradigmatic function in his paraenesis at Thessalonica, a practice which he also finds in Socrates. Secondly, refusal of fees and food and clothing were traditionally linked in Socratic dialogue. Once these connections are recognized, he concludes, the transition between the two chapters is neither abrupt nor surprising[16]. However, Hock does draw attention to the importance of the apology and the relation of Paul's refusal of support to his understanding of his apostleship[17]. In his treatment of this, he does not offer any further solutions to the relationship of the two chapters. Recently, W. Wuellner has argued that chapter 9 is one instance of Paul's conscious use of the rhetorical device of digression and an integral part of his argument throughout 6:12-11:1. This enables us to view the interconnection between these chapters in terms of the rhetorical situation rather than of the traditional literary and theological considerations. He suggests that chapter 9 serves firstly as aversion from the previous topic and then to 'prepare the Corinthians to be favourably disposed to the task of judging (10:14-22) on the basis of the proofs presented'[18].

That Paul's refusal to accept support is used as a model in chapter 9 is certain. He applies it explicitly to the idol-meat question in 10:31-11:1. To see this as its primary function though, does not do justice either to the importance of the apology for Paul or the form it takes. Two distinct issues are involved in these chapters though the same notion of freedom appears in each. It is possible that the chapters are simply thematically linked and that chapter 9 has two

---

15 The Sayings of Jesus, 3-40.

16 The Working Apostle, 124-132.

17 Ibid., 132.

18 'Greek Rhetoric and Pauline Argumentation', Early Christian Literature and the Classical Tradition: in honorem Robert M. Grant, W.R. Schoedel & R.L. Wilken, eds. (Paris, 1979), 177-188, espec. 186-187.

equally important functions. It is also possible, as I have previously suggested, that the strong and those whose support he has refused are one and the same[19]. I am of the opinion that in chapter 9 Paul digresses to rebut an invective of inconstancy against him by the hybrists in relation to his refusal of aid and that this invective is closely linked to their expressions of freedom which we find in chapters 6, 8 and 10. This becomes more apparent when, as I shall argue, we recognize that the idea running through these chapters is not freedom only but freedom and slavery. Attention has been given to notions of servility in chapter 9[20], although the extent of the slave analogy has not been probed sufficiently. To my knowledge, no one has suggested that servility is implied in chapters 8 and 10.

I have argued previously that Paul's refusal of support from certain wealthy Christians initiated the hostilities which underlie chapter 9 and which continue throughout 2 Corinthians[21]. His refusal was a serious affront to the status of his would-be benefactors. It is this group of people, the hybrists, who are projecting their interests in the appeals to freedom. G. Theissen has suggested that the 'strong' and the 'weak' are social categories - the strong are of upper status and the weak of lower social status - and that the terms do not simply reflect national or theological perspectives[22]. I argued in chapter 6 that the appeal to freedom by the strong reflects their social status and is of the nature of a defence of their position. It constitutes a cry for the retention of the status quo, of the privileges to which they are accustomed. These must have been in danger of being eroded by this new association with those members in the community of lower social and economic status, though

---

[19] See above 215-216; and refer also to G. Theissen, 'Die Starken und Schwachen', 169-170 who previously suggested this.

[20] Eg., R. Hock, The Working Apostle, 131; Hock sees the notion of servility in 9:16, 19 as referring to Paul's working for wages.

[21] See above, 245-247 and more widely 233-251.

[22] 'Die Starken und Schwachen', 157-158. And more generally, see C. Forbes, 'Strength' and 'Weakness', for the use of these terms by Greek authors and Paul.

primarily by the teaching and practice of Paul. It represents an ideal which had long been at the very heart of their way of life and which remained largely untouched by the gospel. It reflects the problems and conflicts arising from the integration of people of different race, culture and status into one association[23].

In chapters 6-10, freedom is denoted by the catchcry panta moi exestin (6:12, 10:23), the etymologically related exousia (8:9, 9:4,5,6,12a,b,18; cf. the word play in 6:12), eleutheros (9:1,19) and eleutheria (10:29). There terms are traditionally linked in political, social and philosophical discussions in Greek literature, especially from the Classical Age onward. They appear frequently in association with, or imply, terms which denote the antithesis, slavery. I now direct my attention, briefly, to the interrelationship and meaning of these terms in Greek literature.

I cite two early examples in which they appear. Nicias, to urge his soldiers towards victory, reminds them of the unparalleled freedom they enjoyed in their homeland, of the uncontrolled liberty in daily life that all possessed - tēs eleutherotatēs ... tēs en autę̄ anepitaktou pasin es tēn diaitan exousias[24]. Here the concept of eleutheria and that of exousia must be effectively synonymous. Likewise, in Plato's description of the Athenians. 'Are they not free? and is not the city chock-full of liberty and freedom of speech? And has not every man licence to do as he likes?' (exousia en autę̄ poiein ho ti tis bouletai)[25]. Zen hōs bouletai tis, to live as one liked, was the popular formula which guided the citizen of a free democracy and ultimately it became a conventional expression of freedom[26]. Freedom was never intended to be the pursuit of self interest. The well-being of the community and thus the state and its laws always stood

---

[23] So E.A. Judge, Social Pattern, 60; G. Theissen, 'Soziale Schichtung', 264-272.

[24] Thucydides, 7.69.2; cf. Plutarch, 'Lycurgus', 24.

[25] Rep. 557B. 'Licence', of course, in this translation has the older meaning of what one is permitted to do and not the modern connotation of self-indulgence, etc.

[26] Eg., Aristotle, Pol. 6.1. Cf. Isocrates, Panath. 12.131.

over the individual. Only within the limits set by the interests of the community was the individual to enjoy his freedom. Abuse of personal freedom was consistently attacked by writers and the tension between individual freedom and social obligation is a recurring note in Greek literature[27]. However, the assertion of personal worth, class consciousness, and the pursuit of personal advantage proved stronger than social concern. Freedom and its associated terms came to denote and commend the interests of those in positions of wealth and power.

Against this, Aeschylus' words sounded a jarring note. 'Nobody is free but Zeus'[28]. Later in the play even Zeus' freedom was to be restricted by anagkē, the law of necessity[29]. All free men were slaves, not simply to anagkē or the avenging gods but to one another. The king to the masses[30]; the poor man to his master[31]. Conventions and social obligations, one's own passions, bound even the most powerful[32]. But a new kind of freedom was heralded. The inescapable power of anagkē need not touch the soul of any man, whether slave or free. His inner attitude could give him freedom of choice even when confronted with the unchangeable order of life[33]. This inner freedom assured a man of mastery over external circumstance and thus left him truly free to do as he wished.

The Stoics became the main advocates of this ideal and they taught that it was the very essence and principle of a person's existence. Their most impassioned apostle was Epictetus, the Phrygian who was once a slave[34]. For him, as for other Stoics, freedom meant inner freedom, unhindered by

---

[27] See M. Pohlenz, Freedom. chapter 3, 'The Classical Age'. Thucydides, 2.37.2; Plato, Rep. 563D; Laws 700-701; Dio Chrysostom, Disc. 14.13-14.

[28] Prom. 50.

[29] Prom. 515.

[30] Euripides, Iph. 450.

[31] Ibid., 858.

[32] Euripides, Hec. 864-867: 'Ah, among mortals is there no man free! To lucre or to fortune is he slave: the cities rabble or the laws impeachment constrains him into paths his soul abhors'.

[33] Cf. Euripides, Iph. 1551-1560; Alcestis 962; Sophocles, Antig. 821; most influential, Socrates, see Epictetus, 4.1.159-169.

[34] See M. Pohlenz, Freedom, 151-159.

the body and its passions, unaffected by circumstance, knowing no master. 'He is free who lives as he wills (eleutheros estin ho zōn hōs bouletai)[35]. The terminology is the same as in the political or popular notions of freedom but for the Stoics it was synonymous with educated moral autonomy. Only the wise man was truly free. All others, even if free in status, were slaves; fools, who succumbed to one kind of master or other[36]. Dio Chrysostom preserves this distinction in his discourse on 'Slavery and Freedom': 'So that it follows of necessity that while the wise are free and allowed to act as they wish, the ignorant are slaves and do that which is not allowable for them'[37]. He then defines freedom as the knowledge of what is allowable and what is forbidden, while slavery is the opposite. He disagrees with the popular opinion of the majority on freedom - 'that whoever has the power (hotǭ exestin) to do what he wishes is free, and whoever has not the power is a slave'[38]. There are laws, he says, which must be obeyed. It is only where the law has no jurisdiction, that 'the man who has the power (tēn exousian) to act as he pleases ... is free, and the man who on the contrary lacks the power is a slave[39]. One might add, whether he be slave or free.

This traditional language of freedom was used by Dio Chrysostom to describe the rights of a king. He asks: 'Who a keener sense of justice than he who is above the law, who a more rigorous self-control than he to whom all things are lawful (e hotǭ panta exestin?')[40]. The abuse of power by certain of the Principes in the first-century A.D. led to conflict between the notions of principatus and libertas. The law (supra leges) which protected the freedom of the Roman

[35] 4.1.1; cf. 3.24.70; Diog. Laert., 7.121.

[36] Cf. Horace, Sat. 2.7.83: Davus, the slave, says of the wise man: 'Who then is free? The wise man, who is lord over himself'.

[37] Disc. 14.17. It is tantalising to replace the social categories of 'wise' and 'ignorant' with the traditional social antithesis 'strong' and 'weak' which Paul used in 1 Cor. 8-10. It would make good sense of Paul's argument there.

[38] Disc. 14.13.

[39] Disc. 14.14. This theme underlies his discussions in his Discourses 14, 15, and 80.

[40] Disc. 3.10; cf. ibid., 62.2.4.

citizens[41]. Where there was no effective means of forcing the Princeps to obey the law, and if he happened to be somewhat depraved, 'it might easily inspire the belief that everything was permissible'[42]. Against his grandmother's admonition, Caligula retorted, 'Remember that I am permitted to do anything to anybody'[43]. Seneca was similarly aware of Nero's powers which he described as, '<u>Caesar</u> ... cui omnia licent'[44] and 'qui omnia potest'[45]. This understanding of the freedom to act by the Roman writers approximates to the more liberal concept of freedom of the Greeks which they roundly condemned.

The ideas of freedom and slavery are both inextricably bound up in these discussions. However, as we have seen, the form the antithesis takes varies in the passages I have cited. Sometimes the free man and slave are distinguished; sometimes the one person is described as both free (inwardly) and slave (outwardly) or vice versa; sometimes the one man's actions seem to be both free and bound at the one time (the king and his subjects). Thus care must be taken to determine which way the antithesis functions and whether social, ethical, political or philosophical interests are paramount. In all these different contexts, the vocabulary of freedom (or slavery) remains consistent. The meaning is also the same. It is the freedom of choice or decision. The terms indicate both the right and the power of a free man to act as he himself decides and for which he must take full responsibility[46]. The antithesis of slavery is either directly opposed to it or implied. I shall return to the antithesis when I deal with the terms <u>anagkē</u>, <u>hekōn</u> and <u>akōn</u> in 1 Cor.9:16-17[47].

---

[41] See Ch. Wirszubski, Libertas as a Political Idea at Rome During the Late Republic and Early Principate (Cambridge, 1968), 130-136.

[42] Ibid., 135.

[43] Suetonius, Calig. 29.1: memento ... omnia mihi et in omnis licere. Cf. id., Nero, 37.3.

[44] Polyb. 7.2.

[45] de Clem. 1.8.5.

[46] See M. Pohlenz, Freedom, 124-143.

[47] For a further discussion of these ideas, though not dealing directly with our passage, see H.D. Betz, 'Paul's Concept of Freedom in the context of Hellenistic Discussions about the Possibilities of Human Freedom' Colloquy 26 (1977), and the response and recorded discussion.

The appeal to freedom in Corinthians has long been understood as the 'catchcry' of a particular group of people with vested interests. The many attempts to reconstruct the position of this party have been on what might be termed theological lines. The current trend is towards seeing its members as religious enthusiasts. They are pneumatics, for whom 'freedom', allied with 'wisdom' and 'knowledge', is a speculative principle which leads to their detachment from the world[48]. Their ideas and language are said to be closely related to those which were much later taken over and developed by Gnosticism. It has been labelled as 'incipient Gnosticism'[49]. They considered themselves to be superior spiritually, an elite, and, in line with their 'knowledge', free to satisfy their physical and sexual appetites as they saw fit.

Scholars generally determine the meaning of freedom by reference to gnōsis. The enthusiasts have come into a new knowledge as a result of their conversion. Their new knowledge or enlightenment was a liberating gnōsis. Thus the freedom and authority they propound and practise are consequential. In relation to porneia in 1 Cor. 6:13, H. Conzelmann says that it is 'not merely a remnant of pagan custom. It is provided with an active/speculative justification on the ground of' the principle, panta moi exestin[50]. Attempts have been made to determine the historical background and the various influences which comprise this view of freedom. In relation to its historical source, scholars have commented on the formal nature of panta moi exestin and the general philosophical background to which it can be attributed. To this must be added the popular and political. This in itself should act as a deterrent in defining it too precisely. H. Conzelmann has suggested that we must distinguish between its historical source and the Corinthian understanding of it. If possible, to assess to what extent Paul or their Christian faith have

48 Eg., H. Conzelmann, 1 Cor. 16.

49 So F.F. Bruce, Apostle of the Free Spirit (Exeter, 1977), 261; cf. 'protognosticism', H. Conzelmann, 1 Cor. 15.

50 1 Cor. 108.

influenced it[51]. Paul's doctrine of freedom has been proposed as one source. Panta moi exestin has been said to be part of his supposed anti-Judaizing polemic[52]. It is difficult, though to detect any element which might be said to be derived from Paul's gospel. There appears to be nothing particularly Pauline about either the view or practice of freedom of these Corinthians.

The most that we may need to posit the vocabulary and outlook of these people is that of educated Greeks who were conversant with the popular philosophy. We may not be required to look beyond the language of current usage. Rather than being detached from the world the strong appear to be well entrenched in social convention. That they should regard themselves as superior to the weak is not surprising. Power and social predominance are closely linked with moral ascendancy. The contrast of favour and disfavour between the strong and the weak is a common one in Greek literature[53]. Character, moral qualities, education, reputation, wealth and power - these are the things by which those of high social standing command respect (timē, doxa) and through which they exercise influence. These also are the things which commend a man as eleutheros. The strong are superior in every way. Their blatant disregard for the weak, against which Paul so strongly reacts, is proper. In contradistinction, asthenēs not only denotes lowly status and worthlessness but also servility.

The notion of servility is implied in the idol-meat question. Paul advises the strong Christians not to allow their freedom (exousia) to be the cause of the fall of the weak (8:9). For himself, he would never eat meat if it would lead to this (8:13). Thus his counsel to the strong is that they should surrender their freedom for the sake of those who are 'unfree'. This is the antithesis of what they had learned and of what had been ingrained in them by social practice. It is not a question of compromise, which would have been unpalatable enough, but of accommodation of the strong to the weak. Such accommodation

---

51 Ibid.

52 H. Lietzmann, Kor.1 & 2. 26.

53 See C. Forbes, 'Strength' and 'Weakness', 10-39.

would mean the loss of freedom and self-respect. It would be seen by all as a servile act and to be totally inconsistent with the character of people of their standing. It is a protest in this vein which Paul has in mind when he asks: 'For why should my eleutheria be determined by another man's scruples' (10:29b)[54]. Similarly, it underlies their catchcry, panta moi exestin, which also acts as an invidious comparison between themselves and Paul.

In the context of chapters 8, 9 and 10, Paul seems aware that he is once more providing his enemies with further damning evidence to be used against him. However, the charge of inconstancy is not simply that he mixes with people of lower status than himself. Rather, it relates to his continued enigmatic behaviour. The course of conduct that Paul proposes runs counter to Greek standards of morality. He gives qualified agreement to their position and implies that he himself is free in this matter. Yet he adopts the position of the weak. At the same time, he provides three apparently inconsistent courses of conduct (8:10-13, 10:27, 10:28-29a) which appear to be determined by circumstance. This was to be expected. They had become familiar with his calculated and unprincipled character changes; with his inconsistency in matters of friendship and giving; with his multiple changes of character to suit those with whom he associated. Such willing and deliberate inconstancy was not the mark of a free man but of a servile person.

The charge of inconstancy which can be made against Paul at the end of chapter 8 leads naturally to the kind of question (ouk eimi eleutheros;) with which Paul commences his defence of his refusal of aid in chapter 9. Throughout this chapter, terms which denote freedom and slavery control his argument.

---

[54] H. Lietzmann, Kor.1 & 2, 52, sees v.29b as an exclamation on the part of the strong (objecting to the restriction in v.28, 29a) which Paul is citing. Against this on grammatical grounds (such an interpretation seems to require de or alla rather than gar), R. Bultmann, Theology of the New Testament 1 ET (London, 1952), 219, followed by C.K. Barrett, 1 Cor. 243 and H. Conzelmann, 1. Cor. 178. They suggest that it explains vv.28, 29a. However it is better to see v.29b with F.F. Bruce, 1 & 2 Cor. 100, as a question framed by Paul from the strong's point of view and which follows on naturally from v.27; vv.28, 29a form a parenthesis.

(2) Paul as a free man - 1 Cor. 9:1-14.

In chapter 9, Paul uses eleutheros (vv.1, 19) and exousia (vv.4,5,6,12a,b, 18) to defend his apostleship and these terms control his argument throughout vv.1-14. As we have seen, eleutheros denotes status as does the panta moi exestin of Paul's enemies. Paul is free in status as opposed to servile in status. In this regard, he lacks nothing in relation to his detractors. In the background and giving impetus to his apology is the charge of wilful inconstancy. The antithesis of servility is in the mind of Paul and his critics alike and sharpens the definition and direction of his assertion of his freedom. In vv.1-2, his freedom is integrally linked with the kind of apostle some think him to be and the nature of his relationship with the Corinthians. Keeping in mind the nature of the charge against him and the threat it has posed to his relations with the Corinthians, Paul's argument in these verses may run as follows. 'I am a free man; I am an authentic apostle, not a fraud; I am your apostle'[55].

Freedom in Greek literature means freedom of choice or decision and exousia when used in this sense indicates both the right and the power of a free man to act as he himself decides. This is the meaning of exousia in vv.4-6 where Paul uses it of his apostolic rights. He, like other apostles, has the right (exousia) to eat and drink, to marry and to be financially maintained by the community if he so chooses. Attempts to explain the fascinating insights into the early church which Paul gives in these verses have diverted attention away from his intended emphasis. It is the possession of exousia which is of ultimate importance to him. In relation to the gift which he had been offered, it meant his freedom to accept or refuse[56].

It has been suggested that the three rights which he lists may relate contextually to the controversial issues of food, marriage and money[57] or indicate unfavourable comparisons

[55] For Paul's use of ἑώρακα, see above 275 n.52

[56] On freedom as the main emphasis see H. Conzelmann, 1 Cor. 153.

[57] So J.C. Hurd, Origins, 70-71.

which have been made against Paul by his detractors[58]. They could simply be Paul's way of stressing his freedom in a way familiar to the Corinthians. Freedom under Greek law comprised four elements. These four freedoms represent the analysis of individual freedom by the priests of Apollo and are contained in over 1000 manumission inscriptions found at Delphi and are dated between 200 B.C. and 75 A.D. W.L. Westermann lists them as follows:
'(1) He is to be his own representative, his own master, in all legal matters, without need of any intervention by a second party. This is the legal expression of freedom. (2) He is not subject to seizure as property. He cannot be taken into custody, except by the process of the laws according to free men. (3) He may do what he desires to do. (4) He may go where he desires to go, or, in a variant form, he may live where he desires to live'[59]. The first two characteristics - status as an individual; protection from illegal seizure or arrest - are the two possessions a free man must have and must retain. They are his intrinsic rights. The last two elements - the free choices of economic activity (i.e., earning his livelihood) and of movement - 'seem rather to have been classed as privileges available to a free man than as inalienable rights. The disposal or the retention of these two privileges was evidently regarded as a matter of the freedman's option. The choice must be his'[60].

I am not suggesting that Paul is alluding to these inscriptions in his outlining of his freedom[61]. However, his emphasis upon his status as a free man as constituting certain rights and the absence of restrictions must have struck a familiar

---

[58] So D.L. Dungan, The Sayings of Jesus, 6-9.

[59] 'Slavery and the Elements of Freedom in Ancient Greece', Quarterly Bulletin of the Polish Institute of Arts and Science in America 1 (1943), 341.

[60] W.L. Westermann, 'Two Studies in Athenian Manumission', Jnl. of Near Eastern Studies, 5 (1946), 92-93. In practice, the free man usually contracted some part of his control of these options so that he could live. Cf. id., 'Between Slavery and Freedom', The American Historical Review 50 (1945), 216-218.

[61] Though Paul's third right (9:6) resembles the intention of the third element of freedom in the inscriptions: he may earn his living as he pleases.

chord with the Corinthians, many of whom would have been masters, freedmen or slaves[62]. Corinth may well have been the eastern 'clearing house' during the first centuries B.C./A.D. for the slave trade[63] and private and public acts of manumission continued to be a frequent occurrence in Corinth during the first century A.D.[64]. Manumission seems to have been a point of contention among the Corinthians and Paul had just commented on it in 7:21-22[65]. In the attempt to refute the charge of inconstancy against him, and in anticipation of developing the slave analogy in relation to his apostleship, it is possible that Paul is asserting his freedom by appealing to familiar forms.

Paul certainly appeals to widely recognized social and religious customs to affirm positively his right as an apostle to be supported. He refers to the rewards due to the soldier, the vigneron and the shepherd for their labour (v.7); the witness of Mosaic law (vv.8-10); principles of religious practice, universally held (v.13); and a commandment of the Lord (v.14)[66]. R. Hock is correct when he says that in the context of chapters 8 and 9 the function of Paul's argument is to make the apostolic right as secure as the strong's right to eat meat offered to idols[67]. exousia for both Paul and his enemies has the same meaning.

---

[62] See S. Scott Bartchy, First Century Slavery and 1 Corinthians 7:21 (Missoula, 1973), 58-62.

[63] Ibid., 58 n.185.

[64] Ibid., 94-95.

[65] Paul appears to have been well acquainted with Greek and Roman (and Jewish) laws and customs regarding slavery; so S. Scott-Bartchy, First Century Slavery, 50-62. See also, F. Lyall, 'Roman Law in the Writings of Paul - The Slave and the Freedman', NTS 17 (1970), 73-79, who is concerned to show that while Paul was familiar with both Greek and Roman laws of slavery, he was primarily influenced by Roman law in his reference to the slave and freedman.

[66] For a Jewish background to the elements and form of Paul's argument see D.L. Dungan, The Sayings of Jesus, 9-12. For a Greek background, see R. Hock, The Working Apostle, 128-129: 'sophistic reasoning'; Robertson and Plummer, 1 Cor. 180; J. Andrew Kirk, 'Did Officials in the N.T. Church receive a Salary?, ET 84 (1973) 105.

[67] The Working Apostle, 128-129 and see n.44; cf. also D. Daube, The New Testament & Rabbinic Judaism (London, 1956), 395-396.

Paul then has argued in vv.1-14 that he is a free man who possesses the right and power of choice. He has the same rights as other apostles but the option is his as to whether he will exercise any one of them. In relation to gifts, he rigorously defends his right to receive or to refuse them from whom and whenever he chooses. His behaviour is consistent in every instance with his being a free person.

(3) Paul as a slave - 1 Cor. 9:16-18.

Having heard Paul's passionate version of the conventional assertion of his freedom, a Greek would have been startled, to say the least, by Paul's recourse to the institution of slavery to describe his apostleship. These verses explain why he did not exercise his right to be supported in Corinth. His argument is as simple as it is astounding. 'As an apostle I am a slave who has no rights at all.' The vocabulary of slavery is represented by the terms anagkē, akōn in association with its antithesis hekōn, and oikonomian pepisteumai. The presence of slavery has been noticed before in these verses but only in a general way[68]. The extent of the vocabulary and its function within the dispute has not. Numerous theological, ethical, mystical and psychological interpretations have been made[69], but given the limitations of this discussion, I will confine myself to two recent works, those of E. Käsemann[70] and R. Hock[71].

Käsemann centres his attention on anagkē, the Greek philosophical concept of necessity or destiny. He argues that it must retain its philosophical sense. Paul uses it to 'delineate the character of the divine power as sovereign, inexorable and ineluctable'. However, Paul is speaking as a Jew, not as a Greek philosopher. Thus it is not the impersonal force or chance of the Greek anagkē or Roman fatum but the manifestation of divine power in the gospel. The gospel as

---

68 Eg., F.F. Bruce, 1 & 2 Cor. 85-86; C.K. Barrett, 1 Cor. 209-210.

69 Many of these interpretations are outlined by E. Käsemann, 'A Pauline Version of the "Amor Fati"', New Testament Questions of Today ET (London, 1969), 218-227.

70 Ibid.

71 The Working Apostle, 120-132.

anagkē has radically and successfully challenged Paul and made him its servant. In his ministry, it exercises upon him a force like that of destiny. His destiny is the gospel: he is not a free agent, he can demand no reward, he can only bow to it or rebel against it[72]. Käsemann's exegesis of this passage presents two major problems. First, the Jewish orientation of anagkē. Second, he suggests that it can be best understood if it is divorced from the chapter as a whole and thus from the dispute between Paul and his opponents. It amounts to a personal, joyous tribute to God[73]. Undoubtedly, Paul does use technical Greek terms in a Jewish or original manner[74]. He does, also, as our present context shows, use key words with their normal everyday meaning. It is said, too, that he had a penchant for digression, though here, apparently, a digression within a digression. I suggest that an interpretation which allows anagkē and its associates their standard Greek meaning (and in this case, as the natural antithesis of eleutheros and exousia) within the context as a whole is to be preferred.

This is the value of Hock's interpretation. He places chapter 9 against a background of the traditional debate over the philosopher's means of support in Greek literature. The sophist's argument in favour of charging fees is advanced in vv. 7-14. The counter argument of rejecting fees and working as an alternative means of support takes place in vv. 15-18. He notes the many parallel terms between Paul's argument and Socratic reasoning. Misthos, 'reward' or 'salary', is a technical term in these discussions for the fee charged by sophists for their teaching. Socrates did not charge a fee because he considered the real gain (kerdos) from teaching to be a friend, not money. His practice allowed him to converse with all men, both rich and poor. He is said to have spent (dapanō) his own resources in order that anyone who wished could converse with him and be benefitted. Hock suggests that

---

[72] 'Amor Fati', 228-235.

[73] Ibid., 234-235.

[74] Eg., hilasterion, Ro.3.24; see C.E.B. Cranfield, The Epistle to the Romans Vol.1 (Edinburgh, 1975), 214-218; C.K. Barrett, The Epistle to the Romans (London, 1971), 77-78. For Paul's originality, see A. Dihle, 'Demut', RAC 3 (1956).

that Paul's argument - that his preaching the gospel free of charge (adapanon) allowed him to gain (kerdainō) more converts - is virtually the same. Similarly, he notes the importance of eleutheros, anagkē and doulos to both Paul and Socrates, though he notes that Paul's use of these terms is somewhat different[75].

I suggest that not only are the terms used in a different way, but that the whole direction of his argument differs from Socrates. First, for Socrates, the acceptance of fees (misthoi) would have placed him under compulsion (anagkē) to teach anyone who had the fee. Compulsion is the essence of slavery and he would thus have made himself a slave (doulos). By refusing a fee, he preserved his freedom (eleutheros)[76]. He remained free and self-sufficient at all times and avoided servile dependence. Paul, by contrast, is not arguing that he will not on any occasion accept misthoi. He has defended the right of himself and others to live by the gospel and on occasions he has done so himself. Neither is he arguing that to receive a salary or gifts would make him a slave or a dependent of others. He had no fears of this, apparently, with the Philippians. The obvious distaste for compulsion and slavery in Socrates is quite reversed in Paul's case. He describes himself as a slave in bold, explicit terms to explain why he uses his freedom as he has done. Socrates' refusal was directed towards self-sufficiency, self-control and endurance and away from dependence. We may talk about him in terms of moderate asceticism, poverty and persecution, but not servility. The vocabulary is common to both Paul and Socrates but their usage differs. Even though in discussions of this kind in Greek literature opinions differed as to what was meant by the same language, such diversity cannot account for the use that Paul has made of the terminology in vv.15-23.

Second, if Paul is drawing the defence of his conduct from the practice of freedom loving sophists, then it is one which his detractors would understand. I doubt, though, if Paul's use of these terms made much sense to them at all as a defence of a sophist's right to refuse fees and work for a living.

---

[75] The Working Apostle, 129-131.

[76] Ibid., 59; cf. Xenophon, Apol. 16; Mem. 1.2.6, 1.6.1-3.

Hock has suggested that though Paul drew upon sophistic arguments in favour of charging fees in vv.7-14, he recognized them as unconvincing: 'For a philosopher in the Socratic tradition the appeal to other occupations was not persuasive because philosophy was not like any other occupation. Those who accepted the comparison and sold their wisdom were termed kapēloi[77]. Assuming that sophistic reasoning does underlie this passage, Paul at least advanced it in the correct form. He should have been far less satisfied about his use of sophistic language in vv.15-23 to defend his right of refusal.

Finally, the appeal to the common language and the practice of non-charging sophists does not account for the wealth of servile terminology and its use by Paul, the interplay between freemen and slave and its culmination in vv.19-23, nor to the charge of inconstancy against Paul. Analogies drawn from slavery and freedom were extremely popular and were used in relation to numerous forms of behaviour. I have already shown that the ideas suggested by panta moi exestin, eleutheros, eleutheria and exousia are interrelated and describe a man of free status with the right and power of choice. I suggest that the terminology anagkē, akōn and oikonomian pepisteumai in vv. 16-17 represents the traditional antithesis of this and denotes a man of slave status[78].

---

[77] The Working Apostle, 127-129.

[78] The traditionally associated terms, of anagkē, hekōn and akōn, are found in social, ethical and philosophical contexts. In view of my assumption that we are dealing with invectives relating to Paul's social status, I shall briefly and primarily examine these terms where they are used with a social sense in Greek literature. A strong case can be made for a philosophical emphasis in 1 Cor. 9:16-17. R.F. Hock, 'Paul's Tentmaking', 558-560, sees the triad as expressing the Cynic-Stoic problem of fate and free-will. This would suggest that Paul has the Stoics' concern of harmonizing divine decision with free will. Unlike the Stoics, he willingly submits to anagkē which, in this instance, means preaching the gospel free of charge. Hock, somewhat inconsistently, however, allows emauton edoulōsa (v.19 - which he suggests belongs to vv.16-18) sociological sense, referring to Paul's plying a trade, the word douloō reflecting a common upper class prejudice against just such work. The question must be raised as to whether the social idea of servility is the primary focus throughout these verses. For a recent attempt to explain this language and the issues in the wider context of chapters 8-10 in terms of the Stoic-Cynic tradition as adapted by Hellenistic-Judaism, see R.A. Horsley, 'Consciousness and Freedom among the Corinthians: 1 Corinthians 8-10', CBQ 40 (1978), 574-589.

'The ideas of douleia and anagkē are almost inseparable in Greek, the word anagkē being constantly used to denote both the state of slavery as such and also the torture to which slaves were subjected'[79]. In Homer, the enslavement of a man is described in terms similar to Paul's: anagkē shall be laid upon thee against they will'[80]. Similarly, in Aeschylus, Cassandra is yoked to anagkē: 'Yield to necessity and take upon thee this novel yoke' (zygon)[81]. The sight of slaves under the lash suggested the idea of a drove of oxen; thus zygon is the metaphor traditionally associated with douleia and anagkē[82]. Paul in describing his apostleship as anagkē gar moi epikeitai, is drawing upon familiar imagery to describe himself as a slave. This is confirmed by its frequent association with akōn in describing a slave's lack of rights and power.

Hekōn and akōn are frequently opposed in Greek literature[83]. They are commonly used in association with anagkē[84], eleutheros and doulos in both philosophical and social discussions. The contrasting social conditions of both free and slave are described in these terms in the following passages. 'Free-willed I die ... Let me stand free that I may die free... For I shame slave to be called in Hades who am royal'[85]. The same

---

[79] W.G. Headland and G. Thomson, The Orestia of Aeschylus II (Cambridge, 1938), 345; for anagkē as the state of slavery: Aeschylus, Ag. 1040-1044; Pers. 590; Cho. 74-76; Euripides, Hec. 1293-1295; Cr.488; possibly, though it could be logical necessity, Dio Chrysostom, Disc. 14.11. For anagkē as the torture of slaves: Herodotus 1.116; Antiphon 6.25.

[80] Il.6.458.

[81] Ag. 1070-71.

[82] Zygon douleias: Sophocles, Aj.944; cf. Herodotus, 7.8.3; Plato, Laws 770E; Demosthenes, 18.289; Aeschylus, Ag. 953, 1624; in Paul, Gal. 5:1 (cf. 1 Tim.6:1). zygos anakēs: Euripides, Or.1330.

[83] Eg., Homer, Il. 4.43, 7.197; Sophocles, Ant.276; Ph. 771; Aristotle, EN. 3.1.1-5.22; EE. 2.8.6-9.4.

[84] Eg., Crates, 56.11 (from A.J. Malherbe, The Cynic Epistles (Missoula, 1977), 56-57: 'To the degree that doing something under compulsion is worse than doing it willingly (hekōn)', where the discussion concerns nomos and philosophia; Epictetus 4.1.11. Cf. also M. Pohlenz, Freedom, 124-128; N.G.L. Hammond, 'Personal Freedom and its Limitations in the Oresteia', in Aeschylus, M.H. McCall Jnr., ed. (Englewood Cliffs, 1972), 102-105.

[85] Euripides, Hec. 548-552; cf. id., Or. 1169, 1171; Fr. 247N. See also D. Nestle, Eleutheria (Tübingen, 1967), 65.

sentiment underlies Aeschylus' assertion that 'of free choice no one takes upon him the yoke of slavery'[86]. The distinction is keenly felt by Xenophon: 'We must differentiate ourselves from our slaves in this way, that, whereas slaves serve their masters against their wills akōn, we, if indeed we claim to be free, must of our own free will hekōn, do all that seems to be of the first importance'[87]. In these passages hekōn and eleutheros are synonymous and are opposed to akōn and doulos. The ideas of honour and shame are connoted by these contrasts.

Hekōn, like exousia and panta exestin, denotes freedom of decision[88], and akōn designates a person performing an act under compulsion[89]. The popular notion of freedom, to zen hōs bouletai tis, is used in conjunction with eleutheria, exousia and hekōn and appears to be synonymous with panta exestin. With the addition of the negative μη, it describes with akon and anagke the situation of a slave. Aristotle records the common view of eleutheria as to zēn hōs bouletai tis while douleia is to zēn hōs me bouletai[90]. In similar terms to douleia, he defines anagkē, in the sense of compulsion, as: 'an external principle that checks or moves a man in opposition to his impulse'[91]. This definition forms part of his assessment of a decision as a person's own act for which he must bear responsibility. Throughout, hekōn and boulesthai are opposed to akōn and anagkē[92].

Boulesthai indicates the spontaneous will of the freeman. It is significant that in the Delphic manumission documents

---

86 Ag. 953.

87 Cyr. 8.1.4; cf., the use of these terms in a philosophical context, Epictetus, 4.1.1; 4.1.128.

88 Eg., Aeschylus, Eum. 550; 'Whoso of his own free will and without constraint is righteous'; Pr. 266: 'Of my own will, aye, of my own will I erred'; cf. id., Pr. 220; Sophocles, OC. 935.

89 Eg., Sophocles, Ant. 276: 'So here am I unwillingly not willingly'.

90 Pol. 6.1; cf. Dio Chrysostom, Disc. 15.24: a person is a slave hōste exeinai autọ chrēsthai ho ti bouletai.

91 EE 2.8.11.

92 EE 2.8.9-13; cf. Hippocrates, VC. 11 where akōn is opposed to boulesthai.

the verb used to express the desire to have the freedom of action and mobility is ethelein, never boulesthai. 'The new freedoms are the abilities to fulfil emotional desires, those things which one's heart prompts one to do. This is the essential meaning of ethelein whereas boulesthai would invoke the rational elements of planning and of provision for carrying out that plan. Ouk ethelein denotes a longing to do something without the right and will power to accomplish it. What the slave does is, therefore, done unwillingly (akōn). What the free man does he does of his own volition (hekōn)[93].

What the slave wished for were the four elements of freedom which distinguished the free man from the slave. The major personal restrictions which determined full slave status are the reverse. '(a) In all legal actions the slave must be represented by his master or by some other person legally empowered by the owner; (b) he is subject to having hands laid upon him by anybody; that is, he is subject to seizure and arrest; (c) he cannot do what he wishes to do but must do what his master orders. That means that freedom of choosing his activities is denied to him. (d) He cannot go to those persons or places to which he may wish to go, live in the domicile in which desires to live, or determine his polis residence and affiliation'[94]. It is to this total lack of rights of the slave to which Paul is alluding by his use of anagkē and akōn. He has been made a slave and as such possesses no rights. He is subject entirely to the will of another.

This is the antithesis of what Paul has argued in vv.1-14. The use of hekōn retains the notion of freedom of choice and acts as a true counterfoil to anagkē and akōn. However, we could have expected something more fitting than misthos as an accompaniment, such as to zēn hōs bouletai tis or panta moi exestin. The association of hekōn with misthos suggests a free man working for another, for hire. 'In the Greek scale of values the crucial test was not so much the nature of the

[93] W.L. Westermann, 'Slavery and the Elements of Freedom', 27. For the semantics of hekōn and akōn he cites R. Maschke, Die Willenslehre im griechischen Recht (Berlin, 1926) 2-10. Cf. M. Pohlenz, Freedom, 124 n.27.

[94] W.L. Westermann, 'Slavery and the Elements of Freedom', 26-27.

work (within limits, of course) as the condition or status under which it was carried on. The wage-earner, the free man who regularly works for another and therefore lives under the restraint of another is a rare figure in the sources'[95]. Therefore, Paul, while introducing this notion of freedom, has chosen to maintain the theme of servile status. As against akōn/oikonomian pepisteumai, the option to accept restraint belongs to the free man. Misthos may simply draw attention to one aspect of the dispute; he had refused the offer of support and chosen to work for wages while in Corinth. The references to the free wage earner, though, is controlled by the preceding euaggelizō. The sense then is that if he preached the gospel by his own choice, he has the right to a wage. That is, if it were only a matter of freedom and nothing more.

The combination, hekōn/misthos, contrasts with the true nature of Paul's apostleship, expressed in akōn/oikonomian pepisteumai. Oikonomos is used often to describe a slave who was appointed to positions of trust and provides a natural follow-on from the notions implied in anagkē and akōn. Paul could simply have said, 'I am a slave', but he has preferred to liken his apostleship to that of a trusted slave[96]. The appointment of trustworthy slaves by their masters to positions of managerial responsibility was a common practice, either over a household[97], a private business[98], or as

---

[95] M.I. Finley, 'Was Greek Civilization Based on Slave Labour?', in Slavery in Classical Antiquity, M.I. Finley ed. (New York, 1968) 148. Cf. Aristotle, Rhet. 1.9.27; A. Burford, Craftsmen in Greek and Roman Society (Bristol, 1972), 26ff.

[96] See J. Vogt, Ancient Slavery and the Ideal of Man ET (Oxford, 1974), 129-145, 'The Faithful Slave', though he deals mostly with the relationship of trust between a master and slave. Cf. R. Bultmann, πιστεύω', TDNT 6 (Grand Rapids, 1964) 175-178; C.K. Barrett, 1 Cor. 209, who says the language recalls the appointment of either slaves or freedmen as imperial secretaries; F.F. Bruce, 1 & 2 Cor. 86.

[97] Eg., Lk.12:41-46, where a trusty and sensible (v.41) slave (vv.43,45, 46) is appointed steward by the lord to manage other slaves. Cf. Josephus, Ant. 12.199-200; Inscriptions: IG5 (1) 40, 1235; IG Rom.4.1699; TAM 2.518 (Pinara).

[98] Eg., Demosthenes, 36.43-44, of Pasio, the slave, who was appointed bank manager: 'He gave proof to the bankers, Antisthenes and Archestratus, who were his masters, that he was a good man and an honest, and so won

secretaries or accountants of the emperor[99]. Self-respecting free men were unwilling to accept positions in which they had to obey the orders of an employer[100] and slaves and freedmen were preferred for managerial positions. Masters not only knew their characters and could rely on their obedience, but could punish them should they disobey instructions[101]. Paul had already referred to his apostleship in these terms in 1 Cor.4:1 - ... en tois oikonomois hina pistos tis eurethē. In 9:16-17 then, Paul has described himself as a slave without the right or power of choice, but yet a trusted slave who intends to fulfil the position given to him. οὐαί μοί (v.16), I take to be the cry of alarm of a trusted slave who is aware of the consequences should he fail in his obligations[102].

Paul's question, tis oun mou estin ho misthos, in the light of the slave imagery seems superfluous. A slave, in most instances, could expect no salary, as Paul and his readers were well aware[103]. The most he could hope for was manumission on his owner's initiative; the reward for the faithful fulfilment of his task by an appreciative owner. This is not in Paul's mind. D.L. Dungan says Paul is speaking facetiously. 'What are the wages of someone who is not entitled to any?

---

their confidence ... in moneymaking the best capital of all is trustworthiness'. Cf. Ibid., 36.28-29; Xenophon, Mem. 2.5.2, where Nicias is both slave and manager of a silver mine. See also G. Horsley, New Documents Illustrating Early Christianity, 3 (North Ryde, 1983), 39, for the οἰκονόμος πιστός. His master erected a tombstone in return for his 'good life and industrious servitude'.

99 See P.R.C. Weaver, 'Social Mobility in the Early Roman Empire: The Evidence of the Imperial Freedmen and Slave', P&P 37 (1967) 14-20.

100 Cf. Xenophon, Mem. 2.7.1-5; Aristotle, Rhet. 1.9.27: 'and not carrying on any vulgar profession is noble, for a gentleman does not live in dependence on others'.

101 So A.H.M. Jones, 'Slavery in the Ancient World', in Slavery in Classical Antiquity, M.I. Finley ed., 2; cf. P.R.C. Weaver, 'Social Mobility', 13.

102 Cf. Lk. 12:47-48, 16:1-12. See F.F. Bruce, 1 & 2 Cor. 85.

103 Slaves were hired out for wages as a source of income for their masters, were left free to hire themselves out or to take on a second job in their spare time and to retain some of their wages, or were allotted a part of their earnings as artisans or skilled workers in their trade. Legally they had no right to this money which properly belonged to their masters. See C. Mossé, The Ancient World at Work ET (London, 1969), 86-91; W.L. Westermann, 'Slavery and the Elements of Freedom', 20-22 for 'pay-bringers'.

Why, to do the work for free.' He suggests that the pun may have been lost on the Corinthians and most certainly wasted on centuries of sober-sided Christian exegetes[104]. I rather think that Paul is being provocative and, if anything, would have riled his enemies. Especially as he applies the slave imagery in this verse to his refusal of the gift and the exercise of his freedom in relation to it. He argues that as a trusted slave he cannot receive wages. Rather his 'wages' consist of his fulfilling the duties of his stewardship, preaching the gospel without cost in Corinth. This means in the circumstances, his choice to refuse his right to financial aid.

In his defence, Paul has drawn on two traditionally opposed concepts of status, that of the free man and of the slave. One of honour the other of shame. He is a free man who has the right and power to act as he chooses (vv.1-14). He is a slave who has no rights and is bound to carry out his obligations (vv.15-18). It is the analogy of the slave which he puts forward as the determining factor in how he will exercise his rights as a free man. His freedom is subject to that to which he is enslaved. The gospel determines how he will act in any given situation. Freedom is not the ultimate value for him as it is for his status-conscious critics. Paul has refused their offer and chosen to work for wages in Corinth. He considers that to do otherwise would place an obstacle in the way of the gospel (v.12b). Neither does he at any time in the future intend to change from this, and feels strongly enough about it to call it his 'boast' (v.15). What he does elsewhere may differ, as his opponents are very well aware.

I have suggested that Paul is refuting a charge of inconstancy. He has been accused of not acting as a free man should, of behaving in a wilful, servile manner. He has asserted, in response, his status as a free man in a conventional manner. At the same time, he has taken up the ridicule and used it to describe his apostleship in terms of the basest servility, the status of a slave. This is a radical self-

---

[104] The Sayings of Jesus, 23.

description. I know of no parallel in Greek and Roman literature. The Greeks often see a thing together with its antithesis. But they are always opposed. Free in status means not being servile in status. If not stated it is always understood.

M. Pohlenz cites an example of a seventh century B.C. slave who tried to set aside social prejudice. It is an example that holds good throughout Greek literature. 'The social cleavage between free men and slaves remained and it called for a high degree of self-confidence when Archilochus, in a seventh century B.C. poem, openly defied all prejudice about rank by saying that he lived in poverty and that his mother was a slave. In that age the fundamental claim was thus put forward for the first time that a man and his work are to be judged not by extrinsic accidents of birth but by his intrinsic quality. Archilochus was bold enough to assert himself a free person'[105]. The paradox, though a slave, yet free, was to become a familiar notion in Greek philosophy[106]. But inner freedom, especially that of the 'noble' slave, is far from Paul's thought[107]. The horror felt by the nobleman, Critias, at Archilochus' blatant disregard for convention, though, is not far from that which must have been felt by Paul's enemies.

A fitting climax to his assertion of his free status would have been a kind of peristasis catalogue in reverse, covering his achievements and moral excellence. Perfect development and self-appreciation were the keys to the Greek social and ethical values. These are the things which determined the nature of the free man's aid to others. The notion of service as a slave would have been an abhorrent thing to him for it would have involved the submission of his will and freedom to

---

105 M. Pohlenz, Freedom, 9.

106 Eg., Euripides, Fr. 831, 511; Hel. 730; Ion. 854; Sophocles, Fr. 854. 854. See also D. Nestle, Eleutheria, 120ff. on Epictetus 4.1.1ff and 3.24.64ff.

107 For the figure of the 'noble' slave who possesses freedom of the mind, see, Euripides, Hel. 729. As I argue throughout this thesis, Paul does not invert the traditional notions of shame. For him they always remain shameful, see above 133-135, 210f and chapter 9.4, 'self-derision'.

another[108]. It is this, as I have suggested, which lies at the heat of the strong's self-concern and disdain for the weak, and the unfavourable comparison they make with Paul. A free man could be ridiculed as a servile person, and often was. In return, he will assert his free status and vigorously attack his opponents in like manner. If unable to defend himself, he would retire in shame and dishonour. He will never denigrate himself in servile terms. Paul's playing out of this analogy of shame is a blatant, deliberate and provocative act. It would be abhorrent to a free Greek or Roman. It would be particularly offensive to his opponents who have claimed that Paul acted in a servile manner and over against whom they have asserted their own freedom.

(4) Paul as a flatterer: I Cor. 9:19-23 as invective.

The use of freedom and slavery was a familiar contrast and Greeks would have understood an antithetic use of these terms. Paul's application of both these concepts to himself must have seemed startlingly different. In 9.19, he again embraces these traditionally opposed notions to describe his apostleship - *eleutheros gar hōn ek pantōn pasin emouton edoulōsa* - and continues it throughout vv.20-22. *eleutheros* picks up the theme of freedom from vv.1-14 and *douloō* the slave analogy in vv.15-18.

Since H. Chadwick's seminal work on vv.19-23[109] a number of articles have appeared[110], though scholars generally have not

---

[108] Cf. Philo, de Praem et Poen. 24.137.

[109] '"All Things to All Men" (1 Cor.IX.22)', NTS 1 (1954-55) 261-275.

[110] Eg., R.N. Longenecker, 'All Things to All Men', Paul Apostle of Liberty (Grand Rapids, 1964), 230-244; G. Bornkamm, 'The Missionary Stance of Paul in 1 Corinthians and Acts', in Studies in Luke-Acts, L.E. Keck and J.L. Martyn eds. (London, 1968) 194-207; C.H. Dodd, 'Εννομος Χριστου', in More New Testament Studies (Manchester, 1968), 134-148; H.L. Ellison, 'Paul and the Law - "All things to All Men"' in Apostolic History and the Gospel, W.W. Gasque and R.P. Martin eds. (Exeter, 1970), 195-203; D.L. Dungan. The Sayings of Jesus, 25-26, 33-39; P. Henry. 'All Things to all Persons', New Directions in New Testament Study (Philadelphia, 1979), 158-165. No systematic and extensive work was done until S.C. Barton's 'All Things to All Men' (1 Corinthaisn 9:22): The Principle of Accommodation in the Mission of Paul, (247 pp.), unpublished BA. Hons. thesis, Macquarie University, 1975. An article based on it has been published: S. Barton 'Was Paul a Relativist?', Interchange, 19 (1976), 164-192. The recent

recognized the importance of the passage for our understanding of Paul. Most have understood these verses as an attempt by Paul to explain his behaviour in the light of criticisms which have been made against him at Corinth. His detractors have been said to have denounced his stance as one of 'ambiguity, conformism, opportunism, and unprincipled vacillation'[111]. Numbers of passages in Paul's letters have been cited as evidence of this kind of misunderstanding of Paul by others[112]. As if in recognition of the dilemma of his enemies, but protective of Paul, scholars have chosen to describe his behaviour as flexible[113], chameleon-like[114], apparently inconsistent or contradictory[115].

Most interpreters refer to these verses as constituting Paul's general missionary strategy[116], and, more particularly, as embodying a principle of accommodation[117]. The inclusive nature of his accommodation has also been noticed encompassing many basic differences of religion, culture, sex and social status[118]. D. Daube has suggested that this principle is derived from Jewish missionary practice[119], but this is objected to by S.C. Barton who sees it as a radical expression

---

article by P. Richardson, 'Pauline Inconsistency', NTS 26 (1980), 347-362, does not move outside the broad framework of previous discussions though Richardson applies the 'accommodation principle' more comprehensively to both missionary and church life. In Galatians, he fails to note the nuances of accommodation in Gal.1: 10 and 4:12. See my discussion above 155, below 316.

111 G. Bornkamm, 'Missionary Stance', 197.

112 Eg., 2 Cor.1:13-24, 5:11; Gal. 1:10, 5:11.

113 G. Bornkamm, 'Missionary Stance', 197.

114 H.L. Ellison, 'Paul and the Law', 195.

115 S.C. Barton, All Things , 27; J.C. Hurd, Origins. 128.

116 Eg., D.L. Dungan, The Sayings of Jesus, 27-28.

117 Eg., S.C. Barton, All Things , 16.

118 See, Ibid., 9-25; G. Bornkamm, 'Missionary Stance', 196; D.L. Dungan, The Sayings of Jesus, 33-34.

119 The New Testament and Rabbinic Judaism (London, 1956) 336; Cf. G. Bornkamm, Paul ET (London, 1971) 10-12, who suggests that Paul was an Orthodox missionary of the Jewish faith to the Gentiles of the Diaspora before his conversion.

of Paul's self-understanding as an apostle[120]. D.L. Dungan inquires as to the origin 'of this astonishing sense of transcendence' and lets his net down on the Hellenistic side of the boat. His haul is both interesting and close to the mark. 'Is this', he asks, 'the proud boast of a Peregrinus, both capable and yet apparently also driven to adopt one after the other a protean succession of self-identities in the course of a half-triumphant, half-desperate search for apotheosis?' Or is it the language of an apocalyptic visionary, of the radical relativism of a Diogenes the Dog, or a kind of tolerant Epicurean universalism[121]? The difficulty in establishing a source for 'all things to all men' may be due to its having been considered almost singularly as a principle or strategy. Although, undoubtedly, it is characteristic of Paul's behaviour, I suggest that the description of it as a principle is misleading. It may not have arisen with Paul at all. H. Chadwick thought it conceivable, though not demonstrable, that the phrases, 'a Jew to the Jews' and 'a Gentile to the Gentiles', were contained in a charge-sheet against him. Paul, consistent with his practice elsewhere, is quoting from his adversaries, in an ironical tone[122]. I suggest we should look for the answer in this direction.

It is difficult to deal with inconsistency of this kind even in western cultures of today where social conventions are far more flexible and tolerant than that of the Greeks. Yet scholars have noted with some misgivings the anomalies in Paul's behaviour and have tried to explain them by an appeal to a 'higher consistency', obedience to the gospel[123]. Yet the full impact of his behaviour upon those in his own socio-cultural situation must be felt if we are to understand these verses. It is from the Corinthians' viewpoint that we must

---

120 All Things , 204-216; he stresses that the distinctively Christian elements in Paul's experience are crucial in the formulation of this principle and argues against Daube's view on the grounds of the degree of accommodation (206) and methodology (208).

121 The Sayings of Jesus, 34. See S.C. Barton, All Things , 201-203, who rejects a Hellenistic source for the principle.

122 All Things , 263.

123 So F.F. Bruce, 1 & 2 Cor. 88.

ask our questions. What images would Paul's behaviour evoke, especially in the minds of his hostile opponents? What conventions would he contravene? Which common pattern of behaviour can best explain the presence and the interconnection of the various elements in chapter 9 and its context - the notions of freedom and slavery, the hostility, the apparent inconsistency in Paul's behaviour. In line with their understanding of 'all things to all men' as a missionary strategy, scholars have generally ignored its specific context and its connection with Paul's refusal of the gift, and have sought to apply it as a means of interpreting his behaviour elsewhere in his writings and in Acts[124]. It is critical that it be examined where it arises and its connection with the dispute as it continues throughout the Corinthians correspondence.

I have argued that the charge of inconstancy that has been made against Paul is directed against his inconsistent behaviour, especially in relation to gifts. The question, though, is what form did this charge take? I suggest that we are dealing with the familiar character of the servile flatterer, the one who deliberately adapts his conduct to that of others for his own ends. The erratic, unpredictable person, with his anomalies of character, placed Greeks and Romans in a grave dilemma for which they struggled to find an answer[125]. What they sought in a man was a fixed and steadfast character, consistency in behaviour and constancy in relationships. To be a friend of one person meant a 'thoroughgoing likeness in character, feelings, language, pursuits and dispositions'[126].

I will summarize briefly from chapter three the popular conception of the flatterer. Like the cuttlefish or the chameleon, he adapts to his surroundings. Versatile, pliant and readily changeable, he can assimilate and accommodate

---

[124] S.C. Barton, All Things , and H. Chadwick, 'All Things', deal with other problems throughout 1 & 2 Corinthians but not specifically with the problem of financial support. D.L. Dungan, The Sayings of Jesus, 25, applies it directly to the 'command' of the Lord in 1 Cor.9:14.

[125] For details, see above, 88-89.

[126] Ibid., 25-26, 71, 86.

himself to many persons and circumstances. He is a skilled role-player, with a capacity for infinite changes of style to suit changed circumstances and associates with good and bad alike. He is not to be trusted, is insincere, and a false friend. His words and acts are intended to bring immediate pleasure (though he when required can also speak with the frankness permitted only the closest of friends) and are harmful to those with whom he associates. Everything he does is for his own gain; he is a charlatan and a coward. Servility, shame and dishonour are always present. His behaviour is slavish, his words ignoble and servile and he debases himself in the most degrading manner[127].

Freedom and flattery are implacably opposed. I quote the pertinent contrasts from Plutarch. 'it is necessary to observe the uniformity and permanence of his tastes, whether he always takes delight in the same things, and commends the same things, and whether he directs and ordains his own life according to one pattern, as becomes a free-born man and a lover of congenial friendship and intimacy; for such is the conduct of a friend. But the flatterer, since he has no abiding character of his own to dwell in, and since he leads a life not of his own choosing but another's, moulding and adapting himself to suit another, is not simple, is not one, but variable and many in one.' And again, of the flatterer: 'so by making himself like to all these people and conforming his way to theirs he tried to conciliate them and win their favour ... the flatterer is nowhere constant, has no character of his own ...' Of the actions of free men he says that they: 'yet maintained everywhere their own proper character in dress, conduct, language, and life'[128].

What was required was that a man should remain true to his character in all circumstances of life, uniformly consistent in life as a whole and in individual actions. Versatility in the face of the various contingencies of life was not usually denigrated and sometimes was admired, and changes in character,

---

127 Ibid., 72-82.

128 Ibid., 82ff, for the full quotation.

often permanent, due to compulsion or force of circumstance were tolerable. But the free man who deliberately and consciously changed his character to that of others for the sake of advantage was regarded as abjectly servile and deserving of ridicule. Unlike the slave who has no choice in the matter, the flatterer willingly surrenders his freedom to another - something it is said that a truly free man could never do[129]. Against this background, we can recognize the Corinthians' predicament over Paul's behaviour.

Kolakeia, 'flattery', in 1 Thess.2:5 is the only explicit reference by Paul to the practice of the kolax. He appears to be familiar with the popular contempt for certain philosophers as flatterers. In his paraenesis in 1 Thess.2:1-13, in which he presents himself as a model to be emulated, there are many striking parallels in language and thought with Dio Chrysostom's denigration of them[130]. He claims that he has not spoken out of error, was not motivated by impurity, did not speak with guile, or to please men[131]. He did not resort to flattery, use his cloak for greed, nor seek glory from anyone[132]. The characteristics of the flatterer proved to be a popular source for invective against Epicureans and certain types of wandering philosophers who composed speeches for display alone. It is possible that Paul implies that his rivals in 2 Corinthians were of this ilk.

It is also possible that Paul is alluding to the philosopher-flatterer in Ro.16:17-20. He warns his readers against those who 'create dissensions and difficulties in opposition to the doctrine you have been taught. For such

---

129 Ibid., 84-89.

130 See A.J. Malherbe, 'Hellenistic Moralists', 22-27 (author's typescript); id., 'Gentle as a Nurse', 203-217.

131 On the deception of sophists, see Dio Chrysostom, Disc. 4.2; 32.9; 48.10; 77/78.33; cf. Plato, Mem. 92A; Euth. 277B; Xenophon, Hunting 13.14.8.

132 Cf. Dio Chrysostom, Disc. 48.10, 77/78.33-35: where the philosopher is said to have changed his character and become a flatterer. See also Ibid., 32.10 for those in the guise of philosophers who brought reproach upon philosophers in general; Lucian, Fisherman 34-37; Runaways 21. For the use of doxa and kerdos in relation to the false philosopher, see Dio Chrysostom, Disc. 32.10.

persons do not serve our Lord Christ but their own appetites, and by fair and flattering words they deceive the hearts of the simple-minded'. Written from Corinth, it may provide us with a cameo of the situation there, especially that of 2 Corinthians[133].

Much of the language used against the philosopher-flatterer is derived from the criticism of the flatterer. It is against this general background of the flatterer that vv.19-23 are to be understood. Here we are dealing with Paul's multiple changes of character and the deliberate surrender of his freedom to all kinds of people. In v.19, he reasserts his apostleship in terms of freedom and slavery. Free from all. Slave of all. The servile element is developed in a series of six sentences each of which is accompanied by a final clause (hina) which expresses the motive or purpose for the servility. It is his use of douloō in v.19 which determines the kind of servility involved in the ensuing verses. Emouton edoulōsa[134] suggests a conscious effort on his part to make himself slave of all. It describes the act of a free man who willingly enslaves himself to all people (pasin) without distinction. This is a different kind of servility from that in vv. 16-17. There his slavery is externally imposed. Here it is self-imposed. This description is similar to that of a man of free status who contracts himself into slavery. That also is voluntary servitude, but it is temporary and limited. The person surrenders his rights to economic activity and movement[135]. While he becomes slave of one master, Paul is slave of all. The notion of self-imposed servility is inseparably linked with diversity of conduct[136].

The diversity of his behaviour is underlined by his listing of four distinct categories of people to whom he accommodates.

---

[133] Eg., 2 Cor. 4:2; 11:1-4, 12-15.

[134] Edoulōsa is probably a constative aorist describing the totality of Paul's act. So J.H. Moulton, Prolegomena to the Grammar of New Testament Greek (Edinburgh, 1906), 109.

[135] See W.L. Westermann, 'Between Slavery and Freedom', 218.

[136] Cf. Plutarch, Mor. 13 B.C., where after tersely describing the inconsistent behaviour of flatterers, he continues, 'freeborn by freak of fortune, but slaves by choice'.

They represent a vast range of social and religious customs. He became a Jew to the Jews; as if under the law to those who are under the law; as if outside the law to those who were outside the law; and weak to the weak[137]. This is not the universalism of a Socrates who, by refusing fees and avoiding the implied compulsion, is free to converse with anyone he wishes[138]. Nor is it the calculated tactics of a Cleon who renounced his friendship with the best and presented himself as a man of the people, associating with the most unpretentious and becoming the spokesman for the poor and disaffected[139]. Something more comprehensive is involved. Paul does not provide us with any insight into the contrasting words and actions such accommodation would involve him in. Only from chapters 8 and 10 in relation to the weak do we know the nature of this behaviour and certain Corinthians' reaction to it. Paul's inclusion of the weak is quite deliberate. The emphasis, though, is on diversity and change. The structure of these verses indicates that the notion of self-imposed servility is retained throughout. Emouton edoulōsa is implied in the verb egenomēn in vv.20, 22a,b. Both notions of servility and diversity, are conjoined in the all embracing statement: τοῖς πᾶσιν γέγονα πάντα.

In three concessive participial clauses, Paul makes it clear that he does not undergo a change of character. He is free (v.19); he is not himself under the law (v.20); he is

---

137 S.C. Barton, All Things , 9-16, sees these four groups of people as religious categories: Jews; Jewish Christians who still observe the law of Moses; Gentiles; weak Christians. While the religious component undoubtedly comprises a large part of the activities of these people, I see no reason to restrict Paul's meaning to it. Paul's behaviour here encompasses social conventions as his conflict with his enemies shows. I have also suggested that asthenēs is a status term rather than theological or national. Further, the emphasis is upon diversity of behaviour; He clearly does not intend the specifically mentioned groups to be an exhaustive catalogue as the inclusive nature of pas shows. For hoi asthenes as denoting 'those in socially depressed situations' see C. Forbes 'Strength' and 'Weakness' 83.

138 Cf. Xenophon, Mem. 1.6.1-3; Plato, Euth. 30; R. Hock, The Working Apostle, 131.

139 Cf. Plutarch, Mor. 806F-807A. See also Diodorus Siculus, 20.63.1, where tapeinos is used to describe the role adopted by Agathocles to win the favour of the lower classes to the disgust of his peers.

not outside the law of God (v.21). That is what he has consistently maintained throughout the argument. Paul considers that at no time is his free status impinged upon by his behaviour. To his enemies, these assertions would appear to be of the nature of a candid confession: 'I am not really the many things I make myself out to be'. This would confirm them in their opinion of him as a counterfeit and complement the notions of servility and shame.

Paul's purpose or motive for adopting this style of life is repeatedly stated, in five final hina clauses. He does it so that he might gain (kerdēsō) those to whom he accommodates[140]. The verb, kerdainō, or the noun, kerdos, is used with either a good sense or a bad sense. In a derogatory sense, it is used to describe sophistic moneymaking; of sophists, who by charging fees, appeared to be concerned only with monetary gain. These are the so-called philosophers denigrated by Dio Chrysostom as flatterers, who were concerned only with their own profit (kerdos) and reputation (doxa) and would use any means at their disposal for these ends[141]. This is similar to the ōphelia motive of the flatterer[142] or the mercenary behaviour of Plutarch's flatterer: 'So by making himself like to all these people and conforming his ways to theirs, he tried to conciliate and win their favour'[143]. By contrast, Socrates is said to have considered the real gain (kerdos) from teaching to be the winning of a good friend, not money. R. Hock sees this Socratic motive behind Paul's use of kerdainō. Preaching the gospel free of charge allowed him to gain more converts[144]. It is possible that Paul is playing on the word. His opponents have accused him of having ulterior motives and throughout 2 Corinthians Paul has to defend himself (as we shall soon see in detail) against charges of

---

140 Eg., hina ... kerdēsō, vv.19, 20a, b, 22; with kerdainō, v.21.

141 Disc. 32.10; cf. Xenophon, Hunting 13.8; Isocrates, Ag.Soph. 4; R. Hock, The Working Apostle, 63-72.

142 Eg., Aristotle, EN 2.7.13; 4.6.9.

143 Mor. 53A.

144 Xenophon, Mem. 1.2.7. See R. Hock, The Working Apostle, 131.

deceiving people and of seeking their property. What is implied by the use of kerdainō and the allusion to the characteristics of the flatterer in vv.19-23 becomes clear and critical in 2 Corinthians. From this aspect, kerdainō formed part of the charge against him. However, Paul takes up the good sense in v.23 by linking it with sōzō in a sixth final clause.

This is characteristic of Paul's responses in his conflict with his enemies in Corinth. He frequently takes up certain of the shame elements and develops them seemingly to the detriment of himself and to the enhancement of his detractors. Having done so, he equates these elements with his apostleship and the gospel. In vv.15-18, he adopts servile imagery to explain why he has used his freedom as he has at Corinth. Notions of shame and the gospel are closely linked. In v.23, a seventh final clause indicates that Paul acts in this shameful way, not only so that the Corinthians may be saved, but that he himself might participate in the gospel. His use of to euaggelion in v.23 parallels its use in v.12b and v.18a where it stands for the gospel as 'an effective force or agent'[145]. In the context of chapters 8-10, it means that he considers that his refusal of the gift of his working for wages and his conduct toward the weak has advanced the effectiveness of the gospel in Corinth.

In conclusion, in vv.19-23 we are dealing with invective. Paul's enemies have accused him of being a servile flatterer, of having no will of his own. He is all things to all men for his own advantage. He is a counterfeit who is not to be trusted[146]. Rather than respond in kind or deny the accusations, he takes up the language of the invective and the

---

145 H. Schütz, Paul and the Anatomy of Apostolic Authority (Cambridge, 1975) 52-53. He reasons that it cannot be the hindering of the content of the gospel or the damaging of his own delivery of it. Euaggelion must therefore refer to the gospel as a 'force or agency to accomplish something, having a purpose toward which it proceeds'.

146 It is not possible to say whether 'all things to all men' was formulated by Paul's enemies or whether it was his summary of the invective. I am of the opinion that it is a term of derogation used by his opponents against him. The impressive structure of these verses and the rhetorical flourish undoubtedly is Paul's.

notions of shame in a bold and most provocative manner to describe his work as an apostle. At no stage does he devalue the status of a free man. While holding to it for himself, by using two different notions of servility (one externally imposed, the other self-imposed) he explains how and why he has used his freedom in relation to the points in dispute. Allied with the notions of shame and dishonour and in the face of the charges of servility against him, it represents an extremely unconventional counter to his enemies' view of themselves. It is the antithesis of their own status values and is a serious affront indeed.

Paul returns to this in 10:23-11:1 where he asks the strong in language drawn from the invective to emulate his example. He asks them not to offend Jews, Greeks or the church of God. On his part he tries to please all men (πάντα πᾶσιν ἀρέσκω). ἀρέσκω, 'to please' or 'to accommodate', and often with the nuance of service, has a bad sense when used in connection with the flatterer. It is difficult to attribute a good sense to it when associated with panta pasin[147]. In Paul's description of the philosopher-flatterer in 1 Thess.2:4, he stresses that he does not seek to please men (οὐχ ὡς ἀνθρώποις ἀρέσκοντες). Similarly, in Gal.1:10, a passage often referred to in connection with 'all things to all men'[148], Paul denies that he seeks to please men in his preaching (ἢ ζητῶ ἀνθρώποις ἀρέσκειν; εἰ ἔτι ἀνθρώποις ἤρεσκον, Χριστοῦ δοῦλος οὐκ ἂν ἤμην)[149]. It appears, then, that Paul is speaking tongue in cheek as he did in 9:19-23. The qualification, μὴ ζητῶν τὸ

---

[147] For the terms ἄρεσκος and ἀρεσκέια, see above 73, 78. Cf. the negative sense in the similar phrase in Diog. Ep. 11, in which the writer claims eunuchs rather than philosophers pander to the masses (tois pollois areskontes).

[148] Eg., H. Chadwick, 'All Things', 261-262; S.C. Barton, All Things, 108.

[149] Paul has been accused of inconsistency in his teaching and practice of circumcision. See S.C. Barton, All Things, 107-124. It is interesting to see his use of two servile notions - ἀρέσκειν, δοῦλος - in Gal.1:10. Both terms are used to describe the flatterer and Paul refers both to himself in 1 Cor.9:19 as having made himself slave of all and in 1 Cor.10:33 as seeking to please all men. In Gal.1:10 the terms are opposed. He is not seeking to please men for to do so would mean that he could not be a slave of Christ.

ἐμαυτοῦ σύμφορον ἀλλὰ· τὸ τῶν πολλῶν, ἵνα σωθῶσιν, appears to be unnecessary otherwise. His request that they imitate him and his intimation that his behaviour was modelled on Christ (11:1) would have offended them greatly.

In 2 Corinthians we are confronted with Paul's reaction to a bitter invective against him by his enemies and their new associates. His relationship with the Corinthians is in danger of breaking down altogether as a result of it. At the heart of and comprising most of the invective is the figure of the flatterer. Paul was soon to regret his impetuosity in the present conflict. In the future, charges of this kind were to be met with a blanket, 'No!'.

(5) Paul as a flatterer in 2 Corinthians.

2 Cor.1:13-24 has been called the locus classicus for the attacks on Paul for his versatility[150]. Paul is said to be accused of vacillation in regard to his change in travel plans, a charge which he strongly rebuts. What has made this, which on the surface appears to be so trifling, the centre of such controversy? Altered plans may cause some inconvenience and disappointment to others but in themselves they should not be unexpected or unacceptable. This incident can only be understood against the background of hostility between Paul and his enemies. The accusations are of the same kind we have noticed in 1 Cor.9:19-23 and key terms in the accusation and in Paul's defence can be explained by an appeal to the figure of the flatterer.

In vv.12-14, Paul is talking in a general way about his relations with the Corinthians. This is the first of a number of passages in 2 Corinthians where he shows himself to be perturbed that the Corinthians don't understand him. He assures them that there are no hidden meanings in his letters; they are quite straightforward. This is akin to the common accusation against the flatterer that he knowingly says things contrary to his own opinion or acts contrary to his real

150 H. Chadwick, 'All Things', 262.

character. His word then is not to be trusted[151]. Paul tells them he has always behaved toward them and everyone else with simplicity (ἁπλότης) and sincerity (εἰλικρίνεια). ἐιλικρίνεια is also used by Paul in 2:17 to describe his behaviour as distinct from the questionable behaviour of those who preach for a fee. This is a critical issue for Paul. Judging from his response, it appears that the Corinthians had serious misgivings about him, and even mistrusted him. This attitude had been fostered over a period by his opponents, though Paul's own enigmatic behaviour must have puzzled even his most loyal supporters at times. He is now faced with serious accusations against his character and a threat to his authority which is having a disturbing effect upon many in Corinth. His defence here is the first sign in this letter of a bitter and protracted struggle with his opponents for the loyalty and affection of the Corinthian Christians.

The change in his travel plans is blown up out of all proportions by his opponents who have been able to show that his conduct in this matter simply fits the pattern. The charge against Paul is one of inconstancy. He makes his plans to visit Corinth with ἐλαφρία (v.17) which can be translated as 'fickleness', 'levity' or 'unsteadiness'. This mark of inconstancy is more elaborately framed in the same verse as τὸ Ναὶ ναὶ καὶ τὸ Ου οὔ[152]. Scholars generally refer this specifically to the way in which Paul changed his mind over his travel plans. He says 'yes' at one moment and 'no' the next[153]. However, the words should be taken as a whole. I suggest that here we are dealing with a familiar description of the flatterer in the form of invective. These words recall

---

[151] For this point, see above 78-82. It is possible that Paul here has been accused of presenting a different character in his letters to the one he reveals in person. Letters were regarded as substitutes for the writer's presence, according to ancient authors, and, though style and tone could be adapted to the circumstances and mood of the addressees, it should reflect the personality of its writer; so A.J. Malherbe, Ancient Epistolary Theorists, 15-16.

[152] Scholars have noted the similarity between this saying and Matt.5:37 and James 5:12 though they agree that the thought is quite different.

[153] Eg., H. Chadwick, 'All Things', 262; F.F. Bruce, 1 & 2 Cor. 181; C.K. Barrett, 2 Cor. 76.

Gnatho's self-description in Terence's play, The Eunuch: negat quis nego; ait aio[154]. Cicero quotes these words to describe the pliant and erratic soul of the flatterer[155]. In association with this quotation, Cicero uses many terms which parallel our passage. Flatterers are 'fickle and falsehearted men who say everything with a view to pleasure and nothing with a view to truth'. Their hypocrisy 'destroys sincerity' and their soul is 'fickle, changeable and manifold'[156]. They are contrasted with a true friend who has 'stability, sincerity and weight'[157]. The denigration and terms, the contrast with a true and loyal friend, are traditional. I suggest that both Cicero and Paul's enemies are drawing upon the same background. The phrase from Terence must have become a familiar and popular way of describing a flatterer. In this instance, Paul's enemies have seized upon his travel alterations to further accuse him of being a flatterer and thus persuade others against him. Such behaviour was typical of a man whose word is thoroughly unreliable.

Given the background of this invective, Paul's response is not surprising. He appeals to notions of constancy. First, God is faithful (pistos, v.19). There is nothing fickle about him. By implication, his apostle's word, whether in relation to travel plans or the gospel preached to them, is reliable[158]. Second, and in a similar vein, God is described as 'the one who makes us steadfast' (ho bebaiōn hēmas v.21). It has been suggested that throughout vv.18-20 Paul denotes 'constancy' or 'solidity' by a variety of words - pistos, nai, amēn, and possibly bebaios - which reflect the same Hebrew root[159].

---

[154] Eun. 250-253.

[155] de Amic. 25.93.

[156] Ibid., 25.91-92; cf. ibid., 17.64-18.65 where fickleness (levitas) is contrasted with loyalty (fides). It is not possible, says Cicero, for a man to be loyal whose nature is 'full of twists and twinings' (multiplex ingenium et tortuosum).

[157] Ibid., 25.95.

[158] Cf. C.K. Barrett, 2 Cor. 76.

[159] See W.C. van Unnik, 'Reisepläne und Amen-Sagen ...' in Studia Paulina in honorem J. de Zwaan (Haarlem, 1953) 215-234.

Though he moves his defence onto theological grounds (he rests his impugned reliability upon God's faithfulness in Christ), his choice of pistos and bebaios reflects a conscious effort to distinguish himself from the character of the flatterer. In discussions of the flatterer, that which distinguishes a man of quality from the flatterer, among other things, is pistos and bebaios. The flatterer is notoriously lacking in both[160].

A number of passages in which the flatterer is alluded to need to be considered briefly. First, is that of the philosopher-flatterer. In 2:17, Paul contrasts his sincerity as an apostle to the many who hawk the word of God (οἱ πολλοὶ καπηλεύοντες τὸν λόγον τοῦ θεοῦ). κάπηλος, 'retailer', was used frequently to derogate sophists who charged fees[161]. Traditionally allied to this charge of merchandising is that of deception[162]. In 4:2, Paul avers: 'we have renounced disgraceful, underhanded ways; we refuse to practise cunning or to tamper with God's word'. Paul in these two passages may be contasting himself with his rivals. He refers to them in 11:13 as 'false apostles, deceitful workmen, disguising themselves as apostles of Christ. Some exegetes believe, in view of the connection with the question of financial support in 11:7-11, that this description of Paul's rivals puts the dispute in the context of support among philosophers and sophists[163]. I have argued against vv.7-11 being interpreted in this way. The question of Paul's behaviour in relation to gifts remains the central issue between himself and his enemies as it was in 1 Cor.9[164]. The charges of merchandising and

---

160 For details, see above 86, espec. n.88; for pistis, . Cf. Euripides, Iph.331-333.

161 See R. Hock, The Working Apostle, 54-56. For my discussion of this phrase as an instance of Paul's own invective against his opponents, see below 346.

162 For the relation between 2:17 and 11:13 see C.K. Barrett, 'ΨΕΥΔΑΠΟΣΤΟΛΟΙ' (2 Corinthians 11:13)', in Mélanges Bibliques in hommage au B.P. Béda Rigaux, A. Descamps and A. de Halleux eds. (Gembloux, 1970) 383-385.

163 See R. Hock, The Working Apostle, 140; H. Windisch, Der Zweite Korintherbrief (Göttingen, 1924), 100-101; id., 'καπηλεύω', TDNT 3, 605.

164 For details, see above 176.

deception can be accounted for in the figure of the philosopher-flatterer of whom we have a composite picture in 1 Thess.2:3-6. That his rivals received gifts from the Corinthians is not doubted but it is only one aspect among a number of considerations which I have considered in chapter 6. The rival apostles were most successful in persuading many of the Corinthians away from Paul to themselves and their friends. Their own message has been well received, they have created a good impression (11:3-5,20), their invective against Paul has been damaging to him in his relations with the Corinthians. In the three passages I have considered (2:17, 4:2, 11:13) Paul appears to be responding with his own invective.

Second, Paul is deeply troubled that the Corinthians do not understand him. I have pointed to their misgivings about him in 1:12-14 and his assurance that he has always acted towards them with frankness and sincerity. He makes numerous attempts to clear himself in their eyes and to restore his relationship with them. He appeals to the initial relationship of trust established between them by recommendation (3:1-3, 5:11-12, 10:18, 12:11). They have trusted him and they of all people ought to know him. Accordingly, he refuses to recommend himself to them a second time. To do so under the circumstances would be seen to be an admission of guilt on his part. I have dealt with this aspect at length previously in chapter seven. However, it must be stressed that his frequent reference to 'recommendation' points clearly to a deterioration in the trust relationship established at the outset of his ministry and still apparent in his first letter. That it is almost always opposed to the hostile alliance and its relationship with many of the Corinthians suggests that the alliance is the cause of this breakdown in relations. Integrally linked with this is the charge of inconstancy.

Third, in two passages Paul explicitly refutes accusations against him of deception and in another he takes precautions to guard against such charges eventuating. In 7:2-3, in a context in which Paul shows the stress and anxiety the breakdown with the Corinthians has caused him, he pleads: 'Open your hearts to us; we have wronged no one, we have corrupted no one, we have taken advantage of no one'. In the immediately preceding peristasis catalogue, he makes a poignant reference to their mistrust and suspicion: 'We are treated as imposters, and yet are true; as unknown, and yet well known' (6:8b-9a). The suspicion of the Corinthians are real at this point. While Paul qualifies his pleading with, 'I do not say this to condemn you', he has deeply felt the withdrawal of their affection from him (6:12-13). While they themselves have not made the accusations, they have proved susceptible to the invective directed against him.

In his second explicit refutation of the charge of deception, 12:13-18, Paul links the accusation and the subsequent disaffection with the question of his conduct in money matters. He asks, 'For in what way were you less favoured than the rest of the churches, except that I myself did not burden you'. And somewhat ironically, 'forgive me this wrong'. He then proceeds to refute charges of deception against him and his co-workers. He has not been crafty nor acted with deceit. Neither has he sought their property.

In relation to the collection, Paul is anxious to preclude the possibility of such charges arising (8:16-23). 'We intend that no one should blame us about this liberal gift we are administering, for we aim at what is honourable not only in the Lord's sight but also in the sight of men' (vv.20-21). Accordingly, he outlines the characters of three men who will soon visit Corinth for the collection: Titus, a known quantity to the Corinthians (7:15, 8:6); a brother 'famous among all the churches for his preaching of the gospel' and appointed by them specifically to the collection (vv.18-19); a brother who has been thoroughly tested and approved in many matters (v.22). Paul would not have had to take these elaborate precautions simply to offset invective. The preparations clearly point to the ambivalence of the Corinthians towards Paul. I suggest that the long delay over the collection (v.10) is evidence of this.

The enthusiasm with which the Corinthians originally embraced the idea (v.11) had given way to a growing disinclination to contribute born of suspicion in the face of concerted attacks upon Paul by his enemies. That Paul could now envisage the completion of the collection is a measure of the success of

Titus' endeavours on his behalf (7:5-16). The caution expressed in chapters 8 and 9 suggest that there are many matters which still need to be resolved between himself and the Corinthians before he again wins their full confidence. One slip in this crucial issue would spell complete disaster for Paul and a final triumph for his enemies.

Finally, one characteristic of the flatterer remains to be considered, that of being tapeinos. The servile use of this word is frequent in Greek literature and it is one of the most popular terms used to denigrate the flatterer[165]. Tapeinoun and its cognates are not always used by Paul in this sense in 2 Corinthians, though the nuance of servility is generally present[166]. But where it forms part of the invective and comparison of his rivals, disparagement is intended. Paul's opponents have drawn attention to another aspect of his inconstancy. They say he acts in a mean manner (tapeinos) when with them, but he is bold (tharreō) towards them when away (10:1). This charge is stated more fully in v.10 as: 'For they say, "His letters are weighty (βαρεῖαι) and strong (ἰσχυραί) but his bodily presence is weak (ἀσθενής) and his speech of no account (ἐξουθενημένος)"'. ταπεινός and ἀσθενής are status terms and are often contrasted this way with other status terms such as ἰσχυρός in Greek literature[167]. Here, they are virtually synonymous and refer to the base posture or servile status which he adopted while with them. Tapeinos is often associated in this way with other terms which imply servile status in descriptions of the flatterer. He is said to be 'insignificant and mean' (ho mikros kai tapeinos)[168] and given to 'abasement and servility' (to aggenes kai tapeinon)[169]

---

[165] For details, see above 74-75.

[166] Eg., 7:6, ho tapeinos, where it is better to read 'the downcast' expressing his dispondency though an interpretation in terms of 'the lowly in status' is possible; 12:21, God may humble (tapeinō) me before you', where the humiliation is willed by God, though it may be caused by failure at the hands of his enemies.

[167] See C. Forbes, 'Strength' and 'Weakness', 38-39; see my discussion of these terms in chapter 9f.

[168] Plutarch, Mor. 65E.

[169] Ibid. 66D. C.K. Barrett, 2 Cor. 247, is correct in suggesting that the sense of tapeinos in v.1 is the same as its pairing in Xenophon, Mem.

It is to this inconsistency in conduct to which the invective is directed. One can almost hear his enemies saying, 'Look at him. When he is with us he is ever weak and servile. When he is away he writes letters as if he were a man of quality'.

This is the second time that Paul refers to criticism over the way he writes his letters. On both occasions, he is accused of acting inconsistently. In 1:12-14, I have suggested that Paul is charged with writing in a manner which was contrary to his real character. He gave a different impression in his letters to what they had come to expect of him in person[170]. The element of truth which underlies the invective makes it all the more persuasive. In both these passages, Paul refers to his supposed inconsistency as acting κατὰ σάρκα. In 1:17, it is equivalent to saying at the same time, 'yes, yes, and no, no'. In 10:2 it describes the ταπεινός/θαρρέω antithesis. It is possible that this is his way of alluding to the inconstancy of the flatterer. In his defence on this issue, he again appeals to constancy. 'Let such people understand that what we say by letter when absent, we do when present' (v.11).

tapeinoō (11:7) is used with a social sense in association with Paul's conduct in regard to gifts and forms one of a series of comparisons between Paul and his rivals throughout chapters 10 and 11 in which Paul is consistently seen in an unfavourable light. Some have argued that tapeinoō denotes servile status but refer it to Paul's demeaning himself as a worker while in Corinth[171]. It is used in this way of the lowly status of a wage-earner in Greek literature[172] and undoubtedly his working for wages contributed to the overall picture that his enemies formed of him. But the primary consideration here, as in 1 Cor.9, is his inconstancy over

3.10.5, with ἀνελεύθερον, 'servility', and its contrast with μεγαλοπρεπὲς, 'nobility', and ἐλευθέριον, 'dignity'. Cf. similar contrast in Epictetus' description of the flatterer, 4.1.54-55: ταπεινὸν εἶναι ... μὴ εἶναι ἐλεύθερον.

170 H.D. Betz, 'Paul's Apology' 5, is correct in his observation that the apparent inconsistency between Paul's letters and his appearance causes suspicion also against his writing: 'the contradiction is strange indeed, the suspicion is thus justified'.

171 Eg., H. Windisch, 2 Kor. 334; R. Hock, The Working Apostle, 136; id., 'Paul's Tentmaking', 561-562.

172 Eg., Lucian, Dream 13: kai panta tropon tapeinos.

gifts. I do not wish to suggest that all the invective should be subsumed under the notion of the objectionable flatterer, and I will deal presently with it in its other forms. However, the figure of the flatterer provides the most consistent explanation for the number of charges of inconstancy directed against Paul by his enemies. Against this familiar background, we have been able to account for the kind of charge of servility which was made against Paul; the antithesis of freedom and slavery and associated terms; the breakdown in the relationship and its concomitants of suspicion, mistrust and ambivalence on the part of the Corinthians and the supposed deception on the part of Paul. We have been able to see from the point of view of others how Paul's inconsistent behaviour provided a fertile ground for invective, one in which there was always an element of truth. We can also see how the Corinthians themselves were susceptible to conventional forms of invective based on a character with which they were readily familiar.

c. Paul in comparison with his enemies.

In 2 Cor. 10:12 Paul claims that his enemies have made themselves the measure of apostleship and presumably have compared him unfavourably with themselves. He writes, 'Not that we venture to class or compare ourselves (συγκρῖναι ἑαυτούς) with some of those who commend themselves. But when they measure themselves by one another and compare themselves with one another (αὐτοὶ ἐν ἑαυτοῖς ἑαυτοὺς μετροῦντες καὶ συγκρίνοντες ἑαυτοὺς ἑαυτοῖς), they are without understanding.' I shall argue that the technique used by Paul's enemies and indeed himself, despite what appears to be his denial, is that of the rhetorical device of sygkrisis, 'comparison'[173]. As I have shown previously, sygkrisis was a method by which a person amplified his own virtues and achievements and depreciated those of his enemies. By comparing himself with people of outstanding character or deeds or a standard of

---

173 This has previously been noticed by H.D. Betz, 'Paul's Apology', 14. But independently of Betz and in conjunction with C. Forbes, I had come to similar conclusions.

excellence he attempted to display his superiority. The economiastic topics, which included everything that was commendable in Greek and Roman society, are numerous: virtues such as justice, courage, self-control, magnanimity, liberality, gentleness, practical and speculative wisdom; physical qualities such as beauty, stature, agility, might and health; social standing, which included a man's city, race, upbringing, pursuits, affairs and connections[174].

It is extremely difficult to determine what was the standard or measure Paul's enemies have set. It will become clearer as we proceed that both they and Paul resort to some of the traditional topics. We can assume that the ones used to derogate Paul represent the contraries of the values by which they consider themselves to be superior. It is also hard to ascertain which of the topics belong to his opponents' sygkrisis and which to Paul's, as he engages in self-derision. 2 Cor. 10-12 comprises his response to his detractors and we only get glimpses of the things his enemies said about him. In this section, then, I shall restrict myself to those comparisons which Paul explicitly attributes to them. First, these self-recommenders use their own standard for apostleship. I have suggested previously that the various elements may have formed part of the praise section of their recommendations[175], though the actual comparison formed part of their invective against Paul after their arrival. Secondly, I shall argue the standard consists of values which require an apostle to be a cultivated man and that these values are shared by both parties to the alliance. Friendship initiated by recommendation would most probably have required that they possess common interests and pursuits.

Thirdly, the comparison which the rival apostles initiated - 'they measure themselves by one another and compare themselves with one another' - is between themselves and Paul rather than, as some think[176], between themselves. There can be no doubt

---

174 For details, see above 53-55.

175 Ibid., 274-276.

176 Eg., F.F. Bruce, 1 & 2 Cor. 232; C. Forbes, 'Strength' and 'Weakness' 85.

that they consider themselves to be superior to Paul. The nature of sygkrisis and Paul's quoting of their dispraise show that they were endeavouring to persuade others of their superiority. This, in fact, is implicit in their immoderate conduct; they measure themselves by their own standards whereas Paul and his associates will not boast beyond measure (v.13)[177]. They have made themselves the measure of apostleship and judged Paul to be inferior. The phrase en heautois heautous metrountes does not mean, as C.K. Barrett suggests, that they lacked 'any objective standard of judgement' or that they used 'no standards at all'[178]. Rather it means that they themselves represented the measure. The use of the familiar encomiastic topics suggests that they submitted to a standard which the Corinthians would readily recognize and accept. This is essential to Greek persuasion. It is true that they did not submit themselves to Paul's criteria for apostleship, though he, as we shall see, well understood theirs and conducted his own comparison on a point for point basis. Fourthly, the intention of dispraise is to dishonour an opponent and the comparison of the rival apostles was aimed at humiliating and shaming Paul before the Corinthians. His use of the terms aischynesthai (10:8) and atimia (11:21) implies as much and the idea of shame dominates his own comparison.

Fifthly, the derogatory remarks seem to consist of the encomiastic topics of physical appearance, education and achievements. In relation to the first two of these, Paul relates: 'they say, "His letters are weighty and strong, but his bodily presence is weak, and his speech of no account"' (10:10). While the invective here points to his inconsistency of character and I have included it under my discussion of the character of the flatterer[179], the comments about his personal bearing and style of speech belong also to the theme of comparison. In 11:5-6 he responds: 'I think that I am not in the least inferior to the superlative apostles. Even if I am unskilled in speaking (εἰ δὲ καὶ ἰδιώτης τῷ λόγῳ), I am not

---

[177] For details, see above 199-202.

[178] 2 Cor. 262-263.

[179] For details, see above 323-324.

in knowledge (ἀλλ᾽ οὐ τῇ γνώσει)'. The phrases ὁ λόγος ἐξουθενημένος and ἰδιώτης τῷ λόγῳ both refer to Paul's apparent lack of rhetorical training. His formal presentation lacks skill. Either voiced separately or implied in the above charge is the further one that he is ignorant or foolish. While Paul may be prepared to concede that his speech does not compare favourably with that of his rivals, in no way is he prepared to admit deficiency in knowledge[180]. The association between eloquence and education is a familiar one in Greek and Roman authors. Isocrates taught that the ability to speak well was the clearest indication of understanding[181], while Cicero regarded the precepts of rhetoric as a proper part of a liberal education[182] and defined eloquence as the art of speaking with knowledge, skill and elegance[183]. He comments, 'it is made easily discernible whether the speaker has merely floundered in his declamatory business or whether, before approaching his task of oratory, he has been trained in all the liberal arts'[184]. Wisdom also was inseparably linked with knowledge and eloquence. Isocrates said, 'nothing done with intelligence is done without speech, but speech is the marshal of all actions and of thoughts and those most use it who have the greatest wisdom'[185].

It is possible that dispraise of this kind underlies Paul's words in 2 Cor.5:13: 'For if we are beside ourselves (ἐξέστημεν), it is for God; if we are in our right mind (σωφρονοῦμεν), it is for you'. Most modern commentators have

---

180 H.D. Betz, 'Paul's Apology', 7, says that λόγος refers to both content and to presentation of content. In the phrase ἰδιώτης τῷ λόγῳ, λόγος relates to formal presentation while γνῶσις is the content of the λόγος. However, he suggests that 11:5-6 belongs to Paul's defence and is not another accusation.

181 Antidosis 253-257.

182 De Or. 1.32.146.

183 Ibid., 2.2.5.

184 Ibid., 2.16.73. Cf., G. Kennedy, The Art of Persuasion in Greece, (London, 1963), 7: 'It is not too much to say that rhetoric played the central role in Ancient education'.

185 Nicolas 5ff., Antidosis 257; cf. similarly, Cicero, de Or. 2.2.6, and the contrasts, Plato, Phdr. 239A: 'But the ignorant is inferior to the wise, the coward to the brave, the poor speaker to the eloquent, the slow of wit to the clever'.

applied the antithetical terms *ekstēnai* and *sōphronein* to ecstatic and rational behaviour, that is, to speaking with tongues and sober instruction[186]. They assume that Paul is either referring to the problem of tongues in 1 Cor.12-14, especially to the distinction he makes in 14:1-19[187], or to his visions and ecstatic experiences in 2 Cor.12:1-6[188]. The classical scholar, H. North, has observed that the antithesis here between madness and self-control functions in the same way as in contemporary Greek usage[189]. The verb *ekstēnai* appears to have the same meaning as the more common antonym, *mainesthai*[190]. *Mania* describes a wide range of irrational conduct and is translated by such terms as 'madness, insanity, enthusiasm, inspired frenzy and passion'. It is either directly opposed to *sōphrosynē* or, oddly, combined with it in the form of the oxymoron, *mania sōphrōn*. These uses provide us with the two possible interpretations of v.13.

First, I have suggested that Paul was accused of being uneducated or ignorant because of his failure to speak well. The connection between *sōphrosynē* and other praiseworthy intellectual notions, such as *sophia*, is frequently made in Greek authors. Both *sōphrosynē* and *sophia* belong to those components of virtue which commend a person as noble and worthy of praise. Their contraries, the vices, render a man disgraceful and open to blame[191]. *Sōphrosynē*, as I have shown, is a moral and intellectual notion which on occasions approaches *sophia* in meaning[192]. In his Memorabilia, Xenophon mainly uses it in the moral sense but he makes it clear that Socrates

---

[186] So E. Käsemann, Legitimität, 61-66; F.F. Bruce, 1 & 2 Cor. 207; C.K. Barrett, 2 Cor. 166-167.

[187] See R. Bultmann, 2 Kor. 150-151.

[188] Ibid., 150; F.F. Bruce, 1 & 2 Cor. 207.

[189] Sophrosyne, 317.

[190] Cf., Acts 26:24-25 where Paul's response to Festus' remark, that his efforts to gain advanced knowledge has made him μανία, is: οὐ μαίνομαι ... ἀλλὰ ... ἀληθείας καὶ σωφροσύνης.

[191] So Aristotle, Rhet. 1.9.1-6.

[192] See above 192-193. It basically means 'soundness of mind' and is translated by terms such as 'moderation, self-control, sanity, prudence' and the like.

did not distinguish between it and sophia[193]. He opposes mania to both sōphrosynē[194] and sophia[195] without distinction. In the latter passage, it refers to a special kind of ignorance and not to ignorance per se. It is the vice of self-ignorance, the fault of not knowing oneself which leads to delusion about oneself and one's abilities. He defines it as the 'name they give to errors on matters of common knowledge'. When opposed to sōphrosynē and sophia in this way, mania is a form of hybristic behaviour[196].

A similar range of ideas is present in Plato's analysis of the nature of the ridiculous. He defines it as the name given to the particular vice of self-ignorance, the opposite of the Delphic maxim, gnōthi sauton. This vice takes the form of self-delusion: it is the ignorance of those who think they are richer, possess better physical qualities, and are wiser than they are. When such self-ignorance occurs in the strong (dynatoi), it is detestable for it injures others; but if it occurs in the weak (asthenēs) it is merely ridiculous[197].

In 2 Cor.5:10-12, Paul is comparing his apostleship with that of his rivals. They judge apostleship according to appearance (en prosōpō), and not as Paul implies he would, according to heart (en kardia). I suggest that the comparison involved here is the same one as in chapter 10 and that en prosōpō kouchōmenous refers to those socially accepted values by which they have assessed themselves to be superior to Paul. The notion of judgement is also present. Paul believes that what he is is known to God to whom he must answer and, hopefully to their consciences. In addition we have the very important relational concept of recommendation in this passage which is so central to chapters 10-12. In short, we appear to have a preview of those things which Paul takes up in greater detail in later chapters. It is in this context that we should

---

193 3.9.4-6.

194 1.1.16.

195 3.9.6.

196 See above 193f, and in particular the references to Heraclitus Fr. 116DK quoted there; see also H. North, Sophrosyne, 124, 128.

197 Phil. 48B-49E. Cf. Diodorus Siculus. 9.10.1-3.

view the opposing notions of <u>ekstēnai</u> and <u>sōphronein</u>. Paul appears to be responding to invective. He must have been accused of assuming a position at Corinth for which he hadn't the appropriate qualities, of claiming too much for himself, of not knowing his limitations. By comparison, we can assume that his enemies are characterised by <u>sōphrosynē</u> and other allied virtues. In his defence, he says that whether their invective is true it is for God (θεῷ) and themselves (ὑμῖν) to judge[198].

There can be no doubt that invective of this kind could follow on from a more specific charge of being unskilled in rhetoric. There is, moreover, a hint that Paul is alluding to rhetoric in v.11 when he states that his task is to persuade men, albeit in accordance with God's standard. The term, <u>peithein</u>, is synonymous with rhetoric. A similar idea to <u>ekstēnai</u> may underlie Paul's description of his boasting in 2 Cor.11:23 as παραφρονῶν λαλῶ, 'I speak as a madman'. There though this notion of 'foolishness' or 'ignorance' refers to the role Paul adopts to become like his rivals and forms part of his subtle innuendo against them.

Secondly, the concept of <u>sōphrosynē</u> is closely related to the doctrine of the three characters of rhetorical style - the plain, the middle, and the grand. The style of the <u>sōphrōn</u> avoided the vices of excess and defect and was marked by moderation and restraint and demonstrated a feeling for <u>to prepon</u>. <u>Sōphrosynē</u> was the necessary accompaniment of all three styles, though among Greek-speaking Romans it was regarded as characteristic of the middle or temperate style[199].

---

198 The majority of commentators maintain the distinction between the ecstatic and the rational. The former is towards God; the latter is towards the Corinthians; neither for his own benefit. This notion of selflessness is evident in the following verses (vv.14-15), 'living no longer to themselves'. However, I suggest that invective is implicit in v.13 and that it is linked to the ideas of judgement, comparison, recommendation and boasting in the preceding verses. The datives, θεῷ and ὑμῖν, have the same idea as the preceding θεῷ δὲ πεφανερωμέθα which refers directly to Paul's preaching: 'we persuade <u>(pathō</u>) men' (5:11).

199 So H. North, 'The Concept of "Sophrosyne" in Greek Literary Criticism', CP. 43 (1948), 10-12, and generally, 1-8. She suggests that it was possibly due to a misunderstanding over Cicero's use of temperare, 'mix, mingle, or temper', to describe a combination of the plain and grand styles. It was also considered characteristic of the Attic style (plain) as opposed to the more elaborate Asian style of oratory.

It is also, together with the adjective, sōphrōn, and the verb, sōphronein, applied to the intellectual and ethical qualities of the speaker which enable him to avoid excess and follow the precepts relating to rhythm, choice of words, metaphor, figures, and so on[200]. It is possible then that we have a further insight into Paul's rhetorical style of speech. Passionate, excessive, impulsive, intense, unrestrained by custom and precedent, undisciplined by study and practice. By comparison, his rivals, who were most likely rhetorically trained, were characterized by praiseworthy restraint and showed due deference to rhetorical convention.

The oxymoron, mania sōphrōn, also relates specifically to rhetoric. Sōphrosynē, as the rational element in composition, was regarded by some Greek writers as inferior to and the antithesis of mania which signified the madness or enthusiasm of poetic inspiration. In particular it was unfavourably contrasted with the Platonic theia mania, the madness derived from divine influence. Other writers used it as the equivalent of theia mania and it became 'endowed with a more profound meaning and indicates poetic enthusiasm controlled by reason and thus subordinated to the rules of art'[201]. In particular, it was characteristic of the grand style of rhetoric in which force and intensity, the supreme virtues of this style, were regarded as inseparable from stylistic sōphrosynē[202]. There are certain similarities between Paul's rehtoric and the grand type. E.A. Judge has asked whether in fact Paul might have used it[203], while E. Norden contends that Paul's rhetoric was akin to the Asianic style which was so popular in the cities of Asia Minor[204]. Judge concludes, however, that it is

---

[200] Ibid., 17.

[201] Ibid., 14.

[202] Ibid., 13-16.

[203] 'Paul's Boasting in Relation to Contemporary Professional Practice', ABR. 16 (1968), 38-40.

[204] Die Antike Kunstprosa (Leipzig, 1909), 476 n. 1; cited by E.A. Judge, 'Paul's Boasting', 41. Asianism was affected by foreign ways of thought and speech and was regarded as inferior to Atticism which was so highly regarded by many cultured Romans and Greeks. See H.F. North, '"Sophrosyne" in Greek Literary Criticism', 8-9; G. Kennedy, Persuasion in Greece, 301-303.

'difficult to see in Paul a willing exponent of the grand style'[205].

A major difficulty in identifying Paul's rhetoric is that we do not have any of his speeches available for appraisal. We only have his letters which, if we are to accept the invective as having some objectivity, were regarded as being more rhetorically effective than his speech[206]. As I will show in the next chapter, we do have some indication of Paul's spoken rhetoric in the contrast between the eloquence of the hybrists and his speech as displaying power in weakness (1 Cor.2:4; 4:19-20). He says he consciously avoided speaking καθ' ὑπεροχὴν λόγου η σοφίας (1 Cor.2:1) or ἐν πειθοῖς σοφίας λόγοις (2:4) and he was properly judged to be ineffective and unskilled by rhetorical standards. By comparison his letters displayed some of the praiseworthy qualities (baros ischys) and revealed something of the emotional intensity and force which characterised the grand style. But this type along with the other two was to be tempered by sōphrosynē, had its appropriate function, and was subject to the precepts of rhetoric. Given the derogation of his speech and personal appearance, the traditional association of sōphrosynē and rhetoric and Paul's blatant disregard of the latter in his speech, and the notion of mania as uncontrolled enthusiasm, the contrast of ἐκστῆναι and σωφρόνειν as a device of invective may suggest that Paul ignored the required restraints, disregarded the proprieties and was carried along by his own impetus. There was mania but no sōphrosynē in his persuasion of men.

The disparagement of Paul's personal bearing, hē parousia tou sōmatos asthenēs, is possibly a concomitant of the dispraise of his rhetorical style. The link between the attributes of physical strength and beauty and both eloquence and intelligence is uniformly attested by Greek and Roman

---

205 'Paul's Boasting', 40.

206 The description of his letters as βαρεῖαι καὶ ἰσχυραί (10:10) is not unlike Cicero's of the grand style as weighty, grand and emphatic (gravis, grandis, vehemens), Or. 21.68-69.

authors from as early as Homer[207]. Superior physical qualities - agility, strength, beauty, health - commended an orator, enhanced his speech, and moved the audience in his favour[208]. Physical defects and illnesses were subject to scurrilous attacks and ridicule and had a great impact upon the victim and the onlookers[209]. People were willing to listen to a 'clear voiced orator' until his defects were demonstrated[210] or he would simply appear as an utterly ridiculous person because of his warped and deformed body[211]. It would be most difficult to believe that Paul's illnesses and battle scars did not receive close and eloquent attention from his enemies, possibly provoking Paul to such extended comment on it. We can also assume that in their sygkrisis they praised their superior strength of body and nobility of mind.

The remaining element of the rival apostles' sygkrisis relates to the encomiastic topic of achievements. In 2 Cor. 11:12 Paul speaks of 'those who would like to claim that in their boasted mission they work on the same terms as we do (καθὼς καὶ ἡμεῖς)'. The precise meaning of this verse is difficult to establish[212]. Most commentators consider boasting kathōs hēmeis consists of a claim to apostolic status based upon the apostolic right to support. The rival apostles, unlike Paul, accepted financial aid from the Corinthians but in doing so have left themselves open to the damaging criticism that they were frauds and deceivers[213]. To safeguard their reputation they either sought to induce him to accept the Corinthian offer and thus bring him on an equal footing with

---

[207] See C. Forbes, 'Strength' and 'Weakness', 10-73, who has investigated the notions of strength and weakness in Homer, Diodorus Siculus, Dionysius of Halicarnassus, Josephus, Dio Chrysostom and Plutarch. Cf. also more generally, E.C. Evans, 'Physiognomics in the Ancient World'.

[208] Cf. Auctor ad Herennium 3.10; Seneca Ep. 95.65. Physical merits, see Lucian, Salt 35; Rl.Pr. 15, 16, 19, 20, 23.

[209] For details, see above 64-66.

[210] So Homer, Il. 2.216-219.

[211] Ibid., 2.212; cf. Lucian, Ind. 21, 23.

[212] See the discussion, P.E. Hughes, 2 Cor. 390-392.

[213] For my discussion of this passage, see above 175-176, 239-240.

with themselves[214], or, according to the more popular view, have used his refusal as evidence that he is not a legitimate apostle or an inferior one at best[215].

In my opinion it is most unlikely that the meaning of the phrase kathōs hēmeis should be limited to a claim to apostleship, particularly one for which the criterion was either acceptance or refusal of support. First, the rivals had no doubts about their apostolic status. Rather they are concerned with demonstrating their superiority over Paul and thus justifying their position as the apostles in Corinth. Secondly, as I have argued at length previously, it is difficult to see how in principle Paul could discredit them for accepting gifts from the Corinthians. He had accepted gifts from elsewhere and it was his refusal in the face of this which led to the hostilities and invective against him. His rivals were highly esteemed by the Corinthians for accepting their offer[216]. Undoubtedly Paul's refusal was of fundamental importance to his understanding of his apostleship in Corinth and therefore would become a point of comparison in his sygkrisis. For him, it was proof of the love he had for them as their parent apostle no matter what they thought to the contrary[217]. To them, his refusal was a sign of an inconstant, untrustworthy, unloving friend. It is possible in view of this that we ought to include Paul's comparison on this issue as part of his shame theme. His ironic introduction to the matter suggests this is the case: 'Did I commit a sin in debasing myself ...?' (v.7; cf. 12:13b).

I suggest that kathōs hēmeis has to do with the question of who is the apostle of Corinth rather than with apostolic status. It is a question of authority rather than legitimacy. Does Paul any longer have authority in Corinth? This is the substance of his response in 10:13-18. He was the founder

---

214 So P.E. Hughes, 2 Cor. 390.

215 Eg., C.K. Barrett, 2 Cor. 282; A. Plummer, 2 Cor. 307; J.H. Bernard, The Second Epistle to the Corinthians, Expositors Greek Testament (Grand Rapids, 1967), 103.

216 For details, see above 175-176, 239-240, 245-247.

217 Ibid., 247-251.

apostle, the first to reach them with the gospel of Christ (v.14). His rivals, by comparison, boast eis ta ametra in other men's labours (v.15) and of work already done in another's kanōn (v.16). It is doubtful that they could have taken credit for Paul's achievements. It was an indisputable fact that Paul founded the church in Corinth and it would have been ridiculous for them to have claimed this. Rather they are boasting that their achievements among the Corinthians far surpass his. As Theon said about this topic: 'Among a person's actions we should prefer the finest, those with the best and most durable results, opportune actions that avert great harm, and ones chosen freely'[218]. We do not have any clear indication as to what these may consist of though some scholars feel that as Christ's (10:7) they have laid claim to excelling Paul in the 'signs of an apostle' (12:12)[219].

We do know that in Paul's own comparison where he states that he is a superior servant of Christ he proceeds to list all the 'worst' things rather than the finest. It is certain though that these cultured men have won over the Corinthians from the parent apostle. His defence to this challenge to his authority forms part of his own sygkrisis and I shall take this matter up again in the next chapter.

What then do we know about the rival apostles and Paul from this analysis of their sygkrisis? At this point it is necessary to outline certain difficulties we face with the material. In relation to the objections raised against Paul's speech and appearance, E.A. Judge comments: 'It is not clear to us precisely what kind of social and literary prejudices inspired these complaints. But a convincing explanation of them would probably do much to open up the picture of Paul's place in the society of his day'[220]. We have identified the use of the rhetorical device of comparison and the popular topics of eloquence, intelligence, physical stature and health, and achievements[221]. This suggests that we must place

---

[218] Ibid., 54.

[219] See the discussion in H.D. Betz, Sokratische Tradition, 70-100.

[220] 'St. Paul and Classical Society', 19.

[221] Cf. Aulus Gellius, 1.13.10; Pliny, NH. 7.43.139-140.

the rival apostles within the mainstream of Graeco-Roman cultural convention. Two major difficulties confront us as we endeavour to describe them more exactly, - the enmity relationship and the nature of comparison. First, we are dealing with invective and we do not know how true the details are. Betz, however, suggests that the accusations against Paul are objective and responsible observations, not calumny, which were submitted as a formal report to the Corinthians[222]. Most scholars are prepared to accept, to one degree or another, that Paul was idiōtēs tǭ logǭ. Somewhat inconsistently, they rush to defend Paul's integrity against the accusations that he is fickle, insincere and greedy. But this is to ignore the fact, namely, that both kinds of abuse are malicious invective which arose out of a hostile relationship.

I have said that there may be good grounds for judging Paul to be inconstant by Greek standards of morality. However one only needs to point to a real or imagined defect in a person's character and one is at once led on to comparing it with similar defects or shameful stock characters. Quintilian describes one formal kind of argument called 'apposite' or 'comparative': 'A conjecture as to fact is confirmed by argument from something greater as in the following sentence: "If a man commit sacrilege, he will also commit theft"; from something less, in a sentence such as "He who lies easily and openly will commit perjury"; from something equal in a sentence such as "He who has taken a bribe to give a false verdict will take a bribe to give false witness"'[223]. In a similar fasion, Aristotle argues: 'We must also assume, for the purposes of praise or blame, that qualities which closely resemble the real qualities are identical with them; for instance, that the cautious man is cold and designing'[224].

The character of the flatterer was open to allegations of this kind and indeed was frequently appealed to in this way. If Paul can be called inconstant then he can be attacked as a flatterer and all those defects which traditionally make up

[222] Sokratische Tradition, 44-45.

[223] 5.10.87.

[224] Rhet. 1.9.28.

this stock character can be properly ascribed to him. With _sygkrisis_ a person resorted to amplification or depreciation of common virtues or vices. If Paul is unskilled in rhetoric then he is also ignorant or uneducated. With regard to eloquence (_logos_), it is not clear what concession to the invective Paul is making, if any at all. The concessive form of Paul's reply (εἰ δὲ) (11:6) leaves room for doubt. He could simply be making a concession to debate[225]. Our analysis of his responses in the next chapter may enable us to see whether there is any basis to this dispraise of his speech. However he refutes the implied charge of ignorance. He lacks nothing in knowledge.

His physical appearance is another matter. There can be no doubt that Paul suffered from ill health and physical injury. A severe affliction in Asia just prior to the writing of this letter (which interfered with his travel plans) (2 Cor. 1:3-11) and his peristasis catalogues (1 Cor.4:9-13; 2 Cor. 6:4-10; 11:23-33) bear eloquent testimony to various kinds of adversity and persecution. There is evidence to suggest that he also suffered from a socially debilitating disease or disfigurement[226]. Undoubtedly these things would have been made the butt of illiberal jests and malicious laughter.

There are parallels between the _sygkrisis_ in 2 Cor.10-12 and what are generally considered to be criticisms of Paul in 1 Cor.2:1-5. Paul's lack of eloquence had long been a contentious issue between his enemies and himself. He states that he purposefully avoided using rhetoric when he first preached in Corinth and sought 'power' in those things which were the very antithesis of rhetoric - 'in weakness, in much fear and trembling'. All of this occurs in a context of comparison and rivalry in which Paul's enemies, the hybrists, consider themselves superior. However, the deliberate way in which he adopts the antithetical position and his conscious avoidance of rhetoric 'keeps our question tantalisingly alive'[227]. Thus caution is necessary if we are to come closer

---

[225] So E.A. Judge, 'Paul's Boasting', 37-38.

[226] Eg., 2 Cor.12:1-10, Gal. 4:13-15; See my discussion, 153-154.

[227] E.A. Judge, 'Paul's Boasting', 40.

to the truth about Paul and the rival apostles. Our understanding of the nature of comparison and encomium may help us draw some tentative guidelines.

First, though we have no recorded statements of the rival apostles' views of themselves, on the basis of point for point comparison we can assume that they have attributed to themselves those qualities which are the very opposite of the defects they have found in Paul. Secondly, because of the process of amplification and depreciation, of praise and dispraise, we may need to modify the image that they have created for Paul. The gap between him and his detractors may be narrower than they would have the Corinthians believe. Thirdly, we must remember that many of the terms used in their invective, and of the topics of comparison in particular, indicate the status as well as the character of the person[228]. Fourthly, a related convention of rhetoric requires a ridiculer to be free of the faults he found in his opponent and free from serious faults and physical defects himself. Else he himself would be held up to ridicule by his intended victim and audience alike[229].

d. Summary

We are then ready to make some preliminary conclusions. The rival apostles are probably rhetorically trained (their dispraise of Paul on this point would have been ridiculous otherwise) and have attributed to themselves those virtues and deeds which belong to the traditional ways of measuring a person's greatness. Together with their Corinthian associates who shared these values, they have expected an apostle to be a man of culture, basing this on those qualities which they have ascribed to themselves in an open and unashamed self-display. They have depicted Paul as a socially and intellectually unacceptable person who fails to meet the standards of apostleship which they best exhibit. His speech is unrestrained

228 Cf., E.W. Bower, Ἔφοδος and Insinuatio in Greek and Latin Rhetoric', CQ. 8 (1958), 225. See also, C. Forbes, 'Strength' and 'Weakness', generally.

229 Cf. Plutarch, Mor. 88F; 542D. See also Aristotle, Rhet. 2.6.19; M.A. Grant, The Laughable, 139.

and impulsive and betrays his lack of education and the accompanying social graces. His physical appearance is ridiculous and shameful as befits a fool. He is inconstant and not to be trusted; a servile flatterer who deliberately changes his character to accommodate to others for his own advantage.

We have had sketched for us in invective a picture of Paul which has more than an element of truth in it from a Greek standpoint. The Corinthians found it persuasive for they responded favourably to his rivals and against him. However, the charcoal is not altogether convincing and before we can apply the pigments we need to examine in fine detail the perspective that Paul gives us of himself and his enemies in his response to the invective.

Chapter 9

PAUL'S RESPONSES

Taking Paul's disavowal of rhetoric in 1 Cor. 2:1-5 at face value, we should expect to find no evidence of its conventions being used, consciously at least, in his letters. Perhaps we should distinguish between his preaching and his writing, for his remarks refer directly to the former and his enemies draw a distinction between his ineffective speech and the weight and strength of his letters. The classically educated Fathers saw clearly that Paul's letters did not conform to the classical standards of the Greeks[1]. In addition, his renouncement of 'disgraceful, underhanded ways' and 'cunning' (2 Cor. 4:2) implies that he does not resort to the traditional tricks or devices of rhetoric employed by the formally trained orator. But the very deliberateness of his reaction against rhetoric raises more problems than it solves. 'If he knows how to reject it so forcefully', asks Judge, 'is he not perhaps turning its subtleties against itself?'[2]. The force of this question becomes more apparent when we see that Paul competently uses a number of the traditional techniques - non-naming, comparison, self-praise, self-derision and innuendo - in an attempt to derogate his enemies and win the Corinthians' confidence. I shall deal with his use of each of these devices separately before attempting to draw more precise lines within which we may view Paul and his enemies.

a. Non-naming.

It is a striking feature of Paul's 'undisputed' letters

---

[1] See E.A. Judge, 'Paul's Boasting', 41-44. That formal rhetoric was the standard by which Paul's enemies conducted their comparison has been assumed by most scholars and in this present study also. However, I suggest later that we cannot be certain of the standard by which this rhetoric has been, or should be assessed.

[2] Ibid. 40.

that, though he mentions numerous friends and associates by name, he never once names an enemy[3]. Judge comments that his rivals 'are regularly damned (and is not this too part of the rhetorical art?) with anonymity'[4]. He cites Paul's reference to them in Rom. 16:17-18 - 'those who create dissensions and difficulties' - a passage which I have already described as a cameo of the situation in Corinth[5]. He resorts to a periphrastic construction like this on a number of occasions in his letters to describe his enemies[6].

Periphrasis or non-naming, as a rhetorical device for describing an enemy, was used to great effect by Augustus in his Res Gestae. The only Romans he names (apart from consuls whose names are used for dating) are those related to him in some degree of sonship[7]. There are five occasions where the passage appears to be crying out for a name and where all the readers are aware of the persons indicated by periphrasis[8].

a. He condemns the legitimate government of the consul Antony as 'the tyranny of a faction' (dominatio factionis)[9], while contrasting his own usurpation in terms familiar to public admiration. b. He refers scathingly to Brutus and Cassius

---

[3] Id., 'Scholastic Community ii', 127-135, who lists from the traditional Pauline corpus the names of 80 individuals who 'between them formed his platform and retinue'. By contrast, in the disputed letters, Paul names his enemies on two occasions, in 1 Tim.1:19-20 and 2 Tim 4:14.

[4] Id., 'Paul's Boasting', 41.

[5] See above 311-312.

[6] Periphrasis (περίφρασις; Latin equiv., circumscriptio, circumlocutio) is defined by Quintilian as a circuitous mode of speech which, in oratory, expands a simple thought or word for purposes of ornament; eg., 8.6.59-61; cf., 9.1.35; 9.3.91; 9.4.124. It is often used to conceal something which was indecent, though the reverse is true for the non-naming of enemies; cf. Aristotle, Rhet. 3.6.1-3; Cicero, de Or. 3.54.207; Or. 41.204.

[7] Eg., Gaius and Lucius, 2.14; M. Marcellus, 4.21; T. Nero, 5.27.

[8] I am grateful to E.A. Judge for drawing my attention to these references and his commentary on them, taken from a paper delivered at Macquarie University, 1979, as part of the School of History's Continuing Education Program of Ancient History.

[9] RG. 1.1; Factio, 'faction, clique', was always used with a pejorative sense and was opposed to the amicitia of good men; eg., Caesar, BC. 1.22.5, 'the clique of the few' used by Caesar to derogate his opponents as oligarchs and it was a popular expression used by those excluded from the ruling clique. See also, M. Gelzer, Nobility, 'Factions', 123-136.

as 'those who slew my father' (Qui parentem meum [interfecer] un[t][10]. By not naming them, 'he makes them available for caricature as moral stereotypes defined in relation to himself. The whole exercise is essentially one of comparison' and he 'contrasts their criminality with his concern for correct procedure'[11]. c. He refers to his enemy Lepidus as 'a colleague still living' (vivus conlega) and presents himself with an opportunity to denigrate his record[12]. It enabled him to contrast Lepidus' irregular behaviour in securing the chief pontificate with his own strict concern for legality in the face of concerted popular demand that he assume that priesthood. d. He again alludes to Antony as 'my antagonist in the war' (cum quo bellum gesseram)[13]. He makes a moral contrast between the anonymous Antony who robbed the temples of the provinces of Asia and had given them to Cleopatra and his own beneficence and piety in returning the temple objects. e. He implies that his unnamed enemy, Sextus Pompey, is a pirate: 'I freed the sea from pirates' (mare pacavi a praedonibus)[14]. Sextus' fleets were mostly manned by runaway slaves but to treat the war as one against pirates and slaves served the purpose of discrediting him by banishing him to anonymity behind servile and cruel people. In alluding to his victory and its consequences in this way, Augustus was able to claim subtly that his position rested on the 'free will' and 'demand' of the Roman senate and people rather than legal process or his exercise of force[15].

[10] Ibid., 1.2.

[11] So E.A. Judge, see above, n.8.

[12] RG. 2.10.

[13] Ibid., 4.24; cf. Dio Cassius, 51.17.

[14] RG. 5.25.

[15] So E.A. Judge, see above n.8. For other instances of non-naming and allusions to it, see Plutarch, Lives 'Aemilius Paulus', 31.5: 'a man without a wound, and whose person is sleek with delicate and cowardly effeminancy'. Cf. Cicero, Ad Fam. 1.9.20: 'and at this time certain persons, indeed those very persons whom I often hint at but do not name'. Ad Fam. 1.9.10: 'the comments of a certain clique were brought to my ears - you ought to suspect immediately whom I mean' (i.e., the extreme optimates who were jealous of Cicero); Caesar, BC. 1.22.5: 'the clique of the few'; Cicero, Att. 1.13 - of Piso: 'the "peace-maker" of the Allobroges'; of Clodius: 'a man in woman's clothes'; of Pompey: 'your friend - you know who I mean; the man who, you say, began to praise me as soon as he feared to blame me'; 2:22 'that little Beauty'.

We are now in a position to detail several characteristics of the rhetorical device of non-naming of enemies. a. It takes the place of a name of a person who is well known to the readers; b. it makes the person available for caricature; c. it is an exercise in comparison, usually according to the conventions of praise and blame; d. it is always used pejoratively; e. the intention is to shame the enemy. A number of different conventions may be implied by this technique. First, it was the traditional aspiration of a person of rank that his name, words and deeds should live on after him. Non-naming condemns him to anonymity and allows for the disparagement of his accomplishments. At the same time the denigrator enhances his own reputation and honour. Secondly, to name an opponent in conjunction with abuse or serious charges which threatened his status or dignity would have been understood as a declaration of an open feud. It is possible, then, that the Greek and Roman reluctance to create new and, especially, powerful enemies underlies this device. It provided them with a powerful and damaging form of invective which avoided offending according to the conventions of enmity[16]. Thirdly, where a person had been publicly named and abused, he could commend himself as a man of dignity and restraint by not retaliating in kind. By not naming his detractor, he does not enter into the same game, so to speak. His periphrastic response is all the more damaging as a result. Fourthly, in many instances, avoidance of names altogether reveals existing enmity[17]. It should be clear though that in each instance, non-naming is a form of invective and is clearly understood as such by all concerned. It draws upon the traditional topics or themes by which praise and dispraise

---

16 For fear of creating enmity by naming of an enemy, see Cicero, Qu.Fr. 2.3.3-4. Pompey thought Crassus was plotting to kill him but was careful not to name him publicly.

17 Non-naming in Cicero may indicate a lack of assurance in a person's relations with his superior, or hostility, or great intimacy. See J.N. Adams, 'Conventions of Naming in Cicero', CQ. 28 (1978) 145-166, esp. 163-164.

are attributed and is a powerful form of persuasion.

I have remarked previously that Paul had more sponsors in Corinth than in any other city. Apart from his travelling associates and fellow apostles, Paul names five of his intimates in 1 Corinthians, all of whom should probably be ranked among his patrons - Crispus, Gaius (1:14), Stephanus (1:16; 16:15, 17), Fortunatus and Achaicus (16:17). To these we should add Chloe[18]. In addition, he includes in his closing remarks his Corinthian friends of long standing, Aquila and Prisca, who were with him in Ephesus (16:19). None are named in 2 Corinthians where Paul reveals himself to be in a protracted struggle with his enemies.

From what we have seen of the nature of friendship and enmity relationships in his society, a number of interesting questions arise. First, why was Paul so humiliated by the hostile alliance during his second visit? Usually the more numerous a man's friends the more able he is to withstand his enemies. Paul did not lack powerful intimates in Corinth. However, I have suggested that most of the other Corinthians had committed themselves to the few, powerful men who opposed Paul[19]. Second, had some of Paul's friends also changed sides or were they, too, in some doubt over Paul? Did they in fact support him during his humiliating experience at the hands of the hybrists on his second visit? Third, had they been silenced by the now dominant faction?[20] Fourth, does Paul avoid mentioning their names because he does not wish to involve them further? Their association with him should have involved them in the bitter enmity[21].

We know that all of his friends did not withdraw from him. He names three of them (Gaius, Erastus and Quartus - Rom.16:23) in a letter which was most likely written at Corinth, after the completion of the collection there. We might assume, then,

---

[18] For details, see above 147; cf. 144.

[19] Ibid., 261, 262-265.

[20] A situation not unlike that in 3 John; see A.J. Malherbe, 'In 'Inhospitality', 222-232.

[21] See above 38, 44-45, for the expected involvement of friends in an enmity relationship, though a true friend may wish not to place a burden on them.

that his not naming his friends in a similar way in 2 Corinthians indicates a situation akin to either of those implied by the third and fourth questions. Thus Paul presents a lonely and desperate figure in 2 Corinthians, either unable or unwilling to call upon those traditional ties without which a man was open and vulnerable to a powerful enemy.

There are six occasions in 2 Corinthians and one in 1 Corinthians where Paul's periphrastic description of his enemies conforms to the characteristics of non-naming. a. In 1 Cor. 4:18-19, he refers to the behaviour of his arrogant enemies as ἐφυσιώθησάν τινες and then more precisely to them as τῶν πεφυσιωμένων, 'those arrogant people'. φυσιόω is almost exclusively used by Paul in relation to certain of the Corinthians and always in a pejorative sense. In this context it refers to arrogant behaviour which goes beyond the bounds of moderation[22]. In fact, behaviour of this kind is the dominant theme in the instances of non-naming in 2 Corinthians. At the same time he implies that their arrogance comprises an over-confidence in eloquence and that they lack real power, the power of the kingdom of God which he possesses. b. Paul alludes derogatorily to his rivals in 2 Cor. 2:17 as οἱ πολλοὶ καπηλεύοντες τὸν λόγον τοῦ θεοῦ. Both οἱ πολλοί, 'the many', and καπηλεύω, 'hawk, peddle' (bad sense), belong to the rhetoric of invective used by philosophers against the fee-charging sophists[23]. In contrast, Paul speaks with the sincerity of a commissioned apostle in the sight of God and as the representative of Christ. c. The arrogance of his enemies is again alluded to when Paul refers to them as τοὺς ἐν προσώπῳ καυχωμένους καὶ μὴ ἐν καρδίᾳ (5:12). He portrays them as people who judge apostleship according to appearance (socially accepted values) and represents himself, in comparison, as a faithful and trustworthy preacher of the gospel. d. On two occasions Paul describes his opponents as 'self-recommenders' - τισιν τῶν ἑαυτοὺς συνιστανόντων (10:12); ὁ ἑαυτὸν συνιστάνων (10:18). There can be no doubt about whom he is speaking. He had previously compared himself with them

[22] See above 204-206.

[23] See above 176, 320-321.

in similar terms (3:1) and he has kept the notion of recommendation prominently before the Corinthians (3:1-3; 5:11-12; 6:4; 10:12,18; 12:11). The periphrasis, 'self-recommenders', may be as close as we can come to giving a name to the rival apostles. On each of the occasions Paul uses synistanō, he alludes to his unique relationship with the Corinthians as their founder-apostle[24]. On these two occasions he denigrates his rivals as immoderate boastful men who do not know their limitations in stark contrast to his own restraint, his achievement as an apostle in Corinth, and his recommendation and approval from God. e. The invective is evident in his derogation of his enemies as ὁ ἐρχόμενος who ἄλλον Ἰησοῦν κηρύσσει (11:4)[25]. These interlopers, just as the serpent led Eve astray, would corrupt their 'sincere and pure devotion to Christ' (terms which do not reflect the Corinthians' true situation but add weight to Paul's disparagement of his rivals as seducers) (v.3). In comparison, he presents himself as a jealous parent-apostle who betrothed them to Christ and who cared only to keep them chaste. f. Finally, they are the οἱ θέλοντες ἀφορμήν (11:12), who boast of their superior achievements in Corinth[26]. He then proceeds to castigate them in the strongest terms, damning them as 'false apostles, deceitful workmen, disguising themselves as apostles of Christ' (v.13). The use of these notions of falseness, deceit, and masquerade is significant, for the boaster was traditionally conceived of in terms of pretence and deception[27]. Against them, he placed his consistent but contentious boast that he has never taken offers of support from the Corinthians as evidence of his love for them (vv.7-11).

From these examples we can see that Paul's use of non-naming corresponds to the characteristics which appear in the Res

---

[24] Ibid., 271-272.

[25] While Paul uses the singular here, the reference is most certainly to the visiting apostles.

[26] See my discussion, 334-336.

[27] See Aristotle, EN 4.3.36; 4.7.1-6 for the characteristics of the chaunos and the alazōn.

Gestae[28]. There can be no doubt that the Corinthians and, indeed, Paul knew the names of the unnamed opponents. The periphrastic construction has enabled him to denigrate anonymously the conduct of his enemies and compare it with genuine apostolic behaviour as exemplified by himself[29].

b. Comparison (σύγκρισις)

I have previously outlined in detail the rhetorical exercise of σύγκρισις[30] and have argued that it was used by Paul's enemies to praise themselves as ideal products of education and beauty and to portray Paul as a socially and intellectually unacceptable person[31]. As a background to Paul's use of this device I shall briefly recall its essential characteristics. a. It is an exercise in amplification and depreciation; b. it uses the traditional topics comprising the virtues, physical qualities and social excellences and their contraries; c. it compares persons or things which are similar on a one for one basis, i.e., by individual pairs or groups; d. it attempts to demonstrate equality, superiority or inferiority by i. praising both thus showing that they are equal in all respects; ii. praising both but placing one ahead, or praising the inferior so that the superior will seem to be even greater; iii. praising one and utterly blaming the other; e. in general, selection is from the finest deeds which were done freely and without coercion and are unique and difficult; f. the intention is to praise and blame, to persuade the hearers to favour one and to disapprove of the other.

Paul's comparison is conducted with notable moderation and

---

[28] For examples in Paul's other letters, cf., Rom. 16:17 (already cited); Gal.5:10 ὁ ταράσσων ὑμᾶς ... ὅστις ἐὰν ᾖ; 6:12, ὅσοι θέλουσιν εὐπροσωπῆσαι ἐν σαρκί; 2:12, τοὺς ἐκ περιτομῆς.

[29] It may be thought that the absence of offenders and enemies' names reflects Paul's humanity. But it is difficult to understand how Greeks or Hellenistic Jews who are hostilely disposed towards him could consider being termed 'arrogant', 'peddlers' and 'self-recommenders', etc., in association with other disparaging remarks and comparison, as anything but invective or that Paul intended it as anything else.

[30] See above 53-55.

[31] Ibid., 325-339.

restraint. He commences it by saying that he would not dare (tolmaō) class or compare (egkrinō, sygkrinō) himself with the self-recommenders (10:12). He concludes it by claiming that he was forced (hymeis me ēnagkasate) into retaliatory comparison because the Corinthians failed to commend him (12:11). The irony in his opening remark clears the way for his own sygkrisis. The verb tolmaō, 'to be bold, to presume', and the noun tolma, 'boldness', are used pejoratively to denote hybristic behaviour[32]. This is its context in 10:12-18 in which Paul draws upon traditional notions of excess to describe his enemies' conduct. The irony is stressed by his appeal to his own moderation: he would not boast beyond measure but would restrict himself to the appointed limits. The emphasis upon his restraint is maintained throughout the comparison. As C. Forbes says, Paul's comparison seems to be of the type which places him ahead of the Corinthian leaders, but without "blaming them utterly". He does not attack them directly during his boasting for 'to do so would have destroyed the form'[33]. On the one occasion he does denounce them fiercely (11:12-15), it is anonymously, which, as I have already suggested, commends the speaker as a man of dignity.

The connotation of hybris is also implicit in Paul's use of tolmaō in 11:21. With some irony he states, 'But whatever any one dares (tolmaō) to boast of - I am speaking as a fool - I also dare (tolmaō) to boast of that'. The subjects of such boldness are the encomiastic topics of origin, ancestry and pursuits (vv.22-23). His concluding remark also has a rhetorical flourish about it. It was one of the techniques of rhetoric that the orator should seem to deal reluctantly and under compulsion with something he is really anxious to prove[34]. Paul not only tells the Corinthians that they have forced him to boast but suggests that it is necessary (καυχᾶσθαι δεῖ) (11:30; 12:1) for him to do so if he is to

[32] Either used in association with or implying hybris, see Sophocles OC 1029-1030; Plato, Apol. 38D; Thucydides, 3.45.4. See also the vocabulary of hybris, H.G. Robertson, 'The "Hybristes" in Aeschylus', 374.

[33] 'Strength' and 'Weakness', 86, 88.

[34] So Cicero, de Or. 2.43.182; cf., Plutarch, Mor. 542E; Quintilian 11.1.2; Demosthenes, 18.128.

enter into comparison with his rivals.

There are several places throughout 10:12-12:13 which make it appear likely that Paul entered into comparison with his enemies in accordance with the common convention of comparison[35]. First, the things of which Paul, speaking as a fool, boasts are similar to the common topics or their contraries: his Hebrew origins, his Israelite descent, his ancestry going back to Abraham, his service to Christ, hardships (11:22-23), visions and revelations (12:1-10) and achievements (vv.12-13). Second, his comparison is point for point. 'Are they Hebrews? So am I. Are they Israelites? So am I. Are they descendants of Abraham? So am I. Are they servants of Christ? I am a better one'. From here on the individual pairing is broken off and he boasts singularly and at length of things which make him a better servant of Christ. Forbes suggests two reasons. On the one hand, Paul may be 'deserting the strict *sygkrisis* form in order to give examples of his virtues. On the other, he may be "evening the balance" by supplying *his* side of the comparison, because he feels that the material they have been using for their side of the comparison misrepresents his whole position'[36]. The latter, as I shall show shortly, is to be preferred. However, 'the formal difference' as Forbes comments, 'between these two possibilities is minimal. Either way, only one side of the comparison is given'[37]. The comparison, though, is implicit throughout, as he commences the peristasis catalogue with the comparatives, ἐν κόποις περισσοτέρως, ἐν φυλακαῖς περισσοτέρως (11:23).

Third, Paul attempts to prove his superiority as an apostle according to the various proofs mentioned in (d) above. He denies at the outset that he is inferior to *hoi hyperlian apostoloi* (11:5) and prepares the way for a *sygkrisis* style proof of his own superiority[38]. 'Even if I am unskilled in

---

[35] Much of the following argument is drawn from the discussion of C. Forbes, 'Strength' and 'Weakness', 84-92.

[36] Ibid., 89.

[37] Ibid.

[38] Ibid., 90.

speaking, I am not in knowledge' (11:6). As I have said before, the concession that he is unskilled in eloquence in comparison with his rivals may indeed be factual, or it may simply be a concession to debate. What is important for Paul is that he is at least their equal in knowledge, a fact, he suggests, which should be plain to the Corinthians. He then stresses the aim of his comparison: to remove the ground from under his rivals who have boasted that their superior achievements and qualities prove that they should be the apostles in Corinth. He denigrates them anonymously as vain boasters and false apostles, unworthy to be compared with himself. He appears to be adopting the 'blame utterly' line, and the form is complemented by the non-naming which also conforms to the conventions of individual comparison. Clearly, Paul is stating the superiority of his own apostleship over that of his rivals. Characteristically to substantiate it, he chooses that what is shameful, his refusal of the offer of support. It provides ample warning of the self-derision in which he is about to indulge in the ensuing comparison.

He proceeds to demonstrate his equality with his enemies on a one for one basis. He is equally a Hebrew, an Israelite, a descendant of Abraham (11:22). It is just conceivable that the questions are purely rhetorical (i.e., not requiring an affirmative answer) and that the rivals do not have this Jewish ancestry. But it is hard to understand in what way Paul could establish himself as superior by such a comparison, unless Jewish ancestry was of first importance to the Corinthians, many of whom were themselves Jews or had been sympathetic to the Jewish religion. It is better to see him following a strict comparison of point for point equality before placing himself ahead of them in the thing which really matters. 'Are they servants of Christ? I am a better one' (ὑπὲρ ἐγώ) (11:23).

At this point he breaks from the strict comparative form to advance proofs of his superiority as a servant. The question in <u>sygkrisis</u> is always who is the better man and we could properly expect a review of all his 'finest' deeds. But he deliberately pictures himself as the 'worse' man. He boasts of all 'the wrong things - events forced on him by necessity, apparent failures, imprisonment by legal authorities, humiliations'[39] - things which mark him as a man of shame according to socially accepted values. He does not boast of the matters of which he could truly boast without being a fool, of visions and revelations (12:1,6). Rather he boasts of the socially debilitating illness which was given him - his 'thorn in the flesh', 'his weakness' - to prevent him from becoming conceited. I shall return to this parade of shame shortly. In conclusion, he repeats his claim that he is not inferior to <u>hoi hyperlian apostoloi</u> and that all the signs of an apostle were displayed by him when he was with them. His only 'wrong' was his refusal of the gift.

It is necessary to notice the context into which Paul places his boasting. He has described the 'hybrists' who boast beyond measure as being 'without understanding' (<u>ou syniasin</u>) (10:12), i.e. suffering from a failure to know themselves. This view of his enemies is evident in his comment in 11:19 in which he justifies his foolish boasting: the Corinthians being wise themselves ought to accept him all the more as a boaster for they 'gladly bear with fools' (i.e., the hybrists). The phrases, οὐ συνιᾶσιν, εἰς τὰ ἄμετρα, and ἄφρων, are almost equivalent in meaning. As Betz correctly observes, in Hellenism such behaviour belongs to the category of ἀλαζονεία. The ἀλαζών, 'boaster', is regarded as a fool but he is not to be confused with the truly ignorant, the person who is uneducated. As I have shown, the fool is the person who has lost the awareness of his own limitations and indulges in shameful self-praise and excessive forms of behaviour[40]. It is only by adopting the guise of a fool of this kind that Paul can enter into a retaliatory comparison (11:1,16,17,21; 12:11). He considers immoderate boasting to be foolish. Unlike his enemies he will not boast beyond measure but will keep to the appointed limits. By playing the fool so deliberately, by accusing his opponents of being fools, and by his use of the rhetorical devices of irony and reluctance and his own commendable moderation, he makes it

---

[39] Ibid., 90-91.

[40] H.D. Betz, Sokratische Tradition, 74-75; and see my summary of <u>hybris</u>, 193-194.

patently obvious that in adopting the role of the fool for the sake of boastful comparison he is lowering himself to the level of his opponents.

There can be no doubt that the intention of Paul's sygkrisis is to discredit his enemies and at the same time to demonstrate his superiority as an apostle according to his own criteria of apostleship. Paul, though, is playing a dangerous game. Self-praise is fundamental to comparison. Implicit in his description of his rivals as measuring and comparing themselves is the criticism that they have indulged in excessive self-laudation. There were rules, however, by which a person could justify praising himself and techniques for doing it in such a way as to avoid the offence usually associated with it. It remains to be seen whether Paul's moderation and reluctance to boast reflects a conscious effort to abide by these conventions.

c. Self-praise

Self-praise (περιαυτολογία, lit., 'to speak about oneself') was always regarded as odious or offensive[41], and especially so because it was considered to involve dispraise of others[42]. Yet, as we have seen, it was fundamental to the exercises of commonplace, encomium and comparison. It was not suprising then that 'How to Praise Oneself Inoffensively' was a topic of the rhetorical schools. Plutarch in his essay 'On Praising Oneself Inoffensively' discusses the subject in moral terms and gives a number of circumstances which justified self-praise, and devices for doing it inoffensively and avoiding blame. It is excusable, he says, to mention good character and accomplishments a. if it will help a person accomplish a worthy end[43]; b. if a person is defending his good name, when answering a charge or on trial, in peril, or when slandered or wronged[44]; c. if a person shows that to act in a contrary manner to that which he has been charged would have been

[41] Plutarch, Mor. 539A-B; 547D; Aristotle, Rhet. 2.6.2,11; Quintilian 11.1.22; Dionysios of Halic., ad Pomp. 755.

[42] Plutarch, Mor. 547E; Quintilian 11.1.16.

[43] Plutarch, Mor. 539E.

[44] Ibid., 540C-541E.

shameful[45]; d. if boasting of one's care and worry over others[46]; e. to inspire others to emulation where some advantage accrues to the hearers[47]; f. to humble and subdue the headstrong and rash[48]; g. to overawe public and private enemies and to raise the spirits of friends[49]; h. where imitation has been aroused by the mistaken praise of evil, then self-praise may be used 'to divert the hearer's purpose to a better course by pointing out the difference'. Such praise is 'good and helpful, teaching admiration and love of the useful and profitable rather than of the vain and the superfluous'[50]. Plutarch suggests several devices which make self-praise acceptable: a. if a person is forced to praise himself then he should give the credit in part to God and in part to chance and not attribute it all to himself[51]; b. if a person is praised for the more noticeable qualities (eloquence, wealth, power) he should transfer it to more moderate qualities such as a worthy character or a useful life[52]; he should include minor shortcomings, faults and failures with his self-praise[53].

Paul appears to abide by a number of these recommendations. As Betz suggests, he does not conflict with them at any point and in fact closely coincides with some of them[54]. First, he boasts only because he is forced to defend himself against invidious comparison (11:30; 12:1,11). Second, he boasts of his care and concern for the Corinthians (11:2, 10-11,28,29; 12:14-15) and stresses that his defence has been for their upbuilding (12:19); cf. 10:8). Third, he wants them to know that his boasting is intended to divert them from his enemies

45 Ibid., 541F-542A.

46 Ibid., 544C-D.

47 Ibid., 544D-E.

48 Ibid., 544F.

49 Ibid., 545A; cf., Quintilian 11.1.23.

50 Plutarch, Mor. 545D-546A.

51 Ibid., 542E; cf., Quintilian 11.1.22.

52 Plutarch, Mor. 543A-E.

53 Ibid., 543F-544C.

54 Sokratische Tradition, 75-79.

and their values to 'the gospel he preached to them' (11:1-4). Fourth, he engages in self-praise to refute and shame his enemies (11:12,18,20) and to humble the Corinthians (11:14-18)[55]. As to the devices, he gives the credit to God for his visions and revelations (though this may be coincidental as it is a common characteristic of Paul, but not of the hybrists in 1 Cor.4:7) and tempers his boasting of them by including his weakness, σκόλοψ τῇ σαρκί (12:1-9). Similarly, he moves from the finer points of self-praise to 'lesser' qualities and achievements (11:22-23)[56].

Paul appears then to have conducted his self-praise with studied propriety and his dispraise of his enemies with rest restraint and moderation. This is a most important consideration in view of the excess to which he accuses his opponents of going. Does he consciously conform to these rules of rhetoric, and if so how does he know of them? Plutarch was simply giving literary and moral form to rules which were presumably contained in rhetorical handbooks, though not the extant examples. But the contents of these books were well known beyond the schools and the rules of self-praise both reflected and reinforced the traditional values and customs, especially that of moderation in all things. The question as to whether he is observing the rules of Greek rhetoric should be assessed in conjunction with his correct use of the devices of non-naming and comparison. I suggest that terminology such as 'coincidental' or 'unconscious usage' or 'naturally eloquent' no longer suffice to explain the rhetorical character of Paul's style. I shall return to this question again. Forbes notes that Paul is well aware of the odium attaching to self-praise. Yet he considers that while nearly all of the precepts in Plutarch could be seen as applicable to Paul's boasting, he grants none of them. 'For him boasting is always foolish, for it misses the essential point'[57]. This

---

[55] See above 247ff, for Paul's use of the familial metaphor to shame the Corinthians.

[56] I have already suggested how vv.23b-33 might be understood as a singular development of comparison.

[57] 'Strength' and 'Weakness', 91.

is true in principle, but in deliberately playing the fool he still observes the rules and it is in this guise that he appears to avoid compromising his claim that he would not boast beyond limit.

Paul's excessive self-depreciation presents us with a previously unrecognized dilemma. Self-derision, in varying degrees, was regarded as the worst form of praising oneself. In his discussion of this subject Quintilian comments: 'and yet I am not sure that open boasting is not more tolerable, owing to its sheer straightforwardness, than that perverted form of self-praise, which makes the millionaire say that he is a poor man, the man of mark describe himself as obscure, the powerful pose as weak, the eloquent as unskilled and even inarticulate. But the most ostentatious kind of boasting takes the form of actual self-derision. Therefore leave it to others to praise us'[58]. Here he reiterates a previous warning that the speaker should not boast or speak arrogantly or indulge in self-derision 'which is the final and most ostentatious form of boasting'[59]. Quintilian reflects a popular point of view. Aristotle compares the ἀλαζών and the εἴρων, the 'boastful man' and the 'mock-modest man'. The former exaggerates his possessions, abilities or other good qualities as much as the latter depreciates his. Both extremes are censured as being either an excess or defect of the mean, but the boaster to a greater degree. He boasts for base gain while the self-depreciator wants to avoid pretence[60]. A moderate use of self-depreciation in matters which were not too commonplace or obvious 'had a not ungraceful air', suggests Aristotle, and may even be fitting for a great-souled man when speaking about himself and his inferiors[61]. To a point it could be both witty and skilful, but beyond that it became ridiculous and shameful[62]. There is a hint of disapproval in Aristotle's comment that Socrates 'mostly disowned

---

58 11.1.21.22.

59 9.1.8.

60 EN, 4.7.13-15.

61 Ibid., 4.3.28; 4.7.16.

62 Id., EE 2.3.10; 2.7.5.

qualities held in high esteem'[63].

The magnitude of Paul's self-dispraise leaves him open to accusations of this kind. His derision of himself as a socially humiliated person in 1 Cor.4:8-13 would hardly have impressed the Corinthians. His statement, 'I do not write this to make you ashamed', may indicate that he was aware of the social implications for the Corinthians. Though he could be accused of engaging in 'that most ostentatious kind of boasting' in 2 Corinthians, two factors suggest that he would have appeared as a ridiculous and shameful figure. First, his self-derision is too extensive, too sustained (2 Cor.6:4-10, 11:23-33). Second, he could boast of the finer things but chose elements of dispraise which, unlike the ostentatious boaster's claims, were true. The Corinthians could not have said to him, in terms of the perverted form of self-praise, 'You are not these things, but this'. I doubt that even his affected ignorance could have lessened the Corinthians' sense of embarrassment and shame over Paul's self-ridicule.

d. Self-derision

As we have seen, Paul's self-derision in 2 Cor.10-12 belongs to his foolish sygkrisis. He boasts of the very opposite things from those which we would expect. He concedes he has points which he could compare more than favourably with

---

[63] EN 4.7.14. Socrates was regarded as the master of 'purposed self-depreciation', so M.A. Grant, The Laughable, 125-126. It has been suggested that Paul's role-playing belongs to this tradition which has its origins in Socrates' apology before the Athenians. See H.D. Betz, Sokratische Tradition, 79-89. How familiar Paul or the Corinthians were with this tradition is difficult to say. It is a literary convention which would seem to require a fairly high level of literary culture, the equivalent of the tertiary stage at least, though it may have circulated at a popular intellectual level. This is the crux of the problem. We do not yet know the level of Paul's literary and rhetorical culture. See A.J. Malherbe, Social Aspects, 29-59. It is not for this reason that the Trial of Socrates analogies are inadequate as a background for Paul's apology. For the various arguments against, see E.A. Judge, 'St. Paul and Classical Society', 35; 'St. Paul and Socrates', Interchange 14, (1973), 106-116; A.T. Lincoln, 'Paul the Visionary: the Setting and the Significance of the Rapture to Paradise in II Corinthians XII:1-10', NTS. 25 (1979), 206-210. However Paul does appear familiar with the Socratic-Cynic conventions of the true philosopher. See A.J. Malherbe, 'Gentle as a Nurse', 203-217; R.F. Hock, The Working Apostle, generally. For this reason it is feasible to suggest that Paul was aware of Socrates' apology.

his rivals and emphatically claims he is not inferior to them in knowledge, signs and visions. The concept of shame is characteristic of Paul's description of his apostleship in the Corinthian letters[64] and dominates his comparison in 2 Cor.10-12. A number of explanations have been offered to account for it. Betz suggests that Paul is advancing the σχῆμα of the true philosopher within the Socratic-Cynic tradition. Though the Cynic was denounced for his 'shameful' σχῆμα by his more conventional opponents, traditionally the sophists, he used it in return to discredit them and to prove that he was the true philosopher[65]. The Cynic turned upside down all values. The traditionally shameful - slavery, exile, poverty, begging, lowly birth - were called honourable and the mark of the true philosopher. The traditionally honourable - success, noble birth, wealth, beauty - were regarded as dishonourable[66]. In favour of the Cynic context is the use by Paul of peristasis catalogues to delineate his shame (1 Cor.4:9-13; 2 Cor.6:4-10; 11:23-33). This was a characteristic form in which the Cynics couched their hardship and suffering[67]. Forbes has also called Paul's self-derision a 'curious inversion'; Paul used the conventional form of comparison but 'inverts the content'[68].

There is no doubt that Paul boasts of the contraries but 'inversion' is inadequate to describe what Paul is doing. Inversion was a common and popular form of satire and would have been readily recognized by many of the Corinthians[69]. Unlike the Cynics who spoke satyrically about those qualities which were suspect for a free man and made them 'honourable'

---

[64] I have considered most of these passages, 1 Cor.2:1-5; 4:9-13; 9:16-18; 19-23; 15:8; 2 Cor.2:14; 4:7-9; 6:4-10.

[65] Sokratische Tradition, 44-57.

[66] Ibid., 51; see Ep. Diogenes, 32.4, 34.1.

[67] See R. Hock, The Working Apostle, 115-119.

[68] 'Strength' and 'Weakness', 87, 92; see also, J.H. Schütz, Anatomy of Apostolic Authority, 236 n.1.

[69] See E. Segal, Roman Laughter, 99ff, for the inversion of freedom and slavery as an example of the traditional comic reversal of the everyday Roman value system in the theatre.

his weaknesses always remained shameful to him. There is none of the Cynic appeal to live life at its hardest and most painful according to the doctrine of αὐτάρκεια[70]. Paul deeply feels his humiliation.

R.F. Hock, in a recent article, pointed to the inclusion of Paul's work in the peristasis catalogue in 1 Cor.4:12 and correctly states that it functioned 'to exemplify how foolish, powerless and despised he was in the eyes of many, including his own'. He concludes that Paul 'experienced his working as we should expect an aristocrat to have done, namely, as something slavish and demeaning'[71]. Hock's argument supports the view of Paul as a member of the socially privileged classes. He, untypically for someone of his rank, had chosen for his own reasons to work for wages and felt a considerable loss of status. Work remained shameful to Paul as did the other elements in his shame theme. His peristasis catalogues are 'not the mark of a man who took punishment and humiliation as part of his ordinary lot in society ... the formal recital of affronts is itself a deliberate embarrassment to those he is addressing as well as the mark of his own sensitivity to questions of status'[72]. There is no reversal of values. To make the dishonourable honourable for the sake of boasting would be self-defeating[73]. Paul boasts in his shame and appears to agree with his enemies that these things are truly disgraceful. There is little of the Cynic spirit in his parade of shame. There is even less in his admission that he prayed three times to have his thorn in the flesh removed from him.

E.A. Judge considers that Paul's boasting should be under-

---

[70] Cf. Phil.4:11 where Paul's contentment is acceptance of both plenty and the shame of having nothing. See my discussion, 234-235, espec. 235 n.227. Cf. 255-256, where I suggest that Paul's acceptance of gifts from other churches would have met with the disapproval of Cynics.

[71] 'Paul's Tentmaking', 562.

[72] So E.A. Judge, 'Paul as a Radical Critic', 192.

[73] This is consistent with the pattern which Paul states about God's choice of τὰ μὴ ὄντα (1 Cor. 1:26-28). God chose the socially weak to shame the strong in society. Boasting then can only be ἐν κυρίῳ (v.31). It is this pattern which Paul himself experiences and uses to shame his enemies in Corinth.

stood as a parody of the rhetorical convention of self-display[74]. S.H. Travis concurs with Judge and recalls the work of A. Fridrichsen who noted the similarities between 11:23-33 and Graeco-Roman eulogies such as the Res Gestae. He notes that while Paul follows the accepted pattern of self-display he 'chooses for eulogy items that in the eyes of his opponents, at least, are to his discredit'. He concludes that Paul's catalogue 'is a carefully calculated reductio ad absurdum of the whole Graeco-Roman attitude to boasting', fittingly brought to an anticlimax by the basket incident[75], which Judge had previously shown to be a parody of the award of the Corona Muralis given to the soldier who was first up the wall to confront the enemy. Paul was the first down[76]. This view seems to suggest that Paul knew the conventions of self-display, a distinct possibility. Here our judgement is clouded for though these conventions undoubtedly existed, no systematic treatment of them survives[77]. It is my opinion, however, that the dominant literary form in vv.23-33 is that of sygkrisis[78], and that Paul is responding to malicious invective. He is ridiculing himself rather than parodying his opponents' self-glorying. Judge suggests himself that a difficulty with viewing this as prody is that Paul 'takes his "foolish" boasting with too much anguish for us to assume it was merely a mockery, unless of course the interjections are themselves a part of the irony'[79].

I have not been able to find anything which resembles Paul's sustained self-derision in Greek or Roman authors[80]. Such details are quite common on the lips of an enemy as indeed

---

74 'Paul's Boasting', 47-50; 'The Conflict of Educational Aims in NT Thought', JCHrEd. 9 (1966), 44-45; 'St Paul and Socrates', 114.

75 'Paul's Boasting in 2 Corinthians 10-12', Stud.Ev. 6 (1973), 529-530.

76 'Conflict of Educational Aims', 45.

77 See E.A. Judge, 'St. Paul and Classical Society', 35; cf. id., Social Pattern, 57-59.

78 See also, C. Forbes, 'Strength' and 'Weakness', 84-85, who also reached this conclusion.

79 'Paul's Boasting', 47; 'St. Paul and Classical Society', 35.

80 Plutarch, Mor.634D alludes to the practice of some comic poets who take away the bitterness of their remarks by ridiculing themselves, but I have not been able to develop this further.

could be expected. There are though two interesting passages which may help us understand what Paul is saying about himself. The first is from Pliny the Elder's Natural History, Book 7, in which he eulogizes the character and achievements of eminent people such as Julius Caesar, Pompey, and Sergius. In stark contrast, he lists Augustus' adversa, the reverse of the Res Gestae. It seems to be a systematic dressing down of Augustus by Pliny and is perhaps unparalleled in Greek and Roman literature. I quote it in full: 'Also in the case of his late Majesty Augustus, whom the whole of mankind enrols in the list of happy men, if all the facts were carefully weighed, great revolutions of man's lot could be discovered: his failure with his uncle in regard to the office of Master of the Horse, when the candidate opposing him, Lepidus, was preferred; the hatred caused by the proscription; his association in the triumvirate with the wickedest citizens, and that not with an equal share of power but with Antony predominant; his flight in the battle of Philippi when he was suffering from disease, and his three days hiding in the marsh, in spite of his illness and his dropsical condition (as stated by Agrippa and Maecenas); his shipwreck off Sicily, and there also another period of hiding in a cave: his entreaties to Proculeius to kill him, in the naval rout when a detachment of the enemy was already pressing close at hand; the anxiety of the struggle at Perugia, the alarm of the battle of Actium, his fall from a tower in the Pannonian Wars; and all the mutinies in his troops, all his critical illnesses, his suspicion of Marcellus' ambitions, the disgrace of Agrippa's banishment, the many plots against his life, the charge of causing the death of his children; and his sorrows which were not solely due to bereavement, his daughter's adultery and the disclosure of her plots against her father's life, the insolent withdrawal of his stepson Nero, another adultery, that of his grand-daughter; then the long series of misfortunes - lack of army funds, rebellion of Illyria, enlistment of slaves, shortage of manpower, plague at Rome, famine in Italy, resolve on suicide and death more than half achieved by four days' starvation; next the disaster of Varus and the foul slur upon his dignity; the disowning of Postumius Agrippa after his adoption as heir, and the sense of loss that followed his banishment; then his suspicion in regard to Fabius and the betrayal of secrets; afterwards the intrigues of his wife and Tiberius that tormented his last days. In fine, this god - whether deified more by his own action or by his merits I know not - departed from life leaving his enemy's son his heir[81].

These are the shameful things which Augustus hides from posterity but are the substance of his enemies' invective. Why Pliny constructs this list of contrary matters, even to the exclusion of Augustus' political offices, is puzzling indeed. Perhaps he opposed Augustus' political preeminence or his view of virtus[82]. Whatever his reason, clearly his intention is to shame Augustus posthumously. Though it recalls readily to mind the Res Gestae, it cannot be called a parody. The conventions which operate at this point belong to invective and in this list of adversa we appear to have a skeletal frame of invective. Pliny has constructed an image of Augustus from all the contraries which circulated about Augustus so that the Res Gestae is no longer believable. What Augustus and his supporters have said about him is untrue. It is conceivable that Paul is quoting his enemies in 2 Cor. 11:23-33 who had intended that Paul's 'failures' should weigh heavily against him.

The second passage is a clear case of glorying in weakness and shame. Plutarch records the words and actions of Marcus Servilius against those who wanted to deprive Aemilius Paulus of the due rewards of his victory. '"But", said he, "to such great power is malice brought by you that a man without a wound to show, and whose person is sleek from delicate and cowardly effeminacy, dares to talk about the conduct of a general and his triumph to us who have been taught by all

---

[81] NH. 7.45.147-150. I am thankful to Dr. G. Maslakov for bringing this passage to my attention.

[82] So G. Maslakov, Tradition and Abridgement: A Study of the exempla tradition in Valerius Maximus and the Elder Pliny, unpublished Ph.D. thesis Macquarie University, 1978, 348-357. Maslakov notes the accumulation of disaster words and comments, '... he is presented as a victim of fortuna and of his own inadequacies. Pliny gives us a man totally at the mercy of events ... Augustus is continually subject to fear and anxiety, not once exhibiting resolution or leadership'.

these wounds to judge the valour and cowardice of generals". And with these words he parted his garment and displayed upon his breast an incredible number of wounds. Then wheeling about, he uncovered some parts of his person which it is thought unbecoming to have naked in a crowd, and turning to Galba, said: "Thou laughest at these scars, but I glory in them before my fellow-citizens, in whose defence I got them, riding night and day without ceasing"'[83].

When a Greek or Roman was the victim of such slanderous assertions as Paul was, a number of responses were available to him. For example, he could respond in kind, a mutual invective so to speak, though he would commend himself by acting with restraint and resorting to subtle rhetorical devices such as innuendo or insinuatio[84]. If the charges were true or could not be denied then the accused might simply choose to ignore them and move his defence to less damaging ones. He might give a tacit if qualified admission but then point to more worthy considerations[85]. Alternatively, as was characteristic of Cicero, he might turn the charge aside by a jocular reply, 'making the thing seem deserving of laughter rather than censure'[86]. Great honour attached to the person who could successfully refute his opponent's charges. But no self-respecting person boastfully paraded his shame before his enemies.

The extraordinary nature of Paul's action can be judged by the conventions which governed standard practice in these matters. Greeks and Romans shunned any course which exposed themselves to contempt and ridicule, especially at the hands of their enemies. It was generally held that a person's misfortunes should be concealed as much as possible. Enemies

---

[83] Lives. 31.5-6; For scars on the front of the body, in contrast to the back, as a mark of honour and valour, see Pliny, NH. 7.28.101 - of Lucius Siccius Dentatus, 'having the distinction of 45 scars in front and none at all on his back'; Plutarch, Lives 1.6; Cicero, de Or. 2.28.124.

[84] Cf. Cicero, Inv.Ag.Sall. 1.1-3. For the extended use of innuendo in literary form to avoid direct accusations, see I.S. Ryberg, 'Tacitus' Art of Innuendo', TAPA 73 (1942), 383-404; for insinuatio, see E.W. Bower, ''Ἔφοδος and Insinuatio', 224-230.

[85] Demosthenes, 37.52-55.

[86] Aulus Gellius 12.1.

were said to be ever vigilant seeking every opportunity to take advantage of misfortune and a popular corollary of the maxim, 'help your friends and harm your enemies', appears as 'friends share one's joys while enemies gloat over one's misfortunes'. Nothing was more feared than the mocking laughter of a triumphant enemy[87]. On the subject of misfortunes, the notions of shame are implicit in Plutarch's comment that it distresses people to talk of lost lawsuits, of children burned, and of any unsuccessful business deals[88].

Paul's responses in 2 Corinthians must be viewed in the context of the enmity relationship. Paul has been the victim of a successful and damaging invective. He has been humiliated before the Corinthians. His breaking off from the traditional point for point comparison in 11:23 leads to his revealing those things of which the laughable and shameful consist. One wonders as Paul lists his shame what more an enemy could achieve by ridicule. It is as if Paul is saying, 'You have compared me unfavourably with yourselves and found me to be lacking in the social graces and achievements required of an apostle in Corinth. While I could show myself to be superior to you, I glory in my deficiencies, for my humiliation and shame are the marks of my apostleship and God's approval'. In the enmity relationship in Corinth, Paul is willing to allow his apostleship to be judged on the basis of failure and weakness. We know, however, that this was not all that his apostleship comprised as he himself reminds the Corinthians. They owed their existence to him (10:13-14; 11:2) and they knew of his knowledge (11:6) and of the signs of an apostle which he performed among them (12:12).

e. ὕβρις as Innuendo.

I have dealt briefly with the notion of hybris in 2 Cor. 10-12 earlier, especially in relation to 10:12-13, and hinted at the contribution it can yet make to this argument. It forms an important part of Paul's response to his enemies and

---

[87] For details, see above 46-47.

[88] Mor. 630F. Cf. Euripides, Hipp.403-404. See also Philo, Flaccus 18.150-20.175 for Philo's depiction of Flaccus' shame at his complete reversal of fortune and for the contrasts between honour and shame.

he appears by the use of the rhetorical device of innuendo to create the impression that they are guilty of hybristic behaviour. Scholars have suggested that Paul is being forced into competition with his enemies by the Corinthians. Judge, followed by Travis, likens Paul's position to Favorinus who, after 'initially being lionised' by the Corinthians, was treated by contempt. The response of Favorinus, unlike Paul's, was 'an elegantly self-centred reprimand of them after he was restored to favour'. Judge concludes, 'at this level of society self-admiration, including of course its deceptive asteistic refinements, was absolutely de rigueur. As Paul himself complains, he was despised for not indulging in it (II Corinthians 11:20-21) ... Paul found himself a reluctant and unwelcomed competitor in the field of professional "sophistry" and ... he promoted a deliberate collision with its standard of values'[89]. Similarly, in a later article, Judge contends that Paul 'faced the excruciating demands that he assume the role of leader in the socially acceptable sense ... his own followers and converts insisted that he adopt a more presentable position in society than he was willing to do'[90].

Judge correctly appraises, in my opinion, the cultural level of the conflict, though I doubt that demands were made on Paul to enter into competition with the rival apostles. Rather he fell out of favour with them because of his refusal of the gift[91]. The turning of friendship into enmity and the disfavour with which they came to view him is important for our understanding of his responses. As we have seen, the Corinthians allied themselves with his rivals by mutual recommendation and the friendship which was initiated by it was a consequence of the enmity relationship of the hybrists with Paul, not of his cultural deficiencies. It is clear enough though that the Corinthians cultural background

---

89 'Paul's Boasting', 46-47; cf., id., 'St. Paul and Socrates', 115: 'It is an anguished angry reaction against an attempt to make him magnify himself falsely'; S.H. Travis, 'Paul's Boasting in 2 Cor.10-12', 528-529.

90 'Paul as a Radical Critic', 197.

91 For details, see above 242-246.

and values predisposed them towards the self-recommenders, who utilized the situation to their advantage. Paul speaks as a Greek who has suffered rejection and humiliation at a level where it was felt most deeply in that culture.

Betz notes some of the nuances of *hybris* in chapters 10-12. First, by taking *kauchasthai dei* (11:30; 12:1) and *hymeis me ēnagkasate* (12:11) literally, rather than as a rhetorical device, he considers that Paul was being forced into self-praise by his enemies and thus open to the charge of *hybris*. He avoids this by boasting as a fool and by abiding by the rules of self-praise[92]. Secondly, he correctly observes that in 12:1-10 Paul deliberately keeps within the limits (*dio hina mē hyperairōmai*) (12:7) when speaking of his visions and revelations[93]. Thirdly, he recognizes in 10:10-18 Paul's appropriation of ideas derived from the old Delphic religion, such as 'man's nothingness' (*oudenai*; cf. 12:11, *ei kai ouden eimi*) and the maxim (*gnōthi sauton*), 'know thyself'. He suggests that Paul's awareness of his nothingness keeps him from *eis ta ametra kauchasthai* and thus constitutes an example of *sōphrosynē* rather than of *hybris*. By contrast, it is his enemies who have gone beyond the bounds by boasting of their achievements in Corinth and breaching the rules. He concludes that the thought and language conforms to the Greek humanistic ethical tradition[94].

Betz' definition of *hybris* is too narrow. It is drawn from the Platonic Socrates and antisophistic polemic and, in particular, the Delphic-Platonic notion of *gnōthi sauton* and its relation to human limitations. We have already examined at length the familiar Greek notion of *hybris* in which I pointed to the predominantly social usage of the word in Greek authors, to the wide range of activities it connotes and the extensive vocabulary associated with it[95]. I have argued that Paul resorts to the notion to describe an important characteristic of his wealthy opponents in 1 Corinthians and I have

---

92 Sokratische Tradition, 72-78.

93 Ibid., 95.

94 Ibid., 127-132.

95 See above 182-194.

suggested that we might refer appropriately to them as hybrists. The familiar maxims, gnōthi sauton and mēden agan, as I have shown, were two of the most common topoi associated with the ideal of sōphrosynē and are fundamental to our discussion of hybris, though the ideas implicit in them are present in the earliest use of hybris and sōphrosynē[96].

I have also argued that in 2 Cor. 10:12-13 Paul is using the same conventional language of moderation to commend his own apostolic behaviour, and of immoderation to discredit his enemies. They have boasted of their superiority over Paul in regard to the social graces and achievements in Corinth and have attempted to shame and humiliate him before the Corinthians[97]. Betz is correct in his claim that Paul is accusing his opponents of hybristic behaviour. He is wrong, though, in his assumption that it is a reaction to his opponents' attempts to cause him to praise himself and thus open him to the charge of hybris. It makes little sense for them to accuse Paul of hybristic behaviour if they themselves are boasting of their superiority. As in 1 Cor.4:6-13, the ideas are Paul's and form part of his invective against his opposition. The idea of hybris is the same when used firstly against the wealthy Corinthians and secondly against their friends, the rival apostles. Throughout 2 Cor.10-12, Paul derogates his rivals as hybrists and portrays himself as a man of restraint.

2 Cor.10:13b-16 is extremely difficult to interpret and the nuances present in the various terms permit a number of possibilities. I suggest that the ideas of moderation and hybris in the preceding verses, 12-13a, are sustained throughout this passage, though other nuances are present. Paul writes: we 'will keep to the limits God has apportioned us (kata to metron tou kanonos ou emerisen hēmin ho theos metrou) to reach even you. For we are not overextending (hyperekteinomen) ourselves as though we did not reach you; we were the first to come all the way to you with the gospel of Christ. We do not boast beyond limit (ouk eis ta ametra

---

[96] Ibid., 191-193.

[97] Ibid., 198-203.

kauchōmenoi), in other men's labours; but our hope is that as your faith increases, our field (kata ton kanona hēmōn) among you may be greatly enlarged, so that we may preach the gospel in lands beyond (hyperekeina) you without boasting of work already done in another's field (en allotriǭ kanoni)'.

The main difficulty lies in the precise meaning of kanōn in vv.13b, 15 and 16. Some scholars give it the sense of 'standard of judgement', a criterion (success, qualifications, legitimacy?) for assessing one's status as an apostle[98]. Barrett agrees with this interpretation in part but protests against the exclusion of reference to 'appointed areas of apostolic work'. He suggests that kanōn has a 'fundamentally spatial', though not exclusively geographical, sense such as 'limit', 'boundary' or 'province', especially in vv.15 and 16, and sees the dispute in terms of Paul's understanding of Gal. 2:9-10[99]. These differences in interpretation highlight the problem, for kanōn does seem to admit of these various meanings, though I am cautious about allowing Gal. 2:9-10 and Rom. 15:23-29 too much leeway in determining its meaning in this passage. I have said earlier that kanōn, like metron, is used by Greek authors with a moral sense to denote the limits of appropriate conduct and can be translated as 'standard' or 'measure'[100]. It is likely that a moral nuance is implicit in its use here and that it indicates praiseworthy conduct though it is more likely that metron supplies the moral note and that in this passage we should make a distinction between the two terms.

In the passage Paul is comparing himself with the rival apostles whose hybristic behaviour is implied by the phrase eis ta ametra, 'beyond measure' or 'beyond the bounds', i.e. 'immoderately'[101]. We have seen what this excessive behaviour

---

98 Cf. W.G. Kümmel, Kor 1 & 2, 209; E. Käsemann, Legitimität, 49; against Käsemann, see J.H. Schütz, Apostolic Authority, 170-171, though he is wrong in his opinion that the rival apostle's kanōn has no substance outside their person.

99 'Christianity at Corinth', BJRL 46 (1964), 293-294; id., 2 Cor. 265-266, 267-268. Cf. similarly, F.F. Bruce, 1 & 2 Cor. 232-234, 'field'; A. Plummer, 2 Cor. 287-288, 'province'; H. Windisch, 2 Kor. 310.

100 See above 200-201.

101 ametra is almost the equivalent of hyper metron.

involves in our discussion of *eis ta ametra*. Their standard, so to speak, was one of Greek respectability, comprising the norms of a cultured society. The rivals present themselves as the ideal products of education, leisure, beauty and action. *Eis ta ametra* connoting immoderate behaviour is opposed directly to *kata to metron tou kanonos* in v.13. *Kata to metron* must then imply moderation. In relation to his *kanon*, he will boast in an acceptably restrained manner. But in what does his *kanon* consist? In the immediate context, that is indicated by the phrase *ephikesthai achri kai hymōn*, which is loosely attached to *emerisen*. Paul believes that his mission to Corinth was assigned to him as a measure by God (*emerisen hēmin ho theos metrou*). His having been appointed to come to Corinth is validated by the very existence of the church. He was the first to reach them with the gospel of Christ. This dual thought of appointment and approval is repeated again in association with appropriate boasting in vv.17-18: '" Let him who boasts, boast of the Lord". For it is not the man who commends himself that is accepted but the man who the Lord commends'.

H.W. Beyer is partly right when he says that 'Paul does not appeal to an exclusive right to come to Corinth but to the historical fact that it was granted to him to do this[102]. But while Paul may not be laying down his rights to ethnic, geographical or theological territory, he appears to be claiming something more than an 'historical fact'. The verb *merizō* which he uses must be given more weight within the context of *sōphrosynē* and *hybris*. I suggest it reflects the Greek notion of one's appointed lot or vocation in life in which one must abide[103]. Paul will boast according to his assigned measure, which includes Corinth. There seems to be no doubt that Paul's *kanōn* is inseparably linked with his understanding of his apostleship in Corinth and in his comparison in chapters 11-12 he precisely defines what kind

---

[102] 'κανών', TDNT 3, 599.

[103] Rom.12:3 for a similar context, and see my discussion 199; cf., also 1 Cor.7:17, where *merizō* is associated with the calling of God and one's lot in life as being circumcised, of the uncircumcised or a slave.

of apostle he has been while there. A characteristic of his understanding of his mission, including his coming to Corinth, is seen in the rather vague sentence, 'so that we may preach the gospel in lands beyond you (hyperekeina hymōn), without boasting of work already done in another's field' (10:16). In broad terms, he conceives of his apostleship as one which breaches frontiers. This is however indicated by hyperekeina[104] rather than by kanōn. The sentence appears rather to be framed with the dispute in Corinth in mind than with some wider missionary strategy, and is intended to contrast the hybristic behaviour of his opponents with his observation of the limits. The second clause specifically contrasts the conduct of the self-recommenders with Paul's. His calling to which he limits himself is to found and build up churches in areas where other apostles have not been. The rival apostles overstep the boundaries in that they arrogantly parade themselves in the area of his calling.

Thus there does appear to be a geographical implication in Paul's use of kanōn. Recent epigraphic evidence sheds new light on the problem. Judge cites the use of kanōn in an early first-century edict in which it refers to 'the comprehensive schedule' of requirements for transport and billeting services in a particular region. He continues 'The kanōn in itself is not a geographical concept, but the services it formulates are in this case geographically partitioned'. He suggests that edicts such as this would have been familiar to Paul and his colleagues in their travels and used the term to express 'their understanding of the way God had measured out their respective territorial commitments'. The edict both protected an individual's responsibilities or allowed him the right to negotiate an exchange with others. Judge comments, 'It is the sensitivities aroused by just such an issue which lie behind Paul's rather complex protestations about the requirements of the kanōn under which he is serving. He reflects the older spirit of the liturgical system as a

[104] The idea of direction should not be pressed (eg., west from Corinth) though we know that Paul later expressed a similar idea with specific locations in Rom. 15:23-29. Cf. J.H. Bernard, 2 Cor. 99; C.H. Barrett, 2 Cor. 268; H.W. Beyer, 'κανών', TDNT 3, 599-600.

competition in honour through duty fulfilled. To go beyond one's limit would deprive the next man of his turn'[105].

As I have said previously, the standard or measure by which Paul's enemies, and apparently many of the Corinthians, have judged him to be unfit for his kanōn consists of moral and cultural values. But it is a kanōn which he will not reliquish under any circumstances, no matter how shameful he appears to the Corinthians or to himself.

The comparison which Paul is endeavouring to make in 10:12-18 is not primarily between the two kanones. Rather he is contrasting his own and his enemies' conduct in terms of moderation or excess. Positively, he presents himself as a man of moderation. He will keep to the divinely appointed limits of his apostleship. Negatively, he points to his restraint. He will not dare compare himself with his rivals who have made themselves the measure of apostleship and have compared him unfavourably with themselves (v.12). He will not boast beyond limit (vv.13, 15); he did not overextend himself; he did not boast of his achievements in the kanōn of another (v.16). The implication in each instance is that his enemies acted with excess. Their behaviour is blameworthy; his is praiseworthy and in keeping with and worthy of the recommendation and approval of God.

The superiority which his enemies claim is twice alluded to in Paul's comparison: 'I think that I am not in the least inferior to these superlative apostles (tōn hyperlian apostolōn) (11:5; cf. 12:11). Scholars are divided as to whether, as the majority consider, hoi hyperlian apostoloi refers to the false apostles (11:13) or to the apostles in Jerusalem. Käsemann considers that two distinct groups are implied, the Jerusalem apostles and their representatives. He considers it most unlikely that Paul would describe himself as 'not inferior' to people whom he later describes as servants of Satan[106]. Bruce similarly says that hoi hyperlian apostoloi 'could not well be applied to men of lower apostolic status'

---

[105] E.A. Judge, 'The Regional kanōn for Requisitioned Transport', New Documents 1, G.H.R. Horsley ed., 36-45.

[106] Legitimität, 20-30.

than the Jerusalem apostles[107]. The term hyperlian, is generally translated as 'super' or 'superlative', and depending on the viewpoint adopted, it has either a good sense or is used ironically[108].

I would like to suggest a new point of view in support of the pseudapostoloi and hoi hyperlian apostoloi being identical. The controlling literary form in 11:4-12:13 is that of comparison and, as we have seen, Paul conducts his comparison according to the rules. In 11:5 he prepares the way for proof of his own superiority. He has already implied that his opponents have behaved hybristically by using familiar notions of excessive behaviour to denigrate them. I suggest that hyperlian is a further instance of Paul's vocabulary of hybris and forms part of his invective against them. hyperlian can be translated as 'beyond measure' or 'excessively', and in a context of hybris is used pejoratively[109]. It does not differ greatly in meaning from eis ta ametra or hyper metron. These are the apostles who have gone beyond the bounds, who consider themselves superior to Paul in eloquence and the associated graces. Thus hoi hyperlian apostoloi is a further instance of Paul's use of innuendo to disparage his enemies: they are nothing more than shameful hybrists.

But how does Paul enter into comparison with the hybrists, especially as he has said he would only boast according to the set limits? We have seen the various explanations of Paul's foolishness - of the fool within the Socratic-Cynic tradition and of the parody of conventions of self-display[110]. I have previously commented on the category of the fool in Hellenism

---

107 1 & 2 Cor. 236-237; cf., C.K. Barrett, 2 Cor. 30-32, 277-278, 'Paul's Opponents', 242-244.

108 Cf. J.H. Bernard, 2 Cor. 101, who says hyperlian seems always to be used with an ironical sense in Greek literature, though I have not been able to substantiate this.

109 lian has a wide range of applications but used pejoratively it conveys the idea of excess; eg. to lian Euripides, Phoen. 584; Andr. 866; Hipp. 264 (where to lian is compared unfavourably with mēden agan); used in association with hybris, eg. Lysias 24.15, 25; used as almost the equivalent of hyperbolē, eg. Aristotle, EN. 4.7.15; 7.4.5; 10.6.6. Cf. also Solon 5:8 - mēte lian, 'not too much', as a saying implying moderation, the opposite of hyperlian in 2 Cor.11:5, 12:11.

110 See above, 357-360.

to which Paul is alluding. He becomes the alazōn, the person who has lost the awareness of his own limitations[111]. This means that in his comparison he becomes a hybrist himself; he adopts the same kind of behaviour which he has attributed to his opponents. The key verse is 10:12. He has said that their excessive arrogance shows that they are 'without understanding'. This is the characteristic failure of the hybrists in Greek authors, a failure which, in the words of the Delphic maxim that is Homeric in origin, is a failure to know themselves, to know their human limitations, and is the opposite of metron gnōmosynēs, that conduct which knows the limit of everything. This is the same failure in self-knowledge of which Paul accused his enemies in 1 Corinthians[112]. It seems as if they have sought out friends, according to Paul, after their own kind.

The connection between 'foolishness' and 'boasting' and other hybristic notions is consistent throughout Paul's comparison. First, he makes it clear that in reality he is not foolish (11:16) nor does he boast with the Lord's authority (v.17). Second he stresses that he adopts the role of the fool to enter into comparison with his rivals. In 11:1, he commences his foolish comparison with, 'bear with me in a little foolishness (aphrosynē), and later repeats this request, 'accept me as a fool (aphrōn)' (v.16). He concludes the comparison with, 'I have been a fool' (gegona aphrōn) (12:11), but only under compulsion. Third, his 'foolishness' is intended to mirror the hybristic conduct of his rivals. He wishes them to accept him as a fool in order that he too may boast (11:16). The emphasis is upon emulation: speaking as a fool, 'since many boast of worldly things, I too will boast' (v.18); and again, 'But whatever anyone dares (tolma) to boast of - I am speaking as a fool (en aphrosynē) I also dare (tolmō kagō)' (v.21). The combination of ideas in this last passage in particular - tolman, kauchasthai, aphrosynē - is strong evidence that hybris is in Paul's mind.

111 Ibid., 352-353.

112 Ibid., 205.

This is more clearly borne out in v.23 where Paul moves from equal comparison to boasting of his superiority. 'Are they servants of Christ? I am a better one (hyper egō) - I am talking like a madman (paraphronōn) - with far greater (perissoterōs) labours, far more imprisonments ...' The adverbial use of hyper to indicate Paul's superiority[113], of paraphronōn (the notion of lack of self-knowledge or ignorance of matters of common knowledge)[114], to qualify such presumption on his part, and the comparative perissoterōs, together suggest the theme of hybris which I believe runs throughout these chapters. There can be no doubt that, though he avoids direct accusation, Paul is speaking about the rival apostles. With himself as the foil, he creates the impression of them as arrogant, insolent and shameless men.

Fourth, in this context there is that very puzzling allusion to his opponents' behaviour. To the Corinthians he says, 'For you gladly bear with fools (aphrones), being wise (phronimoi) yourselves! For you bear it if a man makes slaves of you, or preys upon you, or takes advantage of you, or puts on airs, or strikes you in the face. To my shame (atimia), I must say, we were too weak (asthenō) for that' (vv. 19-21). Though it is couched in terms of a rebuke to the Corinthians, the primary focus in the passage is still the comparison between Paul and his enemies. It is most apparent who the 'fools' are. He justifies his asking them to bear with his 'foolishness' on the basis that they have gladly borne with his rivals[115]. Precisely what they have put up with is difficult to say. The conduct he refers to, though - misuse of power and privilege, exploitation, arrogance, abuse and violence - is characteristic of hybris. Behaviour of this kind is said to be typical of

---

[113] A characteristic term used either to introduce a prepositional phrase or as a compound with other words to express hybristic behaviour, see above 197 n.111.

[114] paraphronōn, lit., 'to be beside oneself', I suggest reflects the more common hybristic notion of mania, 'madness', irrational behaviour due to an error in common knowledge which is traditionally opposed to sōphrosynē and associated notions such as gnōthi sauton. See above 194 and 328-333.

[115] See however C.K. Barrett, 2 Cor. 290-291, who thinks that Paul is referring to himself.

superior social status[116] and we have seen that his rivals reflect the standards of this level of society. Paul's behaviour as an apostle was the antithesis of this. atimia and asthenō are social and moral terms[117] and appear to reflect aspects of the invective against him in which his 'weakness' is compared unfavourably with their 'strength'. His personal appearance is weak (asthenēs); his speech is without weight (exouthenēmenos) (10:10); he is (tapeinos) (10:1; 11:7). It is arrogant and abusive conduct of this kind which must have led to his humiliation and shame at their hands before the Corinthians. Apparently the Corinthians have not been offended by such behaviour and have readily submitted to the hybrists. The 'destructive' nature of his rivals' conduct was perceived and felt by him alone.

The comparison between the hybrists' 'power' and Paul's 'power in weakness' is an important one throughout chapters 10-13. Though he is accused of being weak by their standards, by God's standard he will be destructive of their attitudes. On two occasions he defines his task in relation to them and alludes further to their characteristic pride. 'We destroy arguments and every proud obstacle to the knowledge of God, and take every thought captive to obey Christ, being ready to

---

116 For details of hybristic behaviour in Greek authors, see above 182-189. For Paul's adoption of the shameful position of a socially disadvantaged person in 1 Cor. 4:10-13 as a direct contrast with the Corinthian hybrists, see 210-214. Of particular relevance to this discussion is the following passage from Lysias 24.15 which captures many of the characteristics of hybris.

"I expect you, gentlemen, to distinguish clearly between those people who are at liberty to be insolent (hybristais) and those who are debarred from it. For insolence is not likely to be shown by poor men labouring in the utmost indigence, but by those who possess far more than the necessaries of life; nor by men disabled in body (tous adynatous tois sōmasin), but by those who have most reason to rely on their own strength; nor by those already advanced in years, but by those who are still young and have a youthful turn of mind. For the wealthy (hoi plousioi) purchase with their money escape from the risks that they run, whereas the poor are compelled to moderation (sōphronein) by the pressure of their want. The young are held to merit indulgence from their elders; but if their elders are guilty of offence, both ages unite in reproaching them. The strong (tois ischyrois) are at liberty to insult (hybrizō) whomsoever they will with impunity, but the weak (tois asthenesin) are unable either to beat off their aggressors when insulted, or to get the better of their victims if they choose to insult.

117 For my discussion of these terms, see above 210-211, below 385-389.

punish every disobedience, when your obedience is complete.' (10:5-6). In relation to boasting of their superior achievements, he says he will continue with his shameful practice of refusing offers of aid and, in so doing, will cut the ground from under them (11:12). Further, he will restrain himself no longer when next he visits Corinth. Three times he warns that the 'weight' which he displays in his letters he will display against his enemies and, if necessary, against the recalcitrant Corinthians if they do not put themselves to the test before he arrives (10:2,11; 13:2-3).

The contrast between the two kinds of power is retained throughout. His power will be displayed in weakness rather than in any socially acceptable sense (13:2-4). Nevertheless, it is real power; it corresponds to the weakness of Christ which is not weakness but the power of God who gave him the 'authority to build up and not to destroy' (13:10; 10:8) (as he implies his opponents have done). But he does fear that if the Corinthians do not accept what he says in his letter and fail to support him again, that God will humiliate him and he will prove powerless and ineffective (12:21). It is significant that when Paul speaks of the destructive power of his enemies it is in the context of foolishness, and when Paul emulates them he speaks as a fool and not with the Lord's authority (11:17).

Finally, we come to a very complex passage , 12:1-10, in which Paul suggests that he, if any one, has grounds to be a hybrist but instead acts with restraint. This is a much discussed passage and I intend to restrict my discussion to the notions of _sōphrosynē_ and _hybris_ which appear in it[118]. Only Betz has referred to the language of _hybris_ in this passage[119] and none, other than Forbes, has elicited the social implications of such terms as _astheneia_ and _dynamis_[120].

---

[118] For various discussions, among many others, see H.D. Betz, Sokratische Tradition, 89-96; A.T. Lincoln, '"Paul the Visionary"' 204-220; H. Saake, 'Paulus als Ekstatiker', NT 15 (1973), 153-160; J.J. Thierry, 'Der Dorn im Fleische', NT 5 (1962), 301-310; G.G. O'Collins, 'Power Made Perfect in Weakness: 2 Cor. 12:9-10', CBQ 33 (1971), 528-537.

[119] Sokratische Tradition, 95.

[120] 'Strength' and 'Weakness', 91-92.

I will examine firstly the notions of *sōphrosynē* and *hybris* in vv.1-6 and, secondly, the constraint of God imposed upon him in vv.7-10. First, Paul readily admits that he would be justified in boasting of the extraordinary visions and revelation he experienced. He initially discusses it in the third person 'to avoid any hint that he sees it as something he possesses, of which he could boast'[121], but then takes the cudgels on his own behalf. If he wished to boast, unlike his preceding 'boasting', he would not be a fool (*aphrōn*) but would speak the truth (*alētheia*) (vv.5-6). That is to say, he would not transgress the limits of self-knowledge, as his enemies have consistently done.

The association of the ideas of *kauchasthai*, *aphrōn*, *alētheia* is characteristic of discussions of *hybris*. Aristotle refers to *alazoneia*, 'boasting, arrogance, pride', as the excess (*hyperbolē*) of the mean of *alētheia*, 'sincerity, truth'[122]. As I have said before, the *alazōn*, 'boaster', is the *aphrōn* who has lost the awareness of his own limitations and pretends to praiseworthy qualities which he does not have or only possesses in limited measure[123]. The reason for Paul's restraint (though futile boasting would have been excusable under the circumstances and was indeed as far as it went, carried out with notable restraint), was so that no one would think of him above (*hyper*) what they saw in him and heard from him (v.6b). I suggest that *hyper* also alludes to the notion of *hybris*. Paul will refrain from boasting about his visions and revelation so that no one will have an exalted opinion of him. Decisions such as this cost Paul dearly in his relations with the Corinthians. His personal appearance and speech failed to impress them and they regarded the posturing hybrists as superior. His attitude to this point in the passage conforms to the best traditions of *sōphrosynē*.

Second, Paul concedes that it would have been possible for him to have succumbed to *hybris* himself. Thus God imposed upon him the thorn in the flesh to prevent him from being too

---

[121] Ibid., 91.

[122] EE 2.3.4.

[123] See above 352-356.

elated (hyperairōmai) by the excess (hyperbolē) of revelation (v.7)[124]. The translations and various commentators have not given enough weight to the two hyper compounds, hyperairōmai and hyperbolē, in this context. Hyperairō is generally translated as being 'too elated'[125] or 'unduly exalted'[126]. The theme of hybris throughout chapters 10-12 requires a stronger interpretation and I suggest that the hyper compounds are specifically used with this in mind. He has previously used epairō with hypsōma with a pejorative sense[127] of the hybrists (10:5) and Betz correctly translates hyperairō in terms of 'Überheblichkeit', 'presumption' or 'arrogance'[128], a sense that it bears in 2 Thess.2:4. Hyperbolē may also have a negative nuance. It is mostly translated quantitatively as 'abundance'[129] or qualitatively as 'so marvellous' or 'preeminence'[130], a meaning it has in 2 Cor.4:7. It is possible that Paul is playing upon the various meanings of the word. Hyperbolē was the familiar term used for the 'excess' of the mean[131] and Paul may be alluding to it. We have seen that he resorts to the conventional language of moderation and excess in the previous chapters and these ideas provide the background to the interplay between the terms kauchasthai, aphrōn, alētheia and hyper in 12:6. It is permissible then to translate the first section of 12:7 as 'There was given me a thorn in the flesh so that I would not become arrogant by the excess of revelations'.

To this point Paul's use of innuendo has been admirable. The favourable components of praise and blame have been firmly established. He has commended himself as a man of restraint and moderation in regard both to his attitude to his visions

---

124 See C.K. Barrett, 2 Cor. 305, 313-314, for a discussion of the textual problems in v.7.

125 Eg., RSV.

126 C.K. Barrett, 2 Cor. 305.

127 Ibid., 252.

128 Sokratische Tradition, 95.

129 Eg., RSV.

130 C.K. Barrett, 2 Cor. 305, 313.

131 See above 191-192, 197 n.111

and revelations and the devices which he uses to speak about them. At the same time, he has been able to disparage his enemies. This forms part of his comparison and the contrast between his conduct and theirs is patently obvious, especially as it draws to a conclusion the theme of hybris in chapters 10 and 11. The visions and revelations at first (vv.1-4) appear to form a notable departure from his resolve to boast in his weakness (11:30). But the futility of boasting even about these is apparent to Paul. His prefatory remarks indicate as much. He must boast (kauchasthai dei); but he will gain nothing (ou sympheron)[132]. The phrase, ou sympheron, according to Schütz means not only that he gains nothing by boasting but that it will not 'contribute to the common good' of the Corinthians[133]. We have seen though that kauchasthai dei is a rhetorical device[134] and it is possible that in the context of praise and blame that ou sympheron functions in a similar way.

To sympheron, 'the useful', is a technical term which describes one of the techniques of deliberative and epideitic rhetoric. The former aims to persuade people about the useful and harmful (to blaberon) and the latter to attribute praise and blame. It is closely related to what is good and thus praiseworthy according to common values. These forms of rhetoric are intended to persuade the audience or judge that a particular 'course of action is useful and advantageous, that is good and praiseworthy and ought to be chosen, or that another course of action is useless and disadvantageous, that is bad and deserving of censure and ought to be avoided'[135]. Paul could then be saying, 'I must boast. Nothing good can come of it but...'. If indeed, as most scholars believe,

---

[132] For a discussion of the textual problems, see C.K. Barrett, 2 Cor. 305; H. Lietzmann, Kor 1 & 2, 152.

[133] Apostolic Authority, 236-237, who reflects upon the meaning of sympheron in relation to oikodomein in 1 Cor. 6:12 & 10:23. R. Bultmann, 2 Kor. 220, suggests that it recalls the proviso ou kata kurion lalō in 11:17.

[134] See above 353-355.

[135] So E.E. Ryan, 'Aristotle's Rhetoric and Ethics', GRBS. 13 (1972), 296-302; and more generally, D.L. Clark, Rhetoric in Greco-Roman Education, 133-140.

his rhetorically trained rivals boasted of their own visions and revelations, ou sympheron, coupled as it is with kauchasthai dei, may imply that their conduct was both harmful and blameworthy. It is entirely possible that they themselves had resorted to this device to persuade the Corinthians to favour them, for the useful, the good and the praiseworthy proceed by amplification according to the economiastic topics. On a topic which Paul could in truth point to his superiority, he acts with due restraint, in stark contrast to the excessive pride of the hybrists.

What Paul considers useful and the object of acceptable boasting is his weakness - 'on my own behalf I will not boast, except of my weaknesses' (12:5; cf. v.9). The movement from a point of superiority in his comparison to the shameful is the same as in 11:23. Unlike his visions and revelations which are completely out of character with what people see in him and hear from him (v.6), the 'thorn in the flesh' must have been known to the Corinthians and made the subject of much ridicule[136]. It must have been a deeply humiliating experience for Paul following, as it did, his visions and revelations of the Lord. I have suggested that it must have been a socially debilitating disease or physical disfigurement, which in his society and especially in an enmity relationship would have prevented him from displaying excessive pride. He would simply have appeared the more ridiculous[137]. Instead, as Forbes comments, 'He will boast of his weakness - everything that kept him from becoming conceited, everything that would appear to the Corinthians as humiliating and ridiculous'[138]. In terms of the comparison, Paul is deriding himself as the 'worse' man according to the Corinthian values and glorying in that fact.

In conclusion, then, we have been able to detect in chapters 10-12 the theme of hybris developed for the purpose of invective. Though comparison is the controlling literary device upon which Paul conducts his defence, he resorts to

---

136 See above 334, 338.

137 Ibid., 153-154.

138 'Strength' and 'Weakness', 91.

innuendo to disparage his opponents as hybrists. This enabled him to use subtly a popular theme of dispraise against them while conforming to the rules of comparison. At the same time he commends himself as a moderate man. We have seen before that their friends in Corinth had been similarly described by him and it would be fitting from his point of view to describe their friendship as an alliance of hybrists. The notion of hybris has shed new light upon many of the terms and ideas which Paul uses and we can now speak in terms of a vocabulary of hybris. In particular, it gives us a popular and social context into which we can place his 'boasting' and 'foolishness'. It is most fitting, in view of the cruel treatment he has received at the hands of the hybrists over a long period of time, that he should include in the summary to his comparison: 'For the sake of Christ, then, I am content with weaknesses, insults (en hybresin), hardships, persecutions, and calamities; for when I am weak, then am I strong' (12:10).

f. Persuasion

This is an extensive topic and I intend to deal with it briefly and suggestively by drawing together some of the strands which have appeared in the previous chapters. The Greeks and Romans defined rhetoric as persuasion or, more particularly, 'as the faculty of discovering the possible means of persuasion in reference to any subject whatever'[139]. The successful speaker was the one who had understanding and command of the three sources of persuasion - logical reasoning (logos), human character (ēthos) and the emotions (pathos). His aim is to win the favour and admiration of his hearers by appealing primarily to their various emotions and inducing them to believe that he was a man of good sense, good moral character and good will. At the same time, he endeavoured to turn their feelings against an opponent, if one was involved[140].

In pursuit of persuasion, Greek rhetoricians constructed

---

[139] Aristotle, Rhet. 1.2.1.

[140] I have considered these matters previously, see above 56-57; see also D.L. Clark, Rhetoric in Greco-Roman Education, 24-58.

an elaborate system of techniques of argument, style, arrangement, and so on, the practice and theory of which in Roman times were established by the school training[141]. The choice which the speaker presented to the auditors was usually based on aesthetic or emotional preference[142]. When he addresses a popular audience, 'he will base his persuasive arguments on notions possessed by most people ... he will adapt his methods to his audience'[143]. Certain proofs were more suited to popular audiences as they could be more easily followed. Aristotle advocated the use of popular and frequently quoted maxims as a means of persuading an uneducated crowd and enhancing the reputation of the speaker as a man of moral quality. Maxims carried a great deal of weight for they represented the opinions which most people held about themselves. Because they were common they seemed to be true[144].

Preconceived ideas, then, were of fundamental importance to the speaker in his attempts to persuade his listeners to some particular course of action or opinion. It is interesting to note that among the maxims which Aristotle uses as examples, he includes 'the most popular sayings' such as "Know thyself" and "Nothing in excess", two of the fundamental concepts to which, as we saw in the previous section, Paul alludes in his invective against the hybrists[145]. Ryan comments on Aristotle's belief that deliberative and epideictic rhetoric played an important role in shaping social attitudes: 'the members of the society become habituated to find value in certain types of action and not find value in others, to praise certain kinds of men and their deeds and to censure others. There develops in a society a certain unanimity about things which are useful and good which Aristotle, without attributing it to rhetoric, calls "political friendship".

---

[141] See D.L. Clark, Rhetoric in Greco-Roman Education, 67-143, 'The Precepts of Rhetoric'.

[142] However, see Ibid., 118, for the weight carried by proofs which lie outside rhetoric, such as law, witnesses, torture, contract and oaths.

[143] Ibid., 49.

[144] Rhet. 2.21.1-16.

[145] Ibid., 2.21.13.

There develop, too, common patterns of speech about human life and activity, and common opinions about questions of value. There comes into being a set of unwritten laws, such as those telling one how to show gratitude to those doing good to him, to return good to them, and to stand ready to help friends. Finally, and along the same lines, there comes to be a fund of maxims, "old sayings", rules of thumb about what is to be chosen or avoided with respect to human activity[146].

It is difficult for us to grasp how pervasive and influential rhetoric was in Graeco-Roman society. In its schools 'education was almost exclusively education in rhetoric'[147]. The schools were basically conservative or traditional by nature and the same themes and methods were taught almost unchanged for centuries[148] and were reflected widely in the theatre and literature[149], on coins and inscriptions, and imperial sculpture[150], and were popularised by various kinds of wandering preachers and teachers[151]. In classical education, speaking correctly, fluently and clearly involved thinking and behaving appropriately. Formal conventions were adhered to by the speaker and were expected by his audience. The eloquent and well educated speaker won great honours and was esteemed as a leader of society[152].

Though undecided about the level of literary and cultural sophistication of the Corinthians, scholars have noticed the predilection of some of them for rhetoric and its accompani-

---

146 'Aristotle's Rhetoric and Ethics', 302.

147 D.L. Clark, Rhetoric in Greco-Roman Education, 64-65.

148 Ibid., 66.

149 See G. Kennedy, The Art of Rhetoric in the Roman World, (Princeton, 1972), 384-387, and 387-427 for rhetoric in the works of Virgil, Horace, Ovid, and Livy.

150 Ibid., 382-383: key ideas of Augustan rhetoric appear frequently in coins and inscriptions and the orator became a 'standard form in imperial sculpture and the iconography borrows from the rules of gesture and delivery'. See also R. Brilliant, 'Gesture and Rank in Roman Art: the Use of Gestures to Denote Status in Roman Sculpture and Coinage', Memoirs of the Connecticut Academy of Arts and Sciences, 14 (1963), 9-10.

151 A.J. Malherbe, 'Gentle as a Nurse', for various types of transient public speakers described by Dio Chrysostom, especially the Orator-philosopher, 207.

152 See the concluding comments by Quintilian, 12.11.25-30.

ments. But there is a good deal more that has not been clearly enough seen. The rival apostles resorted to the traditional exercise of comparison, and such popular topics of encomium as their social position, power and deeds, to cast Paul in an unfavourable light as a man who lacked culture. In addition they used the popular figure of the servile flatterer to discredit him as an inconstant and untrustworthy person. Paul actually alludes to their use of the tricks of rhetoric (2 Cor.4:2). The majority of the Corinthians were persuaded by it and their susceptibility suggests that they shared a common system of values with the rival apostles. We saw that the main opposition to Paul in 1 Corinthians consisted of wealthy and educated people and their conflict with him has social and cultural overtones. It is feasible to suggest also, in view of their partiality for eloquence, that such Corinthians were educated in rhetoric to one level or another and that their friends, the rival apostles, were professional rhetoricians. The evidence for the social and literary level of the Corinthians who succumbed to their eloquent invective is sparse indeed. The content of the invective does not require that they be sophisticated for it was drawn from the normal speech patterns and opinions of ordinary people[153]. The Corinthians would not have needed to recognize the finer points of comparison and other rhetorical devices for the invective to have been effective.

Yet Paul's letters do appear to demand a reasonable level of education on the part of the reader. We have seen that Paul competently, and even creatively, uses at the one time a number of devices of rhetoric and association with readily recognizable ideas such as hybris and sōphrosynē, and honour and shame. We know that he is engaged in a desperate struggle to win back the hostile Corinthians and that his letters have more effect than his speeches. I assume that at least by describing his letters as bareiai kai ischyrai they mean that they are more persuasive than his speeches. The invective against him does appear to have some element of truth and the Corinthians themselves must have been able to discern a marked

[153] See above 62.

difference between his speeches and letters.

I assume, also, that behind their estimation there must have been some rhetorical standard. But this is the problem. By what rhetorical standard do they assess his letters as bareiai kai ischyrai? The terms ischyros and its antithesis asthenēs, as Forbes has convincingly shown, belong to the 'rhetoric of status' in contemporary Greek literature and are used to ascribe worth on either political, cultural or philosophical grounds. He concludes that Paul's usage conforms to this pattern and that the terms denote 'the value which groups or persons are seen as possessing, in their social context'[154]. We have seen that ischys as 'physical strength' is an important quality for an orator, enhancing his powers of persuasion. Paul lacked this quality, being considered asthenēs, with dire consequences for his speech - ho logos exouthenēmenos. The social nuance is particularly apparent in exouthenō. Paul uses exouthenēmena as a sociological category in 1 Cor.1:28 in conjunction with ta mē onta, as the antithesis of the status term ta agenē[155]. It appears to have this sense in the two other passages in which it is used in this letter[156].

Many of the terms which were originally used of the physical constitution and bodily condition were applied to language. Words used for slender and weak persons were opposed to those describing the strong. Plutarch comments, 'But as the body ought to be not merely healthy but also sturdy, so also speech should be not merely free from fault but vigorous too'[157]. Both ischys and baros are used by Dionysius to describe commendable virtues or qualities which an orator should possess. baros, lit., 'weight, heaviness', is applied to language with the meaning of 'gravity, dignity, impressiveness'. He lists it among the accessory virtues of diction - among which are

---

[154] 'Strength' and 'Weakness', 68, 108-109.

[155] So G. Theissen, 'Soziale Schichtung', 233-235.

[156] 1 Cor.6:4; 16:10, of Timothy. Some suggest that Timothy's youthfulness or timidity is implied, with reference to 1 & 2 Tim. eg. A. Robertson and A. Plummer, 1 Cor. 391. We should also consider that he could be held in low esteem because he was Paul's emissary.

[157] Mor. 7B; cf. ἄλκη, 'strength', Dionysius, de Thuc. 23.360.22; στιβαρός, 'virile', ibid., 24.361.9; ῥώμη, 'bodily strength', de Imit. 3.207.17.

qualities such as 'intensity' and 'sentiment' - 'which to the largest extent reveal the real power (dynamis) of the orator' and 'are productive of so-called eloquence (deinotēs)'[158]. He names it as one of the qualities which lend charm and beauty to language, which together produce good style[159], and says that both Thucydides and Demosthenes shared it[160]. Aristotle uses the word of one of the three kinds of modulation of voice - the shrill (oxeiys), the deep (barys) and the intermediate (mesos) - which, when used properly, 'nearly always help carry off the prizes'[161]. ischys, 'physical strength', is used by Dionysius in the same way as a stylistic quality - forcefulness (deinotēs), strength (ischys), vigour (tonos), elevation (megaloprepeia) - which was characteristic of Demosthenes' eloquence[162]. He lists it among the accessory virtues which reveal the rhetorician's power[163] and uses it in conjunction with other terms which describe physical conditions such as stibaros, 'sturdy, robust, virile'[164].

The Roman authors used a similar range of words such as vis, gravitas and auctoritas to convey these ideas. Cicero speaks of the 'full employment of powerful and weighty oratory' (omnis vis orationis et gravitas)[165], a description which does not appear to differ greatly from that made of Paul's written style. The loftiness, brilliance and weight (auctorites) of Cicero's own eloquence was said to evoke clamorous enthusiasm[166]. He referred to the grand style, the

---

[158] de Thuc. 23.360.10. Translation from W.K. Pritchett, Dionysius of Halicarnassus: On Thucydides, (Berkeley, 1975).

[159] de Comp. 11.37.16; associated with such qualities as 'euphony', 'persuasiveness', and 'dignity'.

[160] de Dem. 34.204.14.

[161] Rhet. 3.1.4; cf., Cicero, de Or. 3.57.215-58.219, for a discussion of modulation of voice.

[162] de Thuc. 55.417.17-18; cf. de Dem. 21.176.2, attributed to Demosthenes. Cf. τὸ ἐμβριθές, 'gravity', de Thuc. 24.363.15, and Longinus, de Subl. 9.3; cf. Dionysius, de Dem. 21.176.3.

[163] Eg., Ep. ad Pomp. 3.239.14ff.

[164] de Comp. 100.10.

[165] de Or. 2.82.334.

[166] Quintilian 8.3.3.

one to which I have suggested that Paul's most closely approximates in tone, as weighty, grand and emphatic (gravis, grandis, vehemens) and thought that this tyle should be used to excite and move the audience[167].

The word dynamis, a more comprehensive term than ischys[168], is more commonly associated with rhetoric. The terms are almost synonymous in many instances and can be used interchangeably to denote 'strength, power, influence', their primary meaning having to do with importance or worth[169]. Aristotle defines rhetoric, in the words of Isocrates, as the dynamis ('faculty, capacity, power') of discovering the possible means of persuasion[170], or the 'faculty' of speech[171]. In the same work, the phrase dynamis tou legein simply means 'eloquence'[172]. Quintilian, in referring to this common definition of rhetoric, i.e., the power of persuasion (vis persuadendi), wished to make it clear that by vis, 'power', he means dynamis[173]. I have mentioned that the accessory virtues, which include baros, ischys, pathos, to prepon, and the like, imparted beauty and vigour and thus revealed the orator's true power (dynamis) and won him fame and glory[174]. The necessary virtues had to be present in each speech or narrative and were directed towards a clear exposition and no nothing more[175]. Without the accessory virtues, his words were in danger of being commonplace and undistinguished,

---

167 Or. 21.68-69.

168 Cf., ad Herr. 3.6.10; the dynameis consists of the physical attributes which are bestowed upon the body by nature: agility, strength, beauty, health.

169 'Strength; and 'Weakness' 64, cf., 33.68.

170 Rhet. 1.2.1.

171 Ibid., 1.1.13.

172 Ibid., 1.6.14.

173 2.15.2-4 ·· vis, 'power', as against potestas, 'capacity', and facultas, 'faculty'; and see his discussion of the 'most celebrated and most discussed definitions' of rhetoric, including his personal preference, 'the science of speaking well', 2.15.1-38.

174 See Dionysius, ad Pomp. 3.239.14ff; de Thuc. 23.360; cf., Cicero de Or. 3.58.219, vis as voice modulation: 'intense, vehement, eager with a sense of impressive urgency' (contentum, vehemens, imminens quadam incitatione gravitatis).

175 Dionysius, de Thuc. 23.360.2ff.

lacking persuasive power or forceful eloquence. Quintilian comments: 'I come now to the subject of ornament, in which, more than in any other department, the orator allows himself the greatest indulgence. For a speaker wins but trifling praise if he does no more than speak with correctness and lucidity'[176]. Roberts suggests that clarity and emphasis were demanded and expected of every writer and could be so easily achieved in the highly inflected Greek and Latin languages that their attainment won no special applause[177]. We have already seen that the term deinotēs is used either as the accessory virtue of 'intensity' or 'passionate force' or of rhetorical skill or eloquence generally and was a quality attributed above all to Demosthenes[178]. The idea of fear is implicit in deinotēs and Longinus couples it with dynamis to describe the awesome or overpowering effect Demosthenes had upon his readers. By comparison, he says, no one fears (phobeitai) when reading Hypereides[179].

It is most significant, then, that Paul opposed his own dynamis to traditional Greek rhetoric which is implied in the phrases, καθ᾽ ὑπεροχὴν λόγου η σοφίας and ἐν πειθοῖς σοφίας λόγοις (1 Cor.2:1,4). Such eloquence is the substance of rhetorical dynamis. It also helps us see what Paul means by preaching 'Jesus Christ and him crucified' in 'weakness (astheneia) and much fear (phobos) and trembling (tromos)'. Forbes has argued that astheneia here is a social judgement according to generally accepted values and that Paul in some way was 'in a socially disadvantaged and humiliating

---

176 8.3.1. For the effect of power of delivery on even a mediocre speech, see ibid., 11.3.5-9.

177 W.R. Roberts, Dionysius of Halicarnassus on Literary Composition, (London, 1910), 27.

178 See W.K. Pritchett, Dionysius on Thucydides, 108 n.4, where he gives the range of meanings and the secondary sources which list the passages containing the word.

179 de Subl. 34.4. deinos, 'terrible, strange, clever', has both primitive and literal associations with the word 'fear'; both Dionysius and Demetrius frequently couple to deinon and to phoberon as almost synonymous terms. Similarly deinos is linked with sophos in authors as early as Herodotus and Sophocles to describe the rhetorically clever and powerful man. So W.R. Roberts, Loeb, Demetrius, 266-267.

position'[180]. The three terms form a trilogy of shame and are a fitting epilogue to the message he preaches. Rather than speak with the persuasive, forceful eloquence of the rhetorician, he presents himself in terms of its antithesis, weak and fearful. The terms in 2 Cor.10:1 and 10, taken from the hybrists' invective, substantiate this image. His presentation and speech are despised as servile (tapeinos)[181], weak (asthenēs) and contemptible (exouthenēmenos). 1 Cor.2:1-5 is the commencement of Paul's theme of personal shame in socio-cultural terms. In each such portrayal, his shame and weakness are directly opposed to the values and interests of his enemies and are the instruments of God's display of power[182]. In 1 Cor.2:1-5 God's power is displayed not simply in the absence of Greek rhetoric but in its very antithesis[183]. The final (hina) clause shows that this was precisely what he intended should happen and it initiates the often repeated idea that it is directly due to the shame of the apostle that the Corinthians owed their existence. Their faith (pistis) was not and could never be ἐν σοφίᾳ but only ἐν δυνάμει θεοῦ.

The ideas expressed by Paul and the terms he uses must lead us to the conclusion that Paul deliberately rejects Greek rhetoric in his preaching of the gospel. The words 'for I decided to know nothing among you except Jesus Christ and him crucified' (v.2) provides eloquent testimony for his reason

---

180 'Strength' and 'Weakness', 79-80.

181 For tapeinos, as a description of style, see Aristotle, Rhet. 3.2.1-2, Poetics 22.1; cf., Dionysius, de Comp. 3:11.15; Aristotle, Rhet. 3.7.2, for similar notions.

182 Eg., 1 Cor. 4:9-13; 15:8; 2 Cor.1:8-10; 2:14; 4:7-12; 12:7-10; 13:3-4.

183 C.J. Robbins, 'Rhetorical Structure of Philippians 2:6-11', CBQ, 42 (1980), 74, comments in passing that Paul's disavowal of Greek eloquence in 1 Cor.2:1 does not include 'the basic principles of correct sentence structure.' His attempt to show that Phil.2:6-11 conforms to the principles of classical rhetoric makes an interesting contribution to the study of Paul's rhetoric, but we must be careful not to apply broad generalizations to Paul's argument in 1 Cor.2:1-5. Such a view does not allow for the distinction between Paul's spoken and written rhetoric. Nor does it perceive the rhetorical significance of terms such as astheneia and dynamis and the social implications posed by the antitheses in these verses. Finally, it does not explain what it is that Paul abandons. Rhetorical eloquence and power consists of both the necessary and accessory virtues. See my discussion above 385-388.

for doing so. The rejection and humiliation of Jesus provides the intellectual and practical basis for the radical schēma of the apostle. As Judge says, 'He was caught up personally with the need to explain how it was possible for the Messiah to be like that'[184]. The whole tenor of rhetoric was incongruous with the gospel which he preached and the way he experienced it at a social level. At the same time, the manner in which he expresses these ideas and his language indicates that he was more than familiar with the rhetorical traditions he was rejecting. It is feasible to suggest that he he may have been trained in rhetoric but had deliberately set it aside.

His letters though are different. The praiseworthy qualities are evident - tharrein, barys, ischyros - providing clear evidence of his characteristic inconsistency. The question though is still with us; what standard do these qualities represent? Can it be that of Dionysius, from whom we have gained some insight into the meaning of these words? It has been said of him that his 'true distinction as a critic is his purity of taste'[185], and that he rejected all post-Attic prose as 'bizarre, eccentric or disorganized'[186]. The rhetorically trained Greek Church Fathers recognized that Paul's letters, however, else judged to be eloquent, did not conform to the classical standards of the Greeks[187]. This also may not have been the standard of Paul's enemies. We have only one extant letter (I Corinthians) on which Paul's critics could have made this judgement, though I suspect the letter in question is his 'painful' letter (2 Cor.2:3-4; 7:8).

On the basis that tharrein, barys and ischyros signify

---

[184] 'St. Paul and Socrates', 111, 113.

[185] So W.K. Pritchett, Dionysius on Thucydides, XXVI. For a similar conclusion with regard to Atticism as the standard of the rivals, see E.A. Judge, 'St. Paul and Classical Society', 35.

[186] So D.A. Russell, Plutarch, 20-21; Dionysius sought to restore the high standard of the Attic Classics but without the pretentiousness of second-century Atticists.

[187] See E.A. Judge, 'Paul's Boasting', 41-42; 'St. Paul and Classical Society', 35. Thus far our attempts to understand Paul's rhetoric have been based upon classical rhetoric. What we need is a study of the first-century Greek rhetoric which was so despised by later Atticists.

persuasive force, we can judge that it had achieved qualified success with the socially conscious Corinthians in a way that his presence and speech did not. Paul attributes their change in attitude directly to it (7:9-11). They were 'grieved into repentance' (v.9). The various elements - the implied harshness of the letter; his claim to be speaking the truth (v.14); the grief and profit of repentance; their fear and trembling (v.15) - reveal all the requirements of parrēsia and tharrein, that frankness of speech and boldness Paul is said to lack when with them[188].

In Galatia, Paul fears his frankness has compounded the difficulty in his relations with the church[189]. In Corinth, it has met with partial success. His buoyancy over their change of heart towards him (vv.7,11), though, needs to be seen together with other unresolved matters which still concern him. He appears to have met with success in regard to a particular unnamed person (tis lelupēken) (2 Cor.2:5-11), (eneken tou adikēsantos) (7:12), or issue (tǭ pragmati) (7:11), but fears many of the old problems will remain when he visits a third time (12:19-21). As I have argued, the Corinthians are still ambivalent towards Paul. They have demanded that he commend himself a second time to them and thereby initiate a new friendship. This he refuses to do. He also had to clear away some of their continuing doubts over his inconsistency of character and his failure to conform to certain social standards. In addition, the rival apostles appear to be still in Corinth and the Corinthians have not broken off these ties. His present 'bold' letter is intended to bring about the Corinthians' obedience so that he need not be a harsh apostle when he is with them. Then he will deal with the others (10:6). Under no circumstances could he resort to worldly weapons - presumably rhetoric and its concomitants - (10:3-4). The schēma remains the same; the power of God will be displayed in weakness (13:1-4) and Paul is faced with the

---

188 For parrēsia and metanoia, see Plutarch, Mor. 56A, where he describes parrēsia as the quality of a true friend who by 'chiding and blaming implants the sting of repentance', though he might be mistaken as an enemy for doing so. See also ibid., 810C.

189 See above 107-109.

possibility of the same humiliation as he suffered before (12:21).

Finally, implicit in such ideas as baros and ischys is that of tone or voice modulation. Scholars have long been confounded by the various and contrasting 'tones' in 2 Corinthians and have used the broad criteria of 'soft' and 'severe' to determine two or more letters or periods of writing to explain the change in voice. I suggest that until we understand more fully the milieu of Paul's rhetoric and the subtelties and nuances which are present in the language, we do not have the basis for making such judgements. Our brief look at the ideas of baros, ischys and dynamis indicates in a modest way the range of tones and emotions which were at the disposal of the speaker or writer[190] and the many and various emotions to which he would appeal[191]. The Corinthians would have been alert and possibly receptive to the subtle and dramatic changes of tone and would have envisaged the traditional and appropriate mannerisms of posture, facial expression and gesture which accompanied them[192].

As we have seen, Paul wished to 'change his tone' towards the Galatians from one of frankness (misunderstood by them as enmity) (Gal.4:20)[193]. It should not surprise us that in a letter the length of 2 Corinthians covering such a range of issues and with the ebb and flow of an enmity relationship, that Paul speaks with a number of voices. We have also seen that in chapters 10-13, Paul employs rhetorical devices which would have demanded changes of expression and voice on the

---

[190] Eg., Aristotle, Rhet. 3.1.4; and espec. Cicero, de Or. 3.57.215-58.219. Cf. Quintilian, 12.10.71, for the various styles an orator would employ in a single speech (eg., he 'will speak gravely, severely, sharply...sarcastically, genially...gently, sweetly...' See also Plutarch Mor. 810C: 'For blame which is mingled with praise and contains nothing insulting but merely frankness of speech and arouses not anger, but a pricking of the conscience and repentance, appears both kindly and healing'. Cf. W. Wuellner, 'Greek Rhetoric and Pauline Argumentation' 183-184, for the use of the primary emotions in 1 Corinthians.

[191] For details, see above 56-57.

[192] Eg., Cicero, de Or. 3.59.220-223. Cf. also ibid., 2.45.189, for the need of the speaker to visibly display the emotions he wishes to evoke in his listeners. For conventions of gesture and their influence upon an audience familiar with them, see Quintilian 11.3.14, 65-87.

[193] See above 155.

part of the person who read his letter to the Corinthians[194]. His painful letter was regarded as being rhetorically effective by the Corinthians generally, though Paul, linking the ideas of fear and powerful rhetoric, says that he does not appear to be frightening (ekphobō) them with his letters. It seems that his enemies have suggested to them that they have no need to listen to his 'weight' by letter when he is absent, for he is so servile when present. Something in his painful letter, though, has turned them around and there should be no reason to believe that they would react in any way but favourably to a further bareia kai ischyra letter.

g. Conclusion

Paul's responses have not added much to our existing knowledge of the rival apostles. Though he does not name them, from his comparison we can be certain that they are Jews who claim apostolic status. Their cultural and social values suggest that they are Hellenists whose relations with the Corinthians are based on those same values. We have seen, also, that Paul uses similar language and ideas as in 1 Corinthians to denigrate them as hybrists.

Our picture of Paul, by contrast, becomes much clearer, though it raises some unresolved questions. First, in regard to rhetoric, his conscious choosing of the antitheses of Greek rhetoric for his preaching of the gospel indicates to us that he was familiar with it, and may even have been rhetorically trained. His preaching approached the grand style in character but lacked a concern for the proprieties. This suggestion became more probable when we saw that his letters possessed certain commendable rhetorical qualities and that he himself used properly a number of rhetorical devices to discredit his enemies and win the Corinthians[195]. We have not been able to determine the standard by which his rhetoric was, or should be, assessed. I suggest that we should look

---

194 In this regard, see E.A. Judge, 'Paul's Boasting', 37.

195 Cf. W. Wuellner, 'Greek Rhetoric and Pauline Argumentation', 177-179, 188, who sees Paul's conscious use of the rhetorical device of digression in 1 Corinthians as evidence of his rhetorical skill. I suggest that 2 Cor.6:14 - 7:1 may be understood in a similar way.

at other unconventional speakers such as Cassius Severus, a near contemporary of Paul, who was known for his powerful oratory and biting wit and lack of restraint. He was not a man of the schools and was, indeed, a severe critic of them, and adopted a new style of rhetoric suited to his age[196]. But it is important to recognize that exponents of the rhetorical art such as Quintilian and Seneca could speak in praise of certain aspects of non-conformist's rhetoric and in a manner not altogether unlike the way in which Paul's enemies spoke of his letters.

Secondly, with regard to invective, there does appear to be more than an element of truth in their dispraise of his physical condition and his refusal to conform to rhetorical dynamis, which rendered him weak in presence and contemptible in speech by Greek standards. Third, Paul's shame has substance to it also, according to accepted social values. His adopting the antitheses of Greek rhetoric follows the same pattern as his use of comparison where he opposes his shame to the honourable things of his enemies. This is a characteristic of his relations with the Corinthians and the rival apostles and conforms to his understanding of the death of Jesus as rejection and humiliation. At the same time, the rival apostles' use of comparison suggests that Paul is a man of

---

196 See M.L. Clarke, Rhetoric at Rome (London, 1953), 105; Cf. Quintilian 10.1.116-117; Seneca, Contr. 3. Pref. 1-7, 12-15; Tacitus, Dial. 26.5. See also, M. Fuhrmann, 'Cassius Severus', Der kleine Pauly: Lexikon der Antike Vol.I, K. Ziegler and W. Sontheimer, eds.(Stuttgart, 1964), 1076, who suggests that Cassius Severus' 'compressed, impulsive and sarcastic style, on the one hand, made a great impression on contemporaries and posterity. Nevertheless, he was criticised for the way his presentation was chopped short and was accused of having injured respectability and good manners as a result of his bitter abusiveness (Seneca, Contr. 3. praef.1ff., 18; Suet. bei Hieron, Ol. 202.4 = fr.69; Tacitus, Dial. 26.5; Quintilian 10.1.116f.). On the one hand, the 'modern Asianic' trend of the empire saw in him its forerunner (Tacitus, Dial. 19) and, on the other, Tacitus has him characterised by Messalla as a transitional phenomenon' (ibid. 26.4-6). Furmann's verdict is that in 'the forcefulness of his attack and in his sharp rejection of school declamations alike (Seneca, Contr. 3 praef. 12ff.) he perpetuates the mentality of the Late Republic. At the same time his harsh manner of speaking with its grasping after points is heavily influenced by the taste of his times' (article translated into English from German). Cf. also M. Schanz and C. Hosius, 'Cassius Severus', Hanbuch der Altertumswissenschaft : Geschichte der römischen Literatur bis zum Gesetzgebungswerk des Kaisers Justinian Vol. 2 (München, 1935), 345-347.

rank, as it would have been ridiculous to have entered into comparison according to the encomiastic topics otherwise. Thus his humiliation and shame is a deeply felt one, practically and intellectually, but one in which he is prepared to suffer and glory. Fourth, we have been able to establish a context in which we can place Paul's notion of the fool, that of the man who is ignorant of his own character, a figure familiar to a tradition which contrasted *hybris* with *sōphrosynē*.

Section 4
CONCLUSIONS AND COMMENTS

I commenced this enquiry into Paul's relationship with the Corinthians with the assumption that it could be explained in terms of Graeco-Roman social conventions. My special interest has been the cause and expression of enmity against him. This approach has illuminated aspects of the conflict which either have not been investigated previously or have been regarded as secondary to theological considerations. In addition, it offers new perspectives and, in some instances, alternative viewpoints to current Corinthians problems. It now remains to reflect on the conclusions which have been reached and to comment on the significant issues which have emerged.

At the outset I argued that, though the common terms of friendship do not appear in Paul's letters, a number of its important conventions are present. I concluded that he conducted his relations with his churches and intimates in accordance with them, though his use of servile terminology suggested that he was redefining the normal pattern of status distinction and discrimination. Contrary to present opinion, the terminology in Phil. 4:15 of 'giving and receiving' indicated that Paul and the Philippians enjoyed a warm and long friendship.

The conventions of friendship and enmity formed the basis of my analysis of the conflict between Paul and the Corinthians. The social implications of recommendation in 1 and 2 Corinthians had not been recognized before and from the study of the recommendation passages, I constructed a broad framework of social relations to describe the conflict: a. Paul in the beginning committed himself to a relationship of trust, i.e., one of friendship by self-commendation; b. his refusal to commend himself a second time and the mistrust of the Corinthians suggested that he was held to be responsible for a breach of that trust; c. his Corinthian enemies and the rival apostles became friends by mutual recommendation and, according to the conventions of friendship, joint enemies of Paul. These last two considerations explained, in part, why it was so difficult for Paul to reestablish relations with the Corinthians and why they continued to doubt his sincerity.

More particularly, Paul's refusal of an offer of aid was the cause of the hostility against him. I asked two main questions: what was the nature of the offer and why did such hostility follow his refusal? A number of factors contributed to my conclusion that it was intended as a gift and, as such, constituted an offer of friendship. Of special significance, firstly, was the idea of gift exchange as a social relationship among people of rank. I argued against the idea of 'salaried' apostles in Corinthians and the Socratic-Cynic analogy of the true philosopher, and indicated the need for further study in regard to money and other gift and service relations in the New Testament. Second, the social implications of gift exchange were important for understanding the connection between Paul's refusal in Corinth and his acceptance of Philippian gifts and the relational nuances which appear in this context.

Within this framework of conventions, Paul's reasons for refusal were consistent with the normal grounds for refusing gifts and services: a. his right as a free man to choose for himself; b. his wish not to burden or injure others by acceptance; c. his analogy of the friendship of parent and child to his responsibility as the parent-apostle in Corinth. His refusal made sense in the context of social division and factionalism in Corinth. I suggested that one of the factions made the offer to Paul and that his acceptance would have placed him under an unwanted obligation. Acceptance, rather than refusal, was the normal custom, especially with powerful benefactors. The refusal of gifts and services was a refusal of friendship and dishonoured the donor. It could be construed by him as a declaration of enmity irrespective of how just the grounds may have been for refusing. Paul would have found it almost impossible, given the intricate nature of friendship and enmity, to remain neutral in the factionalism in Corinth. In fact, his recommendation of his supporters could be understood as his taking sides and may have caused his enemies to seek friends of their own to displace him as the apostle in Corinth.

There was no lack of evidence of the enmity relationship in the Corinthian letters. This study, however, has pointed to the conventional way in which enmity was conducted. I identified the two main forms of invective against Paul: the common figure of the flatterer and the rhetorical device of comparison. His enemies ridiculed him as a servile, fickle and insincere person who consciously adapted to his circumstances and associates for his own ends, and as being socially and culturally inferior to themselves. As well, Paul used a number of rhetorical devices to denigrate his rivals as hybrists and interlopers and to portray himself as a man of restraint.

The analysis of the various devices of rhetoric enabled me to make two important contributions to Corinthian studies. The first relates to the control of the material. Could invective give us an accurate picture of Paul and his rivals? Apart from the serious problem of amplification and fabrication, the normal proprieties of rhetoric could be set aside in an enmity relationship. The difficulties are accentuated by Paul's deliberate and unusual use of self-derision. To be consistent, I had to include all the charges against Paul and his rivals as invective before attempting to draw some tentative guide-lines of interpretation. Of these, the rhetorical technique of sygkrisis is of major significance for understanding 2 Cor. 11:1-12:10. It is the controlling literary form in this passage and Paul adheres to the rules. From the point for point comparison, the movement from equality to superiority, the form of praise and blame, and other related precepts of rhetoric, a more factual picture of Paul and his rivals resulted.

The second contribution deals with the content of the invective. The encomiastic topics of comparison and the figure of the flatterer reflect traditional social and cultural values, as does Paul's lists of personal shame. I concluded from this that the judgement against him was a social one according to conventional values and that the conflict over apostleship was primarily socio-cultural in character. The rival apostles portrayed themselves as cultivated men and made qualities such as position, achievements and eloquence the standard for apostleship in Corinth. In terms of the current debate over apostleship in Corinth, the question is one of authority rather than of legitimacy, but it relates to Paul's social, and not his theological, standing.

The social characters of Paul and the rival apostles which emerged from this analysis were not altogether unalike. I concluded that the rival apostles were Hellenistic Jews who had been educated in rhetoric and belonged to the mainstream of Graeco-Roman cultural tradition. Though Paul disparages them as 'false apostles', they regarded themselves as apostles, superior to him, and were esteemed as such by the Corinthians. Paul's invective of non-naming ensures their anonymity. The pejorative title, 'self-recommenders', is the nearest we can come to naming them but the periphrastic denigration provides an important social insight. Their written self-commendation was the basis of their friendship with Paul's enemies in Corinth. This social and cultural reconstruction of the rival apostles offers an alternative viewpoint to the one which sees them as credentialled representatives of the Jerusalem church and moves the conflict out of the arena of a Jerusalem/Paul antithesis.

The details about Paul are more numerous and complex. First, in relation to the invective, I have suggested that there was some substance to the charges of inconstancy against him according to Greek standards of morality and that it was characteristic of his apostleship. Also, his many humiliating experiences, his socially debilitating disease or disfigurement and ineffectual speech were shameful by socially accepted values. Measured against the favourable qualities of his rivals, they formed the basis of a powerful invective against him. Second, his standard of apostleship provided none of the social graces which the Corinthians valued so highly. Rather, the criteria he advanced were the very antithesis. He described his preaching in terms which were directly opposed to praiseworthy rhetorical qualities and depicted himself as a socially disadvantaged and humiliated person.

My examination of this, however, led me to adopt an entirely opposite view of Paul's education and status. Against current scholarly opinion, I concluded that Paul was trained in rhetoric. His deliberate adopting of the antitheses of rhetoric in his preaching, his adept use of the rhetorical devices, and the accessory virtues which others observed in his letters combine to give a new perspective on his rhetoric. I was also able to suggest that his preaching may have been similar to the grand style of rhetoric, but that he disregarded the proprieties and spoke impulsively and passionately. By comparison, his letters possessed commendable rhetorical qualities. I was not able to determine the standard of rhetoric by which he was judged, but I have shown that notable classical rhetoricians praised the speech of other non-conformists of the rhetorical art in a manner similar to the praise of Paul's written style. A comparison between him and unconventional rhetors of his day may prove rewarding in the attempt to define his rhetoric more clearly.

With regard to his social status, and in support of the growing consensus, my study of Paul's self-derision, especially in his _sygkrisis_ in 2 Cor. 11:23-33, indicated that he belonged to the socially privileged classes. I argued, with E.A. Judge and R.F. Hock, that Paul felt deeply his shame and humiliation and reflected the attitude of a man of rank to things which are traditionally shameful in Graeco-Roman society. The fact that he gloried in them did not suggest a reversal of values, as it did in the Cynic traditions; these experiences were always shameful for him. This view of his status is complemented by his rivals' _sygkrisis_; it would have been ridiculous for them to have engaged in comparison with Paul according to the encomiastic topics unless he was a person of status and education.

Thus both Paul and the rival apostles were most probably social equals and clearly understood the conventions governing honour and shame at this level in society. Unlike his rivals, Paul had deliberately abandoned rhetoric in his preaching and other similar indicators of status in favour of their traditional antitheses. By doing so, he denied himself the normal denotations of leadership, power, position and social standing.

The question arises as to how to relate Paul to Hellenistic society. Familiar ideas such as 'accommodation' and 'assimilation' to Greek culture (referring either to his deliberate missionary policy or his familiarity due to his long ministry in a Greek environment) emphasize Paul the Jew. While there can be no doubt as to his Jewish heritage, there is no evidence in his letters of a progress in Hellenism, conscious or otherwise. Accommodation as a way of describing Paul's behaviour must refer to his relationships with the different ethnic, social and religious groups which made up the heterogeneous communities of the major Greek cities. The socio-cultural picture of him which has emerged from this study is of a well-established Greek who deliberately sets aside certain accepted conventions and has been condemned by his social equals according to those very standards. We saw that Paul spoke of his shame as a Greek from the higher social levels. In fact, the only instance in which he refers to his Jewish background in the Corinthian letters (2 Cor. 11:22-23) is in a context in which his language, ideas and method of argument are consciously Greek.

This social enquiry, then, brings Paul the Greek prominently into view. But to speak of Paul as a Jew or Greek is surely to overly highlight one or the other aspect of Paul as a Hellenised Jew. The picture may become clearer if we knew more about the character of Hellenistic Judaism of the major Greek cities. A comparison of Paul and Philo of Alexandria, though, would suggest that it is a wide framework indeed.

A healthy respect for the dilemma felt by both Greeks and Jews over Paul may help us to be cautious in planting him too firmly in either tradition and may lead us to see something of his remarkable individuality. We have seen that by Greek standards of morality the invective of the flatterer has substance. Primarily, 'all things to all men' reflects the traditional Greek response to inconstancy. But it must also allude to the truly anomalous character of Paul. It is here that we ourselves face a dilemma of definition. How do we describe Paul's inconsistency? I doubt whether this creative and elusive edge to his character can be defined and limited by such terms as 'principle' or 'strategy' or vague ideas such as 'higher consistency'. The chameleon in Paul must be allowed its full range of colours.

I have attempted to outline this problem in terms of the social and literary conventions of Greece and Rome. At the same time an insight has been gained into what must have been the remarkable flexibility, adaptability and openness of Paul. Interwoven with these social and psychological perspectives is the theological one. Paul attributes his behaviour to the gospel he preaches. It was not my intention to investigate his understanding of the gospel on this issue, but it seems to me that such an investigation would show that the gospel itself has a certain relativity for Paul. The interaction between these aspects is a complex one indeed, and it is difficult to determine at individual points which one of them is illuminating the others.

I hinted at this kind of interaction in Paul's experience of shame. It is significant that the important social metaphor of strength and weakness with which he expresses his humiliation has as its theological counterpart the dying and rising motif. This may properly be called his personal theology in the Corinthian letters (if not the most significant, it is at least one of the primary theological ideas in his letters) and relates specifically to his struggle as an apostle.

I have said that the death of Jesus as rejection and humiliation provides the intellectual and practical basis for Paul's expression of apostleship. Or should we say that we have on view a paradigm of a man of rank's individual experience in Greek culture of the death and resurrection of Jesus? I doubt whether a person of inferior status or another socio-cultural setting could have provided us with the same stark social and theological antitheses that are found in Paul.

A similar connection exists between Paul's attempts at social integration in Corinth and his theological idea of oneness or unity in Christ. He introduced into the normal pattern of social relations the notion that Christ's death was a death for all, regardless of status. This was seen generally in his remarkable use of servile terminology to describe himself, his associates and others of rank, and their servitude to others. In 1 Corinthians it is implicit in his attempts to replace the distinctions and discrimination of social standing with his own unconventional idea of communal relations. It was the opposite of Greek ideals of society in which status was regarded as a noble virtue. Its radical demands were ignored by some wealthy Corinthians who insisted on their traditional rights and rejected an apostle who had shamefully abandoned his.

The conflict in Corinth drew from Paul a profound socio-theological statement of his apostleship. Its social character and his experience of it are reflected in his extensive vocabulary of shame and servitude and I suggest that the terms must be allowed their full social weight if we are to understand Paul's theological perspectives.

The social character of the Corinthian community was typical of Greek urban life. The status of Paul's Corinthian opponents became clearer from my analysis of the cause of the conflict. Their excessive behaviour, their attitude towards giving and receiving, the conduct of enmity and the character of the invective were characteristic of the rich and powerful in society. In addition, they sought out by recommendation friends with common pursuits and interests and succeeded in making traditional cultural qualities the standard for apostleship in Corinth. The majority of the Corinthians, though from the lower social levels, possessed a similar system of values. I based this conclusion on two broad considerations: their susceptibility to rhetoric which consisted of conventional themes of invective and their observance of the conventions of friendship and enmity. Our understanding of these has helped explain why their friendship with Paul could so quickly deteriorate into enmity, and why he himself could move them with his own weighty and strong rhetoric.

The idea of _hybris_ enabled me to draw a number of aspects into the social reconstruction of the conflict. It is predominantly a social concept relating to the excessive conduct of the rich and powerful from the viewpoint of those they have shamed. Within its wide range of applications and associated ideas, I have been able to explain terminology, ideas and conduct in 1 Cor. 4:6-13 and 2 Cor. 10:12-12:10. As a result,

I have suggested that Paul's Corinthian enemies and the rival apostles might appropriately be called 'hybrists'. The term represents a familiar and contemporary tradition of long standing in Greek life and thought, something which cannot yet be claimed with any confidence about the primitive gnostic/pneumatic movement. By comparison, it offers a recognizable and more comprehensive context in which to explain the complex of nuances (e.g., status, excess, measurement, moderation, superiority, shame, freedom, knowledge) which appears in the passages.

The common pattern of behaviour enabled me to draw one of a number of links between Paul's enemies in 1 Corinthians and the rival apostles in 2 Corinthians, and may provide an answer to the question which has puzzled commentators as to why gnosticism, said to be so central to 1 Corinthians, is absent in 2 Corinthians. Importantly, I have been able to explain hyperlian (2 Cor. 11:5) as a hybristic notion and to support the identification of these 'excessive' apostles with the 'false apostles' (though this is primarily accomplished by the literary form of comparison). In addition, I have been able to provide a satisfactory explanation of Paul's figure of the boastful fool.

Finally, I suggest that this examination of Paul's relations with the Corinthians has established firm connections between the events and issues in both letters. Based on social considerations, a coherent story has emerged, of Paul's friendship with the Corinthians, its disintegration, the formation of the hostile alliance and Paul's preoccupation with it in 2 Corinthians. In relation to the integrity of 2 Corinthians, our new appreciation of Paul's rhetorical skills and the study of the range of tones and emotions which an orator was expected to employ in a speech or letter, shows that the use of 'harsh' and 'soft' tones as criteria for two or more letters is no longer satisfactory.

SELECT BIBLIOGRAPHY

Principle texts and translations : quotations

Greek and Roman Authors: The Loeb Classical Library, unless otherwise indicated.

Papyrus letters of recommendation: reproduced in Chan-Hie Kim, The Form and Structure of Greek Letters of Recommendation, SBL Dissertation Series 4 (Missoula, 1972), Appendix III.

The Bible: Revised Standard Version of the Bible: New Testament (New York, 1946).

Greek New Testament: The Greek New Testament, K. Aland, M. Black, B.M. Metzger, A. Wikgren, eds. (Stuttgart, 1966).

Spengel, L., ed., Rhetores Graeci 2,3 (Frankfurt, 1966)

Weichert, V., ed., Demetrii et Libanii (Leipzig, 1910).

Secondary Literature.

Adams, J.N.
'Conventions of Naming in Cicero', Classical Quarterly 28 (1978), 145-146.

Adkins, A.W.H.
'"Friendship" and "Self-Sufficiency" in Homer and Aristotle', Classical Quarterly 13 (1963), 30-45.
Merit and Responsibility: A Study in Greek Values (Oxford, 1960)

Balsdon, J.P.V.D.
'Cicero the Man', Cicero, T.A. Dorey, ed., (London, 1964), 171-214.

Badian, E.
Foreign Clientele (264-70 b.c.)(Oxford, 1958).

Banks, R.
Paul's Idea of Community (Sydney, 1979).

Barrett, C.K.
'Christianity at Corinth', Bulletin of the John Ryland's Library 46 (1964), 269-297.
The First Epistle to the Corinthians (London, 1971).
The Second Epistle to the Corinthians (London, 1973).

Bartchy, S.S.
First-Century Slavery and 1 Corinthians 7:21, SBL Dissertation Series 11 (Missoula, 1973).

Barton, S.C.
'All Things to All Men' (1 Corinthians 9:22): The Principal of Accommodation in the Mission of Paul,(unpublished B.A. Hons. thesis, Macquarie University, 1975).

Beare, F.W.
The Epistle to the Philippians (London, 1959).

Bernard, J.H.
The Second Epistle to the Corinthians, The Expositors Greek Testament, W.R. Nicholl ed. (repr. Grand Rapids, 1967).
Best, E.
The First and Second Epistles to the Thessalonians (London, 1972).
Betz, H.D.
Der Apostel Paulus und die sokratische Tradition (Tübingen, 1972).
'Paul's Apology: II Corinthians 10-13 and the Socratic Tradition', Colloquy 2 (1970), 1-16.
Bornkamm, G.
'The Missionary Stance of Paul in 1 Corinthians and Acts', Studies in Luke-Acts, L.E. Keck and J.L. Martyn, eds. (London, 1968), 194-207.
Bower, E.W.
'Εφοδος and Insinuatio in Greek and Roman Rhetoric', Classical Quarterly 8 (1958), 224-230.
Bowersock, G.
Greek Sophists in the Roman Empire (Oxford, 1969).
Brilliant, R.
Gesture and Rank in Roman Art: The Use of Gestures to Denote Status in Roman Sculpture and Coinage, Memoirs of the Connecticut Academy of Arts and Sciences, 14 (New Haven, 1963).
Bruce, F.F.
Apostle of the Free Spirit (Exeter, 1977).
1 and 2 Corinthians (London, 1971).
Brunt, P.A.
'"Amicitia" in the Late Roman Republic', Proceeds of the Cambridge Philological Society 11 (1965), 1-20.
Bultmann, R.
Exegetische Probleme des Zweiten Korintherbriefes (Upsala, 1947).
Der Stil der paulinischen Predigt und die kynisch-stoische Diatribe (Göttingen, 1910).
Chadwick, H.
'"All Things to All Men" (1 Cor.IX.22)', New Testament Studies 1 (1955), 261-275.
Chan-Hie Kim
Form and Structure of the Familiar Greek Letter of Recommendation, SBL Dissertation Series 4 (Missoula, 1972).
Clark, D.L.
Rhetoric in Greco-Roman Education (New York, 1957).
Clarke, M.L.
Rhetoric at Rome (London, 1953).
Conzelmann, H.
1 Corinthians ET (Philadelphia, 1975).
Dahl, N.A.
'Paul and the Church at Corinth according to 1 Cor.1:10-4:21', Christian History and Interpretation, W.R. Farmer, C.F.D. Moule and R.R. Niebuhr, eds. (Cambridge, 1967), 313-335.
Studies in Paul (Minneapolis, 1977).
Daube, D.
The New Testament and Rabbinic Judaism (London, 1956).
Dodd, C.H.
'The Mind of Paul: I', New Testament Studies (Manchester, 1953), 67-82
Dorey, T.A.
'Honesty in Roman Politics', Cicero, T. A. Dorey ed. (London, 1964), 27-45.
Dover, K.J.
Greek Popular Morality in the Time of Plato and Aristotle (Oxford, 1974)
Duff, A.M.
Freedmen in the Early Roman Empire (Oxford, 1928).

Dungan, D.L.
The Sayings of Jesus in the Churches of Paul: The Use of the Synoptic Tradition in the Regulation of Early Church Life (Philadelphia, 1971).
Dunkle, J.R.
'The Greek Tyrant and Roman Political Invective of the Late Republic', Transactions of the American Philological Association 98 (1967), 151-171.
Ellis, E.E.
'Paul and His Co-Workers', New Testament Studies 17 (1971), 437-452.
Ellison, H.L.
'Paul and the Law - "All Things to All Men"', Apostolic History and the Gospel, W.W. Gasque and R.P. Martin, eds (Exeter, 1970), 195-203.
Engemann, J.
'Zur Verbreitung magischer Übelabwehr in der nichtchristlichen und christlichen Spätantike', Jahrbuch für Antike und Christentum 18 (1975), 22-49.
Evans, E.C.
Physiognomics in the Ancient World, Transactions of the American Philosophical Society 59, part 5 (Philadelphia, 1969).
Fee, G.D.
'ΧΑΡΙΣ in II Corinthians 1:15: Apostolic Parousia and Paul-Corinth Chronology', New Testament Studies 24 (1978), 533-538.
Findlay, G.G.
St. Paul's First Epistle to the Corinthians, The Expositors Greek Testament, W.R. Nicoll ed. (repr. Grand Rapids, 1967).
Finley, M.I.
'Marriage, Sale and Gift in the Homeric World', Revue Internationale des Droits de l'Antiquité III, Vol 2 (1955), 167-194.
ed., Slavery in Classical Antiquity (new York, 1968).
The World of Odysseus (Harmondsworth, 1954).
Fisher, N.R.E.
'Hybris and Dishonour', Greece and Rome 23 (1976), 177-193.
Forbes, C.
"Strength" and "Weakness" as Terminology of Status in St. Paul: The Historical and Literary Roots of a Metaphor, with Specific Reference to 1 and 2 Corinthians (unpublished B.A. Hons. thesis, Macquarie University, 1978).
Fuhrmann, M.
'Cassius Severus', Der Kliene Pauly: Lexikon der Antike Vol.1, K. Ziegler and W. Sontheimer, eds. (Stuttgart, 1964), 1076.
Fustel de Coulanges, N.D.
Historie des institutions politiques de l'ancienne France Vol.5 (Paris, 1922).
Gelzer, M.
The Roman Nobility ET (Oxford, 1969).
Georgi, D.
Die Gegner des Paulus im 2 Korintherbrief: Studien zur religiösen Propaganda in der Spätantike (Neukirchener-Vluyn, 1964).
Grant, A.
The Ethics of Aristotle 2 (London, 1885).
Grant, M.A.
The Ancient Rhetorical Theories of the Laughable (Madison, 1924).
Grosheide, F.W.
Commentary on the First Epistle to the Corinthians (Grand Rapids, 1968).
Haenchen, E.
The Acts of the Apostles ET(Oxford, 1971).
Hands, A.R.
Charities and Social Aid in Greece and Rome (London & Southampton, 1968).

Headlam, W.G. and Thomson, G.
The Oresteia of Aeschylus II (Cambridge, 1938).
Hellegouarc'h, J.
Le Vocabulaire latin des relations et des partis politiques sous La Republique (Paris, 1963).
Héring, J.
The First Epistle to the Corinthians ET (London, 1962).
Hickling, C.J.A.
'The Sequence of Thought in II Corinthians Chapter Three', New Testament Studies 21 (1975), 380-395.
Hock, R.F.
'Paul's Tentmaking and the Problem of his Social Class', Journal of Biblical Literature 97 (1978), 555-564.
The Working Apostle: An Examination of Paul's Means of Livelihood (Ph.D. Yale, 1974) Ann Arbor: University Microfilms Inc., 1978.
Hooker, M.D.
'"Beyond the Things which are Written": An Examination of 1 Cor.iv.6', New Testament Studies 10 (1964), 127-132.
Howard, W.F.
'1 Corinthians 4:6. Exegesis or Emendation', The Expository Times 33 (1922), 479-480.
Hughes, P.E.
Paul's Second Epistle to the Corinthians (Grand Rapids, 1962).
Hurd, J.C.
The Origins of 1 Corinthians (London, 1965).
Judge, E. A.
'"Antike und Christentum": Towards a Definition of the Field. A Bibliographical Survey', Aufstieg und Niedergang der römischen Welt Vol.2.23.1, H. Temporini and W. Haase eds. (Berlin, 1979), 3-58.
'Paul as a Radical Critic of Society', Interchange 16 (1974), 191-203.
'Paul's Boasting in Relation to Contemporary Professional Practice', Australian Biblical Review 10 (1968), 37-50.
'St. Paul and Classical Society', Jahrbuch für Antike und Christentum 15 (1972), 19-36.
'St. Paul and Socrates', Interchange 14 (1973), 106-116.
'The Conflict of Educational Aims in N.T. Thought', Journal of Christian Education 9 (1966), 32-45.
'The Early Christians as a Scholastic Community', Journal of Religious History 1 (1961), 4-15.
'The Early Christians as a Scholastic Community: Part II', Journal of Religious History 2 (1961), 125-137.
The Social Pattern of Christian Groups in the First Century (London, 1960).
Käsemann, E.
'A Pauline Version of "Amor Fati"', New Testament Questions of Today ET (London, 1969).
Die Legitimität des Apostels (Darmstadt, 1964).
Kennedy, G.
The Art of Persuasion in Greece (London, 1963).
The Art of Rhetoric in the Roman World (Princeton, 1972).
Keyes, C.W.
'The Greek Letter of Introduction', American Journal of Philology 56 (1935), 28-44.
Kirk, J.A.
'Did "Officials" in the New Testament Receive a Salary?', The Expository Times 84 (1973), 105-108.
Kümmel, W.G.
Introduction to the New Testament ET (London, 1966).

Lacey, W.K.
'Homeric Εδνα and Penelope's Κυριος', Journal of Hellenic Studies 86 (1966), 55-68.
Legault, A.
'Beyond the Things Which are Written (1 Cor.IV.6)', New Testament Studies 18 (1972), 227-231.
Lietzmann, H. and Kümmel, W.G.
An die Korinther 1,2 (Tübingen, 1949).
Lyall, F.
'Roman Law in the Writings of St. Paul - the Slave and the Freedman', New Testament Studies 17 (1970), 73-79.
MacDowell, D.M.
'Hybris in Athens', Greece and Rome 23 (1976), 14-31.
Malherbe, A.J.
Ancient Epistolary Theorists (Missoula, 1977).
'"Gentle as a Nurse": The Cynic Background to I Thess.2', Novum Testamentum 12 (1970), 203-217.
'Hellenistic Moralists and the New Testament', Aufstieg und Niedergang der römischen Welt Pt.2 Vol.26, W. Haase ed. (Berlin forthcoming).
Social Aspects of Early Christianity (Baton Rouge-London, 1977).
The Cynic Epistles (Missoula, 1977).
'The Inhospitality of Diotrephes', God's Christ and His People: Studies in honour of Nils Alstrup Dahl, J. Jervell and W.A. Meeks, eds. (Oslo, 1977), 222-232.
Martin, R.P.
Philippians (Frome and London, 1976).
The Epistle of Paul to the Philippians (London, 1959).
Maslakov, G.
Tradition and Abridgement: A Study of the Exempla Tradition in Valerius Maximus and the Elder Pliny (Ph.D. thesis, Macquarie University,1978).
Mathews, J.
Hospitality and the New Testament Church: An Historical and Exegetical Study (Ph.D. Princeton, 1965) Ann Arbor: University Microfilms Inc., 1977.
Mauss, M.
The Gift ET (Glencoe, 1954).
Moffatt, J.
The First Epistle of Paul to the Corinthians (London, 1938).
Moore, A.L.
1 and 2 Corinthians (London, 1969).
Morris, L.
'ΚΑΙ ΑΠΑΞ ΚΑΙ ΔΙΣ', Novum Testamentum 1 (1956), 205-208.
Munck, J.
'The Church Without a Faction', Paul and the Salvation of Mankind ET (London, 1959).
Nestle, D.
Eleutheria: Teil I, Die Griechen (Tübingen, 1967).
Nisbet, R.G.M.
Cicero in Pisonem (Oxford, 1961).
North, H.
Sophrosyne: Self-Knowledge and Sel-Restraint in Greek Literature (Ithaca/New York, 1966).
'The Concept of "Sophrosyne" in Greek Literary Criticism', Classical Philology 43(1948), 1-17.
Pagels, E.H.
The Gnostic Paul (Philadelphia, 1975).
Pearson, L.
Popular Ethics in Ancient Greece (Stanford, 1962).

Plummer, A.
Second Epistle to the Corinthians (Edinburgh, 1915).
Pohlenz, M.
Freedom in Greek Life and Thought ET (Dordrecht, 1966).
Pritchett, W.K.
Dionysius of Halicarnassus: on Thucydides (Berkeley, 1975).
Rankin, W.M.
'Friendship', Encyclopaedia of Religion and Ethics 6, J. Hastings ed. (Edinburgh,1913), 121-134.
Robbins, C.J.
'Rhetorical Structure of Philippians 2:6-11', Catholic Biblical Quarterly 42 (1980), 73-82.
Roberts, W.R.
Dionysius of Halicarnassus on Literary Composition (London, 1910).
Robertson, H.G.
'The Hybristes in Aeschylus', Transactions of the American Philological Association 98 (1967), 373-382.
Rogers, R.S.
'The Emperor's Displeasure - amicitiam renuntiare', Transactions of the American Philological Association 90 (1959), 224-237.
Rowland, R.T., Jnr.
'Cicero and the Greek World', Transactions of the American Philological Association 103 (1972), 451-461.
Russell, D.A.
'On Reading Plutarch's Lives, Greece and Rome 13 (1966), 139-154.
Plutarch (London, 1973).
'Plutarch: "Alcibiades" 1-16', Proceeds of the Cambridge Philological Society 12 (1966), 37-47.
Ryan, E.E.
'Aristotle's Rhetoric and Ethics', Greek, Roman and Byzantine Studies 13 (1972), 296-302.
Sampley, J.P.
'Societas Christi: Roman Law and Paul's Conception of the Christian Community', God's Christ and His People, J. Jervell and W.A. Meeks, eds. (Oslo, 1977), 158-174.
Schmithals, W.
Gnosticism in Corinth: An Investigation of the Letters to the Corinthians ET (Nashville, 1971).
Schütz, J.H.
Paul and the Anatomy of Apostolic Authority (Cambridge, 1975).
Segal, E.
Roman Laughter: The Comedy of Plautus (Cambridge, 1968).
Sevenster, J.N.
Paul and Seneca (Leiden, 1961).
Süss, W.
Ethos (Leipzig and Berlin, 1910).
Syme, R.
The Roman Revolution (London, 1939).
Theissen, G.
'Die Starken und Schwachen in Korinth: Soziologische Analyse eines theologischen Streites', Evangelische Theologie 35 (1975), 155-172.
'Soziale Integration und sakramentales Handeln: Eine Analyse 1 Kor. 11:17-34', Novum Testamentum 16 (1974), 179-206.
'Soziale Schichtung in der korinthischen Gemeinde: Ein Beitrag Soziologie des hellenistischen Urchristentums', Zeitschrift für die neutestamentliche Wissenschaft 65 (1974), 232-272.
'Wanderradikalismus: Literarsoziologische Aspekte von Worten Jesu im Urchristentum , Zeitschrift für Theologie und Kirche 70 (1973), 245-271.

Travis, S.H.
'Paul's Boasting in 2 Corinthians 10-12', Studia Evangelica 6 (1973), 527-532.
Treu, K.
'Christliche Empfehlungs - Schemabriefe auf Papyrus', Zetesis Festschrift E. de Strijcker (Antwerp/Utrecht, 1973), 629-636.
Vogt, J.
Ancient Slavery and the Ideal of Man ET (Oxford, 1974).
Wagenvoort, H.
Roman Dynamism (Oxford, 1947).
Walcot, P.
Greek Peasants, Ancient and Modern (Manchester, 1970).
Wallis, P.
'Ein neuer Auslegungsversuch der Stelle 1 Kor.4:6', Theologische Literaturzeitung 75 (1950), 506-508.
Weaver, P.R.C.
'Social Mobility in the Early Roman Empire: The Evidence of the Imperial Freedman and Slave', Past and Present 37 (1967), 14-20.
Wessner, P.
Donatus (Aeli Donati Commentum Terenti II) (Leipzig, 1905).
Westermann, W.L.
'Between Slavery and Freedom' American Historical Review 50 (1945), 213-227.
'Slavery and the Elements of Freedom', Quarterly Bulletin of the Polish Institute of Arts and Sciences in America 1 (1943), 1-16.
'Two Studies in Athenian Manumission', Journal of Near Eastern Studies 5 (1946), 92-104.
Windisch, H.
Der Zweite Korintherbrief (Göttingen, 1924).
Wirszubski, Ch.
Libertas as a Political Idea at Rome During the Late Republic and Early Principate (Cambridge, 1968).
Wuellner, W.H.
'Greek Rhetoric and Pauline Argumentation', Early Christian Literature and the Classical Tradition: in Honorem Robert M. Grant, W.R. Schoedel and R.L. Wilken, eds. (Paris, 1979), 177-188.

INDEXES

INDEX OF BIBLICAL AND ANCIENT WRITINGS

I NEW TESTAMENT

II GREEK AND ROMAN

III OLD TESTAMENT, OLD TESTAMENT APOCHRYPHA, JEWISH AND EARLY CHRISTIAN WRITINGS

IV PAPYRUS

INDEX OF SUBJECTS

INDEX OF MODERN AUTHORS

Wissenschaftliche Untersuchungen zum Neuen Testament

Begründet von Joachim Jeremias und Otto Michel

Herausgegeben von Martin Hengel und Otfried Hofius

1. Reihe

41
Mathias Rissi
Die Theologie des Hebräerbriefs
1987. X, 140 Seiten. fadengeh. Br.

40
Carl J. Bjerkelund
Tauta Egeneto
1987. XII, 162 Seiten. Leinen.

39
David G. Meade
Pseudonymity and Canon
1986. VII, 257 Seiten. Leinen.

38
Chrys C. Caragounis
The Son of Man
1986. IX, 310 Seiten. Leinen.

37
Ernst Bammel
Judaica
1986. VI, 331 Seiten. Leinen.

36
Jarl E. Fossum
The Name of God and the Angel of the Lord
1985. XIII, 378 Seiten. Leinen.

35
Erich Gräßer
Der Alte Bund im Neuen
1985. VIII, 345 Seiten. Br. u. Ln.

34
Folker Siegert
Argumentation bei Paulus
1985. VIII, 320 Seiten. Leinen.

33
Markus-Philologie
Hrsg. von H. Cancik
1984. X, 415 Seiten. Leinen.

32
Hildebrecht Hommel
Sebasmata. Band 2
1984. VII, 415 Seiten. Leinen.

31
Hildebrecht Hommel
Sebasmata. Band 1
1983. X, 382 Seiten. Leinen.

30
Seyoon Kim
"The 'Son of Man'" as the Son of God
1983. X, 118 Seiten. Broschur.

29
Heikki Räisänen
Paul and the Law
1983. VIII, 455 Seiten. Leinen.

28
Das Evangelium und die Evangelien
Hrsg. von P. Stuhlmacher
1983. VIII, 455 Seiten. Leinen.

27
Klyne Snodgrass
The Parable of the Wicked Tenants
1983. X, 140 Seiten. Broschur.

26
Folker Siegert
Nag-Hammadi-Register
1982. XXVI, 383 Seiten. Leinen.

25
Gerhard Maier
Die Johannesoffenbarung und die Kirche
1981. IX, 676 Seiten. Leinen.

24
Günter Schlichting
Ein jüdisches Leben Jesu
1982. XVI, 292 Seiten. Leinen.

23
Marcel Simon
Le christianisme antique et son contexte religieux. Scripta varia. 2 Bde.
1981. 1: XX, 370 Seiten; 2: VI, S. 371–852. Leinen.

22
Otto Bauernfeind
Kommentar und Studien zur Apostelgeschichte
1980. XVIII, 492 Seiten. Leinen.

21
August Strobel
Die Stunde der Wahrheit
1980. VII, 150 Seiten. Broschur.

20
Drei hellenistisch-jüdische Predigten
Erl. von F. Siegert
1980. 109 Seiten. Broschur.

19
Gerd Theißen
Studien zur Soziologie des Urchristentums
2. Aufl. 1983. VI, 364 S., Br. u. Ln.

18
E. Earle Ellis
Prophecy and Hermeneutic in Early Christianity
1978. XVII, 289 Seiten. Leinen.

16
Karlmann Beyschlag
Simon Magus und die christliche Gnosis
1974. VII, 249 Seiten. Leinen.

15
Andreas Nissen
Gott und der Nächste im antiken Judentum
1974. IX, 587 Seiten. Leinen.

14
Otfried Hofius
Der Vorhang vor dem Thron Gottes
1972. VIII, 122 Seiten. Broschur.

13
Helmut Merkel
Die Widersprüche zwischen den Evangelien
1971. VI, 295 S., Br. u. Ln.

12
Gerhard Maier
Mensch und freier Wille
1971. VII, 426 S., Br. u. Ln.

11
Otfried Hofius
Katapausis
1970. IX, 281 S., Br. u. Ln.

10
Martin Hengel
Judentum und Hellenismus
2. Auflage 1973. XI, 693 Seiten. Broschur und Leinen.

8
Christoph Burchard
Untersuchungen zu Joseph und Aseneth
1965. VII, 180 S., Br. u. Ln.

7
Ehrhard Kamlah
Die Form der katalogischen Paränese im Neuen Testament
1964. VIII, 245 S., Br. u. Ln.

5
Friedrich Rehkopf
Die lukanische Sonderquelle
1959. VIII, 106 Seiten. Broschur.

J.C.B. Mohr (Paul Siebeck) Tübingen